The Plumsock Papers

The Plumsock Papers

Giving New Analysts a Voice
Institute of the Contemporary Freudian Society Prize Winning Papers

Edited by Paula Ellman and Kimberly Kleinman

IPBOOKS.net
International Psychoanalytic Books

International Psychoanalytic Books (IPBooks)
New York • http://www.IPBooks.net

Contents

Introduction

by Paula Ellman and Kimberly Kleinman

On reading the Plumsock Prize winning papers as a unified body, we wondered if the function of the prize was to encourage a documentation of the culture of the CFS related to incorporation of theories not taught in the curriculum. We also thought that the prize provided a platform for the synthesis of theories that may have been previously viewed as conflicting. Some of our former candidates/current members brought their academic expertise to bear and used their new psychoanalytic knowledge to expand both their "home" field and ours. Many of our authors used the writing experience to document their problem-solving process: how they engaged and treated patients who may in the past have been thought of as unreachable.

The founder of the Plumsock Prize is Edwin Fancher. There is a clear parallel between his role in publishing the Village Voice, which provided a platform for alternative journalism and an entree into alternative theater and other artistic endeavors, and his role in creating what the Plumsock Prize has realized as another platform for original thought.

The Plumsock Award for both Candidates and new graduates has at its core the intention to encourage writing and the expression of psychoanalytic ideas by early career thinkers. The New York /Contemporary Freudian Society has accrued a rich array of papers that bring together theoretical ideas with clinical practice. Each paper, with its unique focus, shows the author's way of linking their clinical work with a specific facet

1

of theory. While incredibly diverse, one profound commonality is that the Plumsock winners each move psychoanalysis forward in development. Each paper was written at a certain moment in time, and each author, in close consideration of clinical process, expounds an area of psychoanalytic understanding, and then adds a new original layer of thinking that further enriches that area.

Churchill, in 2009, integrates his experience as a sociologist and researcher with his psychoanalytic training. Churchill explores the ubiquity of the transference reaction and how this applies to ethnography. He takes up the important question of distinguishing the idea of wild analysis and applied psychoanalysis. The subject matter is an original concept and the term psycho-interactionism is introduced. The author reports that he would now use the title: "Treating the Subject: Toward a Psycho-Interactionist Theory for Ethnography".

Cromer Grayson's paper (2003) presents a case that is a profound illustration of the problems around understanding resistance and engagement. Cromer Grayson digs into the very earliest psychoanalytic writings (S. Freud, A. Freud) and then the classics, including Brenner, and then brings us up to the time she wrote the paper to synthesize theories around enactments and remembering. We understand enactment and resistance as a communication, but it is hard to decipher. However, it is this very understanding that helps us conceptualize the psychic dilemma our patients are caught in. Her review of the literature on acting out reminds us to buckle our seatbelts and to remember that our patients need us even when they seem to not want us.

Finkelstein's paper, Psychosomatic Illness in a Clautro-Agorophobic Patient (Senior, 2015), in reviewing the concept of projective identification, looks closely at the holding function of the mother, without which comes the risk of claustro-agorophobia, 'a nameless dread'. It is the author's presenting clinical material that brings to life the way that psychosomatic expression captures the problem with the clautro-agoraphobic response. A full clinical presentation allows for a close examination of Kleinian projective identification processes, and the mutative impact of psychoanalysis on creating more flexible functional internalized objects.

Goodman's first paper (2001) brings in his expertise in attachment research and synthesizes it with object relations and drive theory. Goodman reviews the theories that construct the mind of the child as it develops in relationship with his/her caregivers and his/her own internal experience. Kernberg's description of borderline psychopathology is implicated in the structure of insecure internal working models. He points out that Attachment theory does not take into account that drives can distort attachment experience.

Goodman's second paper (2002) uses his expertise in empirical studies, Bowlby's attachment theory about internal working models and his knowledge of Object Representations to compare the two models. Goodman asks what is gained by incorporating the two theories. He helps our field begin this process by methodically comparing the basic concepts in each theory, and then empirically demonstrates the conceptual overlap. Goodman makes a case for examining the many theoretical rifts between psychoanalytic theories in the same methodical manner he has applied to object relations and attachment theory. He accurately points out that some theoretical differences may be imagined. Empirical methods may help discover commonalities as well as distinctions between theories.

Hoffman, in On Divergence and Diversity: Regarding Gay Men and the Male-Gendered Pre-Oedipal Good Object (Senior, 2015), explores what makes for gendered choice of primary attachment, and questions the assumptions that the preoedipal early attachment is consistently female. In considering the position of homosexual men, Hoffman takes as his focus both his own personal experience and clinical material from gay male patients. He discusses that the primary object choice may not necessarily be from one's first attachment, but may in fact be a composite that takes on a particular gender for inexplicable reasons. The author cautions the reader not to presume, through overidentification with our patients, certain aspects of attachments. This contribution on the gendered object choice and its relationship to early life experience is a much needed exploration in the area of gender diversity.

Jones' paper, the Role of Concreteness in Chronic Genital Pain (2005), addresses the way that body pain, particularly genital pain, is an expression of concreteness, of something that cannot be yet symbolized. The author's effort in bringing in a series of clinical instances of genital pain in the woman is to illustrate an idea of a continuum of concreteness/symbolization. The author values the crucial importance of the countertransference of the analyst in the clinical work viewing the transference/countertransference enactment as an arena for understanding and intervention.

Jones, in her paper, "Culture Shock—A Factor of Dissociative Identity Disorder" (Senior,2013), writes of her experience with three dissociative disorder patients and considers the contribution of the experience of culture shock in both the creation of a dissociative disorder and in understanding the nature of it. The author considers the good enough early life experience that allows for positive treatment effects in comparison with early life experiences of abuse. The therapeutic process of treatment on these fragmented states is explored. The author raises some interesting questions about identity development, the place of culture in trauma, and the importance of psychoanalysis as an intervention in these instances.

Krass' paper, Fear and Loathing on the Couch: The Intersection of Managed Care and Masochism (2006), considers the crucial place of working in the transference when managed care is a part of a psychoanalysis. Here ideas about "a third" are examined in analyzing the impact of managed care on the analytic process, along with displacements of negative transferences on the third. The author, rather than suffering the masochistic submission to the assault by the managed care company, holds to an analytic perspective of a transferential masochistic surrender by the patient and the understanding of a countertransference that could mirror the patient's helplessness. The author sustains a psychoanalytic perspective and position in this instance of a third party interruption.

Krass, in his paper ,The Rules of Disengagement: The Interaction of Brain and Mind in the Analytic Treatment of Children and Adults with Asperger's Syndrome (Senior, 2010), provides the foundation for an understanding of Asperger Syndrome, and through his clinical presentation demonstrates the crucial importance of the analyst's recognition of intrapsychic conflict in working with AS patients, and the ways that neurological deficits make for particular developments of unconscious fantasy and conflict.

Murphy's choice of Persephone is a terrific metaphor for exploring the conflict present around the development of mature female sexuality and identity (2015). The loss of the mother, not being able to bridge the two worlds due to the loss experienced by the mother, (rather than competition per se) is quite apt. This should be read by every student. The life-giving object becomes the depriving object, and it is only in the integration that the maturing girl does not have to kill herself or her child self. The life-giving mother, due to apres coup becomes the life-depriving mother and the bountiful summer becomes newly understood as the barren winter due to the re-evaluation of the mother through the lens of sexual desire and the need to find an adult partner. This case highlights the psychic danger of female sexual maturity because of the history of the rape of the grandmother, truly fitting with the Persephone myth. This also explores the dynamics of agency as forbidden. and how a female stereotype of passivity is promulgated.

Neumann extends our understanding of the frame in analysis by bringing us into Cyberspace (2012). She highlights the technical difficulties that could cause impingements on the analytic process and clarifies what remains unchanged in the analytic process despite cyberspace. She explicates and addresses the theories that critics have concerning online treatment, concluding that cyberspace is a frontier that deserves further exploration and probably acceptance.

Plotkin encountered a question in the course of her training. She considered analyzing a patient who was significantly older than her. She recognized her resistance, and in consulting with analytic supervisors, she realized that there is a lack of consensus concerning analyzing older patients. She wrote about this experience, identifying obstacles in the patient, in the analyst and in the dyad that create resistances in the treatment of the older analytic patient (1999). Plotkin clarified that an analytic process is not diminished because of age, and that the most significant limitation is psychopathology.

Rockwell in her paper, Reality and the Unconscious (1993)—with a postscript in 2017 speaking to the importance of limiting self-disclosure—articulates the place of the real relationship in the therapeutic alliance . She references Freud in describing the real relationship as the fuel for the development of the transference. There are aspects of the real relationship that serve as a kind of reassurance in the therapeutic process and support the repetition in the transference. There is the new and the repeated, the real and the psychic truth. Clinical vignettes bring a richness to the discussion of the use of the real in the transference work.

Rosegrant's paper, "The Anal World of a Six Year Old Boy" (1995), explores anality and narcissistic grandiosity as means for managing loss, humiliation and trauma. Rich clinical material is provided depicting early unbearable loss that makes differentiation unattainable . The author suggests that the anal world illusion holds the promise that all is flux, in a way which means that no loss is permanent. Questions considered are: Is the child moving into a perversion based on the constellation of the mother's and father's character? What are the specific challenges of examining child development along with adult pathology?

Rosnick's paper, The Imaginary Father (1993), speaks to daughters without fathers and the psychically present imaginary father that supports the development of symbolization. Rosnick begins an interesting exploration of how the crucial importance of being loved by the single parent involves identification with the absent parent. Primitive introjection of the absent parent, wishes to be the exclusively loved object, and a sense of body inadequacy are frequently present with the daughter. Clinical material brings to the fore aspects of relatedness that become compromised and are expressed transferentially.

Schur, in "The Facts of Mind: Thoughts on the Concept of a Taxonomy of Unconscious Fantasy with Special Reference to the "New View" in Psychoanalysis" (2002) brings together a consideration of drive-conflict theory with object relations theory and attachment theory in order to recognize the presence of an enduring structuralization of an inner representational world crucial to formulating a diagnostic picture and treatment plan. Schur wrestles with how the relational view, that was in 2002 the 'new view' in psychoanalysis, values the idea of co-construction and intersubjectivity. The author expresses concern about what he believes is the absence in this "new view" of the capacity to uncover in our psychoanalytic work the unconscious fantasies in the psyche. Schur proposes a taxonomy of internal structures based on the level of differentiation related to primary and secondary processes and revisits the theory of Nachtraglichkeit as a way of accounting for a theory of psychic development that considers the transformations of memory-fantasy and trauma.

Wolf reaches beyond what was the standard curriculum at CFS and uses Bion's Model to understand patients that pose difficulties through how it is difficult for them and for the analyst to think. Wolf metabolizes Bion for the uninitiated, and in so doing demonstrates how the terms

7

and concepts integral to Bion's theories elucidate her work (1999). If you are interested in Bion's theories, this paper provides a clear primer and illustration. This paper may also have contributed to Bion's presence in our current curriculum.

Yumatov explores the literature and brings us through in broad outline the detours we have taken, far from Freud's view that bisexuality is normative (2015) . Psychoanalysis went off track in determining which paths of development were normative, and gender expression, gender splitting and sexual object choice became conflated with part object relating. Yumatov points out the need to clarify the vicissitudes of sexual object choice, the developmental determinants of object choice; the relationship between the synthetic capacity of the mind and sexual object choice; the problems with a simplistic conceptualization of gender and it's expression, and how they relate to problems conceptualizing sexual object choice; how conflating sexual object choice with psychopathology is reductive; and how sociocultural and historical factors impinge upon our capacity to think about these issues. He does this through the lens of bi-sexuality, which is an intellectual coup. Yumatov has drawn upon authors not part of the generally assigned curriculum, bringing scholars to us with whom we are not familiar and also adding his voice to our chorus.

Plumsock Prize Origins and History:

In Honor of Edwin Fancher

by Helen K. Gediman

This entire volume is dedicated in honor of our fellow CFS member Edwin Fancher, who was responsible for securing the grant that established the Plumsock Prize awards. The prize actually grew out of Ed's work as a cofounder and publisher of *The Village Voice*.

In 1955, the year of the launch of this pioneer alternative newsweekly, Ed was invited by his close friend, Daniel Wolf, to take a full-time position at a mental health clinic, but as a lifelong adventurous man, Ed opted to remain as a part-time publisher of the *Village Voice* just as it reached the streets, cheered on by an enthusiastic reading public.

No readers were more enthusiastic than Herbert and Evelyn Lilly Lutz, a couple who lived in the neighborhood. Herbert was a theater lover and was particularly infatuated with the just burgeoning off-Broadway theater, which The Voice promoted. Now, we are getting to answer the question, "How did we arrive at the unusual name, 'Plumsock Prize' for our coveted awards?" Well, in addition to their apartment in Greenwich Village, Herbert and Evelyn also owned a vacation farm on Plumsock Road in Paoli, Pennsylvania. In the 1960's, the Lutz's decided to formalize their charitable activities by establishing a non-profit foundation, which they named The Plumsock fund. Ergo! They asked David Wolf and Ed Fancher to join the board of the Plumsock Fund and to play a role in worthy causes for funding. There you have it!

Now, a few words about Ed's role in creating and developing the Plumsock Fund. During Ed's 19 years at The Voice, he had been in training to be a psychoanalyst at The National Association for the Advancement of Psychoanalysis (NPAP),;and then later at The American Institute for Psychotherapy and Psychoanalysis (AIPP). He soon became interested in joining what was then called the New York Freudian Society (NYFS), now, of course called The Contemporary Freudian Society (CFS). That organization, ours, that is, was at that time only one of four institutes that predominantly trained non-medical candidates in psychoanalysis and became a component society of the International Psychoanalytic Association (IPA).

When Ed was accepted into membership in The New York Freudian Society, he wanted to something useful for the organization and for promoting psychoanalysis, generally. He was very impressed with the creativity of both the candidates and the members of the NYFS, and came up with the idea of asking the Plumsock Fund for a grant of $20,000 to be invested in high-yielding stocks and bonds to provide annual prize money for outstanding psychoanalytic papers by a candidate or a recent graduate of no more than five years. The Society accepted this arrangement and the board appointed a committee chaired by Ed to administer the awards. Papers by candidates were then judged separately from those by recent graduates. Standards for judgment of papers were based on creative ideas and insights into psychoanalytic issues. Once a year, submitted papers were sent to all Plumsock Committee members for their evaluation. Since the source of the funding of these prizes was the Plumsock Fund, the CFS has maintained the Plumsock name for these $1000 prizes.

So far, the Plumsock committee has had two chairs. When Ed stepped down, I, Helen K. Gediman stepped in and formed a committee of seven members, including her as chair, that has remained relatively constant and includes members from Ed's original committee. His policy and procedures have lived on and remained quite stable, with a few changes. We now offer two prizes: the Traditional, which is for candidates and recent graduates of five years or less.; and the Senior, which goes to any member of the CFS who has been a graduate for over five years and who has never published a paper in a psychoanalytic journal or a chapter in a psychoanalytic book. The stipend remains at $1000 and there is no limit on how many prizes are awarded each year, just as long as our treasury, which is not doubled its original capital value, can furnish the prize money to qualified new writers.

Over the twenty-five or more years that the Freudian Society has administered these prizes, numerous awards have been given. Some of the papers have been later published in major refereed psychoanalytic journals. Even those papers that did not win a cash prize often provided an important stimulus for creative thinking along the psychoanalytic journey. Edwin Fancher's dream has continued on as a reality that is until this day as an indisputable source of pride for the Contemporary Freudian Society. We all thank him for his constant support and imaginative enterprise.

Helen K. Gediman, Ph.D., Chair, CRS Plumsock Committee
Members of the plumsock committee: Helen Gediman , Chair.
Members: Phyllis Ackman, Elizabeth Fritsch , Harvey Kaplan, Kerry Malawista, Arnold Richards , Susan Roane

Reality and The Unconscious

by Shelley Rockwell

I communed with all that I saw as something not apart from but inherent in my own immaterial nature. Many times while going to school have **I grasped at a wall or tree** to recall myself from this abyss of idealism to the reality. There was a time in my life when I had to push against something that resisted to be sure that there was anything outside me. I was sure of my own mind; everything else fell away and vanished into thought. (Wordsworth in Moorman, 1965, p. 41)

We want to **live ... only for a moment ... in you** ... there is no book. The drama is in us, and we are the drama. We are impatient to play it. Our inner passion drives us on to this. (Character from *Six Characters in Search of an Author*, p. 218, by Luigi Pirandello speaking to stage manager and actors)

The tendency to experience the world in dualities is an ordinary human characteristic, it contributes to our individual character and makes us who we are. This way of thinking is a crucial part of the young child's world and is the basis for our sophisticated metapsychology. Freud's conflict theory is based on this human proclivity. The clinical manifestations of the struggle between the life and death instinct, as described by Klein and her followers bring this struggle into clear focus.

This paper will explore one significant duality within the psychoanalytic situation; the tension between reality and nonreality. This tension is always there, and is either implicit or explicit, it is underappreciated in our work and theory and therefore its therapeutic potential not fully utilized. Although the central manifestation of this duality is in the transference-real relationship, it is present throughout the psychoanalytic situation.

Historical Background

The polarity between real and unreal has a long history. From the accounts of Helene Deutsch (Roazen, 1985), Hilda Doolittle (1956), and other patients (the Rat Man), Freud had warm, friendly and "real" interactions with many of his patients. This is by now a well-accepted irony. Freud did not follow his own technical advice. The realistic stratum of the analytic relationship was not discussed while Freud was alive. Following his death there was much criticism of this aspect of his technique (Kris, 1948; Zetzel, 1956, 1965). Kris noted that Freud had used "intellectual indoctrination" in his treatment of Lorenz. Lipton (1977) makes the interesting argument that a warm and lively real relationship with the patient was not written about by Freud and his contemporaries because it was generally accepted as distinct from technique, taken for granted and not analyzed, and certainly not seen as part of the therapeutic process.

Near the time of Freud's death Alexander wrote regarding the "corrective emotional experience." Lipton (1977) argued that Eissler's (1953) well-known parameter paper was written in response to Alexander's disturbing ideas. Alexander's suggested that the analyst purposefully act in a manner designed to "correct" or counter the patient's pathogenic childhood experiences—reaction against this was strong then as it is today. Alexander's technique was too skewed toward (false) reality and Eissler's too remote from reality. Both extreme formulations lack a respect for the inherent and necessary tension between real and unreal. Although Eissler advised the necessity of parameters in our work with certain patients, his paper came to define "model" or "standard" technique. Ideal technique places a premium on interpretation, a reification of silence is implied— unless the analyst can make a transference interpretation , it is better to remain silent. In addition to Lipton's point, (Eissler may have been reacting to Alexander's disturbing work) it is possible that an interest in an ideal or standard technique would have been a response to the loss of Freud: reified ideas becoming a substitute for the guidance of a revered and beloved authority.

A moderating movement developed as an attempt to speak to what was excluded in standard technique among some American analysts (i.e. Zetzel, Stone and Greenson) with the concept of the "working alliance," an idea introduced by Sterba (1934). For Sterba the observing ego was equivalent to the "unobjectionable positive transference" (Freud, 1912) belonging to the working alliance, and "the experiencing ego (equivalent to) the transference proper" (Rawn, 1991). Zetzel (1956) believed that the working alliance was part of the transference and it was the job of the analyst to distinguish the neurotic aspects from the alliance. These conceptual efforts represent an attempt to escape the conundrum inherent in "ideal technique."

How then do we understand or conceptualize material which is not part of the transference proper, and not possible or appropriate to interpret? Greenson (1967) meticulously attempts to unravel these three terms; transference, working alliance, real relationship through their relative "genuineness and realistic" characteristics. Apart from these distinctions, Greenson reported that with each deepening or opening-up of the transference there is a potential for the real relationship to develop. Searles (1965) has made this same point. Stone (1967) makes a similar observation, the awareness of the differences between the analyst and the archaic fantasy object is the *condition* for the emergence of the archaic, or primordial transference. For example the patient can "invest the analyst with an immediate aggressive fantasy given a sense of body, vividness, and reality by his living presence" (p. 106-107). The negative transference, when understood, makes room for the "unobjectionable positive transference."

This aspect of reality, as described by Stone and Greenson, specifically the real relationship, provides a reassurance against a full-blown enactment of the transference. In having a "realistic outline" (Stone, 1961, p. 45) of the analyst, patients can consciously and unconsciously compare the distortions of the transference with what is clearly real in the analyst. Often this process goes on quietly, certainly less quietly with a more disturbed patient. It needs little discussion except at times of intense transference flooding or at some pivotal junctures in the treatment. This baseline of reassurance is what allows the "as if" quality of the analysis to be simply that and not a paranoid experience.

The concept of reassurance has had a complicated history. It is natural to need (sometimes the most subtle, unspoken) reassurance when a project of such potential far-reaching change is undertaken as we attempt in an analysis. In the literature on creativity Ehrenzweig (1967) described the creative process as one which first requires the experience of chaos and destruction, chaos before a new form and order can be conceived. There must be something to hold onto while this takes place or one would not have the courage to face this internal challenge. This "holding on" is captured in Wordsworth's description of his need to push against a hard surface in moments of poetic creativity. I am suggesting that the real relationship offers just this, and that the working or therapeutic alliance is an aspect of the real relationship. In order for the real relationship to provide this differentiation and reassurance it must be capable of a separation (even temporarily) from the transference. I suspect that the analyst's holding the frame is itself the basis of "reassurance" and allows a distinct reality of the analyst to emerge from the transference.

Friedman (1969) reviews the literature on therapeutic alliance and argues that the concept is based on an irreducible contradiction: the analyst depends for his influence on "something in the patient which must be dissolved" and "he thus draws for his power on what he is trying to reduce" (p. 142). "The helpful part of the transference is the 'conscious' and 'unobjectionable' positive feeling of the patient toward his analyst" (p. 139). Nevertheless transference is transference and as Stein (1981) aptly described, some patients work cooperatively from the beginning to the end of their analyses. Their working alliance is never or only momentarily threatened, but change seems to fall short in various ways. The unobjectionable part of the transference is ultimately transference and requires activity on the part of the analyst to ferret out the underpinnings of "pseudo-cooperation."

Friedman makes a similar point, arguing that the concept as a way to dodge the inherent paradox (of viewing transference as the source of the therapeutic alliance) does not work; it is an attempt to see the patient as sharing the same motivation, if even just a little, as does the analyst. It is an attempt to postulate a "congruence" between the patient and the analyst "on the analyst's terms." The patient in the concept of the therapeutic alliance is "wrongly endowed with the desire to objectively observe his/her id derivatives, expose unconscious fantasy" (p. 151) and in general be invested in the process of analysis as a process. It is the analyst not the patient who has made this his life's work and is invested for the sake of the process itself. Friedman states that the therapeutic alliance is the achievement, bit by bit of the successful analysis, and is not the fulcrum of treatment as described by Sterba (1934), Zetzel (1956), Greenson (1967) and Freud (1912).

Instead Friedman posits a congruence that can be achieved on more realistic grounds between the patient and analyst:

The work of uncovering repressed material... gives the patient a reason to review settled matters, the reason being a live hope of a better fulfillment... (pp. 148).

there must be some sense in which the patient perceives the analyst's interest as identical with his own current interest... the patient must feel that what he takes as himself, the analyst also to some extent takes him to be... This congruence is the foundation for the noncongruent persuasiveness of the analyst, who in another sense does not settle for what the patient takes as himself... (pp. 150-151).

This formulation removes the therapeutic alliance from the transference as a source of motivation and instead considers the alliance as something built between patient and analyst out of relatively more realistic phenomena. This is what I am calling the real relationship. Friedman's idea of congruence follows Stone's, Searles', and Greenson's finding that the real relationship will grow as the transference deepens and broadens.

Loewald (1980) described a second function for reality. He agreed with Stone and Greenson, that the real relationship is a condition for the emergence of the primordial transference but accentuates less the "reassuring" aspects of the real relationship in the face of the transference and delineates the "nutritive" aspects of the real relationship. The real relationship provides access ("new blood") for the transference. He elaborated on Freud's statement that there were ghosts in the underworld of the Odyssey which "'awoke to new life as soon as they tasted blood'... the blood of conscious-preconscious life, the life of contemporary present-day objects" (1980, p. 248). The living relationship between patient and analyst provides the "blood" which brings the ghosts of transference and the unconscious to life. This idea is dramatically presented in Pirandello's characters' search for an author, a cast which will allow them to "live (if) only for a moment." (1952, p. 218)

At this point my discussion will extend to include more of the analytic situation, beyond the real relationship to what has been called "extra analytic events." Weiss (1975) described the impact of special events, those unforeseen real events such as "a telephone call, knock at the door, a missed session or late arrival by the analyst, a broken elevator … loud disturbing noise … meeting the patient outside of the office setting … etc." as helpful "in mobilizing, highlighting and clarifying transference phenomena" (p. 69). If analyst and patient do not brush off or ignore these disruptions but heed the "clash between the reality knowledge of the analyst and (often silent) regressive transference aspects" (p. 74) there is much to be gained. There is often a sense of surprise and fear, the "safety of the analytic situation" has been momentarily altered, strong feelings and fantasies are stirred. "The transference is suddenly illuminated and a state of confusion and silence" often ensues. "Defensive maneuvers specific for each patient take place to cope … the transference can become too real; too intense and can lead from association, thinking, and feeling into the world of action" (p. 79). Weiss described how pieces of reality can impinge on the analytic situation and, acting like a magnet, pull forward a piece of the transference as Loewald (1980) described transference ghosts seeking the blood of everyday life in order to bring themselves into life.

These bits of reality Weiss calls "special events" and others have called "extra-analytic events" (Tarnower, 1966) come from the outside. There is another class of events which could be termed "intra-analytic events" which are present within the analytic situation and are not random external events. Some common examples include changes in the analyst and analytic situation such as illness, pregnancy, appearance, office location or decor, appointment changed from one time of day to another

In my own experience while pregnant and in reviewing the literature on this topic the single most consistent finding is that pregnancy, like the special events described by Weiss, engenders both shock and often a deepening of the transference experience. This is excluding those I think relatively small number of patients who have such a massive defensive reaction that they either bolt treatment or will not work with their experience of the analyst's pregnancy.

What can be made of these findings, that reality does not disrupt or change the transference so much as it roots it out, (assuming a stable and reliable frame held by the analyst). This can only be true if we are sensitive to these "bits of reality", otherwise there is the tendency on the part of both analyst and patient to pull back from these powerful events, to dismiss them as outside of the work.

The idea that transference experience can be facilitated by real events; that transference is not static, and doesn't automatically or necessarily unfold in all its fullness or in every facet within a particular analysis is an idea akin to the current view of memory. *[Edelman (1987, 1989), Rosenfield (1986, 1988)]*

Bartlett (1932) in his well-known study of memory described memory as "part of an ongoing process of imagination." Bartlett wrote (italics added):

> Remembering is not the re-excitation of innumerable fixed, lifeless and fragmentary traces. It is an imaginative reconstruction, or construction, built out of the relation of our attitude towards a whole active mass of organized past reactions or experience, and to a *little outstanding detail* which commonly appears in image or in language form. It is thus hardly ever really exact, even in the most rudimentary cases of rote recapitulation, and it is not at all important that it should be so (p. 214).

If we think of transference as comparable to memory, or think of transference as schematized memory; we could say that the recollection and experiencing of transference, like memory is "an imaginative reconstruction" and that what stirs the remembering is "a little outstanding detail which commonly appears in image or in language form." This outstanding detail is like the little bit of reality (or sometimes large) that intrudes into the analytic situation and has the power to evoke some piece of transference when we are alert to that possibility. Eich (1980) has demonstrated that memory is cue-dependent, that memory never occurs spontaneously. As with memory it is now outdated to consider transference as something that must be absolutely protected from reality in order to be true and pure. Transference counts on reality, that is a real person called an analyst, to make itself known.

Clinical Considerations

This section will illustrate that the usually quiet but nevertheless pervasive reality actually facilitates, in the two ways described above, the coming forward of the transference and other unconscious material. First, because reality provides a boundary for the unconscious to move or work against, patients are reassured that there are limits to their infantile omnipotence and are therefore more willing to allow the unconscious to be revealed. And secondly, just as reality serves as a kind of illuminating contrast to the patient's unconscious fantasies, it also provides a means for expression of these fantasies. Hence a particular tone of voice, aspect of the analyst's appearance or a chance encounter (Weiss, 1975) may fuel the emergence of the unconscious, most specifically as a vehicle for the transference.

These two functions and their operation will be described in the treatment situation in the following example. I recently heard a senior male analyst present a case of a young, seriously disturbed woman. He reported that she had described her parents as extremely intrusive. A prior treatment was felt to have been unsuccessful. Her method of relating

21

with this analyst was to insist the treatment be once weekly, she set conditions and demands which revealed her expectation that he accept her characterization of him as a "wimp." In reality this analyst has a gentle, intellectual and mild-mannered appearance, yet in talking with him for a few minutes one is impressed by a certain strength, clarity and self-possession that is not "wimpish." The immediate reality of the analyst's appearance and character are used by the patient for her therapeutic ends. His mild-mannered appearance reassures her unconsciously that he is not going to repeat her trauma of parental over-intrusion, she can experience him as differentiated from the original object and from the transference. This aspect of his character provides a reassuring "Wordsworthian" wall or tree, a hard surface for the purpose of differentiation. This allows her to work with this analyst in a way she could not with her former analyst who was more charismatic. Because this process of differentiation is multi-layered, at a deeper level we can assume that the patient senses this new analyst's real strength and is reassured that she will not destroy him. Paradoxically, he is both weak and strong in ways that facilitate her use of him.

The real character of this analyst provides the patient with two advantages. The first is that his mild mannered ways allowed her to defensively devalue his actual strength, power and separateness from her. The devaluation stands in contrast, provides boundary and a proscenium to her transference experience of powerful consuming objects. This allows her to attach with a feeling of safety. A deeper reality of this analyst, which is less available to the patient in her conscious experience, is his strength, maleness, potency and separateness. This strength, that is not compelled to intrude and control, provides her on a deeper level with a reassuring differentiation between her historic experience of strength and a new possibility of strength, that is between the past and present on one hand and a potential future on the other.

As the treatment progresses there will be moments in which the analyst repeats the original trauma through some kind of intrusiveness or over-involvement, that is in the Pirandelloian sense the analyst will inadvertently author a real moment of trauma. Reality always works both ways.

Case of Mrs. A.

The following is a description of a case in which a series of real events elucidated the patient's unconscious in a crucial way. These real events operated in the dual manner just described, as a contrast to the unconscious *and* as a kind of embodying or galvanizing force for the unconscious. The patient, Mrs. A, had been puzzling for some time in that although there was a warmth, sensuality and vitality that was quite winning, she seemed at a deeper level frozen and static. There were inexplicable periods when I felt warded off, bored, and sleepy with her. In times of crisis, particularly to do with separation, she became hard to reach. I began to worry that we might work endlessly but not make much progress. Her external situation improved some, she bought a house, felt she managed her relationships better, but they too did not deepen.

The crisis that shed light on her inner situation began with her sister's life-threatening illness. Upon hearing of her sister's illness my patient planned a week to visit her. She gave the dates she would be out and then in the last session announced the fact that her sister had taken a turn for the worse and she would be away for the entire summer and would not see me again until the fall. I mailed her the bill which included a charge for the two sessions she had originally cancelled. Although she had always been billed and paid for cancelled sessions she was livid that I had charged her for these two sessions. We took this up when she returned in the fall and she refused to pay for those sessions.

23

Unfortunately I had made a real mistake on the bill. Her last session with me had been moved forward one day. I had filled the original hour so did not bill her for it and when writing up her bill did not notice that we had rescheduled the last session and did not bill that either. She was very angry that I could have forgotten, i.e. not charged her for my last meeting of the summer with her. In summary, on the one hand I billed her for two sessions she had not attended and not billed her for the one (final of the summer) she did attend.

I was aware of my anger in the billing error, in using a lightly penciled arrow in contrast to my usual marking in of initials, I was expressing my own sense of loss at her sudden departure. I did not feel certain I would see her again, so in this sense her sudden departure reverberated through me. In not billing for that last session I turned passive to active and did to her what I felt she had done to me.

All of this was dramatized in one particular session. My patient became increasingly agitated. Over and over she came back to the fact of my mistake in not billing her for that last session. She thought that I had been very confused, there must be/have been something really wrong with me. She wondered how I could have made this mistake. Although I had briefly explained how the error had occurred it made no impact on her and she thought we should have a third party consultation. She wasn't sure she could trust me again, could she even continue to see me? She experienced me as unethical and disturbed. I began to feel a bit frantic and confused. This ordinarily very appropriate patient was disturbed by what she called my "poor functioning." Maybe she was right in some way I could not quite ascertain. Finally toward the end of the session I felt convinced I could not reach her, she was deeply paranoid and unrelated. I told her this and with relief she agreed. My salient feeling after this session was that something had broken down. As I studied this reaction further I realized that my denial of a psychotic aspect to this patient had broken down. There was a sense of deep sadness but also many pieces began to fit together. These had primarily to do with her Mother, several odd, bizarre but disconnected incidents relating to her mother came to my mind. Her mother treated her children exactly equal. She sent the most inappropriate gifts, could not remove a single article of her dead husband's possessions from the house and seemed awesomely accomplished at one moment and in the next mysteriously broke down in sobs. It became clear that my patient was in the grip of a powerful maternal transference which had been set off by a real error of mine and the real loss of her sister.

It was the combined effect of these two powerful real events which led to the emergence of a buried psychotic transference, the first and most important being the threatened loss of this much loved sister. These sisters had a special role for one another in that they had been able to depend on each other when their erratic mother was unavailable. The loss of her sister meant Mrs. A would be left alone with a disturbed, confusing mother/analyst. The fear in the transference was ignited by my billing error. My real mistake and confusion were used by her unconscious to express a psychotic element in the way Pirandello's characters were yearning to do with the actors: brought to life, fed and embodied by my error in a particular matrix of grief and loss. On the other hand my real sanity over the prior years (and now as I worked to understand her) did at the end of this tumultuous hour provide a contrast to her psychotic transference, hence she felt I was not as chaotic as her mother or that part of herself which was identified with her mother and warded off by "normalcy." We were for the first time, able to enter into a dialogue about something more disturbed in her. My point is this: the unconscious must have reality to express itself. Reality is not manipulated by the analyst for the patient's benefit as in Alexander's "corrective emotional experience." Reality is simply always present and always used by the patient and my interest is in trying to elucidate this a bit.

Case of Mrs. B.

Another point at which reality plays a part in treatment is through third party benefits. Mrs. B came to me for help with feelings of anger and ineffectiveness. She presented herself as a kind of androgenous ragamuffin and treated me as a wondrous feminine being, her fairy godmother. We had a Cinderella story cast. Her insurance reimbursed an unlimited number of sessions at 90%, hence this reality supported her transference to the analyst as benefactress. It wasn't that I paid her fee, but that she did not pay me. My sense is that this contributed to a lack of urgency in her treatment, a passivity and sense of timelessness. She fostered a mutual admiration society. I found her constant smiling so pressuring and distracting that even though she was a twice-a-week patient I suggested she use the couch. In this instance her unconscious used the real insurance benefits to support and express the fantasy of rescue vis a vis an omnipotent glorious mother. When I observed any break in this transference I would attempt to interpret. She would become subtly threatening when her anger or disappointment in me would be broached. We seemed stuck, she made intellectual progress, her thinking encompassed the more negative aspects of herself but she did not feel them with any conviction. Reality intervened; I think fortunately for the treatment. She became bored with her job (and the idealized transference!) and found a more challenging position. This insurance policy would reimburse only 50% for a limited number of sessions. During the weeks after the first billing with the new insurance her sweetness slowly unraveled. It became clear she was filled with rage, devaluation and feelings of having being exploited by me. She felt I was not and had not done enough for her. The idealization had masked an intensely demanding, greedy and contemptuous part of her which was extracted finally by the real requirement that she make a financial sacrifice for her treatment. Initially the real situation colluded with her defensive idealization and then when the real situation changed it in turn contributed to a break down of

26

this defense. I think that apart from the idealized transference which could not be counted on to help her maintain an alliance with me in the negative transference, this patient had felt I was reasonably helpful and conscientious. She had built a "realistic outline" of me along the lines Stone has described (1961) which was separate from the fairy godmother on the one hand and the wicked stepmother on the other. She repeatedly came back to this "outline," using this reality to help delineate the negative and positive transference, to illuminate them, and help her experience them as her own.

Case of Mr. C.

My final example involves an actual therapeutic intervention which introduced a concrete and dramatic piece of reality. Mr. C reacted with intense transference to my pregnancy. A borderline man, his preoccupation with beating fantasies began as a child. They were present in his night and day dreams as well as part of his masturbatory and sexual activities. These fantasies had a regulating function in his social relations, his role in the beating fantasies would alternate as needed between active and passive so that he would feel either triumphant or submissive. This man was precipitously sent away to boarding school at the age of 11, never to live for any extended period of time at home again, but away at school in the year and at one exotic camp or another during the summer. There is some evidence that his beginning adult sexual development was a threat to his mother, she called his father Big D, D for devil and he was called Little D. This may have led her to sending him away at age 11.

During my pregnancy Mr. C alternated between feeling blissfully united with me, as though it were his baby and terrified at the separation my pregnancy engendered and thirdly enraged at this perceived betrayal.

Repeatedly his desire to destroy (beat) his treatment and gain revenge would take over and he would then pull back from it at the last minute (submit). Given the degree of trauma and disturbance in his relationship with his mother, the move out at age 11 was the culmination of earlier stormy years, he demanded a kind of illusory control over me, breaks in this closeness were very threatening. My pregnancy provided the visible and constant realistic evidence of my bond with my husband, which he had avoided before this point. His destructiveness waxed and waned until my seventh month when he could not contain it anymore. He left a message on my answering machine that he would not return. I realized this was impulsive, but that he would have great difficulty retracting such a triumphant pronouncement and that he could make a final break unless I acted. As he was not answering his telephone I sent him a telegram which said: " I expect to see you for our session tomorrow." He did come in, to both our surprise. In our discussion of this it was clear that my dramatic action felt like a seduction and a beating to him. It was exciting. It represented the extravagant gifts his mother would send him at school and camp to appease him and ease her guilt. It *also* represented my insistence that he not be sent away too soon, that he stay and work this through with me. My action was gratifying in its sexual and aggressive aspects as it hearkened back to the past with his mother, but it also contained a new message for the present and future in that I believed we could both tolerate and live through his grief and rage.

Hence both aspects of reality that I have been describing come into use here. My telegram brought to life his seductive controlling mother but it also served to differentiate then from now in that my demand was not made to stave off separation as it was with his mother, but to insist on deeper work and mastery of his lifelong sense of abandonment. My expectation was that he experience his grief and not do to me what was done to him, thereby maintaining his manic triumph.

Discussion

The paradox of reality in the psychoanalytic situation is in its dual contribution to the forward movement of an analysis. On the one hand the known realistic qualities of and experiences with the analyst allow the patient's unconscious to be partly reassured that the original trauma will not be repeated in its full reality with the analyst, the new carrier of the patient's primary relationship. The analyst's relatively incorruptible position in the analytic situation; one is not particularly seductive, hostile, critical, unreliable, exploitative or controlling serves as a reassuring baseline and differentiation from which the patient can feel it is safe to proceed. On the other hand there are the inevitable real experiences the patient has with the analyst, which galvanize or bring forward the patient's repressed trauma, conflicts and experience. These real events are extremely varied, multitudinous, involving anything as subtle as the analyst's tone of voice, an illness or a chance encounter outside the session as well as those real events that take place in the patient's life, and those which are outside the influence of either analyst or patient.

The paradox of reality is that it serves as both a reassurance that the relationship with the analyst is a potentially new one, and yet the relationship with the analyst inevitably follows psychic fate and in some way small or big repeats the trauma of the patient's childhood.

Perhaps the underlying principle which explains the paradox is that, reality always serves as the thing which is in contrast; the transference can be experienced by the patient in contrast to the relatively realistic and benign relationship with the analyst, and the inevitable realistic "failings" of the analyst can be experienced in contrast to both the generally helpful analyst as well as the real and far greater failings of one's childhood. In other words it is the simultaneous experience of this duality, real and psychic truth, which contributes to psychic growth and can facilitate the crucial experience of integration: past and present, psychic and real.

References

Bartlett, F.C. (1932). *Remembering: A Study in Experimental and Social Psychology*. Cambridge: Cambridge University Press.

Bentley, Eric (1952). *Naked Masks: Five Plays by Luigi Pirandello*. New York: E.P. Dutton.

Brenner, C. (1979). *Working alliance, therapeutic alliance, and transference. J. Amer. Psychoanal. Assn.*, 27: 137–57.

Doolittle, H. (1956). *Tribute to Freud*. New York: Pantheon.

Edelman, G.M. (1987). *Neural Darwinism*. New York: Basic Books.

Edelman, G.M. (1989). *The Remembered Present*. New York: Basic Books.

Ehrenzweig, A. (1967). *The Hidden Order of Art*. Berkeley and Los Angeles: University of California Press.

Eich, J.E. (1980). The cue-dependent nature of state-dependent retrieval. *Memory and Cognition*, 8(2): 157–173.

Eissler, K.R. (1953). The effect of the structure of the ego on psychoanalytic technique. *J. Amer. Psychoanal. Assn.*, 1:104–143.

Freud, S. (1912). Dynamics of the Transference. *S. E.*, 12.

Friedman, L. (1969). The therapeutic alliance. *Int. J. Psychoanal.*, 50:139–153.

Greenson, R.R. (1967). *The Technique and Practice of Psychoanalysis*. New York: Int. Univ. Press.

Kris, E. (1951). Ego psychology and interpretation in psychoanalytic therapy. *Psychoanal. Q.*, 20:15.

Lipton, S.D. (1977). The advantage of Freud's technique as shown in his analysis of the Rat Man. *Int. J. PsychoanaL*, 58:255-270.

Lipton, S.D. (1979). An addendum to the advantages of Freud's technique as shown in his analysis of the Rat Man. *Int. J. Psychoanal.*, 60: 215–216.

Loewald, H.W. (1980). *Papers on Psychoanalysis*. New Haven and London: Yale University Press.

Moorman, Mary (1965). *William Wordsworth: A Biography*. Oxford.

Rawn, M.L. (1991). The working alliance: current concepts and controversies. *Psychoanal. Rev.*, 78(3): 379–389.

Rosenfield, I. (1986). Neural Darwinism: A new approach to memory and perception. *New York Review of Books*, October 9, 21–27.

Rosenfield, I. (1988). *The Invention of Memory*. New York: Basic Books.

Roazen, P. (1985). *Helene Deutsch: A Psychoanalyst's Life*. Garden City, N.Y.: Anchor Press/Doubleday.

Searles, H.F. (1965*). Collected Papers on Schizophrenia and Related Subjects*. New York: Int. Univ. Press.

Stein, M.H. (1981). The unobjectionable part of the transference. *J. Amer. Psychoanal. Assn.*, 24(4): 869–892.

Sterba, R. (1934). The fate of the ego in analytic therapy. *Int. J. Psychoanal., 15:117–126*.

Stone, L. (1961). *The Psychoanalytic Situation*. New York: Int. Univ. Press.

Stone, L. (1984). *Transference and its Context: Selected Papers on Psychoanalysis*. New York: Jacob Aronson, Inc.

Tarnower, W. (1966). Extra-analytic contacts between the psychoanalyst and the patient. *Psychoanal. Q.*, 35: 399–413.

Weiss, S.S. (1975). The effect of the transference of special events occurring during psychoanalysis. *Int. J. Psychoanal.*, 56: 69–75.

Zetzel, E.R. (1956). Current concepts of transference. *Int. J. Psychoanal.*, 37:369–376.

Zetzel, E.R. (1966). 1968: Additional notes upon a case of obsessional neurosis, Freud, 1909. *Int. J. Psychoanal.*, 47:123–129.

Additional Thoughts, October 2017

Today I would take a different stance toward reality and transference. I would like to include a reference by Ignes Sodre who writes that: As analysts we use our whole personality, our perceptions, intellectual understandings and a minutely observed awareness of our emotional states as a fundamental tool for doing the job ... if we weren't all the time being as real as possible a person in the consulting room, it would be like being blind and deaf to what is being communicated in depth. (2015, p. 156)

She continues to say that it makes us no less real when we cannot reveal personal information, etc., the necessity for keeping strict boundaries "around that which is personal" is important because it allows for the "least possible interference with the gathering and reading of the transference." (p.157) What is crucial is whether the patient is in a (more or less) depressive position rather than a persecuted, suspicious state of mind. This enables the patient to take for granted the analyst's concern, and thus a therapeutic alliance, depending on a relationship with a good object, not an idealized analyst or a cruel one, is possible. I believe a therapeutic alliance is based on an internalized good object—some of which the patient is able to bring to the analysis, integrating with what can be developed in the treatment itself.

The Imaginary Father

by Phillida Rosnick

C hildren reared by one parent have distinctive developmental challenges and outcomes which have been reported in the literature. (1, 2, 3, 4, 5) What concerns me here will be certain peculiarities in the ego development of girls reared without a father. I am making a distinction in this paper between the physically present but psychically absent father (6), the intermittently present father (as in a divorce) (7,8,9), the death of a father whom the patient had known (10, 11). and the imaginary father. In conditions where the father has been present and symbolization has taken place, there exists a representation of father. This representation is a combination of the vicissitudes of impulse and defense and the relationship with the mother, all interacting with the press of real life events. But if the child has never seen the father, then the father can be represented only through the mother and through the child's imagination and fantasy. What then are the are the special conditions that pertain to the formation of this paternal representation and to the development of a self-representation for the child?

I plan to report on the analysis of a young woman who never knew her father except through her mother's stories. In the course of the analysis she finds him. and they have a relationship for four years until he dies. This unusual situation has provided an experiment in nature with which to investigate the special developmental challenges for this young woman who had no contact with her father until early adulthood.

There is a small body of literature of analyses of women whose fathers were absent or who disappeared early in their lives. However. Freud (12), in his account of Leonardo da Vinci's life lays out two important developmental deviations. Freud describes: "[h]is illegitimate birth deprived him of his father's influence until perhaps his fifth year, and left him open to the tender seductions of a mother whose only solace he was. After being kissed by her into precocious sexual maturity, he must no doubt have embarked on a phase of infantile sexual activity of which only one single manifestation is definitely attested-the intensity of his infantile sexual researches… [T]he erotogenic zone of the mouth was given an emphasis which it never afterwards surrendered." The dual hazards described here in relation to a man, but just as relevant for women are libidinal over-investment by the parent in the child with subsequent seduction and/or precocious sexual stimulation, and oral fixation in the child. These become a leitmotif in subsequent accounts of analyses of fatherless patients.

There are seven analyses reported in the literature of women who fit the criteria proposed in this paper for having had an imaginary father. They focus on the particular psychic challenges faced by these women. Two are adult analyses reported by Fenichel (13,14), and two are adult analyses reported by Eisendorfer (15). A. Reich (16) describes the superego and self-representation problems of a young woman. Neubauer's (17) is the only report of a child analysis. Finally, McDougall(19), describes an analysis of an overtly homosexual woman.

Fenichel's first case (13), of a woman whose father died the day she was born illustrates oral fixation both in behavioral symptoms and in object relations. He describes that the chief object tie and love object was the mother without stating that the tie was specifically homosexual. She identified with her father and "…mystical union with him, representing at one and the same time sexual intercourse and identification was conceived of as oral union, as communion." "To sum up: the purely fantastic oedipus complex was characterized at all levels of libidinal development by total or partial incorporation, and the object introjected had to be interpreted, according to the stage of the analysis, as father, child, feces, or penis."

As the analysis advanced Fenichel reports, "that the more completely the infantile amnesias were dispelled the clearer did it become that her real experiences with men were relatively unimportant and that the chief object which influenced her real character formation was the one parent whom she knew, her mother." Fenichel discusses the aggressive reactions of this patient to her mother and her disappointments, most notably the lack of a penis and the lack of a father, and her need to repress this anger for fear of loss of love of the only parent she had, and the subsequent displacement of this aggression against all males. For the patient, "no man was the right one".

The second analysis by Fenichel (14), is not reported in sufficient detail to be relevant here except for the description of her presenting symptoms which point again to oral fixation. She was described as an instance of "oral symptom complex" which is described as "(lying) between manic-depressive illness, drug addiction and hysteria." Fenichel describes a symptom picture which would conform nowadays to a diagnosis of bulimarexia (with symptoms of binge eating alternating with starving) in a woman with mood swings and a borderline level of personality organization. The identifications with her mother were omnipresent and intense including choosing the same career as her mother. but she was contemptuous and spiteful towards her. Her "attachment was of a predominantly oral-sadistic character"

Eisendorfer (15) continues to note the dual hazards that Freud had described, namely, an intensification of the libidinal relationship with the remaining parent. and a regression to the oral phase as a reaction to sexual conflict or sexual arousal. For the first time he spells out the nature of the identification of the child with the absent parent. The wish to be loved by mother as the father had been loved establishes a masculine identification in the daughter and a homoerotic love for the mother.

In his first case Eisendorfer describes a 29-year-old woman, an only child. whose father died one year after her birth. He describes an analysis that was highly turbulent and sexualized. "Every emotion became identified with sexuality and in turn was directed towards the mother.. Panic and rage followed each other and swamped any attempt at intellectual understanding". Eisendorter noted an extreme oscillation in her sexual identification. The patient had many openly homosexual dreams in which she had a penis and was having intercourse with her mother or mother figures. "Beneath the passive, inhibited, conscious feminine aspects of her personality there seethed violent defying aggressive masculine elements. She had been unable to develop these two conflicting extremes into a well-rounded personality." He concludes. "One of the important conditions for being loved in these single-parent situations is the identification with the absent parent: a homosexual bond is thus established between the patient and the remaining parent."

In a second case he describes a 32-year-old woman who entered treatment when her mother committed suicide shortly after the patient had left home and married. This woman's father had divorced the patient's mother when the patient was 6 months of age. Of note is the fact that the patient had slept in the mother's bed until her marriage and had mutual masturbation with her mother until shortly before her marriage. "The patient had many dreams in which she played the masculine role, possessed a penis, and engaged in love-making and intercourse with a mother figure .. In one interesting dream the patient is having intercourse with herself: she inserts her own penis into her vagina". The explanation for these alternating identifications lies in a discussion of superego development "In such a setting, in which a severe superego developed as a compensatory factor in order to neutralize the unassimilated id forces, a split personality response was manifested by both patients. Their behavior either was motivated by the id, or after reaching a certain intensity it swung in the opposite direction and was dominated by the superego. Their behavior constantly vacillated between these two poles of reaction." As did their sexual identities. This oscillating, alternately masculine and feminine sexual identification occurs with regularity in this review of cases of analyses of women reared without a father.

A. Reich's paper on "Early Identifications as Archaic Elements in the Superego" (16) makes a further attempt to explain the alternating sexual identities found so often under these circumstances. She reports a case of a young woman with widely divergent selves; a megalomanic phallic self and a deflated, hated self as well as frequent oscillations between the two. This young woman was born several months after her father's sudden death (and after the death of the mother's beloved brother, as well.) Reich notes the patient's early identification with the dead father and his glorified talents. and the desire that she be him and his phallus. She had a fantasy of "standing out like a tremendous obelisk". Reich summarizes: "Any desexualization of the fantasy became impossible. No stable identifications with nonsexual qualities of the objects could be attained because the child was trying to identify with objects that existed in fantasy only. The normal impact of reality on this fantasy object, which would have helped to achieve some degree of desexualization and also to reduce to normal size the figure of the father that was seen in such supernatural dimensions was absent. Hence the un-sublimated phallic character of the ego ideal and its megalomanic scope … She wanted to be a phallus with her whole body … which equalled being a creative genius of monumental proportions admired by everyone around her.… These fantasies, however, were contradicted by her awareness of being a girl. The lack of a penis was experienced as a terrific trauma which caused her to cling evermore tenaciously to this overcathected identification with the father-phallus as such. Thus oral sadistic impulses were aggressively intensified. On the other hand, fear of loss of the mother's love led her to develop strong reaction formations. Finally this ruthless, pregenital aggressiveness was turned against the self as a relentless superego. This became combined with the megalomanic, phallic identification. The end product was a poorly integrated mixture which resulted in the oscillations of self-esteem described above."

Neubauer (17) describes a child analysis of a three and a half year old girl whose father left abruptly during the first year of her life. The mother remarried during the analysis when her daughter was six years old. But unlike the cases presented so far, in which there is persistently described an "arrest at the primary homosexual level" this case "too evades the oedipal conflict. though not through phallic fixation, but through premature flight into latency as an escape from unenduring phallic ambivalence." "With the repression of aggression the castration grievance and all the prephallic grievances which it includes remained unresolved; therefore, an oedipal identification with father or mother was impossible... She remains with a developmental deficiency which stems from the lack of having lived through and mastered the oedipal conflict. Jealousy and rivalry, punishment and guilt, instinctual renunciation with resulting ego expansion-these ingredients are missing to provide an adequate texture of the maturing psyche, with its 'categorical imperative' won only through oedipal participation and solution.

Joyce McDougall (18) describes an adult analysis of a young woman with an overt homosexual identity whose father died suddenly when she was fifteen months old. The by now familiar themes. of severe superego restrictions against aggression to the living parent, of the wish to be the exclusive love object of the mother, and the primitive introjection of the dead father were all aspects in this young woman's analysis. As an explanation for the overtly masculine sexual identity in her patient McDougall states: "in seeking to possess the mental representation of

THE IMAGINARY FATHER - BY PHILLIDA ROSNICK

two parents capable of conferring upon her the status of subjective and of sexual identity, it appeared that the price to be paid was her own castration-the loss of her femininity."

Burgner (19) reports on treatments of both boys and girls who were raised without a father. The conclusions are by now familiar and bear repeating: "These children had problems over establishing a masculine or feminine identity. Fears of incest in the boys and lack of an oedipal father for the girls also hindered sexual identifications. The girls' doubts and conflicts over the mother's femininity (as distinct from the fantasies they had about her underlying sadism to the father) made her a conflictual identifacatory model and enhanced their bisexual problems. It was significant that in all the girls the loss of the father was experienced as confirmation of their inadequate bodies. Their pervasively low self-esteem and dissatisfaction were important factors in their longing for a complete body, a complete family." Also important was the finding that these children were fixated at earlier stages of development," with a corresponding lack of dominance at the phallic-oedipal phases and beyond". She makes a distinction between "triadic" interactions that were essentially pre-oedipal in nature, and the genuine oedipal three object drama. "[T]riangulation" seems developmentally inevitable, but with children raised without a father. the "triangulation" is pseudo-oedipal and "should not be confused with the Oedipus complex proper".

Case Illustration

"And the best and worst of this is
That neither is most to blame
If you have forgotten my kisses

And I have forgotten your name"
Swinburne (20)

I plan to report on an analysis of a young woman, whom I shall call Nora. She had a full brother exactly two years older. Her biological father saw her once at the age of three months and then disappeared from her and her mother's life. Her mother remarried when Nora was six. She and her second husband had two children, a girl and a boy, six and ten years younger than Nora. This man adopted Nora and her brother, changing their name to that of their adoptive father. When Nora was twelve, her mother divorced again and has had no significant relationship with a man since. In college, Nora changed her last name to her mother's maiden name, deleting any patronymic, any notion of a man. When Nora was twenty six and in the eighth month of analysis she looked for her father and found him. They saw each other for four years, until his death.

Nora was twenty five at the time she sought analysis for paralysis in her work and love life. She was a rather eerie looking young woman, with bleach-blond hair cut into an extreme crew-cut. Although she had a slim build, it was curvaceous and feminine. When she wore men's jeans, a boxy man tailored jacket. and oxfords (as she did frequently) it was difficult to discern her gender correctly. Less frequently, she could wear a short skirt and a tight sweater and although gamin, look sexy. She wore her androgynous sexual identity on her sleeve, so to speak.

Nora permitted herself to be seduced by young men who had the reputation for playing around. At the opening of the analysis she was involved in a three year affair with a young man, who was frequently unfaithful to her. She had been "seduced" by this young man, in college, while in the midst of an affair with his best friend, who had been unfaithful to her as well. Many an analytic hour was spent in descriptions of, and in rages against the latest of her boyfriend's conquests, many of

42

whom she arranged to meet. While the relationship was brimming over with jealousy and rivalry, it did not appear to represent triangulation of a genuine oedipal sort.

There was no overt homosexual behavior between Nora and her mother, as in some of the cases reported above, but she and her mother colluded in an unconscious exclusion of males. As a teenager and beyond Nora noticed that when she brought home a young man, her mother ignored him completely, to the point of simply not speaking to him. Once Nora had met her father she noticed an extremely strong resemblance between her brother, Adam, and her father. "Every time I saw my father I saw Adam more strongly and said to my mother, 'How come you never said Adam looked so much like him?' but I don't know. I guess I feel she left him [Adam] out. He hasn't heard half the stories I heard about our father".

Nora was her mother's partner in rearing "the kids", (her half-siblings), including helping her financially after the step-father's departure. (For example, she contributed her weekly paper-route money towards household expenses, taxes, and activities for the younger children.) In doing so she reversed any rivalry with these children who had had a father, albeit briefly, and maintained an exclusive relationship with her mother. After she met her father, she articulated in the following way how she had felt she had unconsciously played her father to her mother: "The ways I am more like my father than Adam, more suited to him, more able to understand him, and understand in ways that I feel are similar to him. As if I somehow understood what my mother understood in him and took it upon myself to be that." She had one overtly homosexual dream in which she associates to her mother as her sexual partner.

In sum, she conformed to some of the deviations in oedipal development described in the review above; specifically, a dramatic and oscillating masculine and feminine sexual identity, a homosexual bond with her mother and a "pseudo oedipal" triangulation in her love life that betrayed a strong pre-oedipal caste.

There were peculiarities in Nora's thought processes such as frank departures from the laws of syntax, cryptic sentence structures. and beginning ideas in medias res. Sessions would start with silence or "blankness" and might go typically like this: "It's becoming increasingly an effort to put together a feeling, of things not being put together. Not being able to think of things. I was noticing on the way over, lurching from one thing to another, images from one time and another, not focusing on anything. Then I started to try and look at things from an overall perspective of kind of how any of these pieces come together and they didn't". She frequently spent whole sessions at a time lost in this at one and the same time overly abstract, overly concrete descriptions of her thoughts. The analyst strained to understand her, but if this digressive and odd thought pattern persisted the analyst "tuned out". She associated this style of thinking with being defective. In the early phases of her analysis this became the subject of some concern in the analyst's mind, culminating in the question of whether analysis was the treatment of choice. While her life was chronically unsatisfying to her and masochistic solutions abounded, she did not show the same kind of disorganization in the running of her daily life that she showed in her thought processes on the couch.

She very characteristically started sessions in a muddle, but might, (or might not) work her way out of it. Sometimes she started an analytic hour with twenty minutes of silence. Underneath the muddle were signs of irritation and hostility toward the analyst. She "started the session in the waiting room" and although she had not stated it directly, made it clear that she resented having to bring the analyst up to date with her words. She startled at hearing the analyst speak. or complained about the analyst intruding herself when the analyst interpreted a displacement and tried to bring an affect into the transference. She made sparing direct or indirect comments about the analyst, and the remarks never developed either within a session or between sessions. While vacations were noted and reacted to by the occasional missed hour or by forgotten dates of the vacation. attempts on the analyst's part to help these parapraxes come alive with feeling were resented or stubbornly defied. She was involved in the analysis which, it seemed, she insisted on conducting on her own. She made almost all appointments, was not late, was cordial to the analyst, paid her bill promptly, and then was gone. The analyst felt alternately actively excluded, or invisible.

It is this "invisible" and ambivalent transference, containing both paternal and maternal elements. which can very easily be mistaken as a transference to the pre-oedipal mother. Its primordial qualities such as her fear of engulfment and identity diffusion and defensive exclusion of the analyst had a particularly maternal pre-oedipal ring.

This is what she knew about her father: that he was Polish, an artist and/or a dancer, that her mother married him several months into a pregnancy with her brother Adam, and that shortly before the birth of Adam, her mother left her father to give birth to and rear her child with her family of origin in a neighboring state. Contact between her parents was intermittent during her brother's infancy, (weekend visits, phone calls, letters), but after a visit three months after Nora's birth, contact was never resumed. She knew nothing of the circumstances of her conception. He lived in New York City and had seen his son several times during his infancy, but had seen her only once.

Her mother was not unwilling to talk about him, but she communicated no affect, no affection, no grief or longing in her words about him. She described him as having had an "indescribable unrelation" to his family members and others. She meant by this phrase he was so "independent" he did not need human contact or acknowledge social or emotional ties of the conventional sort. She predicted that when Nora met him, if he weren't homeless, he would be charming, take her out for dinner, treat her like another interesting acquaintance. and "maybe even make a pass at you." He would not be a father to her.

She decided that even if he didn't want to be her father, even if he was disappointing to her as a parent or a person, she still needed to meet him "to transport him from fantasy to reality." In identifying with a representation that does not have size, shape, or substance, she is identifying with a vacuum. She is left with nothing to go on but her imagination.

To illustrate her lack of a firm sense of self or boundaries she relates the following from the second year in analysis:

She comes to a session frightened and crying because men have been looking at her on the subway, and because she has observed two men accost a beautiful woman in what seemed to her an assaultive way. She said, "I can only learn something if I convince myself that it's isolated, that I'm not being watched ... Richard complains I don't express what I want, of what my idea of having a boyfriend was. And then I remembered an old idea ... seemingly something before I thought about men. And it was more or less some man. Not very well formed. Sort of magical knowing me and understanding me without my saying anything almost. And sort of seeing into me, I guess. Reading from little information what I was good at, or how smart I was, and sort of indirectly being some kind of ticket or permission to be something in a limited, confined, controllable way. And later still I thought I was imagining that was an invisible father."

She got into his apartment building and knocked on his door late one night. He let her in saying "Do I know you?" She answers, "You're my father, I think you're my father." and he replies closing the door behind them, "Well, if I'm your father, then…" She asks him if he knows her name. and he does not, nor does he know his son's name, but he can remember that it is a biblical name. He remembers Nora's mother's first name and she, protecting them both, doesn't press for the last name. Several minutes later he asks her, "What was your name, Lindsey?"

In that remarkable hour and those that followed, she was grounded and a keen observer. She saw him as an eccentric. He is short, with long graying hair and a scraggly beard. He was shy, not socially comfortable as her mother had led her to believe. And his "indescribable unrelation" is far from independence. He was overbearingly needy and demanding. He asked Nora to run countless errands for him because, she saw, he was paranoid and easily agitated if doing it himself. With young children he was inept and shallow. For many following sessions, Nora began "feeling happier than usual and then sad. Not down and depressed. It's pure sad." She mourned in reverse as it were; she mourned the loss of a shared past, not the loss of a shared future.

Her father had been both invisible and had had an "indescribable unrelation" to her and her family. She identified with both qualities. The vagueness in her thought content, the cryptic, often unrecognizable sentences, and the derailing belonged to sexual conflicts she had with this imaginary father, which achieve an unusual intensity since they were all managed in her fantasy and imagination without recourse to reality. This imaginary father was sexualized, thus looking and being looked at, thinking and revealing her thoughts publicly was tantamount to inviting rape. This partially explained the unformed thoughts, the cryptic communications, the resentment in speaking to me in words that was so pronounced at the beginning of the analysis. She wished (and feared) I had some sort of 'magical knowing', and 'seeing into her'.

Another aspect of her thought slippage was an identification with an invisible self. Her "invisible self" is described below in a fleeting thought she has about her boyfriend in the first year of her analysis: "[h]e would be there, be very close or intimate with me and seeing something extremely different. The things that I chose were, that as if to exaggerate it, I would be wearing a white shirt and he would see purple. My hair is short and he would see long. When I think to the original feeling it's exaggerating it, but I was struck. He would be wearing a purple shirt and his hair is long. It was a scary feeling. But as if he's there with himself seeing his shirt and him seeing me I wasn't there anymore." In identifying with a representation that does not have size, shape, or substance. she is identifying with a vacuum. She is left with nothing to go on but her imagination. She "loses herself" in her need for definition from the other. With the reality before her of a father, flawed, but at least with size, shape, and substance, she can distinguish fact from fantasy. This critical capacity to differentiate inside from outside, imagination from reality, spread to other areas as well. This had been the threat in the transference in the opening of the analysis, being engulfed by the analyst/father. It explained why she had been so impervious to the existence of the analyst and had seemed to need to conduct the analysis on her own. It should be noted that the fear of engulfment was from the imaginary father, not the early, pre-oedipal mother.

The first summer after she and her father met they decided to take a trip to Poland together with a study group. During the months before a trip the sexualized excitement between father and daughter reached a feverish pitch and created terror in Nora. In analyzing this it became clear there was an ambiguity in how they addressed each other in public. While they called each other by their first names, it was unclear if she was introduced as his daughter and he as her father to others. The ambiguity of how to describe their relationship, in which they both colluded, contained for the

48

moment the entirety of the incestuous oedipal drama. The "indescribable unrelation" was being transformed into the describable father/daughter relationship. In a reversal of the usual representation, Nora reported "He said 'I was the one he loved and I happened to be his daughter.'" It took her another year before she objectified (clarified?)this further and said, "I am your daughter; therefore you love me."

She did it in the context of the beginning of his illness that was to ultimately end his life. He had a brief stay in a hospital. She started to think about his mortality. She said:"There's something funny about him treating me like a girl. I'm specifically a girl to him. (What's strange?) It's kinda funny he should notice and not have me be both [a boy and a girl] or neither. (she thinks silently) Just a strange sense of being a daughter all over again. The daughter means by definition daughter of the mother. This is completely not that." It was then that she poignantly realized her father didn't want to see his son. He had a daughter and that was who she is to him.

This particular reality, the reality of her father and their now describable relationship, permitted her to explore her sexual identity confusion and intense penis envy. While these issues were worked on in an interesting fashion, they are beyond the scope of this paper.

Summary

I have presented material from one analysis where cognitive difficulties, which raised concerns about the ego strengths of the analysand and questions about the advisability of analytic work, resolved rapidly after the analysand found her father. These difficulties in her thought organization were the result of sexualized fantasies and identifications with her imaginary father and their derivatives in the transference.

The question of her resolution of the Oedipus remains an open one. The analysis is in its fifth year. The analysand has embarked on obtaining a graduate degree and after one semester appears to be doing well. Her achievements to date bring to mind the following quotation from Burgner (19)

"It seems possible that patients who come from families where the father has been intermittently absent in childhood are capable through analysis of reaching certain levels—they are helped to make relationships, albeit with some pre-oedipal dominance, and they are often able to function well in their professional and social lives... But there tends to be a protraction of the original narcissistic interference both in their self-investment and in their sexual identity; they are adhesively and ambivalently tied to the remaining object, and they seem to maintain a certain hopelessness about their adult capacities as partners and parents. A dimension of experience has been denied to them or distorted for them in childhood and, while analysis can go some way of offering them understanding of this deprivation, it cannot—predictably enough—make good the original damage." (19)

References

1. Freud, A., & Burlingham, D. *War and Children*. New York: International Universities Press, 1944.
2. Freud, A., & Burlingham. D. *Infants without Families*. New York: International Universities Press,. 1943.
3. Grossberg, S.H., & Crandall, L., Father loss and father absence in preschool children. *Clinical Social Work Journal*, 1978, 6, 123–133.
4. Aichorn, A. *Wayward Youth*. New York: Viking Press, 1935.
5. Rochlin, G. Loss and restitution. *Psychoanalytic Study of the Child*. New Haven, Yale University Press, 1953, 8, 288–309.
6. Kirshner, L.A., The absence of the father. *Journal of the American Psychoanalytic Association*, 1992,40, 1117–1138.
7. Gardner, G. Separation of the parents and the emotional life of the child. *Mental Hygiene*, 1956, 40, 53–64.
8. McDermott, J. Divorce and its psychiatric sequellae in children. *Archives of General Psychiatry*, 1970, 23, 421–427.
9. Despert, L. *Children of Divorce*. New York, Doubleday, 1962.
10. Bowlby, M. Grief and mourning in infancy and early childhood. *Psychoanalytic Study of the Child*. New Haven, Yale University Press, 1960, 15, 9–52.
11. Bowlby, J. Childhood mourning and its implications for psychiatry. *The American Journal of Psychiatry*, 1961, 118, 481–498.
12. Freud, S. *Leonardo DaVinci and a memory of his childhood*. Standard Edition, JI. London: Hogarth Press, 1910.
13. Fenichel, O, The pregenital antecedents of the oedipus complex. *The Collected Papers of Otto Fenichel, I*, New York, Norton, 1954.

14. Fenichel, O. Specific forms of the oedipus complex. *The Collected Papers of Otto Fenichel, I*, New York, Norton, 1954.

15. Eisendorfer, A. The clinical significance of the single parent relationship in women. *Psychoanalytic Quarterly*, 1943, 12, 223–239.

16. Reich, A. Early identification as archaic elements in the superego. *Journal of the American Psychoanalytic Association*, II, 1954, 218–238.

17. Neubauer, P. The one-parent child and his oedipal development. *Psychoanalytic Study of the Child*, New Haven: Yale University Press, 1960, 286–309.

18. McDougall, J. The dead father. *International Journal of Psychoanalysis*, 1989,70:205–220.

19. Burgner, M. The oedipal experience: effects on development of an absent father. *International Journal of Psychoanalysis*, 1985, 66:311–320.

20. Swinburne, A.C. *An Interlude*, 1866.

The Anal World of A Six-Year-Old Boy

by John Rosegrant

Clinical material from the psychoanalysis of a 6-year-old boy is presented which manifests the creation of an anal psychic world—a psychic world which is blatantly anal in content and characterised by the formal qualities of de-differentiation and interchangeability, which are linked to anal experience and the level of cognitive maturation typical during the anal phase. This case demonstrates the existence at an earlier developmental level of perverse qualities which have previously been identified in adults. In particular, similarities are noted with the fantasies of adult perverts and the Marquis de Sade. Psychodynamic antecedents which have previously been extrapolated from investigation of these adults are confirmed in statu nascendi in this child. Like adult perverts, this boy appears to have created his anal world to defend against acknowledgement of sexual and generational differences. His anal world play is conceptualised as an example of a perverse play style.

The anal world of a six-year-old boy

A 6-year-old boy during the second year of his psychoanalysis presented the remarkable play described below. I shall analyse this play as manifesting

53

the creation of a perverse, anal world which was central to this boy's psychic equilibrium, and which he was able to begin changing only after engaging in a certain kind of therapeutic enactment. This case demonstrates the existence at an earlier developmental level of perverse qualities which have previously been identified in adults.

Session one: Donald brings a board game and states that he had to wait five minutes (he was early), throwing the box on the ground and striking the lid rapidly against my leg; I tell him to stop hitting me and say, 'All that time to have to wait!' He swears at me briefly, then settles into playing the game, cheating outrageously. Ten minutes prior to the end, he notices me glancing at the clock, says 'Oh no, you can't!' turns over the clock, and comes for my watch; I decide to let him remove it (I discuss this choice of intervention below in the section 'The Therapeutic Gain'). I say that Donald wants me not to know the time so I can't end the session; Donald says that is exactly what he is doing. After a bit, I say I will have to guess the time; Donald hides the watch in his pocket but I catch a glimpse, see that it is time, and tell him so; Donald wrestles me and I have to half carry him to the waiting room. Donald returns the watch by sliding it a few inches up my trouser leg.

Session two (two sessions later): Donald brings the same game, puts it on the floor, and flops back on the couch, limbs splayed. I say, 'That's a Donald collapse!' He says yes, that he is broken in a million pieces, so I say I better put him together, and play at this by rapidly moving my hands above him. With a small smile, Donald wails 'Oh no, you put my penis where my nose should be and my nose where my penis should be!' I try again, but he says I put his mouth upside down, then I put his mouth on his belly and his eyes where his nipples should be. My efforts result in jumbled body parts a few more times before I finally get it right.

The rest of the session is an unusually good-natured board game. When I say it is time to stop, Donald grabs me and says that I am in a million pieces; I say that then we would be unable to stop.

Session three (the next session, after the weekend): Donald shows me a loose tooth, then gets out the toy soldiers. One side is losing badly, and I have the leader say they have to try something new, they will—Donald interrupts and says, 'Pee in their pants!' Donald divides the soldiers into boys and girls. A boy wants to watch a girl peeing, and shows her how he can pee farther because he has a penis. He then asks the girl what she has between her legs, and as Donald refuses to speculate, I say she has a vulva and vagina. The boy also wants to see her boobs. After a little competitive urinating, they affectionately fart and poop at each other, including farting into each other's buttocks. The girl has a long vulva but the boy has a longer penis.

War starts between the boys and the girls, with artillery consisting of pooping, farting, barfing and peeing. A girl is captured and has to show her private parts on pain of being shot. I have the girls decide to show what is between their legs because it sometimes scares boys; Donald has the boys pee on the girls so fast that they see nothing. A boy wants the captive's boobs for himself, then the boys burn the boobs off the attacking girls; I say that way they are the same and don't have to feel bad. The boys bury the girls under a pile of poop, then rescue them by using their superior peeing to wash it away. Two boys who do not know what is between a girl's legs examine the captive there, expecting to find boobs, or something big and hairy unless it is a young girl, who would have no hair. The boys shoot off the vaginas of all the girls, then Donald anxiously has them say they have done a bad thing, because now the girls can't pee, and he decides that the boys had missed. A boy sticks a gun up the captive's vagina and leaves it five hours, nervously wondering if she enjoys it. If she has a baby she can pee with her breasts. Two boys drink milk from the girls' breasts, then stretch and pull them off so that they can drink whenever they want; I say then they will never be hungry or lonely. Donald then has these boys successfully fight everyone. Sides change again, and each side has someone with long buttocks who can poop on the others; these two end up pooping into each other's buttocks. When I say it is time to stop, there is a chaotic attack with all manner of excretions and secretions.

Session four (the next day): Donald eagerly says 'OK, the same game of looking at private parts'. The girls are using the bathroom, the boys come to spy. They enjoy smelling farts and poop, and are clearly interested in big buttocks, not genitals. A boy lets himself be seen, but only after putting on lipstick and taping back his penis so that he will be mistaken for a girl. They compare boobs, and although the boy is impressed by the girl's boobs, the boy has big ones too. They begin ingesting each other's farts, piss, poop and vomit, commenting on how delicious it all is, like honey or flowers. The boy especially likes putting his nose in the girl's anus to smell her farts. Donald has a moony expression on his face, and off-and-on is clutching his penis. I have the girl wonder if this is what men and women do when they are in love. They then begin biting chunks out of each other's buttocks and anuses, to their mutual enjoyment. I mention that they are biting each other's private parts. Donald has the boy reveal that he is a boy, saying 'What's wrong with that?' I have the girl say that nothing is wrong with that, she likes boys. Donald has her bite the boy's penis, and then has the boy nervously pee in her mouth.

This scene is essentially repeated twice more with two more pairs. Donald has them say 'We'll show them what men and women do when they're in love!' After his penis is bitten, the boy says he likes it best having his nose in the girl's anus; I say that's better than having his penis bitten because he only has one penis but there are endless farts.

History and clinical background

Donald is the only child his parents had together, but has much older half-siblings; these are the children of his father by a previous marriage,

56

and have always been in the custody of the father. Donald's parents have white collar careers. Both parents have significant character problems, and his mother has begun therapy since Donald started analysis, but his father refuses. His mother is often angry and critical towards both others and herself. His father is emotionally detached and seems baffled by what it means to be a father, showing surprise at evidence that he is important to Donald. Although Donald's parents have stayed together, their marriage has been riddled with anger and resentment for most of his life and is asymmetrical in terms of emotions and power, with his father longing for a renewal of love which his mother rejects.

In addition to the strain trauma and unhelpful identificatory models Donald has experienced from his parents, two other pathogenic factors need to be noted: firstly, Donald has experienced the repeated loss of nannies who were important attachment figures. Both parents work, so after his mother returned to work when Donald was 3 months old, a significant amount of his care was provided by these nannies. Due to external factors, several had come and gone by the time Donald began treatment. Secondly, Donald was vividly confronted with the possibility of injury to the penis because before Donald's birth, his half-brother had his legs and penis badly burned in a freak accident. With startlingly poor judgement, his father tried to assuage Donald's potential anxiety by making sure that Donald had plenty of 'natural opportunity' to look at the damage, such as by urinating with his halfbrother. (It may be speculated that the father was himself coping with considerable castration anxiety.) There was no other evidence of over-stimulation or sexually abusive behaviour.

Donald began treatment at the age of 5 at the insistence of his pre-school. He was violent with other children, pushing and shoving them heedlessly, and talked back to the teachers. His parents also noted that although he used to be sweet and adorable, he was becoming increasingly sarcastic and hard to manage. Testing done by the school indicated superior intelligence.

57

As soon as the analysis began, Donald formed an intense attachment to me, but adamantly refused to acknowledge directly this attachment or his resulting unhappiness when sessions ended. Indeed, anger was the only emotion he would admit to—this one he admitted to proudly. He typically hurried into sessions and played eagerly, but became enraged if I did not follow his instructions precisely, and when I ended the sessions. He firmly maintained that he hated me and that I was stupid, and sometimes hit, kicked or threw things so that I had to restrain him physically. Interpretations of this behaviour in terms of sadness about separation or about his lack of power and control compared to me resulted in silence (if I was lucky) or in increased scorn and abuse. The content of our play was generally a war in which my characters were crushed by his characters, which had a variety of omnipotent powers that changed from day to day. These ranged from exceptional karate skills to magical powers such as fiery breath, flight, gigantic monsters, etc. Interpretations within the metaphor, in which my characters bemoaned their weakness and lack of control, and longed for the admirable qualities of Donald's characters, were usually tolerated, although even these could result in reprimands that I was talking too much. In his controlling behaviour, his omnipotent play, his rage at my interpretive efforts, and his refusal to acknowledge vulnerable feelings or any sort of problem, Donald resembled narcissistic children described by Beren (**1992**).

Donald's anxiety and anger within the sessions gradually abated. It seldom became necessary to restrain him, and the play content changed so that although war continued, characters became much less omnipotent, and Donald and I often co-operatively operated both sides. His unwillingness to refer to his relationship with me or to acknowledge any emotion other than anger continued with little moderation, however. This brings us to the material described initially.

Farty rules

How are we to understand this unusually vivid, even lurid material? First, it is necessary to look at the consequences of these sessions.

The next few sessions were quite similar. Then Donald returned to war and board games, but for weeks maintained a preoccupation with farting: he would suddenly say 'Fart!' (this was not a command, but a representation of farting) or accuse me of farting. This seemed to happen most often when he cheated, so I began to say when he cheated that he was playing by 'farty rules'. Donald was very interested in this idea, and easily recognised the difference between farty rules and grown-up rules. I extended the concept of farty rules to include his misbehaviour at the ends of sessions, which again Donald was easily able to understand. He became intensely interested in what I thought of farty rules, and tempted me to play by them myself. He also talked about my big buttocks, and tried to get me to admit that I farted in sessions, or outside of sessions. This enabled us to talk about how much Donald wished that I were like him, and that there were times that farty rules were most fun but other times that grown-up rules were most fun. We identified that farty rules were most fun when things were not working out for him in the grown-up world, e.g. when he was losing a game, or when he made a mistake. When next he made a mistake at checkers, instead of coldly berating himself or me, and quitting, he stood on one leg and laughed that he was a 'farty chicken leg poop nose'.

Thus, the material described at the beginning appears to have had a salutary effect. From it we developed a language which enabled Donald to engage in a more friendly dialogue with me, talk about wanting us to be alike, accept that he had moments when he was unhappy with himself, and begin to explore the meaning to him of being a child *vis-à-vis* a world of adults.

This pattern, of lurid material in the vein of that presented at the beginning immediately preceding moments of growth, has recurred. Here are two more examples:

Session five (almost three months later, the session before my summer break): I begin by reminding Donald of my vacation, and he applauds. Most of the session is a war between soldiers. Towards the end, some of the soldiers want cake to eat, but the bosses give them poop and pee instead. The soldiers, with great interest, compare the amount of their diarrhoea, then use diarrhoea and pee as bullets. They begin comparing the size of their penises, which they use as weapons; the best warriors have penises that reach across the room. Donald looks at me intently and says 'Wouldn't it be great if we had penises that big? We could fight anybody!' This is the first time he has acknowledged affiliative feelings towards me at a moment of separation.

Session six (one month after the end of vacation): we are playing football, and Donald devises coprolaliac signals from the quarterback to the hiker, for example, 'The other team peed in their eyes and farted out their mouth and poop came out their nostrils and they put their eyeballs in backwards'. Sometimes Donald gives these signals, sometimes he insists that I give them; I comply, although I draw the line at using actual curse words (I discuss this choice of intervention below in the section 'The Therapeutic Gain'). After a while Donald wonders if it is important to control dreams, then sits and tells me four dreams that he wants to try to understand. He is able to see how the dreams include scary feelings that he doesn't want to notice. As we discuss the fourth dream—*He was with a baby-sitter he used to have, she was washing the floor, Donald ate some of the soapy water*—he thinks it means there is something he couldn't say, but that this doesn't make sense because whenever he is mad at his mother it's easy to yell and swear at her. I suggest that nice things are what are hard to say. Donald immediately starts to play soldier, but when I point out he

60

is changing the subject, he sits down and soberly agrees that it is much harder to say nice things than angry things.

The anal world

To understand the clinical material, let us examine it more minutely: in session one, Donald tries to make time unknowable. This is relatively ordinary material, but needs to be kept in mind because I believe it is of a piece with the more shocking material, for reasons which will become clear below.

In session two, Donald's body parts become disconnected and difficult to reassemble properly. Although a mix-up of sexual parts is prominent, non-sexual parts also become rearrangeable. It is as though we fabricate several alternative forms of Donald before getting back to the real one.

In session three, Donald begins by showing me an actually detachable body part, the loose tooth. Then the badly beaten team regresses to the childish behaviour of peeing in their pants. Next follows boys and girls exploring the differences in each other's sexual parts. Then they engage in friendly excretory play, in a way which at first underlines their differences—competitive urination—but then emphasises their similarity, as they identically fart into each other's buttocks. Even the genital difference is lessened, by giving the girl a long vulva. Similar material ensues, but now with a strong aggressive charge, so that excretions are weapons, and the girls must show private parts on pain of being shot. The boys make ambivalent efforts to eliminate the sexual differences, by burning off boobs, shooting off vaginas, or pulling off boobs so that the boys may keep them. The physiology of motherhood is equated with that of babyhood in that mothers can pee with their breasts. Our separation instigates even greater chaos of excretions and secretions.

61

Donald initiates session four by saying we are to play the same game of looking at private parts. For the most part this game has the quality of affectionate lovemaking, as is stated ('We'll show them what men and women do when they're in love!') and as is underscored by Donald's erotic arousal, obvious in his expression and his clutching his penis. At first, interest is in those private parts which boys and girls share—buttocks and what come out of them—whereas private parts which are different are hidden, by the boys wearing lipstick and taping back their genitals, or denied, by the boys also having large breasts. They eat chunks of each other's buttocks, without pain or disgust, and with no evidence of any injury sustained. When the boys' penises are noticed, anxiety increases: the boys are afraid they will be disliked for having this organ, and are nervous when the penis is bitten. A boy comments that what he likes best is having his nose in the girl's anus—an interaction which does not require a penis.

Donald's fantasy world shows striking similarity to fantasies of the Marquis de Sade and of adult patients with perversions, elucidated by Bach & Schwartz (**1972**) and Chasseguet-Smirgel (**1978**, **1981**) as manifestations of an anal world. Anality is obvious in much of the direct, overt content of Donald's fantasies, and I believe that the pervasive theme of interchangeability should be understood as formally anal. By this I mean that such pervasive interchangeability is an anal quality, not only when the interchangeable parts belong to the excretory system, but also when other parts are concerned. To help us keep in mind what I mean by the quality of anal interchangeability, let us revisit this aspect of Donald's play: various excretions and secretions are interchangeable among each other, and also have interchangeable uses: poop, farts, pee, vomit and snot serve equally well as weapons and as savoury foods. Buttocks and the anus themselves may serve as food in addition to serving as excretory organs, and can be bitten off as food for one person without causing pain or injury to the other person, suggesting that they have not really been lost. Sexual parts are interchangeable between the sexes: boys may wear lipstick, hide their penises, have big boobs of their own or steal boobs from girls; girls may have long (penis-like) vulvas, have their vaginas shot off, and their boobs burnt off or stolen. Sexual parts may interchange psychosexual meanings: buttocks may be long and penis-like, boobs may be found between a girl's legs, mothers may pee from their breasts. In fact, virtually all body parts seem to be almost infinitely interchangeable, as I discovered when I tried to reassemble Donald after his collapse in session two.

There is a two-fold bodily basis for interchangeability and de-differentiation being hallmarks of the anal world: first, the anus, buttocks and faeces are common to everyone, male and female, child and adult; second, faeces are fabricated through the process of digesting and reducing various substances to an identical, undifferentiated substance. Bach & Schwartz (**1972**) have demonstrated that the Sadean world is typified by the same kind of interchangeability: any orifice will serve for any sexual act; all sexual acts are also aggressive; any person may serve as the sexual and aggressive object, whether idealised or degraded, stranger, acquaintance, parent or child; not even life and death can be meaningfully differentiated, since death merely results in a trivial rearrangement of molecules into a new life. 'The body contents... [and] the mental products... all become metamorphosed by the fantasy into the standardised parts of an insane anal technology'. Chasseguet-Smirgel (**1978**) has elaborated that a crucial unconscious metaphor in Sade's writings is the passage of his characters through an alimentary canal which results in the reduction of all to faeces: 'The object is... subjected to a process of slow digestion'.

Additionally, the level of cognitive development during this period of life contributes to the child's sense that things and attributes may be interchangeable. The child at this age is first developing objective self-awareness and the awareness of separate objects and calibrating these states with subjective self-awareness; the child is also making the crucial differentiation between male and female (**Bach, 1994**). Since these categories are not yet firmly established, de-differentiation and interchangeability of categories may easily occur. Fast (**1984**) has elaborated on the development of sexual differentiation in this regard. She proposes that although from birth children are socialised to behave according to their gender, their cognitive apparatus originally does not allow them to understand what it means to be of one gender or the other; rather, very young children experience all gender possibilities as open to them, in an undifferentiated manner. Sometime around the age of 2, cognitive maturation allows children to recognise the limits of belonging to their own gender, but the experience of interchangeability of sexual parts and attributes remains within easy 'psychical reach', contributing for example to fantasies of anal birth.

Another aspect common to the anal worlds of Donald and of adult perversions is the idealisation of its creations, particularly but not exclusively anality and the anal products. For Sade, the anus is the preferred organ for intercourse, vastly superior to the vagina. Faeces are idealised by Sade, whereas ideals are treated as faeces (another manifestation of interchangeability in the anal world). Sexual prowess takes on psychotically grandiose proportions, with endless repetitive erections and orgasms. More generally, adult fetishes have a two-fold quality, being either dirty/smelly or shiny/polished/brilliant, the former representing anality directly, the latter hiding it behind idealisation (Chasseguet-Smirgel, 1981). And adults with perversions often insist that their form of sexuality is not only an alternative but superior to 'normal' genital sexuality. For Donald, faeces are sweet as honey or flowers. Pooping and farting can go on endlessly, creating prodigious piles. Penises can be enormously elongated.

Bach & Schwartz (**1972**) analysed Sade's creation of his anal world as a restitutive phenomenon, an attempt to create a self that could survive after experiences of unbearable loss and loneliness. They reconstruct severe narcissistic disillusionment and abandonment trauma in Sade's early childhood and point out that although Sade had engaged in perverse acts prior to imprisonment, the creation of his fully-fledged bizarre perversions only occurred in his writings, after he was imprisoned, and may be understood as an attempt to compensate for his loneliness and humiliation. Anality is an arena for narcissistic compensatory fantasies because anality is the arena for the first major power struggles with parents, and thus potentially for first experiences of power or humiliation, and because the appreciation of the anal products themselves must change from idealisation to devaluation in the course of development. In his anal world, Sade was not weak and alone; rather, he had the complete power over objects and even over reality implicit in the anal transmutations described above.

Unbearable loss and humiliation also appear to be the dangers underlying the creations of adult perversions more generally. This was of course first noted by Freud (**1927**), who understood fetishes to be created as symbols of the maternal penis, in order to disavow the mother's lack of a penis, and thus to disavow the possibility of castration to the man creating the perversion. McDougall (**1972**) and Chasseguet-Smirgel (**1978, 1981**) have expanded this idea by theorising that it is not only the lack of the maternal phallus which is disavowed by perverse people; rather, what is disavowed is the lack of the maternal phallus, the presence of the actual maternal genitals, and the fact that the mature (paternal) penis is needed for sexual relations with the mother. The fetish is an idealised anal phallus that serves to disavow the importance of the genital world generally. By this is meant that the fetish stands for anality experienced as more powerful, desirable, and important than the adult genitalia or adult sexual relations. This formulation is in better accord with the observed occurrence of fetishes than is the idea that they symbolise only the female phallus, because fetishes occur not only attached to women, as we would expect for a symbol of the female phallus, but also attached to men or to the fetishist himself, or even separate from any object—again showing the non-specificity that typifies anality.

Thus, perversions are created to deny the 'double difference', the difference between the genders and the difference between the generations. Through some combination of experience and cognitive maturation, the little boy comes to recognise that he can never be of the same generation as his parents, and that his father has a sexual relationship with his mother that the little boy will never have with her. For the little boy fully to integrate the knowledge of this double difference, he must acknowledge the loss and humiliation of never truly having the mother for himself the way the father does, as well as the possibility of castration for his wishes. He must also acknowledge that he will never possess the female attributes which previously he had assumed to be available to everybody (**Fast, 1984**). The perverse defence against these losses and humiliations is to retreat to an anal world where the double difference is dissolved along with all differences, and where the little boy idealises his creations to protect against a sense of doubt that he might be missing something that other people have.

Donald's play, too, appears to be designed to eliminate the double difference. His elimination of the genital difference is the more obvious, seen in the many examples of interchangeability of sexual parts. His elimination of the difference between the generations, though less obvious, is also of great importance. It is hinted at in the play content of session three, when Donald states that a woman who has a baby can pee with her breasts (thus reducing the adult woman's secretion to a child's excretion), and in the elimination of time (necessary for generational differences) in session one. But I believe its presence was most important in Donald's relationship with me. He almost certainly experienced me as condoning the anal world when I did not restrict the play in sessions three and four. In sessions one, five and six, I was directly located in the anal world, via the elimination of my knowledge of time, our sharing of omnipotent penis-weapons, and my joining in coprolaliac signal calling. Thus, Donald strove to eliminate the generational difference by pulling me into his regression.

Donald appears to have been motivated to eliminate the double difference, and qualities of mine that made me serve as its icon, because of danger situations similar to those described above for Sade and for adult patients with perversions: in his history, we see that Donald experienced significant early object loss in the form of separations from nannies; in the clinical situation, we see that Donald was enraged by the separations from me at the end of sessions and that he was highly resistant to acknowledging attachments to me or anybody else. From the history, we do not know about Donald's learning about female genitals, but it is clear from sessions three and four that some learning has taken place in this area; we also know from the history that Donald was repeatedly exposed to the badly injured penis of his half-brother, reinforcing fantasies about possible damage and loss. In the clinical situation, a significant part of the narcissistic injury that Donald angrily experienced appears to have been simply that I was big and in charge—I scheduled, started and stopped the sessions, I restrained him and set limits when necessary. Donald appears to have experienced my mere presence and existence as evidence of an unattainable adult state of power and strength.

The therapeutic gain

I believe it to be of utmost importance that each upsurge in Donald's expression of his anal world was accompanied by small therapeutic gains—by steps into the adult, genital world that I represented. Let us consider what produced these gains.

A principal factor is simply that since anality was Donald's key regression point—was 'where he was at'—expressions of anality were what he needed to understand and was capable of understanding. Prior comments about Donald's not following rules, or wanting to win so much that he changed rules, were not helpful, whereas he quickly understood and was able to use the enacted concept of 'farty rules'. Expressing affiliation to me as a therapist or helping person would have been too narcissistically threatening, since it would have implied the generational difference—that he was small and needy and I was big and powerful—but affiliation could be expressed as a longing for the shared anal-world attribute of grand penises during session five. However, the type of incipient insight into his dream which Donald showed in session six—recognition that he needed to defend himself from expressing nice feelings—does not seem to fit here, since this insight was expressed in an adult, not anal, idiom; other therapeutic factors must have been at work.

A second factor leading to the therapeutic gain presumably was simply an increase in the 'unobjectionable positive transference' that accompanies the feeling of being understood. Donald was more disposed to understand things in my adult way because he liked me better in this non-specific manner.

I think it may be speculated that Donald also took therapeutic steps because of more specific messages conveyed by our interaction. He invited or demanded that I enter his anal world, and I complied within the play metaphor, while I remained in the adult world in so far as I still made my own choices about what to do, commented on what was going on, and started and stopped the sessions. One specific example of this was in session one, when I joined Donald in enacting that time was unknowable by letting him take my watch, while nevertheless staying in the adult world by commenting that he wanted me not to be able to end the session, and then in fact ending the session on time. A second example was in session six, when I joined Donald in coprolaliac signal-calling but refused to join in cursing, which I judged would be over-exciting and would remove me too far from the adult world; Donald's subsequent move to affectively meaningful dream exploration suggests that my stance at that moment had been helpful.

I hypothesise that our partial enactments were therapeutic because they helped Donald with his 'divergent conflict' (**Kris, 1985**) between his regressive desire to stay in the anal world, and his progressive desire to move towards the adult world. Our interaction gave Donald opportunities to observe that the boundary between my adult world and his anal world was crossable; if I could step down and back up, he could step up. He also had the opportunity to observe that taking steps into the adult world did not have to mean totally surrendering the possibility of anal experience, since I was still able to share it. He was motivated to follow me back towards my developmental level, so to speak, to maintain the pleasure and comradeship that he had clearly felt when I accompanied him to his level. These speculations are congruent with Loewald's (**1960**) idea that an important therapeutic factor is the patient's sense that the therapist recognises in him or her the possibility of attaining a higher developmental level.

Discussion

As we have seen, Donald has created an anal world in many ways analogous to those created by adults with perversions, and even analogous to the anal world of the prototypical pervert, the Marquis de Sade. This 6-year-old's anal world nicely confirms the reconstructions made in psychoanalytic investigation of perverse adults, by demonstrating the expected dynamics *in statu nascendi.* Donald is still very close to the age when it is developmentally optimal to experience and resolve the oedipal triangle, to recognise and accept the double difference. But instead, Donald is investing much of his psychic energy in the perverse solution identified from adult cases.

Does this mean that Donald is at risk of developing sexual perversion? Although extrapolations to the future are always very uncertain, I conjecture that the risk of sexual perversion is not high for Donald, in part because he is taking advantage of analysis, and in part because of indications that he would be unwilling to settle for perversion. Most telling is that despite his resistance to acknowledging it openly, Donald's admiration of me and of other strong men, especially sports stars, is intense and obvious. The narcissistic hurt of not already being one of us has not destroyed his drive to attain our adult strength and status, although it has interfered with realistic movements in this direction by the partial substitution of grandiose fantasies for careful schoolwork and mutual friendships. Donald's wail of dismay when I assembled him incorrectly in session two indicated his conflict around the anal solution.

Furthermore, although Donald's family constellation shows an important similarity to those which are often described in the histories of adults with perversions, it also shows an important difference (although the

70

comparative data are far from conclusive): Donald's mother is angry and domineering and his father somewhat ineffectual and retiring—a power differential that is often depicted in the history of sexual perversions—but there is no evidence that his mother is sexually seductive, as is also often reported (**Bak, 1968; Chasseguet-Smirgel, 1978, 1981; McDougall, 1972**). It appears that an illusory disavowal of the double difference strong enough to require actual perversion for its maintenance is most likely to develop when both the actuality and mythology of the family in which the child grows up discount the double difference, i.e. when the father is weak and uninvolved, and when the mother prefers the child to the father, particularly in a seductive way.

Therefore, Donald's anal world can better be understood as a manifestation of a *perverse play style* with no implication that it will necessarily develop into actual perversion. I intend the term *perverse play style* to indicate play which constructs a certain relationship to reality, the equivalent at an earlier developmental level of the relationship to reality constructed, in adults who are not openly sexually perverse, by means of a 'perverse personality organization' (**Chasseguet-Smirgel, 1981**) or 'the language of perversion' (**Bach, 1994**). The core of this relationship to reality is the maintenance of illusion in lieu of accepting the disillusioning realities of adult life. Such maintenance of illusion requires not only the fantasies that provide its content—these also occur in normal and neurotic constructions (**Bach, 1994**)—but also an experience of these fantasies which imbues them at least at times with belief that is equal to or higher than belief in reality. Steingart (**1983**) called this type of experience of fantasy a 'meaning disturbance', and indicated that its most easily recognised manifestation in childhood is a refusal/inability to shift out of play orientation, or to shift cognitive sets back and forth between play orientation and reality orientation, regardless of reality exigencies and the expectations of objects. Donald's play style may be recognised as perverse because of the conjunction of its anality with a meaning disturbance so defined: it was with great vehemence and intensity of belief that Donald maintained his anality and rejected the adult world (as represented by my efforts at understanding and at communicating empathy), and Donald urgently insisted on enacting his anality: we did not merely play a game that time was eliminated—Donald took my watch. We did not merely play games in which I was assigned the role of a character who talked dirty—I myself had to talk dirty.

Donald would appear to be at risk for a considerably greater-than-optimal reliance on the perverse style. Nevertheless, his use of the perverse style in the absence of actual perversion should alert us to its possible presence in a wide range of people. Indeed, Bach (**1994**) and Chasseguet-Smirgel (**1981**) have indicated that the perverse style is more or less appealing to all of us at different times.

The anal world is nicely designed to defend against awareness of the double difference, but this defence would not have been so available to Donald unless he had specific fixations or developmental lags which made it so. We know that Donald was regularly exposed to the badly injured penis of his half-brother, and it may reasonably be reconstructed that such exposure during the anal period was an important determinant of his openness to the anal world. The castration anxiety accompanying such blatant confrontation with a damaged penis would stir up ambivalence about forming a masculine identity, while the observation of such a differently formed penis would magnify the age-appropriate puzzlement about what a male identity really entails. Such dynamics lead to a turn away from the phallic towards anal drives, and to less clear and definite cognitive boundaries.

The world of the classic anal character type, epitomised by the traits of orderliness, parsimony, and obstinacy (**Freud, 1908**), is the opposite of the kind of anal world that Donald has created. Where in the classic character we find orderliness, we find Donald's world enormously chaotic and befouled; where in the classic character we find parsimony, in Donald's world we find profligate and extravagant fantasies of the exchange of huge amounts of excretions and secretions; where in the classic character we find obstinacy and rigidity, in Donald's world we find limitless flux. I believe these differences are best understood as differences in the respective organising anal experiences: underlying the classical character is the experience of the constricted sphincter, so that people living in this manner are constantly trying to maintain control and exercise 'sphincter morality' (**Ferenczi, 1925**). Underlying Donald's anal world is the experience of the faeces themselves, messy, interchangeable and limitless in that they are ever renewable. Among other things, the classic anal character defends against the experience of the anal world; the hyper-rationality of the obsessional may in part be a repudiation of perverse illusional reasoning.

It is of interest to note that in Donald's playful fantasy that I had reassembled him so that his mouth was on his belly and his eyes were where his nipples should be, he reproduced an image discussed by Freud in his minor paper 'A mythological parallel to a visual obsession' (**1916**). Freud described a 21-year-old male obsessional patient who was preoccupied with this visual image and Freud reported the same image depicted in a Greek myth. Freud's patient would see an image of a naked torso, with facial features painted on the abdomen but lacking genitals, whenever his father entered the room. The patient had had an unusually strong efflorescence of anal erotism, both up until his tenth year, and again during adolescence as a regression from genital sexuality. He now had refined sensibilities and high morals, and although he loved and respected his father, he saw his father as debauched. Freud understood the visual image as a mocking caricature of the father. I believe we can now be more precise. The son, who judging by the length of time that he had experienced a vivid anality, had probably only tenuously established controls over anal world fantasies, created a subtle compromise-formation in which the anal world was both expressed and repudiated: the image of father castrated and with body parts rearranged disavows the double difference by means of anal world interchangeability; at the same time, the temptation to enter the anal world is defended against by mocking its representative, the debauched father.

The mythological parallel comes from the myth of Demeter and Persephone. While searching for her kidnapped daughter, Demeter is too grief-stricken to eat or drink, so her hostess Baubo makes her laugh by suddenly lifting up her dress and exposing her torso to Demeter. Freud explains that ancient sculptures of Baubo show a torso lacking genitals and with a face drawn on the abdomen. Freud drew the general inference that this self-mocking interrupted Demeter's sorrow. I believe that here, too, we can now make the more precise inference that an anal world illusion, promising that all is flux so no loss is permanent, is used to dispel Demeter's tragedy. Inspection of a drawing accompanying the paper leads even more strongly to this interpretation, because the 'eyes' on the torso simultaneously appear to be nipples, but on breasts which are completely child-like, since they consist solely of nipples, with no adult definition. Therefore, the image contains not only anal interchangeability, but also a specific disavowal of the generational difference—the adult Baubo has a child's breasts.

Freud did not explain what psychological meaning underlay the parallel between his patient's image and the mythological image. I believe that the concept of the anal world provides the missing explanation. What my 6-year-old patient is creating now has been created before in Freud's Vienna and in ancient Greece.

References

Bach, S. (1994). *The Language of Perversion and the Language of Love.* Northvale, NJ: Jason Aronson.

Bach, S. & Schwartz, L. (1972). A dream of the Marquis de Sade: psychoanalytic reflections on narcissistic trauma, decompensation, and the reconstitution of a delusional self. *J. Am. Psychoanal. Assoc.,* 20:451–475.

Bak, R. C. (1968). The phallic woman: the ubiquitous fantasy in perversions. *Psychoanal. Study Child,* 23:15–36.

Beren, P. (1992). Narcissistic disorders in children. *Psychoanal. Study Child,* 47:265–278.

Chasseguet-Smirgel, J. (1978). Reflexions on the connexions between perversion and sadism. *Int. J. Psychoanal.,* 59:27–35.

Chasseguet-Smirgel, J. (1981). Loss of reality in perversions—with special reference to fetishism. *J. Am. Psychoanal. Assoc.,* 29:511–534.

Fast, I. (1984). *Gender Identity: a Differentiation Model.* Hillsdale, NJ: The Analytic Press.

Ferenczi, S. (1925). Psychoanalysis of sexual habits. *Further Contributions to the Theory and Technique of Psychoanalysis.* London: Hogarth Press, 1950, pp. 259–297.

Freud, S. (1908). Character and anal erotism. *S.E.* 9.

Freud, S. (1916). A mythological parallel to a visual obsession. *S.E.* 14.

Freud, S. (1927). Fetishism. *S.E.* 21.

Kris, A. (1985). Resistance in convergent and in divergent conflicts. *Psychoanal. Q.,* 54:537–568.

Loewald, H. (1960). On the therapeutic action of psychoanalysis. *Int. J. Psychoanal.,* 41:16–33.

McDougall, J. (1972). Primal scene and sexual perversion. *Int. J. Psychoanal.*, 53:371–384.

Steingart, I. (1983). *Pathological Play in Borderline and Narcissistic Personalities.* New York: Spectrum.

Treatment of the Older Adult:
The Impact on the Psychoanalyst

by Frieda Plotkin

W ork with the elderly challenges analysts in special ways. The author presents clinical material from her practice and from investigative interviews with nine treating analysts who report personal reactions and countertransferences to analytic work with twelve elderly patients. She concludes that the major challenges in work with the elderly come more from the analyst than from the patients. Issues arising from the analyst's unresolved feelings about aging, parents, loss, and death are revived in the treatment of the elderly in an especially intense form. In this paper many aspects of transference are considered, especially those relating to illness, loss, and the problems that flow from identifications of the older analyst with the patient. The affective reverberations in younger and older analysts with regard to the initiation of analytic treatment, the inevitability of moving in and out of real life crises, the sustaining of loss, and, particularly, the impending termination, are presented in the paper.

The material for this paper comes from my interviews with nine analysts, who among them had analyzed twelve "older" adult patients. In addition, I describe my own experience of analyzing an older patient, which led me to an inquiry into why for so many years it was not customary to analyze the elderly. While my examples do give a clinical picture of the patients described here, the focus of this paper is on the experience of the analysts working with these patients: their personal reactions to these analyses and the internal difficulties and complexities that they faced in the work. I will highlight the analysts' difficulties in making the decision to analyze older patients, in tolerating the intense affects involved in the ongoing analytic work with regard to physical illness and loss, and in dealing with termination issues.

There is surprisingly little literature on the subject—perhaps this is an example of the force of Freud's (1905) authoritative long-ago statement that the older patient is not a favorable one for analysis. Since most analysts are acquainted with the arguments presented by these early analysts, and since the definition of "old" has changed markedly over the years, I offer only a scant review of the literature.

Despite Karl Abraham's 1919 paper on psychoanalysis with patients "of advanced years," for many years few analysts concerned themselves with the elderly population. Over time, two divergent views emerged. Otto Fenichel (1945) and George Wayne (1953) described proceeding cautiously and supportively with the elderly. Hanna Segal (1958), Elliot Jacques (1965), Pearl King (1980), and George Pollock (1980) described more insight-oriented approaches. However, in more recent years, believing dynamic psychotherapy to be suitable for older adults, Nemiroff and Colarusso (1981, 1985, 1990) published case reports documenting the older patient's willingness and ability to change. Nevertheless, the determination of how to proceed, and whether the analyst takes a supportive or more heavily interpretive course, has often had more to do with the analyst's attitude than with the patient's need. An informal poll of colleagues taken by Simburg (1985) revealed an interest in whether or not older patients were suitable for analytic work, but Simburg expressed his own curiosity about the analysts' motivation in working with these patients. Similarly, what differences there are (or are not) in work with older as opposed to younger patients has not been sufficiently addressed.

In more recent years several analysts have focused on their own awareness of the affective reactions stirred up in the analyst who works with these patients (Crusey 1985; Settlage, Curtis, and Lozoff 1988). Hinze (1987) noted her tendency to defer to the elderly, and suggested that the difficulty in the work is the analyst's, rather than the patient's. Wylie and Wylie (1987) described their countertransferences, and noted the tendency to collude with the patient's use of age as resistance to cover over other more difficult countertransference issues. Muslin and Clarke (1988) describe the analyst's transference as more flagrant with the elderly since "unresolved business with parental self-objects" (p. 312) complicate the picture. My investigation underscores and expands the theme suggested by these authors: that the analyst's transference is more blatant in work with the elderly, and makes the work more difficult. Although the major problems in work with the elderly are the analyst's and not the patient's, I will also discuss additional conflicts (beyond the evocation of transference reactions) in this work that have to do with a conflictual convergence between reality and psychic reality.

A Case Example

A specific case led to my interest in analysts' responses to older patients. I began treatment with a man in his seventies, and his age engendered in me an almost reflexive initial reluctance to treat him in analysis. However, I pondered the issue further and wondered if my discomfort with the intensity that would arise in the analytic room was in fact complicated by the patient's age. Consequently, I sought consultation regarding analyzability, and in the consultation, the question of age and analyzability became more focused.

The colleague I consulted, a man of about sixty, advised against analysis; he feared that given the extent of this patient's emotional isolation the treatment would take too long, and that the patient might not be able to complete it before the end of his life. Furthermore, he expressed concern about subjecting an older patient to a reimmersion in old and traumatic pain. Another analyst, however, a woman in her seventies (the same age as the patient), wondered why age should preclude the treatment of choice.

Since I found the patient to have some affective availability despite his emotional isolation, and some interest in analysis, and since I realized that I had reacted to the patient's intense feelings of self-contempt and self-reproach with countertransference anxiety (initially dismissed under the aegis of concern about his age) I decided to proceed with a psychoanalysis. To jump ahead of the story a bit, this has proved beneficial for the patient and both challenging and rewarding for me.

The patient was an obsessional man with an erotic transference. Due to his emotional isolation, he initially presented as a man who seemed to choke on his words, of which he had many. I had to wait patiently to hear him, or else I would feel I had forced him to talk. He was stiff and distant. He would sit down and look at my face feature by feature. He often looked at me eye to eye, and then looked away; he looked at my legs more furtively.

My discomfort with the idea of analyzing this man reflected both his discomfort with his impulses and my resonant discomfort. I wondered what it was about his being older that made the unspoken inundation of feelings and impulses fuel my anxieties more than they would if I saw the same symptoms manifest in a younger patient. Was there something more frightening about the passivity of this obsessional man because he was older? Why would passivity in an older patient be more difficult to tolerate? (Perhaps passivity presaged death.) He had lost both parents as a child, and he had an enormous object hunger that he expressed through various modalities including vision, touch, seducing, eating, and smoking. I realized that I had concerns about opening up his enormous hunger, but what difference did his age make? As it turned out, the patient wanted to come close and touch and merge with me, to have intimate contact, as if he could be both sexes. I had become anxious about his regressive potential and covered it over with concerns about his age.

I did have some thoughts about beginning an analysis at his later age, and having to face illness and death with this man. Exactly what would be scary about that? At midlife I surely recognized some concern about the finiteness of personal time. As an only child with few relatives, I certainly had concerns about facing the death of my parents. In retrospect, it is clear that unresolved ambivalence toward my parents coupled with fears of their eventual death prompted further concerns. Don't we all have ambivalence about parents and fears of death? Does the patient's being older concretize the sense of limits?

The Treatment

Let me describe parts of the treatment that were pertinent to the questions I am raising in this paper. In the initial phase of treatment this depressed and obsessional patient could not be anything but mild-mannered on any topic. His ability to experience intensity, however, manifested itself in the emergence of an erotized involvement with the analyst. He would "stay remote and distant in order to be self-reliant and not dependent."

Everything stirred up the early traumas of being left. As he felt the intermingling of grief and love, he would distance and dissociate. However, as the work progressed and he became more aware of using the erotic to cut his depression off, sex and aggression came out more freely. The patient's fear of aggression was the most significant concern. A loosening of identifications and gradual interpretation of defenses against aggression led to the patient's ability to size himself up in relation to me, and to understand the aim of his defenses. He developed an attachment in his treatment that was neither erotized nor felt by him to be childish.

During the course of the analytic work he suffered a life-threatening illness requiring several months of hospitalization and nursing-home care. Throughout the course of his illness and recuperation we maintained our connection by phone and with hospital visits. He returned home and resumed analytic work on our previous four-hours-per-week schedule. His illness left him in need of physical therapy.

Orphaned at an early age, he had become nationally known and honored in his field, and he derived a profound sense of personal identity and self-definition through his professional talents and involvements, so he returned to work as soon as he could. However, upon his return he was told that his office was replacing him. He maintained the option of coming to the office on an occasional basis and otherwise contributing from home. In addition to his physical disabilities, he had now been slapped with humiliation and the pain of diminished status. In light of the patient's clear depression, age, and life stress, medication was indicated, and this was added to his regimen. The depression was less tolerable than it might have been earlier in his life, since he faced a modified retirement at an age that would make other job options unlikely. In retrospect, the patient and I viewed medication as a timely bolster, enhancing his ability to work analytically.

A different patient returned to the office after the illness. I had trouble following him because he was often forgetful. He would lose focus. He was more like the patient he had been in the beginning of our work, getting lost in words and beliefs and ideas. He was easily off-balance, touching the wall to steady himself. I felt his lack of focus and forgetfulness to be functional rather than organic in nature.

My reactions will be described more fully in the discussion section of this paper. However, I will give an example here of the dynamic interaction during the patient's rebound from illness. At one point he began to come late to sessions, complaining of the cold and of tiredness from the walk. My immediate reaction was to collude with his dependency feelings and let issues around the schedule slide, rather than point them out as transference metaphors. But as I thought about it further, I recognized some irritation. Although I steered clear of sounding blaming, I noted an inhibition and fear of injuring this infirm older gentleman.

I then brought up his lateness and waded through his dismissals. The patient told me that although the walk was hard, he faced the "unreal reality of time." He wanted to postpone the separation from work. "I don't work. I smoke more. I am distracted, disconnected." The patient recognized his resentment and didn't want to upset and anger his staff, who were already upset at his leaving. We had been in what Racker (1988) would call a concordant countertransference, in which I had identified with the patient and his conflicts about potential injury to others. We both contributed to the enactment in the analysis.

Unable to recognize the full extent of his anger at first, he was reduced to unsuccessful attempts at symptomatic relief. But as these sessions proceeded affective availability increased and his ability to focus was notable. As material emerged and revived in the transference, he was no longer circumstantial. I was once again the recipient of his falling back in love with the world. He appeared somewhat steadier.

He reported a dream which he would once have found unutterable due to the fear of the wish. In the dream his granddaughter fell from a penthouse terrace. Whereas he once would have defended against the aggression in the dream by an inability to speak, he now related it to his having been fired. He was able to feel conscious anger at his demotion, and not feel choked and disconnected. He appreciated my confronting him with his upset with the aggression in the dream. As a result of our work on the dream, he was better able to confront aggression in his own life. Although he felt "not shining" in the way he had handled his demotion at work, he felt that having shared these life crises with me would help him be more open.

The Study: Methodology

My reactions as I began and continued the treatment of this man and other older patients made clear to me that analysts have specific issues to face in the treatment of the elderly. While transference-countertransference issues are at the heart of every analysis, there is still something qualitatively "more" about the analysis of a person the analyst can think of as "old enough to be one's parent." I was curious about the early analysts' famous caution in working with older patients. My interest led me to conduct a series of taped interviews with nine analysts who among them were treating twelve older patients. I asked a series of standardized, open-ended questions. Follow-up questions depended on the responses received. Each analyst was asked to discuss a specific case. Analysis of the data was thematic.

The nine psychoanalysts interviewed are members of the International Psychoanalytical Association. Seven of them are senior training faculty and members of the American. One was a senior candidate, and another a recent graduate. They had responded to notices about the study in Institute newsletters, as well as to the recommendations of colleagues of the researcher. They work in New York City, Detroit, and Los Angeles, and range in age from forty-two to over ninety.

The patients ranged in age from sixty to ninety-two. Six were described as healthy neurotics with mixed personality disorders. Three of the twelve patients were described as borderline, their pathology ranging from moderate to severe. The two most severely disturbed older adults were undergoing a first analysis. One was so severely disturbed as to have had a thirty-year history of incest with her mother. The analyst felt that "there was nothing else that would help this woman but analysis." A second patient in this category, a mother of four, was described as "having a very poorly defined sense of self, and being scared of everything." A third patient was seen originally as quite "primitive and undifferentiated." Two of these three analysts described their initial reactions to treating these patients in analysis as cautious, and one said he had been almost apprehensive, not knowing what to expect from this "primitive, devouring older woman" (note the condensation of age and psychopathology here). Two other patients had narcissistic personality disorders. One suffered from conversion hysteria. The degree of psychopathology (with its implications for a rather lengthy treatment) was a factor in the analysts' susceptibility to thinking about the "reality of age" as a defense. Other factors, too, such as concerns about limitations in time or possibility also played a role in the stance of some of the analysts interviewed.

The data that resulted were not the kind one subjects to statistical analysis, but were very useful, nonetheless. Once all the data had been organized into coding categories, I determined the logical connections. These analysts believe they have been affected by their work in the manner described below, and I accepted their reports as valid, though without external validation. I made logical inferences from these subjective descriptions of process in the absence of the analysts' associations. I will now present the material from the interviews.

The Data; How Old Is Old?

Analysts all found it convenient to break the patient population into two categories: the "younger old" and the "older old." It might seem reasonable to ascribe these categories to some given age range, but in practice age cannot be quantified in such a simple way. My interviews confirm that it was the fact of infirmity, not chronological age, that determined who was "older old."

Initial expectations and fantasies about age had to be overcome. For instance, the case example above illustrates how my anxiety about age manifested itself in an exaggerated sense of the analysand's vulnerability, and I assumed an overly protective role "for the patient."

The concept of "older old" was introduced spontaneously by several of the analysts interviewed. It is both a psychological construct of the analysts, indicating their discomfort with their patients' fear of loss of vitality, and a realistic fact indicating the actual onset of infirmity. What emerged from the study was a distinction between younger and older "old" on the basis of evidence of continued vibrancy and interest in the world, despite the glimmer of recognition that life is not going to go on forever.

The analysts' idea of "younger old" also emerged spontaneously, without direct questioning. Again, it does not refer to a specific age; it is more connected to a sense of how long in the life span analysis can continue "as usual," without the fragility of age shading the picture. Specifically, in the cases considered, the younger old had all become aware of the insistent progression of time, but in contrast to the older old they thought little about the unpredictability of loss, and there had so far been little change in the quality of their lives.

The question of the relative ages of analyst and patient also came up, with one older analyst stating that age is in the eye of the beholder. This analyst, close in age to the patient, never thought of the patient as older until the patient actually became infirm, because, according to the analyst, the idea of being old is uncomfortable for the analyst.

Challenges to the Analyst's Autonomy

It is ordinarily assumed that the analyst has a good deal of autonomy while working. He can control certain variables. But as he approaches an elderly patient, my interviews suggest that an analyst faces a number of challenges to his independence. The analyst is aware of the danger, although not always able to avoid it. What are these dangers?

The analyst is vulnerable to the narcissistic injury incurred when the elderly person evokes the therapist's own concerns over his own impending aging process. The elderly analyst or the analyst who is ill is especially vulnerable because of his identification with the older patient. With the older adult, the analyst's fears and expectations about both current and potential reality complicate his understanding of psychic reality. Typically, the analytic situation deliberately diminishes the role of external reality in the service of changing the balance of forces to allow for observation of intrapsychic processes. Our interest here is how the analysand's external reality affects the analyst. At some point the patient's actual physical decline may require concessions in the work.

The analysts in my interviews spoke about feeling gratified when they could help patients fulfill dreams that the analysts' parents could not. The ability to help these older patients enhance their lives can fulfill some analysts' longings in relation to their own parents (alive or dead, but certainly alive in the psyche). When the older patient talks about major losses, no analyst is transferentially immune. Also, every analyst is sensitive to the elderly patient who is in a precarious position with relation to mortality. At times of physical crisis more than analysis is felt to be necessary. Because the analyst is a caregiver and gratified by helping someone who is ill, special problems exist in returning to a neutral position after helping the patient through a life-threatening illness. The analyst's separation issues are intensified, as is reflected below in the section on termination.

All the analysts interviewed felt that work with these patients was special. Difficulties arise when analysts like these patients better, or less well, than younger patients, or when they overly "objectify" the elderly patient (that is, when they feel responsible for something in their possession that they imagine to be fragile). To refer to someone as "something in one's possession" implies ownership, dependency, or perhaps a narcissistic replication. This was not explored in my interviews, as the significance struck me fully only afterward.

The Danger of Seduction: Who's Too Old for Whom?

While every analysis has variations due to the specific characteristics of the dyad, these analyses may have features posed by age and life stress in addition to those posed by psychic organization. How many concessions are made in deference to reality, and how many in deference to the analyst's fears? And how do these concerns interact? My interviewees reported that their older patients "appreciated" them more than did younger patients. Since the analyst is more appreciated by these patients, it is easier for the analyst to be seduced by the reciprocal gratification of being "nurturing," particularly at times of crisis in the lives of these patients.

In the present study, while all participants agreed that the unconscious is ageless, subtle differences appeared among the participants with regard to treatment of the older old. Generally the analysts related their experiences of treating older patients to their own self-representations regarding age and accompanying vulnerability. This naturally raises the question: "Who's too old for whom?" The analyst's own feelings of (physical) vulnerability affect, both negatively and positively, how they respond to patients' concerns about disabilities, and how the treatment accommodates these.

Reality as Resistance

Many situations with elderly patients—medical emergencies, for example—create opportunities for reality to be used defensively by the analyst. This is a regular problem in any analysis, but it is sharply heightened in the case of the older analysand. I have mentioned this in my introduction and I will expand on it here. There may be a seductive pull, given the analyst's identification with the patient, not to analyze but to protect, thus overlooking the analysand's often conflicted adaptive potential. While several analysts were adamant in insisting that there were few, if any, changes in their work as a result of the patient's age, one analyst noted the fact that at a certain point concerns with diminished vibrancy (signs of physical decline) affect the analysis. My attempt to see what might have influenced the dissenting analyst's position revealed him to be the only analyst interviewed who suffered lifelong physical illness. He felt that these difficulties influenced his defensiveness against the aging process, and also enhanced his empathic response. This analyst felt that although certain character resistances might diminish with increased age (such as narcissistic personality disorders), and that therefore some patients become more approachable as they get older, people generally focus on narcissistic vulnerability as they become aware of frailty, and shift the focus of the analysis to feelings of fragility.

This analyst's first concern was not to traumatize his older narcissistic patient, and this often inhibited his analytic style. In retrospect, he felt that the problem was much more serious than merely having his style cramped. He felt that he had been frozen in an idealizing relationship to his patient. As a result, given his personal defensive modes, he often felt bored. The treatment ended when the patient began to complain of aches and pains, and to wonder if she weren't too old to continue. She had gotten what she had wanted from the treatment and now preferred the physical comfort of home. It appeared that the analyst's conflicts made it too easy for him to agree.

While the physically vulnerable analyst spoke of experiencing counter-transference irritation with the older old, and felt that his defensively influenced work with these patients became more concretely (and less analytically) issue-focused, the other analysts said that the work with their older patients forced them to think in a less defended way (perhaps because they were not physically vulnerable at that time) about their own mortality, and to grapple with the resulting anxiety. On the other hand, the analyst who had to live with his own physical disabilities revealed not only defensive obstructions. He also revealed an increased thoughtfulness to issues of illusion with the older patient. He was the only analyst who spoke of feeling particularly respectful of preserving illusion when working with the older old. In an interesting mix of insight and defensive rationalization he said:

When you hear an eighty-year-old talking in an illusory way, you want to kind of protect it. You don't want it to be taken away, because the person has to live with his age. I think I would deal with illusion differently in the aging person. Not touch it, whereas with a younger person, you would point out how it's used as a defense.

In his view, "Some illusory experiences are helpful in getting through the difficult time of aging and death." The interviews suggest that analysts who were older, or grappling with illness and more aware of time limitations and their own impending death, had a tendency to think more in terms of the limitations of age, or to feel that time imposed its own framework on their goals.

The Older Patient's Respect for Analysis

If the analysts' views on the desirability of analysis for older patients were mixed, what were the views of the patients? Several patients specifically asked for analysis instead of psychotherapy. Pressures for older patients to be in analysis might reflect the fact that older adults have grown up with a respect for analysis, and perhaps for all authority, which helped to offset the anxieties the patients raised.

Not every positive feature lent itself only to defense, despite the constant potential presented. These older adult patients were more able, under the pressure of time, to open themselves up in analysis. One analyst described his patient as having "a slaking thirst to know himself, and wanting analysis." The use analysts made of such statements involved a mix of defensive and nondefensive reactions more often than only one or the other. For instance, several of the analysts interviewed described attributes of their patients in superlative terms immediately following accounts of nearly unbearable affects faced by the dyad. Object-relational needs of the patients also offset some of the analyst's conflicts. However, this too could be put to defensive use. This was seen most often around issues of termination, as will be discussed below.

The pressure to be in analysis (with the depth of involvement that that implies) was reflective of a wish "not to go it alone," or "to finally be seen or heard"—unlike their experiences with their earliest objects—particularly in the face of death down the line. Also, the attachment to analysis and the analyst, which is filled with vitality (the immediacy of memories and affects from earlier times both good and bad) counterbalances the frailty and loss faced in daily life.

The interview material suggests that the patients' appreciation of their analysts was heightened, or at least that the analysts were more willing to take this appreciation at face value than they are with younger patients. Sicker patients were described as striving for integration and a chance to live. Others often had fantasies of rebirth or of a last chance to "get things right" (such as relationships with children or other loved ones), or gave expression to very strong and long-inhibited or -disconnected parts of themselves: a push for immortality through the analyst's bearing witness.

On the basis of these interviews, it seemed reasonable to consider that the analysts liked the more personal qualities of their older patients because the older adult wanted what the analyst had to offer. Since the patient is more involved with the analyst, the analyst feels more appreciated and enjoys the closeness the patient provides. The analysts' work-ego ideal was bolstered by the patients' enthusiasm for analysis, and fostered useful identifications of analyst with patient that could balance the analyst's moments of anxiety and conflict about vulnerability and death. One analyst described sharing an ego ideal with his patient by saying:

He wants to know himself, and it's an enormous satisfaction to understand himself, even though it's often painful. It brings up the pain of the lost opportunities. But he's still gained so much from understanding himself better. I believe the unexamined life is not worth living, and psychoanalytic understanding is the best way to attain that.

Identification can also have other defensive characteristics in such analytic dyads.

The Illusion of Timelessness

The analyst may join in the patient's dangerous but seductive fantasy that with psychoanalytic understanding comes the chance for a new beginning and immortality. This fantasy is facilitated because analysis involves the patient in a return to a time when time seemed endless and/or meaningless. Another illusion analysis provides is that time to understand the past and repair the present will extend indefinitely. This is so because the intense immersion of an analysis is based in large part on transference issues and on the fact that analysis plays on the illusion of an indefinite future.

In my sample, older persons, given their unique circumstances, experienced a greater sense of loss and depression when such illusions were analyzed than the analysts had come to expect in younger patients. And, because this reaction intersects with the analyst's inner life, the analysis of it threatened the analyst with loss and depression also, particularly where the analyst was older too.

In fact, the analysts' ambivalence and hesitation about termination was noteworthy. Several analysts observed that patients in their seventies emphasize time more. One analyst noted that prior to reaching seventy his patient had lived in a timeless sphere. Sessions were gainful, but slow and drawn out. The patient was said to have used analysis as a timeless playspace after a life of pressured intrusion. At one point in her analysis, after much personal growth and change, the patient at the age of seventy-one became aware of the preciousness of time. As she became more fulfilled, she realized how limited time was, and she wanted more of it for herself. Often, thoughts of "enjoy yourself, it's later than you think," would come to the analyst's mind in identification with this patient. At the same time, he was aware of his own painful reaction to thoughts of the eventual loss of the patient. The analyst described his feeling as, "temporary, but more intense than what I ordinarily feel. The attachment was so strong."

Heightened Transferences

Both transference and defense are heightened with older patients. The analysts in my sample reported greater emotional power in these dyads. While the affective bond varies in its intensity for each patient-analyst pair, in all but two of the cases described there seemed to be a "more than usual" impact of patient on analyst, making for what one analyst described as a "special place" in his heart for the patient. The special place may be the one in which the analyst's unfulfilled longings for parental figures are revived and reworked in relation to older patients. One analyst said that his older patient was so primitive and difficult that it was tempting to dismiss her as untreatable, but several transference factors heightened his continued interest and moderated his aggression. He said that his older patient was referred by an admired supervisor: an older authority figure I wanted to please. So I may have been more responsive to her. Later on I was more responsive than I might have been with such a devouring, difficult patient because she was doing so well, fulfilling wishes that my mother, a Russian immigrant, had wanted for herself, but had been too depressed to achieve.

Another analyst said that he was psychologically readier to see someone a bit older than himself aging only after the analyst had passed the age of his own parents when they died (the analyst is seven years younger than the patient).

The analysts were struck by the "sexuality, vitality, and curiosity" of these older adults. So, when the analysts describe themselves as "strikingly surprised" at the "aliveness" of their older patients, some unconscious ambivalence towards their own parents was manifest. Although the admiration may counter the analysts' feeling of unease about competitive feelings and/or eventual loss, all the analysts felt that these patients distinguished themselves by their persistence in the treatment.

The Difficulty Maintaining Neutrality

I will now concretize some final points about how and why the analysts found it difficult to work with older patients. Analysts are trained to deal with patients' difficulties in facing loss and limitation, and to be able to remain compassionate while maintaining neutrality. But here these issues were more painful than usual for both patient and analyst in the context of the pressing terminal reality. The fact of the patients' actual physical decline was painful for both patient and analyst. However, it impacted on the different dyads in individual ways. There were as many possibilities as there were dyads. One analyst emphasized that one patient's physical decline increased the patient's motivation to change as well as the analyst's enthusiasm. In another case, the patient's declining vision, coupled with gains in the analysis, gave rise to thoughts of termination. While the patient could get someone to drive her to sessions, she had trouble with dependency. Notably, the analyst said she wasn't as deeply bonded with the patient who could not allow for dependency, and the treatment ended. Another analyst described working with his patient intensively almost up to the time she died. He noted that:

The patient kept denying that she was ill. However, she couldn't work well. I simply had to insist that she had to get her husband to take her to the doctor. At certain times, it got very difficult. In the end it certainly was not an analysis.

Thoughts about Death

Thoughts about death are always a part of the treatment after age seventy-five or thereabouts. (I settled upon this age because most interviewees used age seventy-five as a demarcation, although clearly it is not an absolute.) One analyst made a powerful statement about his availability "at the very end," saying:

You can't give up when the patient goes home. So, you don't treat the older patient lightly. It's a sense of a real connection. Depending upon the situation, the usual boundaries of the psychotherapeutic relationship no longer apply. There is a shift to include the family as much as possible, to see the patient more, at unusual times.

Medical Emergencies

It is difficult, but important in this context, to determine where psycho-analysis ends and analytic psychotherapy begins. Fears of death, loneliness, and isolation lead to greater pressure to attach to the analyst as protector, and the analyst may feel a seductive pull to protect rather than to analyze. This is particularly so in the aftermath of medical emergencies. At such times, these analysts indicated that they (ideally) would shift back and forth, becoming more supportive, containing, holding, and interpretive as was necessary. These occasions served as opportunities for consolidating alliances as well as for further exploration of the intrapsychic response to a sense of inner disorganization, disintegration, and annihilation. However, the rebound from supportive to interpretive work was often troublesome. After one analyst had supported the patient through a serious illness, he noted a hesitancy to interpret, recognizing a feeling of "what's the use." This analyst said he had to work through conflicts about feeling responsible for potential injury to an older person.

Difficulties around Termination

Termination of analysis with older patients has unique features. Their sadness is "different." There is more immediacy; all the issues of life and death are "right in the room." An intensity of affect about termination affected the analysts in my sample profoundly. The termination phase brought about the greatest degree of personal disequilibrium that they experienced in the process of treatment. Depth of reflection and some disturbing affect accompanies the decision not to terminate as well, because the awareness of accompanying the patient to a natural end brings with it feelings of uncertainty and pain. Fantasies of separation and abandonment are remobilized for the analyst as well as for the patient at this later phase of treatment. Termination, like the initial decision of whether or not to treat in analysis, appears to be more complex for both members of the dyad than other parts of the treatment. Some analysts and patients put it off.

An analytic termination is always taking place not only during a particular developmental period of the patient's life, but also during a particular period of the analyst's life. The youngest analyst, a forty-two-year-old candidate, said of her eighty-four-year-old patient, "His focus was how to allow himself to feel anchored, and to give that to himself when he couldn't do it before. He was dealing with the final termination, with death." In describing this man as having "really lost out due to his neurosis," this analyst said:

He could have been a multimillionaire. But he couldn't let it happen. He couldn't allow himself children. That kind of loss was very big. It came up as: he's at the end of his life, not having anyone to remember him and he is afraid. There was certainly a lot of sadness and depression that he had never dealt with before. I've never experienced anything like the grief over the fantasy that there would be no child to light a candle for him after he died. There were times when I wanted to say, "But I'll do it for you." I watched him struggle with the sadness, and the helplessness over not being remembered.

The pressure of this termination brought out a multiplicity of wishes in both patient and analyst. The permanence of these losses, occurring as they did at the end of the patient's life, left no possibility of reversal, and was "almost too much [for the analyst] to bear." In addition, the analyst's mother was terminally ill as her patient was terminating. As the analyst described it, she "was dealing with [her own] mother's dying and the pain with him [the patient] was so close. I was learning to separate from everything at once."

Another analyst raised other pertinent issues with impressive honesty when he said:

As the patient leaves I feel like she's taking something away from me. I feel she's taking herself away from me; she's taking her session, her money away from me. I have a lot of that. And I have not been able to sort it all out yet.

This patient was described by the analyst as "grieving at all that's been lost; [she] says 'a piece of ice grabs [her] heart.'" Once the patient had addressed the fact of the diminished period of time available to her, she experienced relief, and hungered for new experiences for which the necessary money, time, and psychological preparedness were now available. The analyst, however, described himself as similar to his patient in having lifelong disappointments and losses to be sorted out, and he experienced the end of the analysis as impacting him in terms of "losing life lived together." This analyst (twenty years younger than his patient) reported his sense of the patient having come to the end stage of life, and feeling closer to the end of life himself. He pointed out that he would have felt differently with a younger patient.

She's such a part of my life, has been there for so long, I can't imagine not seeing her. I can't picture her living her life out without me. I think I have a fantasy about the end of treatment, and the end of her life. I wouldn't have that with a younger patient. She seems at the end part of her life in a real way.

In contrast, a seventy-seven-year-old analyst spoke of the special significance the termination of a treatment had on her. She compared the impact on her of the terminations of her older and younger patients. She is aware that for both the patient and herself, the fact that the analyst is not going to live that many more years is relevant. The robust young patient sees her analyst as frail, and thinks of the analyst's actual fading. As a result, the patient invites the analyst to suggest she continue the process. The analyst has to explore and bear her own feelings about her own "final termination precluding any sort of contact" with the world. Termination brings to mind eventually terminating practice, which in the case of this analyst had been "part of life over half a century." And yet, for this particular analyst the termination with a younger person feels deeper: "You're a part of practically bringing up a young person." This analyst

98

experiences that as different from encountering somebody in the later years of life, "who's probably more shaped up."

It is harder for some older analysts to part with younger patients: that is, to part with eternal youth. This was the case for several analysts who specified that it was also more fun to treat younger patients and be involved with eternal youth. By holding on to younger patients, the older analyst imagines that he maintains his vitality, undoing the frailties and dangers of old age by identification.

Some analysts had to confront the difficulty of ending treatment with those older patients who had suffered early traumatic losses. The concern was that a repetition in the form of the loss of the analyst would be too painful, particularly in the context of an analysis being completed at a later age, with the concomitant loss of relationships due to deaths, fantasy losses, and aging. Exploration of the issue with these analysts at the time of the interviews revealed that it was the analyst, by and large, who had the difficulty. One analyst described his patient as struggling with thoughts that the analyst, like his son, will outlive him, and feeling competitive envy and murderous wishes. The analyst, in confronting countervailing fears and anxieties that related to his struggles with his own father, feared his own mortality: he imagined several of his patients leaving and feared his own aging. To protect himself from his own anxiety, the analyst unwittingly suggested that the work could continue as long as the patient wished. In our interview, the analyst came to the realization that:

It's almost like I'm saying, "We'll be immortal together." All relationships end, and that was a way of perhaps saying, "We could go on forever." So, I'd have to think about that, maybe address that as it appears. "Your father abandoned you. I won't." I'm just thinking aloud. That's something to talk about.

Notably, this analyst had put off treating older patients until both his parents had died. He admittedly shared an area of unresolved conflict with his patient which, if not explored, could lead to putting off ending the treatment. Of course this kind of countertransference dilemma may come up with a patient of any age, but it is perhaps more likely in treatments where analysts and patients face absolute limits of time and opportunity. Notably too, the analyst who found that work with older patients triggered in him too many difficult identifications relating to illness and death allowed his patient to leave when she became preoccupied with her health.

The sample of this study is too small to predict what percentage of analyses with older patients will be brought to termination. Of the twelve cases discussed in this study, three had been brought to treatment termination. Two others ended due to somatic illness, and in one case the patient died. Two patients were not ready to discuss termination, although the analyst thought that one of these patients would eventually terminate. Two analysts addressed the difficulty of bringing the process to an end. One emphasized the helpfulness of maintaining continuity in the face of body changes, infirmity, and so many losses. After all, the analyst is "somebody who knows you well, who still sees you, even through change, as also the same."

Discussion

The analysts I interviewed in this study openly discussed their tendencies toward denial and the wishes for omnipotence that they confronted in treating the elderly. Older patients challenge the analyst with the fact that time, and the possibility of reparation, is limited. But the analyst is conversely confronted with the fact that his time is limited as well, and he may view the patient's time as limited in the service of denying his own limits. On the one hand, the awareness of limited time often impels elderly patients to risk more in a treatment that represents their "last chance" to gain some understanding of lifelong conflicts. On the other, because time clearly is limited and because termination of treatment foreshadows the termination of life and therefore of the analyst's analytic efficacy, it may present a narcissistic injury to the analyst. The analyst may also shift away from an analytic stance with these patients, even if this does not lead to a refusal to treat on the grounds that the patient "would not have enough future years to warrant psychoanalysis."

The limitations imposed by time may not preclude the analyst's gratification and pleasure in the feeling that he worked well. However, he may be confronted by the real issue of the difference between what he expects or wants to accomplish and the lack of time left for the patient to enjoy. Further, there is the question of the patient's time-limited life span as metaphor for the analyst's feeling of limitation in his analytic capacities.

How seriously the analyst takes the analytic needs of a patient with little time left hinges on how strongly the analyst views the patient as "old," or as "older old"; it hinges on whether the analyst views age as a real limiting factor; and it hinges on whether the analyst defends against his own vulnerability by failing to identify with the needs of the patient (for example by saying instead that the patient's character is limited). The analysts interviewed attempted to solve their dilemma by distinguishing between the "old"—whom they believed to be dealing, simply, with familiar analytic issues at a later stage of life—and the "older old"—for whom more limited goals were often thought appropriate.

Since analysts can only imagine the future and do not really know how much longer the "older old" really have to live, a choice of limited goals is not necessarily based on reality, but may serve as a defense against the anxiety these "older" patients arouse in them. When the issue of mortality is brought to the fore, and the analyst is made anxious by frailty, it may lead him to the expectation that he can do less for the patient. Thus the distinction the analysts made between "old" and "older old" was more powerfully influenced by the analysts' own experience of aging and sense of physical vulnerability than by the patients' chronological age, infirmity, or pathology. Corroborating the difficulty analysts have addressing conditions of personal deterioration and death, Stephen Firestein (2000) has noted that analysts have feelings about termination and death that are not entirely resolved by their training analyses. In a panel discussion on the subject at the New York Psychoanalytic Society they were hard put even to imagine their own personal deterioration. Firestein suggests that training analyses, occurring as they do early in the analytic life of the analyst, and usually before the experience of significant loss, do not prepare the analyst to face the "intense affects linked to the reality of expectably permanent separation."

Thus the analyst's countertransference difficulties in empathizing with the patient's fear of death were sometimes experienced out of anxiety as a need to support the patient's illusions, sometimes making it difficult to terminate treatment, and sometimes making it too easy to collude with defense and allow a patient to terminate too early.

The more I reflect on this subject, the more persuaded I am that the analyst's worry about his own durability may be screened by his speculations about the patient's durability.

This paper addresses problems applicable to analysts of any age, and raises the question of whether it might be harder for older analysts, whose vulnerability to physical illness has increased, than for younger ones to accomplish the self-analysis necessary for this kind of work. But it also raises a more general question about the needs our patients fill for us. Several of the analysts interviewed emphasized the older patients' increased personal and human involvement with them. These patients often noted everything about their analysts, and were quick to note changes in the analysts' facial expression and body language. They expressed concern when the analyst was ill.

While this may also be true of "more disturbed" patients, the quality of the investment is different for the two groups. The older patient reads the room less defensively and with more empathy than the more disturbed patient. Analysts responded to this, and were often more interactive. This raises the question of whether and how the patient's real interest in the analyst may interfere with the analyst's ability to self-analyze.

How does one tease out that which, although gratifying and helpful for the analyst, is primarily enhancing rather than diminishing for the patient? This issue has been raised in many analytic contexts, and with regard to the treatment of children, adolescents, and borderline patients, among others. It is not surprising, therefore, that questions come up about what constitutes an analysis with this special population. Particularly when external reality mandates technical modifications, the boundary between psychotherapy and psychoanalysis becomes unclear.

These questions have been raised by other authors about other populations, such as disturbed patients who oscillate in their ability to focus on inner conflict (Stanley Coen, personal communication). Inderbitzin and Levy's (1994) caution against losing sight of the potential for defense that external reality affords has particular applicability to work with older adults, since there are so many opportunities for both analyst and patient to use crisis and loss as resistance. Furthermore, these opportunities to use reality as a defense may be interactively gratifying.

If an older patient has difficulty keeping to the schedule, it may be a piece of acting out or it may be a delay due to physical decline. The analyst may think in terms of conflict and defense rather than face the actuality of the patient's limitation and factor in the meaning to the patient of both the illness and the analyst's reaction to it. It is difficult to do this when the real limitations are subtle and accumulate over time, as the work with my own patient illustrates.

Clearly there is an ongoing need for more in-depth analysis of the problems that confront analysts with patients whose life situations make the distinctions between countertransference and reality more difficult to tease apart.

Conclusion

So what can we learn? When an older patient comes late, does the analyst assume that older or ill patients cannot schedule as precisely as younger healthy patients, and accept this as a real limitation? Sometimes one cannot tell the difference between a real limitation and a resistance until some analysis is done—limitations and resistances may look alike. The analyst has to be flexible, and has to examine the way a real limitation may play into a resistance. It is harder for analysts to treat reality as reality and resistance as resistance when the illness or frailty of the patient triggers their own anxieties. Of course, real limitations may also conform to inner needs and wishes. The analyst may have to analyze himself before he can recognize a possible area of inflexibility and approach it from the point of view of how the lateness may coincide with the patient's fantasies and wishes.

From another perspective, after an analyst has been called upon to act outside the analysis in a real crisis, it may be the analyst who continues unnecessarily in a supportive role to defend against instinctual wishes fostered by the heightened closeness. Although this is true no matter who the patient, it is especially compelling when the analyst has taken responsibility for caring for a patient/parent and may be experiencing heightened fears of aggression. Since such "life crisis" situations are not infrequent with older patients, and since even when they are rare the analyst may fear recurrence, such instances may impose additional stresses on the analyst.

My own experience with patients rebounding from life-threatening illness parallels Abend's statement (1982) about the period just following an analyst's illness being most problematic for the analyst. Abend was referring to a sick analyst, but as the material presented indicates, it may be true as well for analysts with elderly, and perhaps declining, patients.

For instance, with the elderly patient I described above, I found the countertransference issues of this post-illness phase to be especially difficult. It's hard to take away something that has been given during a life-threatening illness, such as supportive interactive contact. In some instances the patient felt punished, and I experienced the change as a deprivation. Also, for quite a while there were times when I did not experience the patient as the same person as he had been. The work was different for a time: I found myself reaching out more. I functioned as a wall that the patient needed to steady himself. He viewed me as a mother bolstering a needy child, and noted relief upon my return to more interpretive work. Obviously, analysis may not be possible in every instance where support has been given. Sometimes support is given when analysis might have been better. The questions are never clean and clear and may never be readily settled, despite their obvious importance.

Another aspect to be considered in the countertransference is the possible reversal of the more common pattern of older analyst and younger patient. Where the roles of analyst as parent and patient as child are disrupted, and the difference between the generations is blurred, the analyst may have to struggle with developmental tasks that have not yet been faced in his own life, or which are being faced simultaneously with the patient. This was seen in the vignette of the recent analytic graduate who was terminating treatment with her eighty-four-year-old patient as her own mother was dying. This can of course be true with any patient/analyst pair. However, with the elderly, where the termination of treatment presages the patient's actual death, the analytic relationship becomes, in consequence, peculiarly intense in a way that may be less striking, or perhaps not even exist, with younger patients.

To conclude: Work with the elderly, from initial diagnosis all the way through termination, revives in the analyst specific unresolved transferences related to aging. These are conflictual activators that serve to remind the analyst of his own mortality and limitations. I hope this paper has made it clear that there are complexities in the treatment of older adults that remain to be addressed; I have in mind particularly an elucidation of the interplay in this patient population between external reality and intrapsychic meanings and constructions. The gratifications in working with elderly patients, including the opportunity to see how conflicts are dealt with and reworked over a life span, are as ample as the challenges, and the work itself underscores the issue of what analysts fear, hope for, and expect from their patients.

References

Abend, S. M. (1982). Serious Illness in the Analyst: Countertransference Considerations. *J. Amer. Psychoanal. Assn.* 30:365–379

Abraham, K. (1919). The applicability of psycho-analytic treatment to patients at an advanced age. *Selected Papers.* New York: Basic Books, 1953, pp. 312–317.

Crusey, J. E. (1985). Short-term psychodynamic psychotherapy with a sixty-two-year-old man. *The Race against Time: Psychotherapy and Psychoanalysis in the Second Half of Life*, ed. R.A. Nemiroff & C.A. Colarusso. New York: Plenum, pp. 147–166.

Eisenstein, S. (1994). The aging of therapists. *How Psychiatrists Look at Aging, Vol. 2*, ed. G.H. Pollock. Madison, CT: International Universities Press.

Fenichel, O. (1945). *The Psychoanalytic Theory of Neurosis.* New York: Norton.

Firestein, S. (1978). *Termination in Psychoanalysis.* New York: International Universities Press.

Firestein, S. (2000). Discussion of J.L. Kantrowitz, "Termination and the meaning of time: Limitations and possibilities." *New York Psychoanalytic Society*, February 22.

Freud, S. (1905). On psycho-therapy. *Standard Edition* 7:257–268.

Gould, R. L. (1990). Clinical lessons from adult development theory. *New Dimensions in Adult Development Theory*, ed. R.A. Nemiroff & C.A. Colarusso. New York: Basic Books, pp. 345–370.

Hinze, E. (1987). Transference and Countertransference in the Psycho-analytic Treatment of Older Patients *Int. R. Psycho-Anal.* 14:465–474

Inderbitzin, L. B. and Levy, S. T. (1994). On Grist for the Mill: External Reality as Defense. *J. Amer. Psychoanal. Assn.* 42:763–788

Jaques, E. (1965). Death and the Mid-Life Crisis. *Int. J. Psycho-Anal.* 46:502–514

King, P. (1980). The Life Cycle as Indicated by the Nature of the Transference in the Psychoanalysis of the Middle-Aged and Elderly. *Int. J. Psycho-Anal.*, 61:153–160

Modell, A. H. (1990). *Other Times, Other Realities.* Cambridge: Harvard University Press.

Muslin, H., & Clarke, S. (1988). The transference of the therapist of the elderly. *J. Am. Acad. Psychoanal. Dyn. Psychiatr.* 16:295–315.

Nemiroff, R., & Colarusso, C. (1981). *Adult Development: A New Dimension in Psychoanalytic Theory and Development.* New York: Plenum.

Nemiroff, R., & Colarusso, C. (1985). *The Race against Time: Psychotherapy and Psychoanalysis in the Second Half of Life.* New York: Plenum.

Nemiroff, R., & Colarusso, C. (1990). *New Dimensions in Adult Development.* New York: Basic Books.

Plotkin, F. (1998). *Treating the older patient: The psychoanalyst's experience.* Dissertations Abstracts International-B. UMI Microform # 9813002.

Pollock, G. (1980). Aging or aged: Development or psychopathology. *The Course of Life: Psychoanalytic Contributions toward Understanding Personality Development, vol. III*, ed. S.I. Greenspan & G.H. Pollock. Washington, DC: U.S. Government Printing Office, pp. 529–585.

Racker, H. (1988). The meanings and uses of countertransference. *Essential Papers on Countertransference*, ed. B. Wolstein. New York: New York University Press, pp. 138–201.

Segal, H. (1958). Fear of Death—Notes on the Analysis of an Old Man. *Int. J. Psycho-Anal.* 39:178–181

Settlage, C. F. (1996). Transcending Old Age: Creativity, Development And Psychoanalysis In The Life Of A Centenarian. *Int. J. Psycho-Anal.* 77:549–564

Settlage, C. F., Curtis, J., Lozoff, M., Lozoff, M., Silberschatz, G. and Simburg, E. J. (1988). Conceptualizing Adult Development. *J. Amer. Psychoanal. Assn.* 36:347–369

Schachter, J. (1990). Post-Termination Patient-Analyst Contact: I. Analysts' Attitudes and Experience; II. Impact on Patients. *Int. J. Psycho-Anal.* 71:475–485

Simburg, E. J. (1985). Psychoanalysis of the Older Patient. *J. Amer. Psychoanal. Assn.* 33:117–132

Wayne, G. J. (1953). Modified psychoanalytic therapy in senescence. *Psychoanal. Rev.* 40:99–116.

Wylie, H. W., Jr. and Wylie, M. L. (1987). The Older Analysand: Counter-transference Issues in Psychoanalysis. *Int. J. Psycho-Anal.* 68:343–352

Thinking About Reverie in Bion's Model of the Mind

by Nancy Wolf

Bion was concerned with thinking. Thinking, in Bion's vocabulary, is possible when an individual can tolerate both desire and its frustration and render them meaningful through representation. But the question arises, what if there are early frustrations which are felt as terrors, terrors that overwhelm the psyche, how do such experiences gain representation? Bion, understanding the defense of projective identification as a communication, posits the reception of projective identifications as the avenue for terror to find a name. Bion understood the defense of projective identification as more than a maneuver to evacuate distress, more than a need to make another bear what is intolerable for the self; he understood it to be a communication with an implicit expectation for the mother to comprehend and also carry the weight of the terrifying experience for the child. When a mother can receive this projected angst and bear it, muse over it, and render it tame and meaningful, and then return it, altered, to her child, now capable of representation, she has mediated and ameliorated the unbearable. This power to transform terror to a bearable state can to a large part be attributed to the tasks the mother performs and the affect she endures in the state Bion names reverie.

Bion relates reverie to our capacity to dream; he radically alters our conception of dreaming in his assumption that we dream while awake and while sleeping and in his assumption that not all dreamwork is meant to disguise experience. Yet Bion retains and uses Freud's explanation of the mechanisms of dream work in his understanding of the dynamics of the mind. I intend to look at Bion's concept of reverie as a central process in his model for achieving mind and thinking, and intend to show reverie as a state of consciousness necessary for processing un-symbolized experience, experience that has been too terrifying to claim and represent.

Bion thought, as Freud did, that we are born with a "rudimentary consciousness" (Bion, 1967, p.116) capable of perception but limited in the capacity for understanding and making meaning. Bion was also well acquainted with our capacity to fragment our experiences into unknowable states; he saw this in his fellow soldiers in World Wars I and II, in his more psychotic patients, and, at traumatic moments in himself. Though Freud and Bion understood the nature of our beginning consciousness similarly, they investigated very different aspects of it. Freud's brilliant understandings address our capacities as symbol makers and are centrally involved in discerning the concealed and conflicted meanings in our communications. But Freud leaves us with few clues as to how to address the non-symbolizing mind. Bion's theories are attempts to understand our pre symbolic nature and failed symbolic capacities. Reverie, in my reading of Bion, is an essential state of consciousness for the development of this thinking and symbolizing capacity.

Thinking, for Bion, is more than a conceptual activity; it is a capacity to experience affective and instinctual states and render them with meaning. In his paper "A Theory of Thinking," Bion says that thinking occurs when a preconception "mates with frustration." (Bion, 1967, p.111.) An example of that mating would be an expectation for the breast and milk which is not met. At that moment there is the beginning potential for recognition of absence, recognition of the absence of the good breast rather than the experience of a bad breast, and thus a space for thinking is created. Thinking cannot occur if the frustration is so great that the painful experience needs to be obliterated from our minds rather than represented; the need to expel the bad breast experience is an example of such obliteration and such expulsion forecloses the experience of missing, wanting and longing. Excessive anxiety can make representation impossible and this flight from thought leaves one with aspects of the terror, unnamed, a state Bion refers to as "nameless dread." (Bion, 1992, p.45.) Bion understands that these early frustrations are so anxiety ridden because they carry threats of annihilation and disintegration which can overwhelm the ego, and as such are "unthinkable." (Bion, 1992.) For Bion, the unthinkable can be known and thought through the containment and the reverie of the mother.

Bion's recognition that projective identification is a mode of communication provides us with an understanding of how a mother can engage in her task of reverie. For Melanie Klein, projective identification is a technique to rid the mind of the intolerable. The defense, as she describes it, is based on the phantasy that psychic contents can be moved from one individual to another. For Klein, projective identification was a means of keeping aspects of experience separate, a means of separating good from bad, through the phantasy of evacuation. Bion recognizes a further dimension in Klein's understanding; Bion recognizes that projective identification is not just a discharge phenomena nor solely phantasy but is a communication, and he thus enables us to see its provision for an interchange between mother and child. Bion, in 1977, told a group of New York analysts that

Melanie Klein said that patients have omnipotent phantasies, that they split off parts of the personality and project them into the breast... I think that is correct... as far as it went. What I am not so sure about is that it is only an omnipotent phantasy. I have experienced the situation in which a patient can arouse in me feelings which have a simple explanation. You could say 'Anybody would know why the patient makes you feel like that; you need to have more analysis.' That is true, but it is not the whole truth. I think that the patient does something to the analyst and the analyst does something to the patient; it is not just an omnipotent phantasy. (Bion, 1980, pp.14–15.)

For Bion, the unthinkable needs a "sojourn" (Bion, 1967, p.116) in the other's mind. Bion gives the name reverie to that sojourn. Projective identification is no longer just about evacuation and discharge; it has become a form of dialogue.

In his book Reverie and Interpretation, Thomas Ogden employs Debussy's understanding of music to explicate reverie. Odgen says "Debussy felt that music is the space between the notes. Something similar might be said of psychoanalysis. Between the notes of the spoken words constituting analytic dialogue are the reveries of the analyst and analysand." (Ogden, 1997, p.107.) Later Ogden continues that "we do well in psychoanalysis to allow words and ideas a certain slippage. This is particularly true of the term reverie." (Ogden, 1997, p.157.) Ogden beautifully describes these personal moments of semi-conscious meanderings of the analyst or the patient in the sessions. Ogden sees these moments as intersubjectively created reveries not as distractions and shows how attending to them promotes and deepens the work of the treatment. It may be Bion's intention as well not to too precisely define reverie; he may think, as does Thomas Ogden, that reverie is a form of thinking we perform in the gaps or spaces between our conscious attention and that it is a mental state on the border between the articulate and the inarticulate. I hope to preserve reverie's evocative nature as I explicate it through a reading of Bion's ideas as they have illuminated my clinical experience.

Reverie enables something inchoate but coded to become visible and meaningful. One can compare reverie to the developing medium photographers use in film development. Bion states that the projected identification can only be received by the mother if the child can hold and then communicate some of the nature of the elements of the terror. These held and then projected elements provide the elementary code comparable to the photographers negative upon which the developing medium, in this case, reverie, works.

Reverie in common usage implies a state of self-preoccupation and self-involvement. In Bion's lexicon, reverie is not self-referential but a mode of thinking on another's experience. Winnicott's concept of "primary maternal preoccupation" (Winnicott, 1956) helps to elucidate something about this state of consciousness which Bion calls reverie. Winnicott recognizes that the mother's primary preoccupation with her infant could be called an "illness" were she not providing a maternal function. (Winnicott, 1956, p.302.) He uses the word "illness" because "a woman must be healthy... in order both to develop this state and to recover from it." (Winnicott, 1956, p.302.) The "illness" aspect of this state relates to the ways she merges with her infant so that she is so sensitive and so one with him that the everyday world dims and her awareness of her own needs diminish. This particular heightened awareness of another seems comparable to reverie. It may be that something occurs in the mother's receptor channels or capacity for links that allows a temporary suspension of mental boundaries so that she can sense and feel aspects of her child's feelings that are not usually accessible to another. This capacity to be outside one's own sensing zone and to be the register of another's without loss of identity or ego functioning is for Winnicott a temporary state of being that the mother lives through pregnancy and for a few months after delivery. For Bion, reverie is not limited in terms of months, though it may be in terms of moments. The reverie of which Bion writes, similar to the maternal involvement explicated by Winnicott, is thus not about withdrawal but about a particular form of preoccupation, a preoccupation with another in mind.

Michael Balint provides another concept which illuminates the reverie experience. He writes of three areas of the mind in his book The Basic Fault; one, he calls the "area of creation." (Balint, 1968, p.24.) In this area, he states that "the subject is on his own" producing something out of himself which could be an artistic creation or a mathematical or philosophical one or even a "gaining of insight or understanding something or somebody." (Balint, 1968, p.176.) Balint describes this area of the mind as being involved with "hazy and dreamlike as of yet 'unorganized' contents," and he states that in this area there are no objects per se, he says there may be pre objects" and he wonders if Bion "faced with the same difficulty … was to call them alpha and beta elements and alpha function." (Balint, 1968, p.25.) But Balint may not have meant area in its concrete sense. It seems that Balint is beautifully describing the process of thinking and the nature of the content of this thinking during reverie. Reverie is not a locale as much as a mode of thinking. Reverie is a mode of thinking which requires an altered state of consciousness, one of a less singularly focused attention involved with less defined contents.

Bion gives the name "beta elements" to "things in themselves" which are not thinkable. Bion writes, "The term 'things in themselves' I hold with Kant to refer to objects that are unknowable to mankind." (Bion, 1962.) It is upon these beta elements that the mother's reverie works. Beta elements are in essence mentally indigestible. They may evoke terror; they are aspects of experiences to which we can react but not comprehend. Without the help of the mother's reverie and containment the individual experiences "nameless dread," (Bion, 1962, p.45) not thought. Beta elements, a category

116

for unknowable phenomena, is a problematic concept because that which cannot be known seems to exist in an ever unreachable sphere, and Bion does ultimately believe that we can only approximate representation and knowledge of emotional experience. (Eigen, 1981, p.62.) In a less ideal realm, we can explain a mother's capacity to transform by her more integrated and mature emotional state of being. We can ascribe the "unthinkable" to the infant; terrors which approach annihilation anxieties for the infant or child may be seen and experienced quite differently by the mother.

I see a young man in psychoanalysis who I will call George. He first entered my office walking with a limp which was the result of a nearly fatal motorcycle accident he had while inebriated. Such self destructive actions, I learned, were frequent, though none quite so close to actual death. To our work, he brought the tortuous sadomasochistic relationship he lived in with his beautiful girlfriend. This young woman seemed to regulate her precarious narcissism through attempts to control her human environment. She would demand his total attention, attempt to orchestrate his sexual responses, and criticize him if he were not perfectly attune to her desires. Her denigratory attacks were unbearable to him; they often provoked him to violence, particularly directed at himself. His violence could be seen as a response to beta elements or uncontainable unknowable pain. If such moments could be experienced at all, they were felt as potential annihilations tolerable only through discharge.

In *learning from experience*, Bion writes of the necessity for the mother to contain the unbearable in order for the child to be able to transform beta elements, elements of which I spoke of as motivating my patient George's aggressive actions. If a mother refuses or continually fails to bear and decode the child's projections, and rejects the projected elements of the unbearable, "then a further burden is thrown on the infant's capacity for toleration of frustration for now its capacity for the toleration of

117

frustration of thought itself is tested ... we have thus approached a mental life unmapped by the theories elaborated for understanding of neurosis." (Bion, 1962, p.37.) For the child has presented the mother with an aspect of his experience which contains the preconceived expectation and the pain of its failed realization. The conjoined elements of the projected desire and frustration are a kind of beginning thinking; Bion sees thinking occurring when preconception and frustration mate, and writes that projective identification is "an early form of ... a capacity for thinking." (Bion, 1962, p.37.) The mother's refusal to receive the projection is destructive to the beginning thinking process and results in the child introjecting a misunderstanding object rather than a thinking capacity. Bion deduces from his adult patients that such an obtuse early object is internalized as "a greedy vagina like 'breast' that "starves its host of all understanding...." (Bion, 1967, p.115.) Ronald Britton in his paper "Keeping Things in Mind" notes that if "the patient, client, child, or someone else ... feels that he cannot 'get through,' that they are making no impact ... an intensification may occur in their effort to project" or there may be a "spiraling violence" or "despair." (Britton, 1992, pp.108–9.) All of these reactions were seen in my patient George.

Bion is saying that we are no longer in the territory mapped by our understanding of neurosis because we are no longer in the terrain where experience is capable of meaning and symbolic representation. A neurotic symptom is evidence of our symbolic capacity; within the symptomatic act are hidden meanings. This capacity to symbolize results from the capacity to bear affective and instinctual experience. It is upon the un-symbolized aspects of our patients' experience that our capacity for reverie is so essential. Christopher Bollas' idea of the "unthought known" (Bollas, 1987, p.277) contains the understanding that we and our patients live aspects of early failures, or overly intense instinctual storms, or projections from parents' psyches, without having the capacity to think about them.

These moments become lodged in our skins rather than experiences we know in our mind.

George was educated and able to recognize layered meaning in the historical texts that he read during his college and graduate school years, yet his capacity for emotional representation and comprehension was frail. From what we have gathered, he was rarely soothed. He was left to cope by himself with agitations and confusions and anxieties, though he was materially well cared for. He coped with these anxieties by finding ways to eliminate them or put them to sleep. As a child he addressed these distresses through activity, and in adolescence, he turned to drugs. He could not mentally register these gaps in providing during his growing up years; he was mostly cognizant of just getting on and of his actions and reactions. Beneath his bravado and his idealization of his uniqueness, he judged himself harshly for his delinquent behavior. He could not have told me the reasons for his wild behaviors; the terror empowering them was not represented. He attributed his sense of total failure in getting something unnameable, but needed, to his own innate unworthiness, and this made his girlfriend's attacks even more unbearable.

Bion's paper "Attacks on Linking," concerns a patient whom he believed was raised by a mother incapable of reverie:

The analytic scene built up in my mind a sense of witnessing an extremely early scene. I felt that the patient had experienced in infancy a mother who dutifully responded to the infant's emotional displays. The dutiful response had in it an element of impatient "I don't know what's the matter with the child." My deduction was that in order to understand what the child wanted the mother should have treated the infant's cry as more than a demand for her presence. From the infant's point of view she should have taken into her, and thus experienced, the fear that the child was dying. It was this fear

119

the child could not contain. He strove to split it off together with the part of the personality in which it lay and project it into the mother.... (Bion, 1967, p.104.)

It seemed to me that George also had annihilation terrors. Over time, through our work, I learned that those fears were awakened by loss or rejection or frustration or failure. Before treatment, his schizoid shell prevented his full experience of these fears, or he regulated them through action; his dangerous escapades were ways to dare physical death. Prior to our work, he alternated between two mental states, one a desire for action often containing a flirtation with dying, the other a more inert state of ennui and boredom. In the bored state where there was no engendered activity, feelings of emptiness and loneliness had the potential to surface. He had hoped that this lover promised a new self state , an enlivened one. Her subsequent attacks were especially destructive and unbearable in light of that hope. His girlfriend's accusations and dissatisfactions were deeply scarring, and he imprinted those wounds on his body through self-inflicted injuries. In these wounding actions he attempted to deal with unthinkable pain through an attack on his body; this attack on his body, preserved and protected his girlfriend. These physical attacks transferred his terror and pain to a somatic registrar and were destructive to his capacity for thought. His body and his fluctuating mood states were the registrar of his "dying" experience. This was how and where he carried his annihilation terror; it was not capable of thought.

It seemed to me that unconsciously George longed for a deep attachment, perhaps even a kind of symbiotic fusion with a loved and loving other. Prior to our work, when need states began to surface, he found ways to annihilate them, but as our work took hold, his internal dilemmas were increasingly enacted between himself and his lover. She treated his needs as he himself had, with disgust and dismissiveness. One of our initial tasks was to begin to help him recognize his longings and desires and to disengage them from the violent rejection both he, and now she, applied to them. We needed to find language for his desires and therefore ours was a highly verbal engagement. I often searched aloud with George for meanings of his experience, wondering with him how some experience might have felt or of what it reminded him. My hope was to provide him with an alive and thinking space. In time his rage states and violent reactions gave way to feeling pain and a beginning awareness of his lover as separate from him and severely compromised. We had begun to tame and transform the beta elements so that they could be available for more than discharge.

My patient's fear of dying was not a knowledge he could hold in mind. His behaviors were often defenses against this terror and were about heightened forms of excitement to counteract his fear. But he communicated to me his intense fear of annihilation which informed each one of his actions. It was behind his pressured speech; it was in his need to recircle and restate a thought or a decision; it was in a warded off emptiness that his movements and his forced humor conveyed. It was this wordless communication that I needed to receive and ponder. My understanding of his terror came about in my clinical reveries; as Bion stated "the patient does something to the analyst." (Bion, 1977, pp.14–15.) I understood that he was over and over again devising a self-cure for something dead or dying within him. Though I spoke to him of his self-destruction and the pain that fueled his rage, it was a long time before I addressed his fear of dying directly. It remained in the texture between us, perhaps in the realm of being contained and tamed; perhaps I knew it for a long time without having a name or language for it.

Three years into the treatment, he was able to talk with me about a pervasive despair which lived with him; but then we were in a different psychological space. He and I had lived through something together. I had been the holder of the living and dying experience. I needed to know both without collapsing into death or artificially engendering liveliness. It had been important for him to feel worthy of living and to experience himself as non-contaminating and yet I needed to hold and not deny his desperation and dying. When he became able to speak of this pervasive despair, he was able to bear some of the emptiness he had fled.

Bion writes, "In short, reverie is a factor of the mother's alpha function. (Bion, 1962, p.36.) Bion seems to be of two minds in the matter of explaining what alpha represents. He wants to create an open category for a not fully known mental process which converts sense data to thinkable experience, and simultaneously he attempts to give this alpha process shape and content. In this latter frame of mind, he writes that alpha function "transforms sense impressions into alpha elements which resemble and may in fact be identical with the visual elements with which we are familiar in dreams, namely the elements that Freud regards as yielding their latent content when the analyst has interpreted them." (Bion, 1962, p.7.) It is with alpha dreamwork that Bion returns us to central aspects of Freud's initial understanding of psychology as Freud was exploring it in The Interpretation of Dreams. I found J.O. Wisdom in his paper titled "Metapsychology after Forty Years" in agreement on this point. Alpha is connected if not synonymous with our capacity to dream. Dreamwork alpha transmutes our experience into something mental and personal as the totality of the sense experience is condensed into, what is for the individual dreaming the experience, an image. Bion has thus applied Freud's understanding of dream-work to explicate and describe the origins of our capacity to digest and represent our experience. This transformation of sense data into visual imagery is for Bion a mental process of digestion necessary for psychic survival and nourishment comparable to our digesting and metabolizing food for our physical existence and nourishment.

Bion distinguishes this dream work from Freud's elucidation of dream work in two ways. He sees this kind of dreaming as a continuous mode of processing experience which occurs while we sleep and when we are awake, simultaneous with other states of consciousness. Secondly, Bion attributes to this dream-work the capacity for representation, for preparation for symbolization, and for memory, and as such, the element of distortion or disguise is predominantly if not totally absent. Bion gives his dream-work the adjective of alpha to distinguish its work from the more familiar nighttime dream work. He further describes it in a passage where he speaks of talking to a friend about a vacation. Bion states that while conversing, he is "sensorially "perceiving the moment in which he is talking and the vacation town of which he speaks and converting all this into "the image of that particular church" in the town. (Bion, 1992, p.180.) He continues,

> I do not know what else may be going on, though I am sure that much more takes place than I am aware of. But the transformation of my sense impressions into this visual image is part of the process of mental assimilation…. By contrast, the patient might have the same experience… and yet be unable to transform the experience so that it can be stored mentally… instead the experience (and his sense impressions of it) remains a foreign body; it is felt a 'thing in itself lacking any quality we usually attribute to thought or verbal expression… the example I have given of the visual image of the church… is not even a symbol. Although once… experienced… there is nothing to prevent its appearance in other contexts fulfilling the functions… associated with symbols. (Bion, 1992, pp.180–181.)

Reverie thus requires the capacity for alpha functioning, or according to Bion, is a factor or component of our alpha functioning. In Bion's example, the image of the church has become his madeleine. According to Bion, sense data impinge on our senses resulting in perceptual registration without meaning registration, until transformed through alpha dream-work to a personal affective image. In another passage, Bion describes a patient's use of the word table, stating that it was not used with both its common meaning and its associations but "as a pure note in music devoid of overtones and undertones as if meaning nothing but 'table,' it came close to meaning nothing at all." (Bion, 1992, p.63.)

This work of alpha function approaches what Freud calls condensation in dream work and as such could be said to belong to the work of primary process thinking. But Bion has already distinguished alpha from primary process by its name and by asserting alpha functioning's attention to the reality principle; the capacity for alpha functioning which the mother provides through her reverie is possible only when frustration can be tolerated, not when it is evaded. James Grotstein, in his paper "Who is the Dreamer Who dreams and who is the Dreamer Who Understands the Dream," writes that alpha function is "more extensive" than primary process, that it results in more than condensation and displacement, that it accomplishes "imaginative re-synthesis". (Grotstein, 1981, p.385.)

Bion states that the mother's reverie bridges "the gap between sense data and appreciation of sense data"; he sees "the perception of psychic qualities as requiring the same treatment as sense data." (Bion, 1967, p.117.) The mother's dreamwork holds the child's experience and moves it from a perceptual registrar to a meaning one. Her dreamt image is a container for both affect and perception. A mother must derive an image from the infant's projection and her comprehension allows her to provide either a name for the experience or a mind state for the infant to arrive at his or her own image.

I was sitting with George who had returned to his earlier fatalistic attitude to his life. The world had been slowly and surely coming alive for him through our work; he was acquiring a growing ability to interact with others and to effect his desires. All this now was profoundly shut down as if it had never been. The meaning of his regression, in the wake of an interruption in his contact with a new girlfriend, came to me in a reverie. Halfway into his third session of the week, I became cognizant of an event, his loss of someone significant in his early care-taking, that he had been told happened to him in his first year of life. My recollection of this experience came to my awareness as if I had been startled into knowing it. There was an unfocused image preceding it or accompanying it, of him in a room alone as a child; it all surfaced so quickly, I cannot take it apart. When I spoke of it and my now understood meaning of his frozen despair, something of his recited past came alive in the room for us both. It seemed we had reached some affective piece of his childhood depression in a way unavailable before. This despair was less fragmented and less dispersed; it was more available for my registration and comprehension; using photography again as an analogy, the negative had a different more elaborated code.

Nonetheless, it had come clear to me as a shock. Some reveries come to our minds more in a series of images available for our musing; they are less startling in their appearance. Many of Ogden's examples of reverie are more reminiscent of daydreams. It may be relevant that this aspect of my patient's history was not in any way represented for him; he had been told of this interruption in his care-taking but he had no aspect whatsoever of it in represented memory. I had to experience what was yet unrepresented and unsymbolized and register it and comprehend it. In terms of projective identification, it was as if he forced the experience of something forever closed and gone into me for me to metabolize and make it knowable, and in my reverie, my alpha function was at work.

Reverie is a kind of musing, a kind of alternative state of conscious-ness, a kind of thinking in a transitional space where we are attuned to the one who has generated our engagement and in contact with our dreaming minds. We have the capacities belonging to alpha functioning similar in ways to the activities of primary process, condensation, symbolization and synthesis; and we can access both earlier represented experiences of our own which illuminate the present projected one and access tools to experience and represent the present experience. But these capacities gain their truthful and relevant use only if they come from an emotional understanding and involvement with the person and his or her projected experience. Reverie at its core is a profoundly emotional experience.

Bion writes that "we may deduce reverie, as the psychological source of supply of the infant's need for love and understanding ...." (Bion, 1962, p.36.) He continues in the same chapter with this question: "when the mother loves the infant what does she do with it? Leaving aside the physical channels of communication, my impression is that her love is expressed through reverie." (Bion, 1962, pp.35–6.) Reverie is thus not an abstract state of mind. It seems to be a kind of contemplation that comes from loving and that provides love. It may be that the capacity to know and bear someone else's confused pain can only result from an intimate involvement. It maybe that our developed capacity to accept symbolic gratification in place of the concrete required the sustenance of love. The work of reverie is accomplished from the actual emotional bearing of another's pain. Bion articulates this when he writes "I am more satisfied with my work if l feel ... I have been through these emotional experiences than I do if the session has been more agreeable. I am fortified in this belief by the conviction that has been borne in on me by the analysis of psychotic or borderline patients. I do not think such a patient will ever accept an interpretation, however correct, unless he feels that the analyst has passed through this emotional crisis as part of the act of giving the interpretation." (Bion, 1992, p.291)

Yet some of our patients do not seem to want our reverie. Bion writes that "the patient has the capacity to exact an emotional relationship from the analyst and reject it… the patient arouses 'untenable' emotion and denies any material that would allow alpha to operate and therefore the analyst to profit by the experience for the patient's benefit… it is essential for there to be an experience for which no benefit can be obtained." (Bion, 1992, p.136) Betty Joseph, in her paper "On understanding and not understanding: some technical issues" (1983), clinically details the maneuvers of patients who oppose understanding and introspection and use us to ensure their eviction of experience. In his paper "The Therapeutic Object Relationship," Mark Grunes speaks of what he calls "empathic impermeability" and defines the experience as follows: "that on some occasions patients leave us with the feeling that we cannot and will never understand anything about them. It is as if we have been internally struck dumb. This experience usually signals some radical and unexpected rejection of primal intimacy." (Grunes, 1984, p.134)

I had such an experience with a female patient named Alice whose creativity and intelligence disguised her profound resistance to the "primal intimacy" of which Grunes wrote. George, the male patient of whom I wrote, presented himself as entangled with his girlfriend so that he handed over to her, what should in an adult have been aspects of his self-functions. Much of our early work was involved in helping him sort out what belonged to him and what to her. As disabling as this relationship was for him, it also was a manifestation of his wish for some version of dependence. Both George and Alice needed and sensed that they needed some kind of experience of dependence and sought them in dysfunctional relationships.

Alice began her treatment in the midst of a break-up from a long time unsatisfactory relationship and in the midst of an infatuation. The new relationship was quickly intense and their love-making provided a fusional and ecstatic connection for her. But the relationship did not survive. She felt tricked and betrayed by her lover, and I think also by me, in my inability to predict the relationship's demise and protect her from the loss. This profound disappointment occurred too early in our treatment to be properly experienced and worked through. It was disruptive to her trust in me rather than facilitative in reviving her fragile trust in and desire for intimate connection. She was thrown back upon her need to remain self-sufficient or, in Bion's language, omnipotent.

Alice kept her emotions at an intellectual remove. She used her fine intellect to examine other's faults when they disappointed her. This technique seemed initially perceptive and well balanced until it became clear that she managed to eliminate her own emotional responses in these understandings and thus divorced her distress from the experience, making it unavailable for tending. The defense left her in many ways anchorless, relying as prominently as it did on her mind alone. A dream where she could accomplish physical feats with only the prowess of her mind seemed to give us further clues as to her relationship with her emotions.

During our short and interrupted treatment, she would not allow my reverie, though she was interested in my ideas on other people in her life. For her I was either the fading mother or the mother she created and controlled; I was never permitted to be of independent emotional use to her. To allow my reverie would have required registering her desperate longing for the reverie mother she never had. It was this refusal of reverie that Bion heeds us to notice, and it is by this noticing that we create a space for reverie where none previously existed. Reverie requires a mental reflective space and it is our recognition of the closure of this space that provides such a reflective space, but here one is to reflect upon its absence.

For Alice to allow my engagement through reverie would have required a belief or hope that her pain could be comprehended by another. It would have required her to register her feelings regarding the failure of

128

her objects or her feelings regarding her perceptions of those failings so that she could transfer aspects of those failings onto or into me. But it felt safer to keep these experiences unlinked. She discharged them as beta elements with neither comprehension nor expectation of relief. She was left with unnamed anxieties and late night terrors and hauntings and with pangs of emptiness. These dissociated and projected terrors could not be named nor tamed nor could they be permanently disowned. In the realm of neurosis, I could have been a bad or inconsistent mother; in a less representational world, I would have been a container and permitted my reverie upon that which I contained. In this realm, though, I could only be a therapist working in my office with no resemblance to anyone of past meaning. It felt safer for her to use the wisdom of self-help books or the readings of tea leaves than to truly use my mind.

Reverie, then, is a state of consciousness where heightened receptivity to another occurs and reverie is a state of consciousness which is facilitated by alpha functioning and facilitates alpha function in those whose projections are dreamt upon by the other. Bion has hypothesized that dream-work is essential to the creation of the psychological mind and Freud begins his understanding of the psychological mind with his interpretation of the dream. Bion brings us back to this initial investigation (Wisdom, 1964), positing that dreaming is the source both of our sanity and of our capacity to render experience internal and meaningful and remembered. Melanie Klein's articulation of the paranoid schizoid position is, as Ogden points out," a psychology without a subject." (Ogden, 1986, p.42) Ogden writes that "there is no interpreting subject mediating between perception of danger and response to it." (Ogden, 1986, p.42) Bion's work on thinking attempts to discern the specific dysfunctions that prevent the development of our subjectivity and our capacity to experience.

Bion, not a theorist we usually think of as centrally interested in aspects of our dependence on one another or in merger-like experiences, has located his concept of reverie in these very areas. Reverie is a mental immersion in the affective and sensory fragments of another's experience which results from an intimacy that borrows from merger-like states of being and requires capacities for both reception and introjection. Each of the patients I have mentioned lacked a primary caretaker, whose love was conveyed through reverie, and each had different variations of incapacities in thinking in regard to their emotional and psychological lives. These early and repeated failures resulted in their attempting to eliminate their need for another. They then try to prevent the analyst's reveries on their experiences and attempt to destroy that mind space in us. This destruction replays their own experience of the dismissal of their projections and the refusal of a resting place in their parent's mind. They know only how to evict distress, not how to experience it and tame it. It then becomes our treatment task to render reverie possible so that mindedness can occur. We need to develop patients' trust in our capacity and willingness to bear their confusing pain and we need to help them with their shame around these confusing and powerful feelings, so that they can allow us the kind of deep mental and affective immersion they need us to have, for our reveries to be the processors of their disruptive experiences. It is the other's reveries, according to Bion, which hold and contain and name the unbearable in our early lives. Without such a kind of early knowing, thinking may be at risk.

References

Balint, Michael (1968, 1979). *The Basic Fault*. New York: Brunner Mazel.

Bion, Francesa, ed. 1980. *Bion in New York and Sao Paulo*. Perthshire: Clunie Press.

Bion, W.R. (1967). *Second Thoughts: Selected Papers on Psychoanalysis*. London: Karnac.

Bion, W.R. (1962). *Learning from Experience*. London: Karnac.

Bion, W.R. (1990). *Brazilian Lectures*. London: Kamac. BION, W.R. (1992, 1994). Cogitations. London: Kamac.

Bion, W.R. (1982, 1985, 1991). *The Long Week-End 1897-1919: Part of a Life*. London: Karnac.

Bion, W. R. (1985). *All My Sins Remembered, Another Part of a Life and The Other Side of Genius, Family Letters*. Abingdon: Fleetwood Press.

Bion, W.R. (1977). *Taming Wild Thoughts*. London: Karnac.

Bollas, Christopher (1987). *The Shadow of the Object, Psychoanalysis of the Unthought Known*. New York: Columbia.

Britton, Ronald (1992). Keeping Things in Mind. *Clinical Lectures on Klein & Bion, ed. Anderson*, Robin. London: Routledge.

Eigen, Michael (1981). The Area of Faith on Winnicott, Lacan, and Bion. *International Journal of Psychoanalysis*, Vol. 62, pt. 4, pp.413–433.

Freud, Sigmund. The Interpretation of Dreams, *Standard Edition*, Vol. IV, 1900.

Green, Andre (1972). The Analyst, Symbolization and Absence. *On Private Madness*, Madison, Connecticut: IUP.

Grotstein, James (1981). Who is the Dreamer Who Dreams the Dream and Who is The Dreamer Who Understands. *Do I Dare Disturb the Universe?: A Memorial to W. R. Bion*, ed. Grotstein. London: Karnac.

Grunes, Mark (1984). The Therapeutic Object Relationship, *Psychoanalytic Review* 71(1), Spring.

Issacs-Elmhirst, Susanna (1981). Bion and Babies. In *do i dare*, Kamac.

Joseph, Betty (1983). On understanding and not understanding: some technical issues. *Psychic Equilibrium and Psychic Change: Selected Papers of Betty Joseph, Spillius & Feldman*, ed., New York and London: Routledge, 1989.

Klein, Melanie (1946). Notes on Some Schizoid Mechanisms. *The Selected Melanie Klein*, Juliet Mitchell, ed. New York: Free Press, 1986.

Milner, Marion (1957). *On not being able to paint*. New York: IUP, 1957.

Noy, Pinchas (1969). A Revision of the Psychoanalytic Theory of Primary Process. *International Journal of Psychoanalysis*, Vol. 50, pp. 155–178.

Ogden, Thomas (1986, 1990). The Paranoid Schizoid Position: Self as Object. *The Matrix of the Mind, Object Relations and Psychoanalytic Dialogue*. New York: Aronson.

Ogden, Thomas (1997). Privacy, Reverie and Analytic Technique. *Reverie and Interpretation, Sensing Something Human*. New York: Aronson.

Ricoeur, Paul. "Language, Symbol and Interpretation" and "The Conflict of Interpretations," Chapters 1 and 2, in *Freud and Philosophy: an Essay on Interpretation*. New Haven: Yale, 1970 (translated by Denis Savage).

Winnicott, D. W. (1956). Primary Maternal Preoccupation. *Through Pediatics to Psychoanalysis, Collected Papers*, London: Hogarth Press.

Winnicott, D. W. (1971). "Dreaming Fantasizing and Living: A Case History Describing a Primary Dissociation." *Playing and Reality*. New York: Basic Books.

Wisdom, J. O. (1981). Metapsychology after Forty Years. *Do I Dare Disturb the Universe?: A Memorial to W.R. Bion*

Empirical Evidence Supporting the Conceptual Relatedness of Object Representations and Internal Working Models

by Geoff Goodman

The proliferation of new developmental and clinical theories broadly termed "psychoanalytic" demands a methodology for making systematic comparisons to establish the commonalities and distinctions among them. This article presents an empirical method for the comparative evaluation of such theories. The Mother-To-Child Object Representation / Internal Working Model Q-sort is a 100-item instrument constructed to assess the quality of the prototypical mother's object representation and internal working model of her child at age five. Object relations judges were asked to sort these items for a complex, differentiated, integrated object representation of a five-year-old, attachment judges for a secure, coherent, freely valuing internal working model of a five-year-old. Judges' criterion Q-sorts in each group yielded a composite criterion Q-sort of the quality of the prototypical mother's mental representation of her child according to each group's theoretical perspective. The Spearman-Brown correlation between the two composite criterion Q-sorts was r = .90, p < .001, suggesting that when confined to a 100-item common vocabulary, judges representing each theoretical construct agreed on the conceptual relatedness of object representations and internal working models. The theoretical constructs of object representations and internal working models share common assumptions in need of further exploration.

The past two decades theories have witnessed a proliferation of developmental and clinical theories broadly termed "psychoanalytic." Attachment theory, proposed in the 1950s by the British psychoanalyst John Bowlby (1969) and later embraced in the 1970s and 1980s by American developmental psychologists (Ainsworth 1979; Ainsworth et al. 1978; Bretherton and Waters 1985), has been reintroduced to psychoanalysts as a contemporary psychoanalytic theory (Fonagy 2001; Goodman 2002; Slade 1999). What is gained by incorporating the insights of attachment theory into the canon of psychoanalytic theories? And what is lost? Can neighboring constructs originating from the many diverse "psychoanalytic" developmental and clinical theories that bombard us in our pluralistic, twenty-first-century community (e.g., critical theory, deconstructionism, hermeneutics, interpersonal theory, intersubjectivity, psychoanalytic feminism, relational psychology, self psychology) be systematically compared with one another to establish the commonalities and distinctions among them? Pine (1990) compared drive psychology, ego psychology, object relations theory, and self psychology in an attempt to synthesize their insights for the enrichment of clinical work. His goal, however, was not to evaluate the theoretical overlap among these four psychologies and thereby determine the unique features of each. Could we devise an empirical method for making such comparative evaluations among theories, even just to dis- cover whether theoretical differences are real or imagined? Perhaps some theoretical controversies could be resolved through a systematic application of such a method.

One such controversy exists between some proponents of psycho-analytic theory and attachment theory. Following the publication of Bowlby's brilliant paper, "Grief and Mourning in Infancy and Early Childhood" (1960), Anna Freud (1960) expressed the sentiments of many eminent psychoanalysts of her day by repudiating Bowlby's presumed neglect of the internal world, declaring that psychoanalysts "do not deal with the happenings in the external world as such but with their repercussions in the mind, i.e., with the form in which they are registered by the child" (p. 54).

These polarized attitudes continue to this day in some quarters. Fonagy (1999) recently observed that "there is bad blood between psychoanalysis and attachment theory" (p. 595). The dynamics of this conflict are complex and historically determined, yet its manifestations are imprinted on many aspects of these two theoretical perspectives as they appear in the current literature. One such aspect affected by this conflict is the theoretical writing about object representations and internal working models. Some object relations theorists (Levine and Tuber 1993, p. 74; Levy and Blatt 1999, pp. 555, 567) and attachment theorists (Bretherton 1987, p. 1075) have expressed their own theory's presumed privileged status by referring to the "static" immutability of the other theory's representational construct, suggesting an imperviousness to developmental change.

Let us review these recent developments of the conflict. Bretherton's criticism (1987) is based on the idea that object relations theory is founded on a fixation-regression model (Zeanah et al. 1989) that inhibits further development. According to Zeanah and colleagues, a "continuous construction model" (p. 657), such as the attachment model, corrects for the errors of the fixation-regression model because a continuous construction model "does not specify the point of origin of various forms of psychopathology or link them to particular developmental phases. Instead, it leaves the question of putative origin open" (pp. 657–658). Coinciding with this idea, clinical intervention focuses not on the meaning and interpretation of specific events occurring within specific stages of psychosexual development or phases of separation-individuation but rather on the meaning and interpretation of ongoing patterns of interaction throughout childhood and into the present, expressed through the transference relationship. Internal working models, therefore, do not represent interpersonal experiences with a caregiver from a particular developmental epoch; rather, they represent an accumulation of these experiences over a person's entire interpersonal history.

In the other camp, the criticisms of Levine and Tuber (1993) and Levy and Blatt (1999) are based on the idea that attachment theory reduces the immense variation in psychopathology to two or three pat- terns of insecurity that fail to make subtle discriminations among levels of clinical functioning and development. For example, a person with a secure internal working model could nevertheless have an unintegrated, undifferentiated object representation or vice versa, depending on the severity of psychopathology. Attachment theorists' abandonment of stage theory is therefore equated with a devaluation of the influences of development—both the accumulation of interpersonal experiences and maturational changes—on the form and severity of psychopathology. According to this view, internal working models can- not capture developmental change because they become increasingly resistant to change (Bowlby 1980) and stable by as early as twelve months (Ainsworth et al. 1978). In an effort to establish a developmental dimension related to the attachment categories, Blatt (1995; Levy and Blatt 1999) specifically suggested that qualitative differences in the representational complexity of the internal working model (differences related to specific developmental epochs) exist both among the three traditional attachment categories—secure, dismissing, and pre-occupied—and within each of the two insecure attachment categories—dismissing and preoccupied.

Levine and Tuber (1993) argued that individuals exhibiting a wide range of clinical and adaptive functioning can nevertheless be classified together in the same insecure attachment category: "If a person with psychotic representations falls into the same nonautonomous [insecure] category as a person who has made a 'generally successful adaptation,' then, we suggest, the [attachment classification] system needs further refinement" (p. 74). Given that the quality of object representations has previously been shown to be associated with level of clinical functioning (Blatt et al. 1991), it is questionable whether any conceptual relatedness is to be found between object representations and internal working models.

Other theorists, however, have postulated its existence. Diamond and Blatt (1994) declared that "working models of attachment and object representations are overlapping, if not identical, modes of conceptualizing the internalized cognitive-affective schemata that form the bedrock of the intrapsychic world, and that in turn shape interpersonal relationships" (p. 77). The idea that object representations "give organization and direction to manifest behavior, including interpersonal relationships, perceptual and cognitive functions, and conceptions of oneself and others" (Blatt and Lerner 1983, p. 213) closely corresponds to the idea that internal working models are "mental representation[s] of an aspect of the world, others, self, or relationships to others of special relevance to the individual" (Main, Kaplan, and Cassidy 1985, p. 68). These mental representations guide "the organization of information ... regarding attachment-related experiences, feelings, and ideations ... [as well as] appraisals of experience ... [and] may be expected to affect language and thought as well as nonverbal behavior" (pp. 67–69). Both theories conceptualize mental representations as cognitive-affective schemata that provide affectively charged information of object, self, and self-in-relation-to-object through the gradual internalization of episodic memories (Stern 1985; Zelnick and Buchholz 1990). From the work of these authors, it

137

would appear that the conceptual definitions of object representations and internal working models might indeed be related.

Preliminary empirical evidence also seems to support the conceptual relatedness of these two theoretical constructs. Levy, Blatt, and Shaver (1998, p. 411) presented empirical evidence that dismissing and pre-occupied individuals have comparable object representations as assessed on conceptual level, differentiation, and scorable attributes—qualities previously defined by Blatt et al. (1992) as the essential structural and qualitative dimensions of object representations. That the two insecure internal working models have comparably low levels of complexity, differentiation, and affective content suggests that less differentiated, less integrated object representations might come in two varieties—dismissing and preoccupied (see Figure 1). It may be suggested, based on their data, that the concept of an insecure internal working model does not obscure, but instead enhances, our knowledge regarding the low end of the complexity of object representation.

Using clinical work to assess the conceptual relation between these two constructs, Diamond et al. (1999, p. 853) reported the case studies of two adult outpatients with a diagnosis of borderline personality disorder. One patient was classified as dismissing, the other as preoccupied. At the beginning of treatment and after one year, both patients were assessed as having comparable differentiation scores on mother and father representations using the Object Representation Inventory (Blatt et al. 1992). Empirical studies using larger sample sizes would need to be conducted to confirm findings such as these.

After reviewing the recent developments of this conflict, two questions need to be asked: Does this conflict—manifested so clearly in discussions about the essence of mental representation—have a clearly defined empirical basis? And does an empirical method exist for making a comparative evaluation of the two theoretical constructs?

The present study seeks to determine whether empirical support exists for the conceptual relatedness of object representations and internal working models. The method used here to measure these constructs is the Mother-To-Child Object Representation / Internal Working Model Q-sort (Goodman and Moon 1995), a 100-item instrument that yields the quality of the prototypical mother's object representation and internal working model of her child at age five (for its initial use in a study, see Moon 1999). The Q-sort approach was used because of its ease of use and its forced-choice methodology, which forces judges to place items in a normal distribution that characterizes both the high and low ends of a construct. Items are placed into nine piles that range from "most uncharacteristic" to "most characteristic" of the construct being defined (see Block 1961). The Q-sort can be used to test the conceptual relatedness of constructs from neighboring theories whose proponents are willing to sort 100 items that encompass the features of the theoretical constructs to be defined.

Two groups of highly respected judges representing each theoretical construct were selected to sort the items according to the prototypical mother's mental representation of her child: object relations judges were asked to sort the items for a complex, differentiated, integrated object representation of a five-year-old; attachment judges were

Structure of object representation (Blatt) complex, differentiated, integrated

Structure of internal working model (Kobak) security (first dimension)

hyperactivating

Figure 1

139

The structure dimension of the object representation (left) and the orthogonal security-anxiety and hyperactivating-deactivating dimensions of the internal working model asked to sort the items for a secure, coherent, freely valuing internal working model of a five-year-old. The hypothesis of this study was that the composite criterion Q-sort of one group of judges would be positively correlated with that of the other group. (A composite criterion Q-sort is a method of aggregating judges' ratings of a proto-typical individual on a variable or variables of interest; see method section below.) Specifically, our hypothesis was that the composite criterion Q-sort defining the prototypical mother's complex, differentiated, integrated object representation of her five-year-old (provided by the object relations judges) would be positively correlated with the composite criterion Q-sort defining the prototypical mother's secure, coherent, freely valuing internal working model of her five-year-old (provided by the attachment judges)—according to the 100- item vocabulary provided by this Q-sort. Support for this hypothesis would then suggest that these two theoretical constructs are conceptually related, and that object relations researchers and attachment researchers need to work together to build bridges between the two theories.

Method

Judges

The judges who provided criterion Q-sorts for this study were selected on the basis of specific criteria. To qualify, judges had to be highly respected within their theoretical community, either object relations or attachment, having published extensively and enjoying a national or international reputation. Judges also had to have established their expertise primarily in one or the other theoretical orientation. Judges who had constructed instruments to assess either object representations or internal working models were especially sought. Equal numbers of men and women within each theoretical perspective were also sought. Finally, selection was based also on having previously established a facility with empirical research (judges needed to under- stand the Q-sorting task and its role in the study).

Each judge was contacted both by telephone and by letter and was requested to provide a criterion Q-sort of the prototypical, or ideal, mother that epitomizes the particular construct for which he or she was Q-sorting (object representation or internal working model). A brief theoretical conceptualization of the construct was included to serve as a general guideline that, along with his or her theoretical and clinical expertise, would determine the Q-item distribution. The dimension sorted by the object relations judges was called "Complexity and Quality of Object Representation," while the dimension sorted by the attachment judges was called "Security-Anxiety." These two brief theoretical conceptualizations were formulated to maximize the distinctions and minimize the similarities between the two constructs. The contrasting theoretical distinctions represented by these two conceptualizations would work against the hypothesis of significant conceptual relatedness. If a positive correlation between the two groups of judges was significant in spite of these contrasting theoretical guidelines, then the finding would be considered highly supportive of the conceptual-relatedness hypothesis.

Measure

The Mother-To-Child Object Representation / Internal Working Model Q-sort (Goodman and Moon 1995), a 100-item instrument, was constructed to yield the quality of the prototypical mother's object representation and internal working model of her child at age five. The first 60 items were designed specifically to assess the security of internal working model; the second 40 items, the complexity and quality of object representation. Each Q-sort item included a statement related to the construct (e.g., "Mother understands child's need for her avail- ability," used to measure security of internal working model), followed by its theoretical opposite ("expresses dissatisfaction over child's need for her availability"), thus providing clarity when placing items into the most uncharacteristic piles. Similarly, the theoretical conceptualizations also contained theoretical descriptions of the lower end of both construct dimensions.

The theoretical basis of the Q-sort items, as well as the theoretical conceptualizations of both constructs, originated in two primary sources: Blatt et al.'s description (1992) of their rating-scale method of coding object representations, and Kobak et al.'s description (1993) of their Q-sort method of coding internal working models. Blatt et al.'s coding system was used because it yields a measure of object representations, whereas other coding systems (Krohn and Mayman 1974; Urist 1980; Westen 1993) yield measures of object relations—a conceptually broader construct. Kobak et al.'s coding system yields a measure of internal working models paralleling Main and Goldwyn's coding system (1994) for the Adult Attachment Interview (George, Kaplan, and Main 1996). Nevertheless, Westen's object relations Q-sort (1993) was consulted, as well as a coding system of parents' internal working models of children (Slade et al. 1993), Q-sorts of attachment security in children (Aber and Baker 1990; Waters and Deane 1985), and Q-sorts of personality development in both children (Block and Block 1980; Schachter, Cooper, and Gordet 1968) and adults (Block 1961). After extensive consultation with a prominent object relations theorist and prominent attachment theorist (neither serving as a judge in this study) to establish face validity on item content and selection, a final set of 100 items was determined.

The Q-sort items were sorted into nine piles ranging from most un-characteristic to most characteristic of the prototypical mother's mental representation of her child, as viewed from the theoretical construct being defined. The items follow a forced-choice distribution in which the five most uncharacteristic items are placed in pile 1, and the five most characteristic in pile 9. Eight items are placed in piles 2 and 8, twelve items in piles 3 and 7, sixteen items in piles 4 and 6, and eighteen items in pile 5, thus forming a normal distribution (for additional information regarding Q-methodology and procedures, see Block 1961). Judges' criterion Q-sorts representing each construct were totaled and then divided by the total number of judges representing that construct to form a composite criterion Q-sort for each construct (Block 1961; J. Block, personal communication, April 30, 1997). These two composite criterion Q-sorts, which reflected the overall perspectives of the two groups of judges, were then used to test the study's hypothesis. Because these internationally respected judges collectively defined this Q-sort instrument, prima facie construct validity was established. Discussing the criterion validity of his own Q-sort for assessing hysteria, Block (1961) wrote, "It is fair to say that the concept of hysteria is nothing more than what a group of competent psychiatrists say it is, and so the usual criterion problem is solved here in a sufficient fashion" (pp. 104–105).

Regarding predictive validity, the Mother-To-Child Q-sort was applied to the interviews of fifty mothers of varied socioeconomic back- grounds regarding their childrearing attitudes and practices, conducted when their children were age five. The clinical and developmental literature suggests that the complexity and quality of parental representations of one's child would be associated with constructs assessed in the child such as positive self-concept (Blatt 1974; Bollas 1987) and selfregulation (Higgins 1989; Maccoby 1959, 1961). Multiple regression analyses revealed that after controlling for mothers' educational level, complexity and quality of object representation (Q-sorted by two independent raters using the Mother-To-Child Q-sort) predicted their children's reports at age twelve of both positive self-concept, standardized coefficient = .25, p = .06, and rule enforcement with peers, standardized coefficient = .33, p < .05 (Moon 1999). Thus, predictive validity of the instrument was supported.

Results

First we tested the internal consistency of each group of judges. The alpha coefficient was .96 for the object relations judges and .94 for the attachment judges. These results suggest that the judges within each group agreed with one another regarding the meaning of the construct they assessed.

Second, we calculated a Spearman-Brown correlation, which measures the degree of association between the two theoretical constructs derived from the two composite criterion Q-sorts provided by the two groups of judges. (The Spearman-Brown correlation was used instead of the more common Pearson product-moment correlation because the mathematical formula used in its calculation takes into account the fact that the item distributions were composited.) The Spearman-Brown correlation was $r = .90$, $p < .001$, a very large association by any standard. Thus, each construct accounted for 81% of the variance in the other construct $(r2 = .90 \times .90 = .81)$, which suggests that the two constructs—object representations and internal working models— are conceptually related.

Third, we conducted a Q-factor analysis to confirm the significant overlap between these two constructs suggested by the significant Spearman-Brown correlation. In this statistical procedure, judges' criterion Q-sorts were treated as separate variables, while the 100 Q-sort items were treated as "subjects," to determine how judges' criterion Q-sorts clustered. Only eigenvalues (a measure of commonality among judges) greater than 1.00 were considered. A one-factor solution (eigenvalue = 10.44) accounted for 74.58% of the total variance. That only one factor (rather than two) was extracted from the data confirms the significant commonality between the two constructs.

The two distributions of the 100 Q-sort items—the common vocabulary used to measure these two theoretical constructs—closely corresponded to each other. When confined to a 100-item common vocabulary, these judges—from two different theoretical orientations— nevertheless agreed on the conceptual relatedness of the constructs. Block (1961, p. 90) first discussed the use of Q-sort methodology to compare and contrast conceptual distinctions in theoretical constructs, and in this spirit the judges selected to test the hypothesis found an appreciable conceptual relatedness between the two theoretical constructs under study.

Even at the item level the two groups of judges matched on many of what they believed to be the 10 most characteristic and 10 most uncharacteristic features of the prototypical mother's mental representation of her child. Table 1 displays the 10 most characteristic items and the 10 most uncharacteristic items for each theoretical construct. The two groups of judges had 40% (4 out of 10) of the most characteristic items in common (boldface items) and 60% (6 out of 10) of the most uncharacteristic items in common (boldface items). If we conclude that the two theoretical constructs are conceptually related, then what do these 10 overlapping items suggest about the prototypical mother's mental representation of her five-year-old?

These 10 overlapping items (see Table 1, boldface items) appear to fall into five distinct categories: emotional availability (items 22, 29, 43), affect tolerance in both self and child (items 30, 34), positive involvement (item 40), coherence of mental representation (items 61, 82, 88), and flexible authority (item 66). Six of these items (22, 29, 30, 34, 40, 43) were specifically constructed to assess internal working models, but were also uniformly endorsed by the object relations judges; the other four items (61,

66, 82, 88) were specifically constructed to assess object representations, but were also uniformly endorsed by the attachment judges. Thus, the five categories identified must be considered salient aspects of mothers' mental representations from both theoretical perspectives.

These 10 items together seem to underscore the importance of coherent, integrated, realistic representations and the ability to modulate affective expression in oneself and one's child. Both object relations theorists (e.g., Kernberg 1986) and attachment theorists (e.g., Kobak and Sceery 1988) have emphasized the lack of representational coherence and affect regulation in the development of psychopathology. Clinicians who conduct parent consultation could focus on these two characteristics that directly affect the quality of parenting—at least according to these two groups of judges.

Most Characteristic of OR prototype
Mother describes child as a complex, integrated, emotional being (describes child using situation-dependent behavioral or functional characteristics [e.g., physical attributes, play activities]).4
Mother tolerates differences in feeling states between child and herself (feels obligated to maintain child's feelings of satisfaction).
Mother appreciates and can empathize with child's less mature developmental status (infantilizes or parentifies child).
Mother is warm or emotionally available to child (is cold or emotionally unavailable to child).
Mother is generally tolerant and forgiving of mistakes and limitations in herself and child (is critical and perfectionistic toward herself and child).
Mother understands child's need for her availability (expresses dissatisfaction over child's need for her availability).

Mother presents an objective and clearly thought-out picture of influences on relationship with child (is unclear or confused about influences on relationship with child).
Mother perceives a connection between her attitudes and behaviors and child's feelings of satisfaction (perceives no connection between her attitudes and behaviors and child's feelings of satisfaction).
Mother describes child's behavior as caused by both environmental events and child's internal thoughts and feelings (explains child's behavior as exclusively state-dependent or trait-dependent).
Mother describes a mutual connection between child's experiences and her experiences (denies any mutual connection between child's experiences and her experiences).

Table 1. The 10 Q-sort items most characteristic and 10 Q-sort items most uncharacteristic of the prototypical mother's mental representation of her child for each theoretical construct—object representation (OR) and internal working model (IWM)

Most Characteristic of IWM prototype
Mother understands child's need for her availability (expresses dissatisfaction over child's need for her availability).
Mother is warm or emotionally available to child (is cold or emotionally unavailable to child).
Mother is generally tolerant and forgiving of mistakes and limitations in herself and child (is critical and perfectionistic toward herself and child).
Mother presents a generally positive picture of child while acknowledging negative feelings (vacillates between positive and negative feelings toward child).
Mother presents a generally positive picture of child while acknowledging negative feelings (attempts to present a perfect or wonderful picture of child).

Mother seems emotionally invested in child (seems detached or uninfluenced by relationship with child).
Mother describes child as a complex, integrated, emotional being (describes child using situation-dependent behavioral or functional characteristics [e.g., physical attributes, play activities]).
Mother is a competent and supportive confidante (is unwilling or unable to listen to child's problems).
Mother is proud of her child and the qualities she or he possesses (is ashamed of her child and the qualities she or he possesses).
Mother is relaxed and comfortable spending time with child (is anxious spending time with child).

Most Uncharacteristic of OR prototype
Mother describes child as an object to control, manipulate, or persecute (mother respects child's autonomy while also maintaining firm, flexible limits).
Mother describes child at different times as all "bad" or frustrating or all "good" or gratifying, either demonizing or idealizing child (integrates both positive and negative aspects of child's personality).
Mother is consumed by feelings of anger toward child (appropriately modulates expressions of anger toward child).
Mother expresses no pleasure in relationship with child (openly expresses the pleasure she experiences in relationship with child).
Mother's description of child contains little understanding of why child feels or behaves as she or he does (description of child contains rich, fully articulated, coherent explanations for child's motives and behavior).
Mother is unconcerned with child's well-being and ability to function (is concerned with child's well-being and ability to function).
Mother describes child as harboring and expressing ill will, spite, or hatred toward others (describes child as doing or disposed to doing good).

148

Mother describes child in sarcastic or derisive manner (provides balanced, realistic picture of child, containing neither idealized nor devaluing descriptions).
Mother describes child as feeling only one way (describes child as having a variety of feelings).
Mother dismisses child's proximity or contact needs as "babyish" or immature, urging child to get involved in the world away from her (supports child's seeking proximity or contact while also acknowledging her or his exploration needs).
Mother describes child as cold, unemotional, or impersonal (describes child as able to communicate warmth toward others and to make others feel loved by her or him).

Most Uncharacteristic of IWM prototype
Mother describes child in sarcastic or derisive manner (provides balanced, realistic picture of child, containing neither idealized nor devaluing descriptions).
Mother describes child as an object to control, manipulate, or persecute (mother respects child's autonomy while also maintaining firm, flexible limits).
Mother's description of child could apply to any child (description of child uniquely distinguishes her or him).
Mother expresses no pleasure in relationship with child (openly expresses the pleasure she experiences in relationship with child).
Mother and child have reversed roles in which child controls mother in either a caregiving or punitive manner (maintains firm, flexible limits while also respecting child's role experimentation).
Mother's description of child contains little understanding of why child feels or behaves as she or he does (description of child contains rich, fully articulated, coherent explanations for child's motives and behavior).

Mother dismisses child's proximity or contact needs as "babyish" or immature, urging child to get involved in the world away from her (supports child's seeking proximity or contact while also acknowledging her or his exploration needs).

Mother is consumed by feelings of anger toward child (appropriately modulates expressions of anger toward child).

Mother lacks confidence that child can rely on her (is confident that child can rely on her).

Mother's specific descriptions of relationship with child contradict generalizations (presents a consistent overall picture of relationship with child that is well-integrated with specific memories).

The findings of this study, however, by no means imply that the two theoretical constructs are conceptually identical. For example, it would be possible to conceptualize the constructs as existing on two different levels of abstraction. Perhaps internal working models psychically represent self- and object representations in interaction with each other. A child might have an internal working model of him- or herself in interaction with the mother during separations and reunions. We would therefore be considering a constellation of three mental representations: a self-representation, an object representation, and a representation of these two representations in interaction with each other. Under this circumstance, the quality of the internal working model would depend on the quality and complexity of the self- and object representations it comprises. Thus, the quality and complexity of object representations and internal working models would complement each other, but these two kinds of representations would be organized at different levels of abstraction (see Goodman 2002). Further research would be needed to test this more subtle hypothesis.

The evidence at the item level also suggests that the two theoretical constructs are not conceptually identical. We observe that the two groups of judges did not match on 50% of what they believed to be the 10 most characteristic and the 10 most uncharacteristic features of the prototypical mother's mental representation of her child (see Table 1, items not in boldface). What clues provided by these nonoverlapping items can we identify that might account for subtle theoretical differences in the pattern of item placement between these two groups of judges?

Upon inspection, the nonoverlapping items selected by the object relations judges as most characteristic and most uncharacteristic seem to focus on the mother's image of the child and the internal and external influences on his or her personality and behavior (e.g., "Mother describes child's behavior as caused by both environmental events and child's internal thoughts and feelings"). The key aspects of the relationship between mother and child seem to be less emphasized. By contrast, the nonoverlapping items selected by the attachment judges as most characteristic and most uncharacteristic seem to focus on just these key relationship aspects (e.g., "Mother seems emotionally invested in child"). The mother's image of the child seems to be less emphasized. As already mentioned, these differences in the pattern of item placement are subtle. Both object relations judges and attachment judges selected "Mother describes child as a complex, integrated, emotional being" (assessing mother's image of child), as well as "Mother understands child's need for her availability" (assessing a key aspect of the mother-child relationship), as most characteristic items. Perhaps both object relations theory and attachment theory could expand their purview to include both object-representational and relational phenomena. This study would seem to indicate that traditional points of conflict such as fixation-regression versus continuous construction diminish in clinical importance when judges empirically define their theoretical constructs using a common vocabulary.

Clinically, the findings suggest that the quality of object representations manifested in the transference relationship could be conceptually related to the quality of the internal working model. According to Bowlby (1973), the internal working model, rather than serving to gratify the infant's needs during the mother's absence, represents a set of expectations that help the infant predict the mother's behavior. Storing in memory how the mother behaves during moments when the attachment system is activated (e.g., when a stranger threatens a sense of security) will assist the infant in adapting his or her behavior to maximize feelings of security and ensure survival. The adaptive function of this attachment system is protection of the child from danger posed by predators or other unknown dangers in the environment. The degree to which the parent provides a secure base from which the infant can explore the environment and to which the infant can return in times of perceived danger determines how securely attached the infant behaves toward the caregiver. The caregiver's responses to the infant's behaviors help determine the infant's expectations of security.

Patient reactions to long weekends, vacations, and the termination process assume a fuller meaning in the context of the manifestations of the internal working model. In treatment, the patient enacts the structure of the internal working model through transference relationships that evolve over time, providing clues regarding the nature of early caregiving relationships, particularly the extent to which the caregiver provided a secure base for the infant when the infant was separated from the caregiver. Interpretations that underscore the incompatibility between (1) patient expectations of rejection, emotional inconsistency, abandonment, or unavailability that emerge in the context of the clinician's leaving and absence, and (2) patient expectations of trustworthiness, reliability, stability, and emotional availability derived from perceived good experiences with the clinician at other times during the treatment, serve to contain and integrate split-off self- and object representations that stimulate the process of creating a whole person. At separations and reunions, psychoanalytic clinicians must pay close attention to the activation of this interplay among the underlying expectations of clinician behavior, patient responses to these presumed expectations, and countertransference pressures to behave in accordance with them. That psychoanalytic clinicians in recent years have already begun to pay close attention to relational phenomena (e.g., Treurniet 1993) suggests that they are already benefiting from exposure to neigh- boring theories such as attachment theory in their clinical work.

Four limitations of this study should be noted. First, although pain-stakingly constructed, the brief theoretical conceptualizations and Q-sort items representing the two constructs that were provided to the two groups of judges might not have accurately captured how some judges within each construct would conceptualize that construct. It is also not known how much impact the theoretical conceptualizations had on the judges' Q-sort distributions.

Second, the lower levels of these two constructs could not adequately be compared, because the conceptual level of object representations is typically coded on a one-dimensional rating scale that measures structure (Blatt et al. 1992, p. 8), whereas the quality of internal working models is typically coded on two orthogonal dimensions, (1) security-anxiety and (2) hyperactivating-deactivating (Kobak et al. 1993, p. 235). Anxiety (insecurity), the low end of the first dimension, can be represented as either hyperactivating (preoccupied) or deactivating (dismissing), the two ends of the second dimension (see Figure 1). Thus, two varieties of insecure internal working model have been identified (preoccupied and dismissing), against only one variety of unintegrated, undifferentiated object representation. Thus, if we are to make an adequate comparison with the internal working model construct, the object representation construct needs further articulation at the lower levels (see Moon 1999).

Third, it is possible that conceptual differences would have been identified had Q-sorts of other kinds of mental representations been used—for example, an adult's mental representation of a parent.

Peculiarities in Q-sorting for the quality of the prototypical mother's mental representation of her five-year-old might have interfered with the detection of real conceptual differences.

Fourth, the nonrandom selection of judges might have biased the sample's representativeness of the object relations and attachment populations. As mentioned, both groups of judges were selected on the basis of a previously established facility with empirical research. But because object relations theorists in general tend to have less expertise in empirical methods than their attachment counterparts, the group of object relations judges in particular might not have been altogether representative of their field.

In conclusion, this study suggests that two theoretical constructs—object representations and internal working models—are conceptually related, according to the two groups of judges who submitted criterion Q-sorts for this study. It is hoped that as a result of this study an exploration of the structure and function of object representations and internal working models will be undertaken. Object relations theory and attachment theory both have proud, respected traditions that can be preserved and augmented through their reconnection to each other. Mutual understanding of the central tenets of both theories is necessary to take this next momentous step.

This study also underscores the usefulness of an empirical method for making systematic comparisons between the constructs of neigh- boring theories and establishing the commonalities and distinctions between them. Only through such rigorous evaluation will we be able to discover whether theoretical differences are real or imagined, which could assist in resolving our disputes with one another. In the present study, theorists from each theoretical perspective chose to use many of the same Q-sort items to characterize their preferred theoretical construct. What other theoretical constructs in our field can we operationalize and put to the test in order to discover both their commonality and their uniqueness?

References

Aber J.L., Baker, A.J.L. (1990). Security of attachment in toddlerhood: Modifying assessment procedures for joint clinical and research purposes. In *Attachment in the Preschool Years: Theory, Research, and Intervention*, ed. M.T. Greenberg, D. Cicchetti, & E.M. Cummings. Chicago: University of Chicago Press, pp. 427–460.

Ainsworth, M.D.S. (1979). Infant-mother attachment. *Am. Psychol.* 34: 932–937.

Ainsworth, M.D.S., Blehar, M.C., Waters, E., Wall, S. (1978). *Patterns of Attachment: A Psychological Study of the Strange Situation*. Hillsdale, NJ: Erlbaum.

Blatt,S.J. (1974). Levels of object representation in anaclitic and introjective depression. *Psychoanal. St. Child* 29: 107–157. [→]<http://www.pep-web.org/document.php?id=psc.029.0107a>

Blatt, S.J. (1995). Representational structures in psychopathology. In *Rochester Symposium on Developmental Psychopathology: Vol. 6. Emotion, Cognition, and Representation*, ed. D. Cicchetti & S.L. Toth. Rochester: University of Rochester Press, pp. 1–33.

Blatt, S.J. Chevron, E.S., Quinlan, D.M., Schaffer, C.E., & Wein, S. (1992). *The assessment of qualitative and structural dimensions of object representations.* Rev. ed. Unpublished manuscript, Yale University. [Related→]<http://www.pep-web.org/document.php?id=psc.035.0107a>

Blatt, S.J. & Lerner, H. (1983). Investigations in the psychoanalytic theory of object relations and object representations. In *Empirical Studies of Psychoanalytic Theories*, ed. J. Masling. Hillsdale, NJ: Analytic Press, pp. 189–249.

Blatt, S.J. Wiseman, H., Prince-Gibson, E., & Gatt, C. (1991). Object representations and change in clinical functioning. *Psychotherapy* 28: 273–283.

Block, J. (1961). *The Q-sort Method in Personality Assessment and Psychiatric Research*. Palo Alto, CA: Consulting Psychologists Press, 1978.

Block, J.H., Block, J. (1980). The role of ego-control and ego-resiliency in the organization of behavior. In *Minnesota Symposia on Child Psychology, ed. W.A. Collins. Vol. 13*. Hillsdale, NJ: Erlbaum, pp. 39–101. [Related→]<http://www.pep-web.org/document.php?id=ifp.003.0198b>

Bollas, C. (1987). *The Shadow of the Object: Psychoanalysis of the Unknown Thought*. New York: Columbia University Press.

Bowlby, J. (1960). Grief and mourning in infancy and early childhood. Psychoanal. *St. Child* 15: 9–52. [→]<http://www.pep-web.org/document.php?id=psc.015.0009a>

Bowlby, J. (1969). *Attachment and Loss: Vol. 1. Attachment*. 2nd ed.. New York: Basic Books, 1982. [→]<http://www.pep-web.org/document.php?id=ipl.079.0001a>

Bowlby, J. (1973). *Attachment and Loss: Vol. 2. Separation, Anxiety and Anger*. New York: Basic Books. [→]<http://www.pep-web.org/document.php?id=ipl.095.0001a>

Bowlby, J. (1980). *Attachment and Loss: Vol. 3. Loss, Sadness and Depression*. New York: Basic Books. [→]<http://www.pep-web.org/document.php?id=ipl.109.0001a>

Bretheron, I. (1987). New perspectives on attachment relations: Security, communication, and internal working models. In *Handbook of Infant Development, ed. J.D. Osofsky*. 2nd ed. New York: Wiley, pp. 1061–1100.

Bretherton, I. & Waters, E., Eds. (1985). Growing Points in Attachment Theory And Research. *Monographs of the Society for Research in Child*

Development 50 (1-2, Serial No. 209). [Related→]<http://www.pep-web.org/document.php?id=jcp.005.0112a>

Diamond, D., Blatt, S.J. (1994). Internal working models and the representational world in attachment and psychoanalytic theories. In *Attachment in Adults: Clinical and Developmental Perspectives*, ed. M.B. Sperling & W.H. Berman. New York: Guilford Press.

Diamond, D. Clarkin, J., Levine, H., Levy, K., Foelsch, P., & Yeomans, F. (1999). Borderline conditions and attachment: A preliminary report. *Psychoanal. Inq.* 19: 831–884. [→]<http://www.pep-web.org/document.php?id=pi.019.0831a>

Fonagy, P. (1999). Psychoanalytic theory from the viewpoint of attachment theory and research. In *Handbook of Attachment: Theory, Research, and Clinical Applications*, ed. J. Cassidy & P.R. Shaver. New York: Guilford Press, pp. 595–624. [Related→]<http://www.pep-web.org/document.php?id=jcp.005.0112a>

Fonagy, P. (2001). *Attachment Theory and Psychoanalysis*. New York: Other Press.

Freud, A. (1960). Discussion of Dr. John Bowlby's paper. *Psychoanal. St. Child* 15: 53–62. [→]<http://www.pep-web.org/document.php?id=psc.015.0053a>

George, C., Kaplan, N., Main, M. (1996). *Adult Attachment Interview*. 3rd ed. Unpublished manuscript, University of California, Berkeley. [Related→]<http://www.pep-web.org/document.php?id=ijp.084.0651a>

Goodman, G. (2002). *The Internal World and Attachment*. Hillsdale, NJ: Analytic Press.

Goodman, G. & Moon, M.Y. (1995). *The Mother-To-Child Object Representation / Internal Working Model Q-sort*. Unpublished manuscript, Cornell University Medical College, White Plains, NY. [Related→]

Higgins, E.T. (1989). Continuities and discontinuities in self-regulatory and self-evaluative processes: A developmental theory relating self and affect. *Journal of Personality* 57: 407–444.

Kernberg, O. (1986). Borderline personality organization. In *Essential Papers on Borderline Disorders: One Hundred Years at the Border*, ed. M. Stone. New York: NYU Press, pp. 279–319. [→]<http://www.pep-web.org/document.php?id=apa.015.0641a>

Kobak, R.R., Cole, H.E., Ferenz-Gillies, R., Fleming, W.S., Gamble, W. (1993). Attachment and emotion regulation during mother-teen problem solving: A control theory analysis. *Child Dev.* 64: 231–245.

Kobak, R.R. & Sceery, A. (1988). Attachment in late adolescence: Working models, affect regulation, and representations of self and others. *Child Dev.* 59: 135–146.

Krohn, A., Mayman, M. (1974). Object representations in dreams and projective tests: A construct validational study. *Bull. Mennin. Clinic.* 38: 445–466.

Levine, L.V., Tuber, S.B. (1993). Measures of mental representation: Clinical and theoretical considerations. *Bull. Mennin. Clinic.* 57: 69–87. [Related→]<http://www.pep-web.org/document.php?id=psc.031.0107a>

Levy, K.N., Blatt, S.J. (1999). Attachment theory and psychoanalysis: Further differentiation within insecure attachment patterns. *Psychoanal. Inq.* 19: 541–575.[→]<http://www.pep-web.org/document.php?id=pi.019.0541a>

Levy, K.N., Blatt, S.J. & Shaver, P.R. (1998). Attachment styles and parental representations. *Journal of Personality & Social Psychology* 74: 407–419.

Maccoby, E.E. (1959). Role-taking in childhood and its consequences for social learning. *Child Dev.* 30: 239–252.

Maccoby, E.E. (1961). The taking of adult roles in middle childhood. *Journal of Abnormal & Social Psychology* 63: 493–503.

Main, M., Goldwyn, R. (1994). *Adult attachment scoring and classification systems.* 6th ed. Unpublished manuscript, University College London.

Main, M., Kaplan, N., Cassidy, J. (1985). Security in infancy, childhood, and adulthood: A move to the level of representation. In Growing Points in Attachment Theory and Research, ed. I. Bretherton & E. Waters. *Monographs of the Society for Research in Child Development* 50(1-2, Serial No. 209):66–104.

Moon, M.Y. (1999). *Longitudinal correlates of mothers' object representations of their 5-year-old children: An exploratory study.* Unpublished dissertation, Columbia University.

Pine, F. (1990). *Drive, Ego, Object, and Self: A Synthesis for Clinical Work.* New York: Basic Books.

Schachter, F.F., Cooper, A., Gordet, R. (1968). A method for assessing personality development for follow-up evaluations of the preschool child. *Monographs of the Society for Research in Child Development* 33(3, Serial No. 119):1–55.

Slade, A. (1999). Attachment theory and research: Implications for the theory and practice of individual psychotherapy with adults. In *Handbook of Attachment: Theory, Research, and Clinical Applications,* ed. J. Cassidy & P.R. Shaver. New York: Guilford Press, pp. 575–594.

Slade, A., Aber, J.L., Cohen, L., Fiorello, J., Meyer, J., Desear, P., & Waller, S. (1993). *Parent Development Interview coding system.* Rev. ed. Unpublished manuscript, City University of New York.

Stern, D.N. (1985). *The Interpersonal World of the Infant: A View from Psychoanalysis and Developmental Psychology.* New York: Basic Books. [→]<http://www.pep-web.org/document.php?id=zbk.016.0001a>

Treurniet, N. (1993). What is psychoanalysis now? *Int. J. Psycho-Anal.* 74: 873–891

Urist, J. (1980). Object relations. In *Encyclopedia of Clinical Assessment*, ed. R.H. Woody. Vol. 2. San Francisco: Jossey-Bass, pp. 821–833.

Waters, E., Deane, K.E. (1985). Defining and assessing individual differences in attachment relationships: Q-methodology and the organization of behavior in infancy and early childhood. In Growing Points in Attachment Theory and Research, ed. I. Bretherton & E. Waters. *Monographs of the Society for Research in Child Development* 50(1–2, Serial No. 209):41–65.

Westen, D. (1993). *Social cognition and object relations scale: Q-sort and TAT data (SCORS-Q)*. Rev. ed. Unpublished manuscript, Harvard University Medical School.

Zeanah, C.H., Anders, T.F., Seifer, R., Stern, D.N. (1989). Implications of research on infant development for psychodynamic theory and practice. *Journal of the American Academy of Child & Adolescent Psychiatry* 28: 657–668.

Zelnick, L., Buchholz, E.S. (1990). The concept of mental representations in light of recent infant research. *Psychoanal. Psychol.* 7: 29–58. [→]<http://www.pep-web.org/document.php?id=ppsy.007.0029a>

Object Representations and Internal Working Models

A Model for Understanding Their Structure and Function

by Geoffery Goodman

I will never leave you or forsake you.–Joshua 1:5

Object relations theory and attachment theory have much in common. For Freud (1905b) the object was initially identified as that part of a caregiver toward whom the infant's libido was directed. The aim of this intrapsychic process was to discharge quantities of libido. Libidinal gratification, which for Freud is originally autoerotic, is more realistically achieved through objects. Freud (1926a) later recognized that the first object—the mother—also becomes identified with the young child's need for security.

This enlarged view of the uses of the object originated from Freud's (1926a) later concern about potential danger-situations in childhood that cause anxiety and contribute to the development of psychopathology. These danger-situations consist of the loss of the object, the loss of the object's love, castration anxiety, and anxiety precipitated by the superego. Later psychoanalytic theorists explored in greater depth the possible relation between danger-situations and the development of the young child's intrapsychic representations of object and self.

This exploration of the relations between early childhood danger situations and the development of object relations headed in two different directions. British psychoanalysts such as W. R. D. Fairbairn (1952) and especially Melanie Klein (1932, 1946, 1952c) believed, contrary to Freud, that infants engage in object relations from birth and that the precursors of what we consider to be the three principal agencies of the mind—id, ego, and superego—also exist from birth. If these precursors exist within the first 12 months of life, then it follows that intrapsychic conflict also exists within this same time frame. According to Klein, from the beginning of postnatal life the aggressive and libidinal drives, unbound by organized mental processes or representations, threaten to overwhelm and destroy the fragile ego. Thus, the early ego defends itself by implementing the primitive mechanisms we know as projection, introjection, splitting, and denial.

It is through these same defensive processes that object relations develop. Because the drives—and the defenses directed against them necessarily contribute to the development of the infant's earliest self and object representations, these earliest images of caregiving experiences encoded into the infant's memory are therefore highly distorted and grotesque caricatures of the object, the primary caregiver, who is split into good and bad object representations. The purpose of splitting is to protect the ego from the overwhelming anxiety created by the terrifying, persecutory object representations that threaten the ego's survival. It is only through integration of these good and bad object representations that depressive anxiety, a more mature level of anxiety that acknowledges dependence on the object and the potential for loss of the object, can be experienced. Object representations can then begin to approximate reality.

The suppositions that the ego, object relations, and intrapsychic conflict exist from birth and help to account for the origin of psychopathology were organized around what became known as the British Object Relations School, which obviously represented a departure from the traditional Freudian (1905b) understanding of early infant development. Yet the emphasis on primitive infantile anxiety's being related to separation and loss directly followed from Freud's (1926a) later theorizing on the origin of anxiety and its function as a signal of external and internal danger rather than as converted libido.

The second direction that emerged from Freud's (1926a) later interest in primitive anxiety was taken by Bowlby (1946, 1958a), who agreed with Klein's departures from Freud but reacted to her emphasis on drives by building an object relations theory without them. Bowlby (1973, 1980a, 1982, 1988) borrowed from ethology and systems theory to construct the idea of the internal working model. The danger-situation most salient for Bowlby was separation from and loss of the primary caregiver. The quality, duration, and frequency of separations and losses have profound implications for the development of future psychopathology. The internal working model begins to develop at birth and continues developing as the attachment behavioral system becomes organized and focused on one person-the primary caregiver. Episodic memories of early experiences of care, separation, and prolonged absence are encoded and organized into a mental representation of the relationship to this caregiver. This working model has adaptive value because it provides an accurate appraisal of experiences, which assists the infant in developing expectations of the primary caregiver that coincide with the infant's own behavioral repertoire.

A primary caregiver who fails to meet the attachment needs of the infant, through frequent or prolonged separations, emotionally un-responsive care, or outright rejection of these needs, activates in the infant defensive exclusion (Bowlby, 1973). The infant defensively excludes painful information about the caregiver or caregiver behavior, such as rejection or prolonged absence to preserve a pain-free internal working model of the relationship to the primary caregiver. In Bowlby's attachment theory, the supposition that the infant needs to exclude these painful caregiving memories from awareness helps to account for the origin of psychopathology. Whereas in Freudian theory repression is used to defend against awareness of drives that threaten to break through and interfere with adaptation to the environment, defensive exclusion is used to defend against awareness of real external situations that threaten to cause mental pain in the infant feelings of rejection by the primary caregiver and the infant's corresponding feelings of unworthiness of the primary caregiver's love.

The existence of the drives and the capacity to appraise experience accurately (at least initially) are the two primary differences between the directions of thought represented by Klein and Bowlby. For Klein, self- and object representations are the drive and defense influenced outcome of interactions with the primary caregiver that develop from terrifying, persecutory, unmodulated images and can become transformed into reality-based, coherent images that consist of integrated drive derivatives. For Bowlby, internal working models are the reality-influenced outcome of interactions with the primary caregiver that develop from initially accurate appraisals of real experience but that can become distorted by the exclusion of certain aspects of experience that protects the infant from experiencing painful feelings. Whereas Klein's infant is born into a grotesque distortion of reality and only gradually becomes aware of reality, Bowlby's infant is born into an awareness of reality and only gradually distorts reality through its selective exclusion.

This fundamental difference between the two theories—and between these two theories and classical psychoanalytic theory—has profound implications for the origin, development, and treatment of psychopathology. One important implication that distinguishes Bowlby's theory from Klein's and Freud's theory is that psychopathology develops because of environmental impingements, not because of endogenous characteristics. Thus, Freud's conviction that psychopathology reflects the earliest stages of normal development and connects us all to the mental suffering of humanity is overturned by Bowlby's idea that psycho-pathology emerges only through deviant environmental experiences. Psychopathology is therefore not a consequence of genetic heritage in conflict with inevitable environmental demands but rather a consequence of a maladaptive environment in conflict with an attachment system that evolved to function in an adaptive environment. The questions posed here are whether any compatibility exists between object relations theory and attachment theory and whether this putative compatibility could produce a more comprehensive theory that encompasses the unique insights of each theory.

Instead of searching for areas of compatibility, object relations theorists and attachment theorists each underscored the merits of their own theory while exposing the presumed flaws in the others' theory. Although not considered an object relations theorist per se, Anna Freud (1960) nevertheless spoke for many of them when she repudiated Bowlby's presumed neglect of the internal world and declared that psychoanalysts "do not deal with the happenings in the external world as such but with their repercussions in the mind, i.e., with the form in which they are registered by the child" (p. 54). Lyons-Ruth (1991), in turn, criticizes object relations theory because "qualitative differences in these patterns (of emotional regulation) are not best represented by the concept of fixation at different points along a single developmental continuum" (p. 16).

Adopting this antagonistic tone, empiricists from both theoretical orientations have continued to emphasize difference over compatibility. For example, object relations researchers (Levine and Tuber, 1993,

p. 74; Levy and Blatt, 1999, pp. 555, 567) and attachment researchers (Bretherton, 1987, p. 1075) characterize each other's representational construct as immutable rather than as evolving over time. The result has been a polarization of positions that has prevented a comprehensive theory from emerging. The model proposed here for reconciling the diverse understanding of the structure and function of object representations and of internal working models relies in part on Kernberg's (1966, 1967, 1975, 1984, 1986a) theory of borderline personality organization (see Figure 1). In particular the three insecure internal working models identified by attachment researchers seem to qualify as belonging within the conceptual category of borderline personality organization because they share many of the features identified by Kernberg as constituting this personality structure.

Otto Kernberg's Theory of Borderline Personality Organization

Initially, self- and object representations gradually develop in relation to each other as a consequence of affectively charged experiences. The components of the internal world "always include a self representation, an object representation, and an affective disposition that links them" (Kernberg et al., 1989, p. 9). Thus, the infant introjects mental representations of connected interactions rather than isolated images. Because of the initially immature capacity of the ego for integration, these libidinally and aggressively charged sets of representations remain split apart. Later, however, these initially unintegrated and affectively unmodulated representations gradually become integrated and modulated as the ego begins to develop a capacity for integration and anxiety tolerance and starts to perceive the aggressive impulses connected to the bad self-

and object representations as less threatening. Kernberg (1986a, p. 299) identified splitting as operating as a defensive process only after the ego has developed the capacity for integration.

In borderline personality organization, splitting is considered the predominant defense mechanism operating to keep good and bad self- and object representations separated from each other. Other primitive defense mechanisms associated with borderline personality organization include projection, introjection, projective identification, denial, primitive idealization, devaluation and derogation, omnipotent control, and narcissistic withdrawal. Kernberg (1987) has demonstrated, however, that some of these defense mechanisms, such as projection, can also be used at higher levels of personality organization. From a diagnostic perspective, borderline personality disorder proper would be considered just one of several personality disorders that display the underlying structure of borderline personality organization. Other personality disorders, such as narcissistic personality disorder, however, might be organized at either a borderline or a neurotic level of the personality, depending on the level of integration of the mental representations, the level of sophistication of the defensive processes, the level of affective modulation, and the ego's capacity for anxiety tolerance.

Kernberg's concept of the pathological grandiose self facilitates our understanding of the possible vicissitudes of borderline personality organization. A condensation of the real self and idealized self-and object representations constitutes the pathological grandiose self, permitting some ego integration at the cost of a deterioration of object relationships. Such patients project unacceptable self-representations onto the external world, leaving them "completely unable really to depend on anybody because of their deep distrust and depreciation of others" (Kernberg, 1986a, p. 292). They can also project the pathological grandiose self onto another person when that person needs to be protected from the individual's derogation.

169

Kernberg associates the pathological grandiose self with the narcissistic and antisocial personalities—"a subgroup of the narcissistic personality" (p. 292)—who react to interpretations as if they were rejections, but demonstrate "a persistent absence of separation anxiety or mourning reactions at weekends, vacation, or illness of the analyst" (Kernberg, 1986b, p. 255). Kernberg emphasizes that borderline personality organization and the pathological grandiose self employ the same primitive defense mechanisms. Indeed, the pathological grandiose self, observed in narcissistic personalities, shares the defensive structure of borderline personality organization because of "the predominance of mechanisms of splitting... or split-off ego states" (p. 246). The distinction between these two pathological organizations is that, because of the pathological condensation of mental representations, the pathological grandiose self:

> compensates for the lack of integration of the normal self-concept which is part of the underlying borderline personality organization: it explains the paradox of relatively good ego functioning and surface adaptation in the presence of a predominance of splitting mechanisms, a related constellation of primitive defences, and the lack of integration of object representations (p. 247)

Thus, structural formation and adaptive functioning differ between the two pathological organizations, but the underlying defensive processes remain essentially the same (for a more detailed discussion of these issues, see Chapter 3).

Mary Main's Contribution to the Understanding of Internal Working Models

Mary Main (Main and Goldwyn, 1994; Main et al., 1985), extending Bowlby's (1973) theoretical work on internal working models and Mary Ainsworth's (1979; Ainsworth et al., 1978) empirical work on their development in infancy, studied internal working models in adults. She and her colleagues found that a secure internal working model (F) is reflected in persons who during the Adult Attachment Interview (George et al., 1996; Main et al., 1985) appear to feel free to explore their thoughts and feelings. Persons with secure internal working models appear relaxed and open; their accounts of relationships to their parents, coherent and organized. By contrast, a dismissing (insecure) internal working model (Ds) is reflected in people who provide little information about their childhood and offer semantic memories of idealized parents combined with episodic memories of rejection. These people limit the influence of attachment relationships and experiences in their mental lives. Also by contrast a preoccupied (insecure) internal working model (E) is reflected in people who appear entangled in past experiences with parents. These people offer passive, vague memories that convey internal confusion, communicated through tangential, rambling, and ultimately unconvincing discourse. An unresolved internal working model (U) is found in people who appear unresolved about significant losses, abuse, or other traumatic events. These people exhibit lapses in their ability to monitor reasoning and discourse only when discussing traumatic events. Finally, the cannot-classify (CC) attachment category is assigned to people who cannot be classified within the original Ds-F-E attachment classification system. Their AAI's appear to contain the marked presence of two different internal working models-either two insecure models (Ds and E) or a secure and insecure model (F and Ds; F and E).

171

Main and Goldwyn (1994) also described subclassifications of the secure internal working model (F1, F2, F3, F4, F5), the dismissing internal working model (Ds1, Ds2, Ds3, Ds4), and the preoccupied internal working model (E1, E2, E3). These subclassifications capture subtle differences among people assessed as having a particular internal working model; these categories also represent distinctions on a continuum ranging from extreme dismissing (Ds1) to extreme preoccupied (E3; see Figure 1,). Finally, the four internal working models identified by Main and her colleagues correspond to the infant attachment categories previously identified by Ainsworth and her colleagues. Secure corresponds with secure, dismissing with anxious-avoidant (A), preoccupied with anxious-resistant (ambivalent; C), and unresolved with disorganized (D). Main et al. (1985) are the first researchers to have found a concordance between the internal working models of mothers and the internal working models of their infants (for a more detailed discussion of these issues see Chapter 4).

The Model: Application of Kernberg's Theory to the Structure

Many of the defense mechanisms identified by Kernberg as operating within a borderline personality organization had already been implicated in the structure of insecure internal working models: for example, "defenses of splitting and denial... [are] apparent in avoidant children, who tend to escape from self-involving affective interactions and who adopt defensive strategies to eliminate any negative affects, such as anxiety and anger" (Ammaniti, 1991, pp. 248–249). Splitting is also clearly observed in resistant (ambivalent) infants whose object representations oscillate between a gratifying mother and an abandoning mother. Explicit

172

incoherence in the AAI's of dismissing as well as preoccupied persons also testifies to splitting of object representations.

I propose that all dismissing (Ds1, Ds2, Ds3, Ds4) and preoccupied (E1, E2, E3) subclassifications and the unresolved classification (U) belong within the conceptual category of borderline personality organization (see Figure 1). The features of the pathological grandiose self reviewed earlier also characterize dismissing persons, who deactivate attachment needs to avoid profound feelings of rejection. The dismissing attachment category has been associated with both narcissistic (Rosenstein and Horowitz, 1996) and antisocial (Allen et al., 1996; Rosenstein and Horowitz, 1996) personality disorders in adolescents and adults, while avoidant attachment in infants has been associated with antisocial behavior in later prepubertal childhood (Cassidy and Kobak, 1988; Erickson, Sroufe, and Egeland, 1985; LaFreniere and Sroufe, 1985; Pastor, 1981; Renken et al., 1989; Sroufe, 1983; Sroufe et al., 1984). Two other classes of psychiatric disorder associated with the narcissistic personality--eating disorders (Davis and Marsh, 1986; Grace, 1990; Masterson, 1995; Richard, 1985; Ruderman and Grace, 1988) and substance abuse (Derby, 1992; Vieira, 1997; Woodham, 1987; Wurmser, 1984)—have also been associated with the dismissing attachment category and rating scales (Allen et al., 1996; Cole-Detke and Kobak, 1996; Fonagy et al., 1996; Rosenstein and Horowitz, 1996).

According to this literature, people diagnosed with either psychiatric disorder focus exclusively on their bodies or on peak bodily experiences in an effort to "divert attention from distress cues and minimize the need for support from others" (Cole-Detke and Kobak, 1996, p. 283). Studies have also shown that dismissing persons deny distress on self-report instruments (Dozier et al., 1991; Dozier and Lee, 1995; Kobak and Sceery, 1988; Pianta, Egeland, and Adam, 1996) and deny their need for psychiatric services (Dozier, 1990). These various findings related to the dismissing attachment category are concordant with findings pertaining to avoidant attachment in children. For example, in a study of loneliness in children ages five to seven who at 12 months had been assessed for quality of attachment, avoidant children reported the least loneliness, while resistant (ambivalent) children reported the most (Berlin, Cassidy, and Belsky, 1995), or missing others. Consciously, avoidant children, like dismissing adults, deny needing or missing others.

In spite of (or perhaps because of) their denial of attachment needs, dismissing persons (Dozier and Kobak, 1992) and avoidant infants (Spangler and Grossmann, 1993; Sroufe and Waters, 1977b) alike demonstrate high levels of anxiety in attachment-activating situations as measured by fluctuations in monitored heart rates and increased cortisol levels. Perhaps Kernberg's (1986b) observation that narcissistic personalities, under the influence of a pathological grandiose self, demonstrate a persistent absence of separation anxiety during analyst absences is incorrect; rather, these people experience separation anxiety intensely but lack any awareness of it. It appears that the dismissing attachment category ideally captures the spirit of Kernberg's construct of the borderline personality organization with the pathological grandiose self.

Similarly, the features of borderline personality organization without the pathological grandiose self also characterize preoccupied persons, who hyperactivate attachment needs through enmeshment and preoccupation to protect against the terror of abandonment (Kobak et al., 1993; Kobak and Sceery, 1988). The preoccupied attachment category and rating scales are associated with borderline personality disorder (Fonagy et al., 1996; Patrick et al., 1994; Rosenstein and Horowitz, 1996) and depression (Cole-Detke and Kobak, 1996; Dozier, 1990; Fonagy et al., 1996; Kobak et al., 1991). The psychiatric literature reveals that these two psychiatric disorders have a high comorbidity rate (Goodman et al., 1998; Gunderson

174

and Elliott, 1985; Gunderson and Phillips, 1991; McGlashan, 1983, 1987; Pope et al., 1983).

From an object relations standpoint, it is when splitting mechanisms fail and the object representation becomes momentarily integrated that a person becomes aware that the bad, persecutory object representation toward which the destructive impulses have been directed is simultaneously the good, loved object representation toward which the libidinal impulses have been directed. At these moments the depressive position gains ascendancy, overwhelming the borderline personality with states of depressive anxiety and consequent feelings of concern and guilt. The condensation of idealized self- and object representations necessary for the development of the pathological grandiose self has not occurred; thus, the borderline personality is more vulnerable to these trial integrations. Nevertheless, mechanisms of splitting quickly resume their operations and, because tegrated and unmodulated of poor anxiety tolerance good and bad representations remain unintegrated and unmodulated.

Because of the superficially adequate ego functioning and surface adaptation afforded those persons with a pathological grandiose self, preoccupied people might appear to have a more primitive personality organization than dismissing persons do. I am proposing, however, that the quality of object relations and defensive processes characteristic of the personality organization of preoccupied persons are identical to those of dismissing persons. Although dismissing persons superficially benefit from an additional defensive structure—the pathological grandiose self—both internal working models are dominated by unintegrated self- and object representations and mechanisms of splitting, projection, introjection, and denial. The unresolved attachment category, highly associated with preoccupied attachment (Adam et al., 1996; Fonagy et al., 1996; Pianta, Egeland, and Adam, 1996; for child and infant studies, see Hubbs-Tait et al., 1996; Lyons-Ruth et al., 1993) would be organized

175

at a lower level of personality organization and consequently would have more unintegrated levels of object representation than even the three preoccupied subclassifications (E1, E2, E3). Unresolved attachment is by definition associated with significant unresolved losses, abuse, or other traumatic events (Main and Goldwyn, 1994).

Kernberg (1986b) inadvertently forecasted the conceptual distinction between the dismissing and the preoccupied attachment categories:

> The absence of the capacity to depend upon others on the part of narcissistic personalities [dismissing individuals), in contrast to the clinging dependency ... in borderline patients [preoccupied individuals], contributes fundamentally to the differential diagnosis of narcissistic personalities functioning on an overt borderline level from usual borderline patients [pp. 255–256].

This new conceptualization of the two insecure internal working models might account for the lack of association reported by Fonagy et al. (1996) between persons who satisfied Kernberg's (1977) structural criteria for borderline personality organization and insecure attachment classification (Fonagy et al., 1996, p. 29). I am suggesting that, because Kernberg identified an underlying personality organization that spans diagnostic categories (borderline and narcissistic), there would be no association between this underlying organization and specific attachment categories (preoccupied or dismissing). Persons classified as either preoccupied or dismissing satisfied structural criteria for borderline personality organization, thus nullifying any association with a specific attachment category.

Although both borderline personality organization and the pathological grandiose self represent two distinctly different structures, they share primitive defensive processes, unmodulated affects, and unintegrated self- and object representations. Thus, on Kernberg's (1977) structural interview, designed to measure those borderline processes that encompass both borderline and narcissistic psychopathology, preoccupied as well as dismissing attachment categories would include people who satisfy the structural criteria for borderline personality organization. This proposed model does not contradict, but rather accounts for, findings of a strong relation between borderline personality disorder and preoccupied attachment (Fonagy et al., 1996, p. 29; Patrick et al., 1994; Rosenstein and Horowitz, 1996).

How do we make sense out of the attachment subclassifications identified within each of the three internal working models? Kernberg (1986a) pointed out that similar personality traits can be organized within a borderline personality structure (unintegrated mental representations, dyadic relations) or a neurotic personality structure (integrated mental representations, triadic relations). Two secure attachment subclassifications, F1 and F2, could represent narcissistic personality features organized at neurotic levels (see Figure 1). These two subclassifications capture such dismissing features as "some setting aside of attachment" (Main and Goldwyn, 1994, p. 135) yet nevertheless represent secure, coherent internal working models. The complexity and quality of object representations among these two subclassifications would be significantly higher than those among the four dismissing subclassifications (D$1, Ds2, Ds3, Ds4) because the two attachment categories-secure and dismissing-are differentiated by two distinct levels of personality organization-neurotic and borderline. Thus, according to this proposed model, narcissistic personalities organized at a neurotic personality organization would receive a secure attachment classification of F1 or F2, whereas narcissistic personalities organized at a borderline personality organization would receive a dismissing attachment classification of Ds1, Ds2, Ds3, or Ds4, depending on the severity of the pathological grandiose self.

The remaining secure subclassifications—F3, F4, and F5—could be similarly accounted for. Those rare persons who, because of a favorable genetic heritage, emotionally sensitive caregiving during childhood, or years of clinical treatment, receive an F3 subclassification are organized at a healthy level of personality organization that exceeds the neurotic and borderline levels. The other two secure subclassifications, F4 and F5, represent hysterical and depressive personality features organized at neurotic levels (see Figure 1). These two subclassifications capture such preoccupied features as "somewhat resentful/conflicted" (Main and Goldwyn, 1994, p. 138) yet nevertheless represent secure, coherent internal working models. Again, the complexity and quality of object representations among these two subclassifications would be significantly higher than those among the three preoccupied subclassifications (E1, E2, E3) because the two attachment categories—secure and preoccupied—are separated by two different levels of personality organization-neurotic and borderline. According to this proposed model, then, hysterical and depressive personalities organized at a neurotic personality organization would receive a secure attachment classification of F4 or F5, while hysterical and depressive personalities organized at a borderline personality organization would receive a preoccupied attachment classification of E1, E2, or E3, depending on the severity of the borderline personality organization.

Bowlby (1973, p. 205) suggested that one can have multiple internal working models, an idea that other attachment theorists support (Bretherton, 1985; Fonagy, 1999a; Main, 1999; Main and Goldwyn, 1994). Certainly, the splitting of self- and object representations into good and bad affective categories suggests a multiplicity of mental representations in all young infants and in older infants and adults whose representations remain unintegrated. The model proposed here, however, considers an internal working model to be an organization of good and bad self- and object representations and defensive processes (see also Sroufe and Waters,

1977a). If the internal working model is secure, then a healthy or neurotic personality structure predominates. Self- and object representations tend to be complex, differentiated, and integrated, while more sophisticated defensive processes such as repression, minimization, rationalization, and sublimination are operative. If the internal working model is insecure, then a borderline personality structure predominates. Self- and object representations tend to be less clearly differentiated and unintegrated, and more primitive defensive processes such as splitting, projection, introjection, and denial are operative.

A borderline personality structure is further categorized by the usual constellation of borderline operations, or by the pathological grandiose self, which consequently determines the category of insecurity, whether preoccupied or dismissing. Both good and bad self- and object representations, and the defense mechanism of splitting, operate within each of the two insecure internal working models. Primitive idealization might signify the manifest object representation of the dismissing attachment category, but object representations of opposite affective valence signified by derogation are sure to be operating at more latent levels (see Bach, 1994). Primitive idealization, a marked characteristic of dismissing persons' depiction of their parents (Main and Goldwyn, 1994), might reflect a defense mechanism against the awareness of envy of the primary caregiver's ability to gratify attachment needs, coupled with his or her intentional withholding of this gratification through rejection. Primitive idealization would thus keep "the potentially envied person on a pedestal and out of range" of envious comparisons (Joseph, 1986, p. 18). On the other hand, splitting without the idealization or depreciation of others might signify both good and bad object representations operating at both manifest and latent levels.

Attachment theorist and researcher Roger Kobak and his colleagues (1993, p. 235) have described the defensive processes of the dismissing

179

and preoccupied attachment categories as defensive strategies of emotion regulation when the attachment system is activated but attachment needs have not been gratified. Dismissing persons deactivate attachment needs by "restricting access to attachment memories, idealizing parents, or devaluing attachment relationships" (p. 233). We can easily imagine, however, that underneath the idealized parental representations lies the devalued parental representations split off from consciousness. These complementary representations both reflect deactivating defensive processes (see Figure 1). Preoccupied persons hyperactivate attachment needs by engaging their parents in hostile, dependent conflicts that represent dramatic attempts at eliciting caregiving responses to attachment needs. We can also easily imagine that underneath the coercive hostility and resentment directed at the parental representations lies the longing for some external evidence of the loved parental representations split off from consciousness. These complementary representations reflect hyperactivating defensive processes (see Figure 1). Kernberg and his colleagues (1989; see also Clarkin et al., 1999) have masterfully illustrated the rapid oscillations that occur between the manifest and latent levels of these self- and object representations in psychodynamic psychotherapy with patients who satisfy structural criteria for borderline personality organization.

Because dismissing persons use deactivating strategies, whereas pre-occupied persons use hyperactivating strategies, it becomes a conceptual quandary to explain the possible existence of multiple internal working models. If, as I have argued, the principal conceptual difference between these two forms of attachment insecurity is the existence of the pathological grandiose self, then how could a person both manifest and not manifest this defensive structure? Perhaps the condensation of the real self and the idealized self- and object representations suggested by Kernberg as constituting the pathological grandiose self was incompletely or weakly formed. Under low levels of stress, when the attachment system is minimally activated, the pathological grandiose self routinely operates to protect the ego from painful feelings of rejection stimulated by episodic memories (or fantasies) of refusal of the parents to respond to attachment needs when those needs were activated. Under unusually high levels of stress, however, when the attachment system is highly activated, the intrapsychic protection afforded by the presence of the pathological grandiose self weakens. The persecutory anxiety and split-off feelings of exquisite vulnerability break through into consciousness, which could thus mobilize a hyperactivating strategy of emotion regulation typically observed in a borderline personality structure without the pathological grandiose self, manifested in such rapidly oscillating attitudes as hostility, manipulation, dependency, and seductiveness.

Under the attachment-activating conditions of the AAI, a person with a weakened pathological grandiose self could demonstrate this loosening of the omnipotent defensive structure while responding to highly stress-inducing questions regarding specific attachment-relevant situations (e.g., bodily injury, fear, loss of a caregiver) or specific childhood memories regarding interactions with a caregiver (e.g., mother, father). Thus, for example, at specific moments perceived as highly stress inducing, the person's discourse could shift from dismissing (Ds) to preoccupied (E). In such cases, a cannot-classify (CC) attachment category, seldom observed in low-risk samples, might be assigned to capture these shifts between insecure attachment categories (Ds and E) or between secure and insecure attachment categories (F and Ds; F and E). AAI coders need to ascertain that no single attachment pattern predominates if an interview transcript is to merit a CC attachment classification (Main and Goldwyn, 1994).

These intrapsychic shifts in borderline personality organization between an activated and a weakened pathological grandiose self, or between a borderline personality organization without the pathological grandiose self and a more integrated personality organization, can also

181

occur in the therapeutic situation in response to interpretation, depending on the patient's ability to tolerate anxiety (see Chapter 10). Steiner (1987) has suggested that in treatment such shifts occur among the paranoid-schizoid position, depressive position, and "pathological organization" (which conceptually resembles Kernberg's pathological grandiose self): "The leading anxiety of the session ... is often connected with a transition or a threatened transition between two of the three states" (p. 77). When two distinctly different internal working models emerge in the AAI in the context of discussion of the two different parents (the cannot-classify attachment category), it is possible that these people have destroyed all the links between the two internal working models (activated in association with the two parents). Why this split needs to be maintained is not clearly understood. Perhaps the integration of the two internal working models represents recognition of the parents' sexual union—frightening, sadomasochistic parental intercourse that would result in the destruction of both attachment figures (see Britton, 1989).

Two distinct internal working models might also be observed to be operating in certain infants. At 12 months, infants assessed for quality of attachment in the Strange Situation (Ainsworth et al., 1978; Ainsworth and Wittig, 1969) sometimes demonstrate an avoidant attachment strategy during the first reunion with the mother (moderate activation of the attachment system); later, however, they demonstrate a breakdown of this strategy during the second reunion (high activation of the attachment system). (For further discussion, see Goodman et al., 1999). It is possible that, as with adults during the AAI, the underlying defensive structure of self-sufficiency and denial of attachment needs weakens, leaving the infant feeling painfully helpless and vulnerable. Attachment researchers are increasingly considering the question of multiple internal working models and their meaning, and research studying persons classified with the CC internal working model is in progress.

Different Levels of Abstraction Proposed Between Object Representations and Internal Working Models

In Chapter 8, I argued that the complexity and quality of both good and bad object representations are comparable within each insecure attachment category, which accounts for the conceptual relatedness between object representations and internal working models found by all previous empirical studies (reviewed also in Chapter 8). I propose, however, that the actual constructs, according to this model, are organized at different levels of abstraction. Just as borderline personality organization refers to the pattern, or organization, of self- and object representations and defensive processes, so, too, do internal working models refer to the pattern, or organization, of self- and object representations and defensive processes. In this sense, the construct of internal working model is conceptually broader or more abstract than the construct of object representation. In other words, self- and object representations represent the building blocks around which personality structures are formed. These representations contain aggressive, libidinal, and self-preservative (attachment) impulses against which the ego defends itself by employing an array of defensive processes. The ensemble of endogenous drives, mental representations, and defensive processes meanwhile constitute a higher level of organization–the organization of personality.

Perhaps previous studies demonstrated a high concordance between assessments of object representations and assessments of internal working models because object representations of a certain level of complexity, of differentiation, and of integration naturally belong to an internal working model of a certain pattern of security or insecurity. As proposed earlier, unmodulated, unintegrated self- and object representations belong to either the dismissing or the preoccupied attachment category (depending on the presence of the defensive structure known as the pathological grandiose self), whereas modulated, integrated self- and object representations belong to the secure attachment category. The congruence between the two constructs would naturally be moderately high, but the level of abstraction would differ. Rudimentary assessments of these two constructs would not necessarily detect this difference in level of abstraction. Internal working models, like personality organizations, consist of the total constellation of self- and object representations as well as defensive processes and endogenous drives. Finally, internal working models, like personality organizations, also determine the structure and function of self- and object representations within their broader, more abstract intrapsychic context.

Theoretical Implications

The model proposed in this chapter encompasses tenets of both object relations theory and attachment theory but also assumes revisions to both theories. One of the revisions suggested by this model is related to the conventional location of borderline psychopathology during the rapprochement subphase of separation-individuation between 15 and 24 months (Kernberg et al., 1989; Mahler et al., 1975), which we now know contradicts the findings of attachment research (see Lyons-Ruth, 1991). The splitting mechanisms characteristic of borderline personality organization-rapidly oscillating perceptions of good and bad caregiver representations—can be easily observed in the ambivalent behaviors of anxious-resistant (C) infants assessed in the Strange Situation at 12 months.

Kernberg's (1969, 1972, 1986a) criticisms notwithstanding, Klein's developmental timetable appears to be a more accurate depiction of the processes that contribute to borderline versus neurotic personality organization, According to Klein (1946, 1952c), integration of good and bad objects into a coherent whole takes place by six months of age, coinciding with the onset of the depressive position, which signifies the infant's recognition of the potential loss of the mother as a loved person and the infant's dependence on her. Whereas Mahler assumed that separation-individuation was the goal of mature development, Klein (like Bowlby) assumed that recognition of the infant's dependence on the mother was the goal. Anxious-avoidant (A) infants and dismissing (Ds) adults deny their dependence on anyone and hold an omnipotent belief in total self-sufficiency. Similarly, anxious-resistant (ambivalent; C) infants and preoccupied (E) adults exaggerate their distress and dependence in a hostile manner to exercise control over the other person. This maneuver does not signify a true recognition of dependence and potential loss originating from the infants' misdirected aggressive attacks in fantasy and behavior.

Klein also assumed that infants begin to form representations at birth, an idea that differs from Kernberg's and Mahler's views that symbiosis—the lack of differentiation—is a normal stage of intrapsychic development. Symbiosis might be viewed instead as a result of defensive processes, consistent with the paranoid-schizoid position, acting to condense idealized self- and object representations to form the pathological grandiose self as protection against a hostile, threatening, and, most important, depriving object world. Merging (as well as rigid maintenance of boundaries) might reflect a defensive process, not the initial developmental phases of normal autism or normal symbiosis. In Kleinian theory, infants struggle to keep good self- and object representations apart from bad ones from birth through six months; by six months the ego has developed sufficiently for them to begin to integrate these disparate representations into a unified whole. Bretherton (1987) laments the lack of "a detailed treatment of precursors to internal working models in early life" (p. 1071), but contributions from Kleinian theory and attachment research can occupy this void.

185

How does this process of integration occur? Although Klein (1952b) assigned influence to the quality of maternal behavior as well as maturational processes, it was Bion (1962, 1967), one of her followers, who articulated a process by which integration or lack of integration takes place. Bion's "K link" represents the process by which an infant engages in affective communication through projective identification (see also Ogden, 1979), activating the mother's capacity to receive and modify the communication through metabolization. The infant projects hostile, persecutory "beta elements" into the mother to control her. The emotionally responsive mother, interpreting the projective identification as a message of distress (e.g., hunger, discomfort, the need for protection), acts as a container for these primitive affects and transforms them through the "alpha function" into modulated, coherent affects. The infant then introjects these metabolized affects, thus accumulating experiences that ultimately form an object representation "capable of self-knowledge and communication between different aspects of themselves" (Britton, 1998, p. 23). Hence, the K link serves the purpose of transforming object representations of extremely negative affective valence into integrated, modulated representations through integration with good object representations. Aggressive endogenous drives meet the facilitating environment to produce complexity, integration, and knowledge.

This process can break down when the mother is unable to engage in the K link with the infant. For example, depressed, low-income mothers of six-month-old infants engaged in little eye contact or smiling during face-to-face play situations; both members of the dyad appeared to act in concert to avoid affective engagement (Cohn et al., 1986). Low-income mothers who during pregnancy tended to deny that their future infants would be bothersome also tended to have infants who exhibited anxious-avoidant behavior in the Strange Situation at 12 months (Goodman et al., 1999). Dismissing mothers, observed during free play and in a series of other interactions with their 10- to 13-month-old infants, were inclined to ignore negative affects, whereas preoccupied mothers were likely to attend to positive and negative affects randomly (Haft and Slade, 1989). It appears, then, that mothers who have insecure internal working models have difficulty integrating their infants' affects, most likely because they themselves have difficulty acknowledging and accepting their own negative affects and integrating them with positive affects into a coherent whole. Defensive processes discussed earlier interfere with their recognition of negative affects in themselves and others.

Dismissing mothers, who deactivate the attachment system, perhaps "dis-attune" to negative affect, interpreted unconsciously as an expression of the infant's attachment needs, and dismiss the signals. Consequently, the infant's negative affects associated with the projected persecutory object representation have no opportunity to be contained or metabolized. On the other hand, preoccupied mothers, who hyperactivate the attachment system, perhaps randomly attune to negative affect, also interpreted unconsciously as an expression of the infant's attachment needs, and ineffectively attend to the signals. Again, the infant's negative affects associated with the projected persecutory object representation are denied the opportunity to be contained or metabolized. In both scenarios, the outcome for the infant is continued use of splitting mechanisms that protect the good object representations from the unmetabolized bad object representations. The aggressive impulses, in conjunction with primitive defensive processes, seriously impair accurate processing of information about the mother, with resultant unstable differentiation and lack of integration and complexity. Herein lies the origin of the intergenerational transmission of psychopathology.

Perhaps the most dramatic illustration of the intergenerational transmission of personality organization comes from the groundbreaking research of Bell and Ainsworth (1972), who assessed mothers' responsiveness to their infants' crying during home observations in the first three months and again in the last three months of the first year. Crying could be considered a behavioral manifestation of irritable, unmodulated affect. The percentage of crying episodes that mothers ignored in the first three months ranged from 4 to 96. Although the mothers' responsiveness to their infants' crying remained stable between the first three months and last three months of the first year, the duration of infant crying between the same two time periods was uncorrelated. Furthermore, mothers who had been most responsive to their infants' crying in the first three months tended to have infants who cried least in the last three months, whereas mothers who had routinely ignored their infants' crying in the first three months had infants who cried most in the last three months. At 12 months, infants were assessed for quality of attachment in the Strange Situation. Securely attached infants had mothers who had been more responsive to their crying in the first three months; the mothers of insecurely attached infants had been less responsive to their crying in the same time period.

In the context of Bion's (1962, 1967) theory, the mothers who acted as containers for their infants' negative affects transformed these beta elements into affects that their infants could more easily metabolize, thus establishing the K link. The mothers who defensively ignored these negative affects intensified their infants' projective identifications, depriving their infants of opportunities for integration and growth. That the mothers' emotional responsiveness was stable across time while the infants' crying was unrelated across time suggests that mothers' emotional responsiveness makes a greater contribution to the process of integration of the object representation than does the initial duration of infants' crying (a possible marker of the intensity of infant aggression). That the intensity of infant aggression is unstable over the first 12 months suggests that variations are not generally genetically based; rather, infant aggression either becomes more modulated (signifying integration) or remains unmodulated (signifying splitting) over the first 12 months, depending on the mother's capacity for affective containment.

In spite of these remarkable findings, De Wolff and van IJzendoorn (1997) concluded from a meta-analytic study that "[caregiver) sensitivity has lost its privileged position as the only important causal factor" (p. 583) in determining security of attachment, a finding suggesting that genetic variations in the intensity of aggression might also contribute (see also Kernberg, 1986a). Regardless of the specific medium of transmission, however, splitting mechanisms form the foundation of borderline personality organization (or Klein's paranoid-schizoid position), which can take the form of narcissistic (dismissing) or usual borderline (preoccupied) personality structures. Integrated (secure) personality structures can advance to the oedipal stage of development and develop a neurotic personality organization (or Klein's depressive position) or healthy personality organization in which dependence on the other person is acknowledged and even welcomed.

Not only does object relations theory need to recognize an earlier developmental timetable and the existence of the ego from birth, but also attachment theory needs to recognize the influence of aggressive and libidinal drives in conjunction with attachment needs (a component of the self-preservative drives). Over 40 years ago, Bowlby (1958b) envisioned a time when infant aggression would be fully incorporated into a comprehensive theory of attachment. That time has come. An infant experiences intense anxiety associated with being alone, or in the dark, or when it finds itself with an unknown person" (Freud, 1926a, p. 136). These experiences of object loss and contact with strangers carry a particular meaning for the infant. The infant acts as an interpreter of his or her experience. The anxiety to which Freud referred might have nothing to do with objective reality; the unknown person could be a distant grandparent meeting the infant for the first time. The perception of danger in this harmless experience has obvious survival-promoting value, but at the cost of a distortion of objective reality.

Such distortions in perception, though prompted by actual experiences, must originate in endogenous characteristics and the defense mechanisms used against them. Klein (1946, 1952c) determined that infant anxiety reflected the onslaught of aggressive forces, defended against through projection. The distorted, threatening meanings that infants attach to often innocuous experiences, such as object loss and contact with strangers, suggest that projection is interfering with an accurate appraisal of objective reality. Attachment theory needs to account for stranger anxiety and the need for proximity and contact as a complex interplay between projected aggression and the activation of attachment needs. The anguish associated with the rejection of attachment needs also originates in the meanings that the infant attaches to this experience. An intrapsychic approach needs to complement the functionalist approach already articulated by attachment theory.

Clearly, object relations theory could benefit from reclaiming the Kleinian developmental timetable, acknowledging that infants begin constructing their representational worlds at birth, and recognizing the supreme importance of the drives as well as the caregiver's containment and metabolization of drive-dominated impulses, which includes attachment strivings—all positions that appear consistent with the findings of attachment research. The goal of psychological development is not separation-individuation from the mother but, rather, interdependence with her the hallmark of the depressive position: "Individuation begins at birth" (Bretherton, 1987, p. 1081).

Attachment theory, on the other hand, could benefit from acknowledging that attachment needs belong to the self-preservative drives and seek gratification, which produces pleasure (Eagle, 1987; Lichtenberg, 1989; Silverman, 1991, 1993; Slade and Aber, 1992). Actual caregiving experiences do become split off and excluded from consciousness, but attachment theory has failed to appreciate that infants interpret these experiences in the context of desires so intense and all-consuming that they distort the perception of external reality. Attachment needs operate in tandem with aggression and libido to distort external reality, which ultimately affects the capacity of internal working models to make accurate appraisals. Self- and object representations begin as split-off, unmodulated fragments; consequently, with affective containment and metabolization provided by the caregiver over the first six months, they become more integrated, coherent structures, developing into complex personality organizations internal working models—that incorporate drives, defenses, and images of experiences influenced by drives, defenses, and external reality. The ability to make an accurate appraisal of external reality begins only after intrapsychic integration has taken place in conjunction with the onset of the depressive position. Young infants are thus not accurate perceivers of external reality—the fatal flaw of attachment theory that object relations theory is prepared to redress.

References

Adam, K. S., Sheldon-Keller, A. E., & West, M. (1996). Attachment organization and history of suicidal behavior in clinical adolescents. *Journal of Consulting and Clinical Psychology*, 64, 264–272.

Ainsworth, M. D. S. (1979). Infant-Mother attachment. *American Psychologist*, 34, 932–937.

Ainsworth, M. D. S., Blehar, M. C., Waters, E., & Wall, S. (1978). *Patterns of attachment: A psychological study of the strange situation.* Hillsdale, NJ: Erlbaum.

Ainsworth, M. D. S., & Wittig, B. A. (1969). Attachment and exploratory behavior of one-year-olds in a strange situation. In B. M. Foss (Ed.), *Determinants of infant behaviour IV* (pp. 111–136). London: Methuen.

Allen, J. P., Hauser, S. T., & Borman-Spurrell, E. (1996). Attachment theory as a framework for understanding sequelae of severe adolescent psychopathology: An 11-year follow-up study. *Journal of Consulting and Clinical Psychology*, 64, 254–263.

Ammaniti, M. (1991). Maternal representations during pregnancy and early infant-mother interactions. *Infant Mental Health Journal*, 12, 246–255.

Bach, S. (1994). *The language of perversion and the language of love.* New York: Jason Aronson.

Bell, S. M., & Ainsworth, M. D. S. (1972). Infant crying and maternal responsiveness. *Child Development*, 43, 1171–1190.

Berlin, L. J., Cassidy, J., & Belsky, J. (1995). Loneliness in young children and infant-mother attachment: A longitudinal study. *Merrill-Palmer Quarterly*, 41, 91–103.

Bion, W. R. (1962). *Learning from experience.* London: Heinemann.

Bion, W. R. (1967). *Second thoughts.* London: Heinemann.

Bowlby, J. (1946). *Forty-four juvenile thieves: Their character and homelife.* London: Balliere, Tyndall & Cox.

Bowlby, J. (1958a). The nature of the child's tie to his mother. *International Journal of Psycho-Analysis*, 39, 350–373.

Bowlby, J. (1958b). Psycho-Analysis and child care. In J. D. Sutherland (Ed.), *Psychoanalysis and contemporary thought* (pp. 33–57). London: Hogarth Press and the Institute of Psycho-Analysis.

Bowlby, J. (1973). *Attachment and loss: Vol.2. Separation: Anxiety and anger.* New York: Basic Books.

Bowlby, J. (1980a). *Attachment and loss: Vol. 3. Loss, sadness and depression.* New York: Basic Books.

Bowlby, J. (1982). *Attachment and loss: Vol. 1. Attachment* (2nd ed.). New York: Basic Books.

Bowlby, J. (1988). *A secure base: Parent-Child attachment and healthy human development.* New York: Basic Books.

Bretherton, I. (1985). Attachment theory: Retrospect and prospect. In I. Bretherton & E. Waters (Eds.), Growing points in attachment theory and research. *Monographs of the Society for Research in Child Development*, 50(1–2, Serial No. 209), 3–35.

Bretherton, I. (1987). New perspectives on attachment relations: Security, communication, and internal working models. In J. D. Osofsky (Ed.), *Handbook of infant development* (2nd ed., pp. 1061–1100). New York: Wiley.

Britton, R. (1989). The missing link: Parental sexuality in the Oedipus complex. In J. Steiner (Ed.), *The Oedipus complex today: Clinical implications* (pp. 83–101). London: Karnac.

Britton, R. (1998). *Belief and imagination: Exploration in psychoanalysis.* London: Tavistock/Routledge.

Cassidy, J., & Kobak, R. R. (1988). Avoidance and its relation to other defensive processes. In J. Belsky & T. Nezworski (Eds.), *Clinical implications of attachment* (pp. 300–323). Hillsdale, NJ: Erlbaum.

Clarkin, J. F., Yeomans, F. E., & Kernberg, O. F. (1999). *Psychotherapy for borderline personality.* New York: Wiley.

Cohn, J., Tronick, E., Matias, R., & Lyons-Ruth, K. (1986). Face-to-face interactions of depressed mothers with their infants. In E. Tronick & T. Field (Eds.), *Maternal depression and infant disturbance* (pp. 31–44). San Francisco: Jossey-Bass.

Cole-Detke, H., & Kobak, R. (1996). Attachment processes in eating disorder and depression. *Journal of Consulting and Clinical Psychology,* 64, 282–290.

Davis, M. S., & Marsh, L. (1986). Self-Love, self-control, and alexithymia: Narcissistic features of two bulimic adolescents. *American Journal of Psychotherapy,* 40, 224–232.

De Wolff, M., & van IJzendoorn, M. H. (1997). Sensitivity and attachment: A meta-analysis on parental antecedents of infant attachment. *Child Development,* 68, 571–591.

Derby, K. (1992). Some difficulties in the treatment of character-disordered addicts. In B. C. Wallace (Ed.), *The chemically dependent: Phases of treatment and recovery* (pp. 115–124). New York: Brunner/Mazel.

Dozier, M. (1990). Attachment organization and treatment use for adults with serious psychopathological disorders. *Development and Psychopathology,* 2, 47–60.

Dozier, M., & Kobak, R. R. (1992). Psychophysiology in attachment: Converging evidence for deactivating strategies. *Child Development,* 63, 1473–1480.

Dozier, M., & Lee, S. W. (1995). Discrepancies between self- and other-report of psychiatric symptomatology: Effects of dismissing attachment strategies. *Development and Psychopathology,* 7, 217–226.

Dozier, M., Stevenson, A. L., Lee, S. W., & Velligan, D. I. (1991). Attachment organization and familial overinvolvement for adults with serious psychopathological disorders. *Development and Psychopathology*, 3, 475–489.

Eagle, M. (1987). *Recent developments in psychoanalysis*. Cambridge, MA: Harvard University Press.

Erickson, M. F., Sroufe, L. A., & Egeland, B. (1985). The relationship between quality of attachment and behavior problems in preschool in a high-risk sample. In I. Bretherton & E. Waters (Eds.), Growing points in attachment theory and research. *Monographs of the Society for Research in Child Development*, 50(1–2, Serial No. 209), 147–166.

Fairbairn, W. R. D. (1952). *An object-relations theory of the personality*. New York: Basic Books.

Fonagy, P. (1999a). Points of contact and divergence between psychoanalytic and attachment theories: Is psychoanalytic theory truly different. *Psychoanalytic Inquiry*, 19, 448–480.

Fonagy, P., Leigh, T., Steele, M., Steele, H., Kennedy, R., Mattoon, G., Target, M., & Gerber, A. (1996). The relation of attachment status, psychiatric classification, and response to psychotherapy. *Journal of Consulting and Clinical Psychology*, 64, 22–31.

Freud, A. (1960). Discussion of Dr. John Bowlby's paper [Review of "Grief and mourning in infancy and early childhood"]. *Psychoanalytic Study of the Child*, 15, 53–62.

Freud, S. (1905b). Three essays on the theory of sexuality. In J. Strachey (Ed. and Trans.), *The standard edition of the complete psychological works of Sigmund Freud* (Vol. 7, pp. 135–243). London: Hogarth, 1961.

Freud, S. (1926a). Inhibitions, symptoms and anxiety. In J. Strachey (Ed. and Trans.), *The standard edition of the complete psychological works of Sigmund Freud* (Vol. 20, pp. 75–172). London: Hogarth, 1961.

George, C., Kaplan, N., & Main, M. (1996). *Adult Attachment Interview* (3rd ed.). Unpublished manuscript, University of California, Berkeley.

Goodman, G., Aber, J. L., Berlin, L., & Brooks-Gunn, J. (1998). The relations between maternal behaviors and urban preschool children's internal working models of attachment security. *Infant Mental Health Journal*, 19, 378–393.

Goodman, G., Hans, S. L., & Cox, S. M. (1999). Attachment behavior and its antecedents in offspring born to methadone-maintained women. *Journal of Clinical Child Psychology*, 28, 58–69.

Grace, P. S. (1990). *Personality characteristics of the mother of bulimics.* Unpublished doctoral dissertation, University of Illinois, Chicago.

Gunderson, J. G., & Elliott, G. R. (1985). The interface between borderline personality disorder and affective disorder. *American Journal of Psychiatry*, 142, 277–288.

Gunderson, J. G., & Phillips, K. A. (1991). A current view of the interface between borderline personality disorder and depression. *American Journal of Psychiatry*, 148, 967–975.

Haft, W. L., Slade, A. (1989). Affect attunement and maternal attachment: A pilot study. *Infant Mental Health Journal*, 10, 157–172.

Hubbs-Tait, L., Hughes, K. P., Culp, A. M., Osofsky, J. D., Hann, D. M., Eberhart-Wright, A., & Ware, L. M. (1996). Children of adolescent mothers: Attachment representation, maternal depression, and later behavior problems. *American Journal of Orthopsychiatry*, 66, 416–426.

Joseph, B. (1986). Envy in everyday life. *Psychoanalytic Psychotherapy*, 2, 13–22.

Kernberg, O. (1966). Structural derivatives of object relationships. *International Journal of Psycho-Analysis*, 47, 236–253.

Kernberg, O. (1967). Borderline personality organization. *Journal of the American Psychoanalytic Association*, 15, 641–685.

Kernberg, O. F. (1969). A contribution to the ego-psychological critique of the Kleinian school. *International Journal of Psycho-Analysis*, 50, 317–333.

Kernberg, O. F. (1972). Critique of the Kleinian school. In P. L. Giovacchini (Ed.), *Tactics and techniques in psychoanalytic therapy* (pp. 62–93). New York: Science House.

Kernberg, O. F. (1975). *Borderline conditions and pathological narcissism*. New York: Jason Aronson.

Kernberg, O. F. (1977). The structural diagnosis of borderline personality organization. In P. Hartocollis (Ed.), *Borderline personality disorders: The concept, the syndrome, the patient* (pp. 87–121). New York: International Universities Press.

Kernberg, O. F. (1984). *Severe personality disorders: Psychotherapeutic strategies*. New Haven, CT: Yale University Press.

Kernberg, O. (1986a). Borderline personality organization. In M. Stone (Ed.), *Essential papers on borderline disorders: One hundred years at the border* (pp. 279–319). New York: New York University Press.

Kernberg, O. F. (1986b). Further contributions to the treatment of narcissistic personalities. In A. Morrison (Ed.), *Essential papers on narcissism* (pp. 245–292). New York: New York University Press.

Kernberg, O. F. (1987). Projection and projective identification: Developmental and clinical aspects. *Journal of the American Psychoanalytic Association*, 35, 795–819.

Kernberg, O. F., Selzer, M. A., Koenigsberg, H. W., Carr, A. C., & Appelbaum, A. H. (1989). *Psychodynamic psychotherapy of borderline patients*. New York: Basic Books.

Klein, M. (1932). *The psycho-analysis of children* (A. Strachey, Trans.). London: Hogarth, 1950.

Klein, M. (1946). Notes on some schizoid mechanisms. In R. E. Money-Kyrle (Ed.), *Envy and gratitude and other works 1946-1963* (pp. 1–24). New York: Delacorte Press, 1975.

Klein, M. (1952b). On observing the behavior of young infants. In R. E. Money-Kyrle (Ed.), *Envy and gratitude and other works 1946-1963* (pp. 94–121). New York: Delacorte Press, 1975.

Klein, M. (1952c). The origins of transference. In R. E. Money-Kyrle (Ed.), *Envy and gratitude and other works 1946-1963* (pp. 48–56). New York: Delacorte Press, 1975.

Kobak, R. R., Cole, H. E., Ferenz-Gillies, R., Fleming, W. S., & Gamble, W. (1993). Attachment and emotion regulation during mother-teen problem solving: A control theory analysis. *Child Development*, 64, 231–245.

Kobak, R. R., & Sceery, A. (1988). Attachment in late adolescence: Working models, affect regulation, and representations of self and others. *Child Development*, 59, 135–146.

Kobak, R. R., Sudler, N., & Gamble, W. (1991). Attachment and depressive symptoms during adolescence: A developmental pathways analysis. *Development and Psychopathology*, 3, 461–474.

LaFreniere, P., & Sroufe, L. A. (1985). Profiles of peer competence in the preschool: Interrelations between measures, influence of social ecology, and relation to attachment history. *Developmental Psychology*, 21, 56–68.

Levine, L. V., & Tuber, S. B. (1993). Measures of mental representation: Clinical and theoretical considerations. *Bulletin of the Menninger Clinic*, 57, 69–87.

Levy, K. N., & Blatt, S. J. (1999). Attachment theory and psychoanalysis: Further differentiation within insecure attachment patterns. *Psychoanalytic Inquiry*, 19, 541–575.

Lichtenberg, J. D. (1989). *Psychoanalysis and motivation.* Hillsdale, NJ: Analytic.

Lyons-Ruth, K. (1991). Rapprochement or approchement: Mahler's theory reconsidered from the vantage point of recent research on early attachment relationships. *Psychoanalytic Psychology,* 8, 1–23.

Lyons-Ruth, K., Alpern, L., & Repacholi, B. (1993). Disorganized infant attachment classification and maternal psychosocial problems as predictors of hostile-aggressive behavior in the preschool classroom. *Child Development,* 64, 572–585.

Mahler, M. S., Pine, F., & Bergman, A. (1975). *The psychological birth of the human infant: Symbiosis and individuation.* New York: Basic Books.

Main, M. (1999). Epilogue: Attachment theory: Eighteen points with suggestions for future studies. In J. Cassidy & P. R. Shaver (Eds.), *Handbook of attachment: Theory, research, and clinical applications* (pp. 845–887). New York: Guilford.

Main, M., & Goldwyn, R. (1994). *Adult attachment scoring and classification systems* (6th ed.). Unpublished manuscript, University College, London.

Main, M., Kaplan, N., & Cassidy, J. (1985). Security in infancy, childhood, and adulthood: A move to the level of representation. In I. Bretherton & E. Waters (Eds.), *Growing points in attachment theory and research.* Monographs of the Society for Research in Child Development, 50(1-2, Serial No. 209), 66–104.

Masterson, J. F. (1995). Paradise lost: Bulimia, a closet narcissistic personality disorder: A developmental, self, and object relations approach. In R. C. Marohn & S. C. Feinstein (Eds.), Adolescent psychiatry: Developmental and clinical studies, Vol. 20. *Annals of the American Society for Adolescent Psychiatry* (pp. 253–266). Hillsdale, NJ: Analytic.

McGlashan, T. H. (1983). The borderline syndrome: II. Is it a variant of schizophrenia or affective disorder? *Archives of General Psychiatry*, 40, 1319–1323.

McGlashan, T. H. (1987). Borderline personality disorder and unipolar affective disorder: Long-Term effects of comorbidity. *Journal of Nervous and Mental Disease*, 175, 467–473.

Ogden, T. H. (1979). On projective identification. *International Journal of Psycho-Analysis*, 60, 357–373.

Pastor, D. L. (1981). The quality of mother-infant attachment and its relationship to toddlers' initial sociability with peers. *Developmental Psychology*, 17, 326–335.

Patrick, M., Hobson, R. P., Castle, D., Howard, R., & Maughan, B. (1994). Personality disorder and the mental representation of early social experience. *Development and Psychopathology*, 6, 375–388.

Pianta, R. C., Egeland, B., & Adam, E. K. (1996). Adult attachment classification and self-reported psychiatric symptomatology as assessed by the Minnesota Multiphasic Personality Inventory-2. *Journal of Consulting and Clinical Psychology*, 64, 273–281.

Pope, H. G., Jr., Jonas, J. M., Hudson, J. I., Cohen, B. M., & Gunderson, J. G. (1983). The validity of DSM-III borderline personality disorder: A phenomenologic, family history, treatment response, and long-term follow-up study. *Archives of General Psychiatry*, 40, 23–30.

Renken, B., Egeland, B., Marvinney, D., Mangelsdorf, S., & Sroufe, L. A. (1989). *Journal of Personality*, 57, 257–281.

Richard, B. (1985). The ideal imaginary object and narcissism in anorexia nervosa. *Etudes Psychotherapiques*, 16, 189–192.

Rosenstein, D. S., & Horowitz, H. A. (1996). Adolescent attachment and psychopathology. *Journal of Consulting and Clinical Psychology*, 64, 244–253.

Ruderman, A. J., & Grace, P. S. (1988). Bulimics and restrained eaters: A personality comparison. *Addictive Behaviors*, 13, 359–368.

Silverman, D. K. (1991). Attachment patterns and Freudian theory: An integrative proposal. *Psychoanalytic Psychology*, 8, 169–193.

Silverman, D. K. (1993). Attachment research: An approach to a developmental relational perspective. In N. Skolnick & S. Warshaw (Eds.), *Relational perspectives in psychoanalysis* (pp. 195–216). Hillsdale, NJ: Analytic.

Slade, A., & Aber, J. L. (1992). Attachments, drives, and development: Conflicts and convergences in theory. In J. W. Barron, M. N. Eagle, D. L. Wolitzky (Eds.), *Interface of psychoanalysis and psychology* (pp. 154–185). Washington, DC: American Psychological Association.

Spangler, G., & Grossmann, K. E. (1993). Biobehavioral organization in securely and insecurely attached infants. *Child Development*, 64, 1439–1450.

Sroufe, L. A. (1983). Infant-Caregiver attachment and patterns of adaptation in preschool: The roots of maladaptation and competence. In M. Perlmutter (Ed.), *Minnesota Symposium in Child Psychology* (pp. 41–83). Hillsdale, NJ: Erlbaum.

Sroufe, L. A., Schork, E., Motti, E., Lawrosky, N., & LaFreniere, P. (1984). The role of affect in emerging social competence. In C. Izard, J. Kagan, & R. Zajonc (Eds.), *Emotion, cognition, and behavior* (pp. 155–192). Cambridge, England: Cambridge University Press.

Sroufe, L. A., & Waters, E. (1977a). Attachment as an organizational construct. *Child Development*, 48, 1184–1199.

Sroufe, L. A., & Waters, E. (1977b). Heart rate as a convergent measure in clinical and developmental research. *Merrill-Palmer Quarterly*, 23, 3–27.

Steiner, J. (1987). The interplay between pathological organizations and the paranoid-schizoid and depressive positions. *International Journal of Psycho-Analysis*, 68, 69–80.

Vieira, C. (1997). Drug addiction and narcissistic disorders. *Revista Portuguesa de Psicanalise*, 16, 91–97.

Woodham, R. L. (1987). A self-psychological consideration in cocaine addiction. *Alcoholism Treatment Quarterly*, 4, 41–46.

Wurmser, L. (1984). More respect for the neurotic process: Comments on the problem of narcissism in severe psychopathology, especially the addictions. *Journal of Substance Abuse Treatment*, 1, 37–45.

The Facts of Mind
Thoughts on the Concept of a Taxonomy of Unconscious Fantasy with Special Reference to the "New View" in Psychoanalysis.

by Michael Schur

"Like so much else in psychoanalysis, phantasy, the main focus of clinical interest, still eludes our full comprehension. Indeed, a satisfactory taxonomy of unconscious phantasies and their derivatives has yet to be drawn up (Moore and Fine, 1990, p.75)."
In Mahony (1997, p.61)

In the course of teaching psychoanalytic psychotherapy, I have become increasingly concerned about the capacity of students to arrive at what used to be called a tentative "psychodynamic formulation." In an earlier era, a central objective of teaching psychological and psychiatric interviewing and assessment was to assist the student to become proficient in arranging preliminary, clinical data into a composite, albeit tentative, understanding of the mental status of the patient in conjunction with his/her putative psychodynamic organization so as to be able to "plan the treatment." Implicit in this teaching was the assumption that the patient's presenting symptomatology could be referenced against the classical metapsychological "points of view," i.e., the economic, dynamic, genetic, structural and adaptive frames of reference. An integrated, psychodiagnostic formulation emerged from the collecting of the clinical data in relation to these points of view. The influence of classical ego psychology was the underpinning of this methodology and it influenced not only clinical interviewing, but also psychological testing to a very considerable extent. But, times have changed. Following the developments in self-psychology (Kohut, 1977), which have lent important influence to its emergence, has been the "relational" movement in psychoanalysis (also known as the intersubjective and interpersonal approaches) best exemplified by the current contributions of Greenberg (1991) and Mitchell (2000), Aaron (1996) as well as Stolorow and Atwood (1992). The fundamental contribution of the relational psychoanalysts appears to be their emphasis on the dyadic, intersubjective communication that reverberates between patient and analyst and its "irreducible subjectivity" (Renik 1993). Indeed, they make strong assertions that the classical perspective for too long relied on the authoritative blank screen view of the analyst to the neglect of the reality of the interpenetration of the deeper layers of the mind by both parties in the therapeutic dyad. (It is worth noting that Freud was well aware of but did not theoretically develop this area of his thinking when he commented in his paper on the Unconscious (S.E. Vol. XIV, p.194) "It is a very remarkable thing that the unconscious of one human being can react upon that of another without passing through the conscious."

However, what appear most disquieting—and even epistemologically and alarmingly radical to those trained in the ego psychological tradition— are the basic claims of the "new view" relational psychoanalysts:

The central philosophical position of the new view theorists concerning the nature of mind is that it is in its entirety interpretively constructed in the context of interpersonal interaction. Because mind is accorded no factuality independent of interpretive construction nothing is held to uncovered or discovered in the psychoanalytic process. According to this view, the mind is not preorganized but rather awaits organization and the articulation of mental contents through interpersonal interaction. (Eagle et al. p. 459, 2001)

Juxtaposed to this constructivist, subjectivist epistemology is the description, again by Eagle, of the epistemic basis of the classical position.

The clearest expression of the "Enlightenment Vision" in psychoanalysis is found in classical theory. In linking the "cornerstone" concept of repression—the essence of which is the failure to acknowledge the truth about oneself—to pathology, and in linking the lifting of repression—the essence of which is increased self-knowledge—to cure, Freudian theory staked its claim to cure on the assumption that there are real contents in the psyche that can be discovered, or at least approximated via psychoanalysis. (Eagle et al., p. 460, 2001)

It is not difficult for those of us trained in the classical tradition to acknowledge that there is an undeniable and persistent influence on the analytic process created by the subjectivity of the analyst which includes his physicality, tone of voice, office furnishings, and most important, his words. Accordingly, the analytic frame is never accurately characterizable as wholly or even largely abstinent, anonymous and neutral. These hallmarks of the classical frame were understood to be more or less ideals

205

or objectives as opposed to being continuously operative clinical realities. It is one thing, however, to recognize and analyze the subjectivity of the analyst (via study of the countertransference) and its influence over the full range of the psychoanalytic process and the patient's psyche and yet, quite another to subscribe to the relational, analytic point of view that there are no "facts" of a patient's (or analyst's) mind separate from the interpersonal, analytic dialogue which constructs and "cocreates" them.

It is interesting to observe that the epistemological assumptions of the evolving relational literature have an interesting temporal contiguity with the cultural relativism, and perspectivism of the past decade. To be sure, relational and interpersonal analytic thinking certainly has a foundation in the Sullivanian theorizing of the 50's in this country. Nevertheless, there is an interesting similarity between the denigration and rejection of authority expressed in the assumption of the "politically correct" sociocultural mores of some current academic settings and the major assumption of the relational school that the analyst is not, by virtue of his training and experience, in a privileged position of authoritative knowledge with respect to his/her patient. To the extent that relational psychoanalysts eschew autonomous psychic reality as a pre-existing constituent of the patient's mind they do bear an interesting similarity to the theses of cultural relativism that are preponderant today. It is also, of note that the "narrative" truth versus "historical" truth juxtaposition broadly corresponds to the distinctions that can be drawn between the "new view" relational analysts and classical ego psychologists. e A recent advertisement for a relational conference this year states that "… all ideas, including psychoanalytic conceptions and accumulated wisdom, are historical, linguistic, political and contextual." This point of view would, by necessity, clash with the assumption that unconscious fantasy* manifests continuity across human history because it represents predictably occurring dimensions of psychic structures that are not political or contextual constructions. For example, the data, which affirm the historical and cross-cultural expressions of the ædipus complex also (footnote: * hereafter UCF) pose a challenge to "new view" assumptions. In that regard it would be of interest to test the assumption that it appears that relational and intersubjective, psychoanalytic theorizing does seem to have emerged from the pens of those more affiliated with academia as opposed to medical, psychoanalytic settings in which an empirical, epistemological realism would be a more essential metapsychological assumption. It is our view that, central to the philosophical and epistemological assumptions of the relational view is the de-emphasis of drive—conflict theory in which it has been assumed that the patient presents in our office because of a pre-existing state of mind which is in conflict over "issues" (as patients are wont to describe them) or as we would formulate—a struggle with some competing intrapsychic forces. It is about these patients that we were taught to assess and establish a psychodynamic formulation. However, as evidenced by a recent presentation at an American Psychological Association conference (2001) entitled:

World Horizons: A Post Cartesian Alternative to the Freudian Unconscious, the following statement is found: Next the authors review a case published by Stolorow nearly thirty years ago and consider how differently it might be conceptualized within their world-horizons view of unconsciousness. What became especially clear, once the residues of drive-theoretical theories of mind were relinquished, was that what could not be known was a function of intersubjective systems, both in childhood and in analysis. Fantasy could now be understood, as the effort to make sense of the gaps created by the not knowing required by the family system … This case restudy illustrates, according to the authors, their contention that consciousness and unconsciousness, no longer seen as regions

of isolated minds, are better understood as shifting emergent
properties of intersubjective systems (p.28)

In this concise statement we find the dismissal of drive-conflict theory,
the dismantling of the concept of repression of the tri-partite theory and
the reduction of our theory of fantasy to what appears to be a simplistic,
conscious, conceptualizing activity of mind, i.e., "the effort to make
sense of the gaps created by the not knowing etc…" Again, in a radical
characterization "isolated minds" is likely an exaggerated reference to
separate psychic entities-patient and therapist.

What we ultimately decipher in these statements is a camouflaged, but
deliberate effort to separate mind from body. We can accept the assumption
that intersubjectivity is always a reference to the psychic interpenetration
of one person by another and the reciprocal, psychic reverberation of the
other. However, conspicuous by its omission in intersubjective, relational
theorizing is the role of the body and its corporeality and attendant, urge-
related requirements. Does the merging of intersubjectivities, as they
are discussed in the relational literature, in fact, reflect a displaced and
attenuated reference to the merging of separate but energically invested
bodily parts and processes? If we are to be theoretically faithful to what
is essentially biologic in psychoanalysis, then we must account for the
body. It's dismissal is either defensive or motivated by pars pro toto
theorizing that attempts to forge the underpinnings of a general theory
of psychoanalysis on insufficient premises.

To regard fantasy, for example, as something akin to a "conceptualizing
activity of mind" is to do violence to a long history in psychoanalytic
theorizing which, from Freud's earliest contributions, has established the
centrality of UCF as a core, constituent factor of mental life. It is true
as Arlow (1969) has commented that unconscious fantasies "embarrass
our methodology" (p.4). This is not, however, scientific justification for

dismissing UCF and its function as a "fact of mind." Conscious and UCFs are "facts of mind" that exist intrapsychically and independently of the intersubjectivity of family systems. When we say that conscious and UCF are representations in the psychic apparatus of unsatisfied or unfulfilled wishes we anchor the theory of UCF in particular in drive theory inasmuch as a wish is a psychological representation, in many instances, of some dimension or derivative of a drive. There are, however, non-drive-structured wishes in the psychic apparatus including those for safety, regulation of self-esteem, avoidance of anxiety and the like. It is, perhaps, this recognition of the distinction between wishes as representatives of drive derivatives and wishes as not motivated by drive energies that has brought the work of the Sandlers (1998) to the attention of those who endeavor to find a rapprochement between classical ego e psychology and the contributions of the British Psychoanalytic Group. Kernberg (2001) summarizes this contribution in suggesting that they:

> ...stressed that unconscious fantasy includes not simply derivatives of libidinal and aggressive drives, but specific wishes for gratifying relationships between the self and significant objects. They proposed that unconscious fantasy thus takes the form of wishes for specific relationships of the self with objects represented by fantasized, desirable relations between self-representations and object-representations. According to this view the expression of impulses and their derivatives is transformed into a desired interaction with an object and a wishful fantasy which includes the reaction of the object to the wishful action of the individual. (p. 524)

Concisely summarized here is the elegant elaboration by the Sandlers of their theory of UCF in which they contend that UCF goes beyond the mere representation of a drive derivative and, in fact, is necessarily interdigitated with a theory of internalized-reciprocal object-relations. What is served in such a contribution is the elaboration of the inner, representational world that is conjoined with the instinctually driven substrate of the individual. Consistent with Arlow's (1980) view of UCF, the Sandlers' also insist on the representational point of view which emphasizes, according to Arlow, that "…at all times we are dealing with a psychological experience, the mental representation of an object, a persistently "internal' experience" (p.5)

The Sandlers' integration of an object-relations theory with drive theory should also be interdigitated with emerging research in attachment theory. As Silverman (2001) has noted we are incorrect in assuming that drive alone can account for the totality of object cathexes. The attachment system has a primitivity that commingles with early libidinal development. As attachment behavior is, essentially, protection from predation, it becomes, early on, involved in serving multiple ends, a protective function as well as a libidinal and object regulating function (c.f.-Silverman). Accordingly, a general developmental psychoanalytic theory must be at least g triangular to include a drive, an object-relations and an attachment theory. It is important, though, while acknowledging the aforementioned necessity for theoretical breadth, to also allow oneself to be comfortable in defining a problem in psychoanalytic theory that can be studied. This avoids the pars pro toto fallacy and yet allows for thoughtful, circumscribed work to proceed. To that end a theory of UCF which elucidates its role and function in the psychic apparatus would appear to be intrinsically useful in psychodiagnosis and treatment. If, as Arlow (1969) says, that the technical role of the analyst is to help the patient distinguish between pathogenic UCF and reality, then, by definition, an epistemological distinction is being drawn between pathologic influences within a patient's mind, and objective, external reality. To that end we ask if there are persistent and consistent mental structures (UCF structures) which exist in mental life. We account for their formulation below.

Positing the congruence of the biologic and representational dimension integrates drive and object-relations perspectives and elucidates the clinical data of UCF that either alone cannot accomplish. (As previously mentioned the integration of the affect regulating function of the attachment system into drive and representational systems is beyond the scope of the current paper.) However, corresponding to this biologic (drive) and representational (object-relation) convergence are what I refer to as the Neutralization-Internalization Axes. Neutralization processes are those ego based processes which account for the de-instinctualization of sexual and aggressive drive energies and which bring that energy into the service of the ego's efforts to create increasing psychic structure. Internalization processes: incorporation, introjection, identification, account for the structuralization of the inner representational world by alteration of this inner world based on interactions with the external object world. Neutralization and Internalization processes work conjointly to establish the capacity for delay of discharge of instinctual tension via the construction of internalized self- and object representations. This establishment of the capacity for delay and renunciation of immediate drive gratification, though, stimulates the development of the capacity for imagination which, begins to serve, in substitute fashion, for instinctual gratification. The fundamental process involved in the genesis of UCF formation is the effort to recapture, via imaginative fantasy activity, a previously gratifying relationship that was lost or relinquished in reality and now becomes a scenario played out in the internal world of self- and object representations. These scenarios attempt to gratify wishes that have become unsatisfied both as a function of the de-instinctualization of drive energies as well as because of parentally established prohibitions against gratifications of drive derivatives. Thus, as external object relations become transformed into internalized self- and object representations the UCF serves as a fulcrum or point of fixation, i.e., it demonstrates that what has been lost in reality can be regained in imaginative UCF. The child's refusal of renunciation of the forbidden wish finds expression in the intractable vestige of the UCF.

The UCF then occupies a locus in psychic life, in psychic structure. The concept of a "pathogenic unconscious fantasy" embodies the hallmark of an epistemology of objectivism and realism, i.e., it is responsible for the creation of symptoms in the realm of psychic reality in the same way that an organic pathogen can disrupt and create symptoms in the somatic sphere. For example, a hallucination is a pathologic disruption within the drive representational systems. The "pathogenic unconscious fantasy" is, equivalently, a disruption within the same systems albeit at a higher level of structuralization and differentiation of the psychic apparatus. If a relational psychoanalyst, in the course of interviewing a seemingly intact patient, gradually becomes aware that the patient is presenting a florid hallucination would that analyst assume that the patient's symptom has been constructed or co-created by the intersubjective communication between the two parties? I think not. Such a symptom can only be accounted for, scientifically, as a pre-existing mental structure—a continuous "fact of mind" for that particular patient.

INTERNALIZATION AXIS

	incorporation	introjection	identification
N E U T R A L I Z A T I O N (A X I S)	L	I	
			H
	I		
	H		

H	I	L
beating fantasy	feces = baby	incorporation of breast
primal scene fantasy	penis = baby	incorporation of phallus
wish for seductin fantasy	body = phallus	breast = penis
non-vaginal impregnation fantasy	vagina = mouth	breast = face
parthenogenetic fantasy	vagina = anus	mouth = urethra
illusory phallus fantasy	imbilicus = penis	mouth = anus
menstruation as castration fantasy	vomitus = fetus	wish/fear of being easten
family romance-oedipal fantasy	phallic woman	
prostitute fantasy		
liebestod fantasy		

That patients present with pathogenic UCF formations is a central assumption of the structural framework, i.e., the Arlow Brenner (1964) and the Gray (1994) Busch (1999) traditions. (The Arlow-Brenner and Gray-Busch approaches would seem to differ on technical posture only, not on the central theoretical assumption of pathogenic UCF). It has been common in the author's supervisory experience that students' abilities in formulating about dynamically active UCF structures is limited by their not having learned (or been taught) about the core UCFs discernable in human psychological experience. As bio-psychological structures,

UCFs express a commentary on the individual's life experiences as they influence character and its formation through ontogenesis. Character structure as well as symptoms are, in fact, significant expressions of the dominance of a core UCF in the individual's psychic life. It is our view that students could be well served in their clinical studies if they were familiarized with a taxonomy (or classification) of developmentally hierarchic UCF structures. Students that are aware of the range of core UCF structures would, over time, become more sensitive to derivatives in the patient's clinical material. Derivatives are approximations or disguised expressions of UCF. Seen economically, a derivative is an expression of cathectic investment. A derivative expresses the degree of pressure on the gradient of repression, i.e., the more the derivative represents the core UCF (conflict) the more intense is the need for repression to be operative defensively. Conversely, the less the derivative resembles the core UCF (is disguised) the gradient of repression requires less counter cathectic force. It is the continual clinical study of derivatives that leads to interpretive possibilities. Students can learn to study the activity of their own and the patient's mind as well as the contents or "facts of mind" by being sensitized to derivatives that are part of the clinical presentation. It can be discerned that this methodology assumes the uncovering or discovery of UCF structure (via study of derivatives) and not the construction or cocreation of psychic structure as in the relational view. The taxonomy below designates core UCF structures as L (lower), I (intermediate), or H (higher) to suggest a rudimentary differentiation in development. (A complex question which we will then address is the manner in which UCF structures accrete or interdigitate in psychic development. Increasing differentiation and maturation in ego capacitates and functions as well as the influence of trauma tend to complicate the study of UCF). A student's knowledge, though, of a basic taxonomy is a potentially rewarding point of departure.

In reviewing the core UCF framework we note that many are characterized (at the lower level of development) by an interchangeability of body parts. This phenomenon is a reflection of the displaceability of cathexis of the primary process. Partial, pre genital instinctual aims are highly mobile and fall to governance by g the primary process. In contrast, the secondary process features of discrimination and differentiation in ego functions can be juxtaposed with the more primitive inclination to condensation of internalized self- and object representations of body parts effected by the primary process. (The mechanism of condensation is a hallmark characteristic of primary process activity). In the assessment of UCF we can, thus, begin to think of the aforementioned categorization of lower, intermediate, and higher levels of UCF structures as representing increasing movement toward secondary process determination of these psychic structures. In relation to UCF formation pathogenesis can be viewed as the intrusion or residual influence of primary process activity into the activity of the secondary process (or some dimension of ego failure with respect to the neutralization axis). Importantly, this point sheds light on the intermingling of contradictory attributes in the UCF (peremptoriness and condensation with structuralization). This partial structuralization which we observe in the organization of the UCF contrasts with dreams in which condensation and displacement are the essential organizing principles in its formation. The UCF is, therefore, both more and less structured by the secondary process when primary process infiltrates are represented in its organization.

It is the opinion of this paper that students studying the process of developing as psychotherapists should be exposed to such a taxonomy. While it is yet unrefined and rudimentary and is only a beginning at considering the theoretical complexities of how fantasy structures continue to evolve (and can also become represented somatically) it is nonetheless a testament to the view that UCF structures can be assessed and discovered as pathogenic dimensions of mental life. It is our view that such a perspective, which rests on an objectivist epistemology, in no way subtracts from the intersubjective resonance in the therapeutic dyad but rather can enrich it by assisting the student to develop as a sensitive decoder of derivative expressions of core UCF structures of their patients and themselves. With regard to the aforementioned evolution of UCF structures we will conclude with a few comments suggestive of further study.

Certainly a major challenge posed to the relational analysts (which they readily acknowledge) is the difficulty they face in ensuring that the "cocreation" of interpretations of the patient's psychic life do not include unwarranted intrusions of unconscious, countertransference fantasies. The technical challenge facing the ego psychological, objectivist analyst is no less daunting with regard to the sensitivity required to Arlow's view that all memory is screen memory. Prior to his discarding the seduction theory, Freud had put great stock in his theory of Nachtraglichkeit (1895) in which he asserted that later events (particularly the emergence of sexual impulses) can reactivate earlier experiences and memories of a sexual nature which could not be experienced as such at the time because of the psychosexual immaturity of the individual. This brief theory of Nachtraglichkeit (or deferred action as it is cumbersomely translated received little consideration and it essentially disappeared with the seduction theory. (Freud returned to it briefly in the Wolf Man case history and in several other contexts but it has had no central theoretical position in the history of psychoanalytic thought.) The Nachtraglichkeit concept has significant, but unrecognized implications for a comprehensive theory of UCF. If pathogenic UCF becomes fixated in development and we become aware of such fixations by a study of the patient's symptoms then we are at liberty to suggest that a patient's current symptomatology may be the patient's effort at reorganization of earlier memory-fantasy amalgams that had not yet attained the opportunity for representation. This should continue to remind us that derivatives are levels of representation of UCF and, accordingly, deeper levels of UCF may have the capacity but not yet the opportunity for representation in psychic life.

There is an unavoidability of potentially enriched, psychoanalytic theory which would emerge from studying the convergence of a theory of memory and a theory of fantasy under the transformational Nachtraglichkeit perspective. The tension created between an individual's developing cognitive-emotional abilities and conflicts and the demands of repression compel us to see fantasy-memory fixations and transformations as the central clinical avenue in a technique emerging from a reinvigorated theory of Nachtraglichkeit. Not only does a theory of Nachtraglichkeit obviate the trap of unicausal theorizing (by avoiding the trap of attributing adult psychopathology to a single cause, e.g., the unempathetic mother linked to narcissistic disorders) but it also demonstrates the promise of an interdigitated theory of psychic development in its considering the transformations to which memory-fantasy, as well as trauma, are subject. It was the poet Rilke who said, "Although the world changes as fast as cloud shapes manifold, all things, perfected at last, fall back to the very old" (citation unknown). It is, in the psychic domain, the study of the reworking of the very old that will constitute an exciting "new view" in psychoanalytic theory.

Appendix A

The analytic patient is a 37-year-old male in his first year of analysis. He has been married seven years. He opens his analytic session by reporting that the previous night his wife invited him to take a bath with her. This is an unusual event since his wife always locks herself in "her bathroom" when she bathes. On this occasion he lets himself into "her bathroom" by unlocking the door with a paper clip that he keeps on top of the doorframe. (He keeps this paper clip handy because she periodically invites him into the bathroom to talk with her when she bathes). On this occasion, though, she behaves in a sexually aggressive manner towards the patient and he states that she has "four or five orgasms." He has none. (In the course of the seven year marriage he has never had an intravaginal orgasm-only coitus interruptus). After the sexual interlude he goes to bed with his wife and quickly falls asleep. He awakens at 4:00 am and feels his sprained right ankle is throbbing. He goes to an upstairs bedroom and plugs in a heating pad, which he wraps around his ankle, and he falls asleep. When he awakens at 7:00 am he remembers the following dream: "I am pursuing an attractive woman into a fancy apartment building. I am ascending a spiral staircase but I lose sight of her and I no longer can follow her. Rather disgruntled I go to my own apartment. I open the door and it is very dark in the apartment. Immediately, a ten foot alligator lunges to attack me. I start to struggle with it; I'm able to close the mouth and wrap an extension cord around it to close it; I struggle but eventually subdue it and I throw it in the shower. Then I wake up."

1. Are there derivatives in the aforementioned clinical and dream material which are suggestive of a core UCF in this patient?

References

Aaron, L. (1996). *A Meeting of Minds*. Hillsdale, NJ: Analytic Press.

Arlow, J.A. (1969). Unconscious Fantasy and Disturbance of Conscious Experience. *Psychoanalytic Quarterly*, 38: 1–27.

Arlow, J.A. (1980). Object Concept and Object Choice. *Psychoanalytic Quarterly*, 49: 109–133.

Arlow, J.A. & Brenner, C. (1964). *Psychoanalytic Concepts and the Structural Theory*. New York: International Universities Press.

Busch, F. (1999). *Rethinking Clinical Technique*. Northvale, NJ: Aronson.

Eagle, M. et al. The Analyst's Knowledge and Authority: A Critique of the "New View" in Psychoanalysis. *Journal of American Psychoanalytic Association*, 49, No. 2, 457–489.

Freud, S. Project for a Scientific Psychology. *S.E.*, Vol. I.

Freud, S. The Unconscious. *S.E.*, Vol. XIV, p.194.

Gray, P. (1994) *The Ego and Analysis of Defense*. Northvale, NJ: Aronson.

Greenberg, J. (1991) Oedipus and Beyond. Cambridge: Harvard University Press.

Kernberg, O. (2001) Recent Developments in the Technical Approaches of English-Language Psychoanalytic Schools. *Psychoanalytic Quarterly*, 70: 519–547

Kohut, H. (1984) *How Does Analysis cure?* Chicago. University of Chicago Press.

Mahony, P. (1997) A Child is Being Beaten: A Clinical Historical and Textual Study. In Person, Ethel S Ed. *A Child is being Beaten Contemporary Freud: Turning Points and Critical Issues*. Yale University Press, New Haven, Connecticut.

Mitchell, S. (2000) Relationality: From Attachment to Intersubjectivity. Mahwah, NJ: The Analytic Press. Orange, D. World Horizons: A Post-Cartesian Alternative to the Freudian Unconscious. *Psychologist-*

Psychoanalyst, Newsletter of Division 39, American Psychological Association, Vol. 20, No. 3, Summer 2001, p.28.

Renik, O. (1993) Analytic Interaction: Conceptualizing Technique in Light of the Analyst's Irreducible Subjectivity. *Psychoanalytic Quarterly*. 62: 553–571.

Sandler, J. & Sandler, A.M. (1998) *Internal Objects Revisited*. Madison, Connecticut. International Universities Press.

Stolorow, R. & Atwood, G. (1992) *Contexts of Being: The Intersubjective Foundations of Psychological Life*. Hillsdale, NJ. The Analytic Press.

The Opening and Closing of Doors: Chronic Syntonic Acting Out

"A Trial of Patience" or "Analytic Havoc"

by Nancy Cromer-Grayson

Received the Plumsock Prize at the New York Freudian Society 2003

Suspense

ELYSIUM is as far as to
The very nearest room,
If in that room a friend await
Felicity or doom.
What fortitude the soul contains,
That it can so endure
The accent of a coming foot,
The opening of a door!
Emily Dickinson

22

This paper is a clinical vignette of a patient who misses appointment after appointment in a manner that is usually understood as counterproductive for an analysis, indicating a very poor prognosis. The case demonstrates how analyzability should remain an open question. When a patient is so uncooperative and resistant as to cause the analysis to take a unique form, what is most important to understand is what the patient is recreating in the enactment. Allowing the patient to create the atmosphere in the analytic setting will eventually resolve the uncooperative behavior, making collaboration and further progress possible. The analyst must accept as a communication whatever the patient brings into the analytic setting until the divergent conflict can be modified by the analysis.

Tolerating an almost intolerable action by a patient can actually foster analytic treatment. In this case the patient, Ms. Anna X, was unable to conform to the recommended regularity and frequency in a way that is usually considered desirable; she was never punctual and missed an inordinate number of scheduled appointments. This is usually considered contra productive and contra indicative for an analysis. The analyst gets discouraged and thinks the door is closed when it is actually opening. The patient is unconsciously enacting something without any awareness of its meaning.

I had worked with many patients who resisted treatment by unexplained absences but until I met Anna, I had never sustained a treatment with such extreme parameters. The frequency of missed sessions made me wonder at times if she was really in treatment and if I was really treating her. I was also interested to note my own countertransference; I was aware of a nurturing instinct that she elicited, which made me more tolerant of her acting out than I might have been with other patients.

Anna's response to having opened the door into herself through our work was frequently punctuated by missed sessions, which I came to understand as a slamming of the door. Many would have felt that this

222

patient was not analyzable; as Daniel Stern puts it, "it wreaks havoc." (Person, et al. p.183) However, as the treatment has progressed, Anna's fear of opening the door has lessened and she has been able to tolerate the experience of being in the room with me for longer periods of time. Over a period of six years, I have grown to regard this form of Anna's resistance as a valuable analytic tool; rather than viewing her enactments as adversarial and detrimental to the treatment, we have used them as a positive opening into her world.

According to Freud (1914): "Only when the resistance is at its height can the analyst, working in common with his patient, discover the repressed instinctual impulses which are feeding the resistance.... This working through of the resistances may in practice turn out to be an arduous task for the subject of the analysis and a trial of patience for the analyst. Nevertheless, it is a part of the work which effects the greatest changes in the patient and which distinguishes analytic treatment from any kind of treatment by suggestion." (p.155)

Anna X was referred for treatment when she was a sophomore in college. Her aunt was a therapist. I was aware of the positive transference that could develop because of this (Anna was close to this stepsister of her mother's); I didn't, however, anticipate to what extent it would help maintain a link to the treatment and to me in the transference when Anna began acting out by missing a substantial number of sessions.

At our first meeting, Anna appeared almost androgynous. She was dressed in an odd assemblage of clothing that smacked of the orphanage. Her hair was reversed bleached (platinum blonde with her natural black showing through), cut short and spiky. Pale and thin, she wore clunky Mary Jane's with striped tights and had a puckish air. She looked rather scary, in contrast to her soft-spoken and somewhat withdrawn demeanor.

In spite of her spiky appearance, Anna exuded a natural sweetness, which, in combination with her youth and extreme isolation, made people respond to her. Regardless, she reported having few friends. She had a mysterious way about her, which I experienced as defensive, a way of keeping the world at bay. It seemed as though she was out of touch with a sense of her own maturity even though she had recently made a major move on her own to New York from the west coast. She had just transferred from a liberal arts college in Seattle to a private art college in New York, which she was attending when we began. She was paying tuition with a limited, educational trust fund that had been set up by her maternal grandmother. She planned to use her trust fund to pay for treatment, although it would eventually run out.

At the time of our first session, Anna was living with her best friend from her hometown; they were attending to the same art college, which created problems. Anna thought that the professors favored her roommate who didn't have time for her. Anna was envious of her roommate's ability to socialize and she often felt excluded. Complicating matters was the fact that her roommate had emotional and financial support from her family; Anna had only the limited funds from her grandmother's trust. While Anna was connected to her family on the west coast, she had never been truly nurtured as her friend had been. Every educational opportunity was of Anna's own volition and this precocious autonomy had been hers since childhood.

Anna's original complaint upon our first meeting was depression. She felt "sad" a lot of the time and worried that the sadness would become overwhelming. She also discussed having panic attacks where she felt she couldn't breathe when traveling on a plane. This frightened her and made her to worry about dying. Interestingly, in our early sessions, she made no mention of her mother except to note that she had died when Anna was six. Just as Anna's absence from appointments was as significant as her presence, so her minimal mention of her mother served to highlight the effect her mother's absence had had on her. Anna's enactments were clearly linked to her mother although she was not yet conscious of this.

At our first session, Anna requested an analysis, citing her maternal aunt's psychoanalytic work. Anna was unclear as to what an analysis entailed and eventually we decided to work at a frequency of four sessions a week. Within the first month Anna had missed half of her appointments. I wondered whether her erratic behavior had to do with an early transference phenomenon or whether it was characterological. McLaughlin (1991) says, "Erratic behaviors literally jump out to meet the eye and beg for recognition." (p.573)

What emerged as a key factor in the analysis was the number of doors that were opening and closing. It grew increasingly evident that the missed sessions were reenactments of Anna's chaotic childhood and movements. Her parents had divorced when she was two, at which point her father moved from Berkeley to Seattle and Anna had little contact with him. Anna's paternal grandparents lived near Anna and her mother and Anna visited them on most weekends.

Anna described her mother as a poet involved with a group that included Andy Warhol. Anna reported that on many nights she had cold cereal for dinner because her mother was more interested in her nightlife than in her daughter. Anna's mother would often return drunk, vomit and leave the four-year-old to clean up and care for her. In a fragmented way, over a period of several months, with many missed sessions, Anna increasingly acknowledged her mother's existence as well the fact that she had been an alcoholic and a heroin addict. At this early stage of treatment, I was aware that Anna's erratic attendance was related to the erratic care she had received from her mother who was notably absent even in her presence. I began to see Anna's missed sessions as an unconscious reenactment of her relationship with her mother.

Anna was six when her mother died in what appeared to be a drug overdose. She then lived with her paternal grandparents with whom she secretly hoped to remain. Six months later, however, her grandparents decided that it was best for her to live with her father. Anna's father was an unsuccessful jazz musician at the time, a hippie who lived with his African American girlfriend, Regina. During school holidays and summers, Anna returned to her grandparents; she preferred their home, but felt conflicted in her loyalties and guilty if she talked to her grandparents about her father's squalid home. Her grandparents reiterated that her father loved her; this discouraged her from discussing the painful atmosphere of his house.

Once again Anna's erratic attendance seemed to be directly related to her early life experience. She had so often been uprooted from the comfort of her grandparents' home, never truly feeling secure and confident in her father's company. My office was another home, but a safer one where she could control her comings and goings by choosing to keep her sessions or not, to call or not.

Anna described her father as a sloppy, overweight man who was not terribly successful. I pictured a Willy Loman like figure, burdened by failure. Her grandparents gave him money to buy and operate a small insurance company. Her "stepmother" (they never actually married) worked at Pizza Hut. Anna reported having been embarrassed by them and by their house. It was on the "wrong side of town" and always a mess. Valued most for her house cleaning abilities, Anna felt neglected. Was Anna making me a new object for the neglect she had felt? Psychodynamically, with her continued absences, she created a feeling of being both neglected and rejected by me, just as she had felt in her various homes.

As a child, Anna was repulsed by the smell in her father's home of cigarette and pot smoke and beer. This smell had a profound effect on her. Issues of location and cleanliness dominated her adult choices of

226

living environments. The odors from the street and in her apartment, were constant sources of anxiety. The area where she lived never seemed to be elegant enough and reminded her of the shame she felt growing up. This had implications for the transference as well; my clean and carefully furnished office was on the "right side of town." Anna's desire to connect with me because of my office's location, the consistent analytic frame I offered, and her fantasy that I was the idealized maternal figure, had implications in the transference. I represented the preferred caregiver in the east; I also represented the grandparents who sent her away. Unconsciously she forced me to neglect her by not coming or calling. She also provoked a countertransference feeling in which I refused to neglect her.

It became strikingly clear that Anna had come east to school in order to connect to her mother's family. (Her mother had a stepsister and stepbrother who both lived in New York.) She also had a step-maternal grandmother who lived in the Boston area. This also affected the transference as our work took place in the east, partly at my office and partly absent from my office. With each holiday, with Anna' family in the west, she returned east with a new struggle around our work, which was at once a refuge and a painful exploration of her past.

After graduation, Anna took odd jobs such as refinishing furniture, waiting on tables, and assisting a designer. This presented problems for her; the smell of the paint and turpentine nauseated her, and reminded her of the odors in her father's home; waiting on tables at a neighborhood coffee shop made her think of her stepmother. Anna was afraid that she might be repeating her life and that she would be trapped in a "nowhere" job. Was she happy in a "nowhere" analysis given her inability to stick to a schedule? And yet, she maintained a rigorous discipline in her own painting. (She had always managed to save enough to pay for "a room of her own", an artist's studio, in which to work on her art.)

This fear of a "nowhere" job was partially resolved when she answered an advertisement in the New York Times for a job with a prestigious magazine. After an extensive interviewing process, she was given the job. Notably, it was a lifestyle magazine with an emphasis on creating beautiful living environments. Starting at a low level, Anna has now advanced to a position where she conceptualizes and executes features.

Although we seemed to be making progress in her analysis, a year after graduation Anna decided to stop treatment for "financial reasons." She returned occasionally and erratically for a session; her payments were correspondingly erratic. About eight months later, she decided to return to her analysis. Through our work, Anna was showing a curiosity about her past and how it affected her present functioning. She desperately wanted more than her parents had had, but felt guilty about this ambition.

At the beginning of the analysis, although committed to a schedule of four sessions per week, Anna was almost never able to come at that frequency or to be punctual. The sessions were mostly filled with her reporting on issues of reality relating to her boyfriend, best friend (prior roommate) and her new dog. She spoke in a flat, expressionless tone. All of her housemates irritated her in similar ways. Her boyfriend wasn't tidy enough. He left his clothes all over, never had the money for rent, and didn't communicate his feelings. They had fun together socially, but she wanted more of a romantic and sexual relationship. She felt guilty when she thought of breaking up with her boyfriend, and angry and sad when her best friend dropped her. I said these movements of the doors into and out of her intimate relationships might remind her of being abandoned by her mother. I thought at the time that this was also connected to me in a growing transference.

Anna controlled 'being dropped' by me by continually missing sessions, which gave her a sense of omnipotence. When I said this. she found it difficult to process and it increased her defensive armor, which resulted

228

in missed sessions. I knew that Anna's acting out was a communication, but clearly, I had spoken too soon. As Freud (1914) said, "…the patient does not remember anything of what he has forgotten and repressed, but acts it out. He reproduces it not as a memory but as an action; he repeats it, without, of course, knowing that he is repeating it." (p.150)

Anna had impulsively bought a new puppy, which required much more attention than she had anticipated. She had not realized the extent of the financial responsibility and the training process was a nightmare. The dog was constantly urinating and defecating in her apartment even after being walked. Trying to work out a shared plan of responsibility with her boyfriend was a positive attempt to assert herself, as were her missed sessions. She was attempting to have a controlled, committed relationship with her boyfriend, her dog and with me.

Throughout this period, however, Anna continued to miss at least one or two sessions weekly, and was almost always late when she did show. She was continually attempting to commit to her analysis in the same way that she was attempting to commit to her dog and boyfriend. Perhaps this is how she viewed her relationship with her father and grandparents. Were they committed to her or were they too conflicted to leave their door open for her? Was this a projection of hers? If so, was she projecting onto all of her objects?

The first dream Anna reported in the analysis was about having been with her grandparents and having said something sassy. Anna was upset because she made her grandmother cry. As her grandmother cried harder, Anna felt really mean, but also annoyed that her grandmother was so upset. Thinking about this dream, I wondered if she was worried about my uncovering terrible things about her in the analysis. This led me to believe this was part of the enactment in her missed appointments.

Both of these situations (with Anna's boyfriend and in the dream about her grandmother) seemed to be repetitions of her past. Now twenty-four, she went to a nice office each morning, but returned each evening to a neighborhood she didn't like and a home that wasn't kept in a way that made her comfortable. She felt burdened by cleaning up after her dog and boyfriend. This was a reminder of visiting her grandparents who lived in a consistently organized and clean house, and having to return to her father and stepmother's foul-smelling environment. I said to her that this dichotomy was being replicated in the contrast between my office and her home, and that this could contribute to her comings and goings and missed appointments. She commented that I am consistently here for her, but then justified her erratic schedule with external realities.

At this time, Anna told me that she was behind in rent and ashamed to run into her landlord. This was also happening with me. As Stein (1973) says, "…the acting-out pattern continues as before and it may, for a time, become more flamboyant, a development which is likely to be disconcerting even to the most unflappable of analysts." (p.349) Anna was consistently testing my staying power and endurance through her wildly inconsistent schedule.

By this point, Anna was arriving late to every session, missing more sessions than ever before, and was delinquent in payment. Some weeks she missed only one session, but other weeks she missed two or more without even calling. There were even occasions when she would miss the entire week of her analysis. However, Anna also did call sometimes to let me know that she had woken up too late to come. At such moments, I questioned whether we had reached an impasse, whether the door would remain permanently immobile. My counter transference was fury. Gaddini (1982) expresses it when he says that, "The degree of empathy that such a situation requires from the psychoanalyst is out of the ordinary. Continuously subjected to frustration the psychoanalyst may in fact collude with the defenses organized around the self, and think that nothing is happening and nothing relevant can happen. If instead he is able to notice through indirect signs (in dreams, behavior, associations) that a certain amount of work is unconsciously being carried out, he may feel pleased and may want to tell his patient the good news." (p.59)

At the same time as I felt furious, I felt compassion for Anna's need to enact with me her opening of one door and closing of another. I was aware that she was experimenting with my endurance to see if I too would become a disappointing object who could not keep the door open for her. I wondered if her intermittent disappearances were expressions of her unconscious need for me to share her childhood experience of abandonment. I often felt lost and unsure of how to proceed, just as I imagined Anna so often felt. I had to maintain my conviction that there was something powerful in allowing her to reenact her unconscious conflict.

As Gaddini (1982) adds, "…(The analyst) must make himself available and reliable for that unconscious part of the patient that is working. He must help it not to come out into the open but, on the contrary, to protect its clandestineness. He must learn to discover and to decipher the incoming messages, without making them public. He must accept a kind of communication which is, and must remain, a one-way communication. In other words, he must accept a clandestine therapeutic alliance. The only return communication which is worthwhile is that his clandestine ally comes to trust him, to make up his mind that there is somebody out there that is able to understand him and protect him, someone he can count on, when, properly grown up and strengthened, he can come out of his clandestineness less terrified. The psychoanalyst will have to know how to wait for this to happen." (p.60)

Just as I would arrive at what I thought to be an understanding of the pattern to Anna's missed sessions, the pattern would change. Even Anna was becoming aware of the ever-shifting pattern. "It's weird that I missed two sessions last week because I was feeling good. Now that I've been doing this for a while it should be routine. I'm not sure why I forget like that." Although she was somewhat aware, she was not conscious of this being a repetition of her past. However, I continued to mention that she might consider this a possibility and she began to have some openness to that. Although this new understanding did not affect her comings and goings, we were more able to talk about it.

In another session, she said: "I don't know why I keep messing up the times. I'm excited about coming. I guess in my subconscious I don't want to come. I do like coming four times a week. Everyone I know who is in therapy wishes they could come four times a week. My friend thought it was great to come so often because it gives you more time to focus on things that don't get buried." Nevertheless, Anna denied any connection between missing her sessions and her past, describing herself instead as tired and having overslept or forgotten our appointment. As Smith (1997) said, "…activity can be viewed through an infinite variety of lenses." (p.15)

The technical dilemma I faced here was how best to handle Anna's difficulty in maintaining the appointment frame of the analytic treatment. Should I insist on more prompt and regular attendance? Should I mention it at all? Should I call when she did not arrive or wait to hear from her? "In analysis, resistances are best analyzed, not overcome by suggestion or by some corrective emotional experience. That is to say, their nature and origin are to be understood and, when understood, interpreted to the patient." (Brenner, 1979 p.149)

As a child, Anna had longed to be nurtured by her mother, but had lost both her mother and her memories of her. Anna had then wanted to live with her paternal grandparents, but was pushed out the door and told that she was to live with her father and stepmother. When she was with her father, she looked forward to vacations and summers with her grandparents. As an adult, even when she had a roommate (human or canine) she projected her abandonment issues, ridding herself of dog,

232

roommate, and boyfriend. Even in the transference, she tried to do this with me, freeing herself of burdens in a way she couldn't have done with her own family.

Anna's experience of her two vastly different childhood homes affected the transference enormously. At times, I was the good grandparent. At other times, especially during periods when she was not showing up, I suspected I was a negative object who promoted growth and self-discovery, which created intolerable conflict for Anna. She felt as torn in our work as she had felt as a child and recreated that feeling within the analytic hour, in both her presence and her absence.

There are, of course, other clinicians who believe that not prohibiting acting out can counteract the therapeutic work. "…(Acting out) tends to counteract the recognition and organization of an inner space; it tends to counteract recognition of one's autonomy and one's real dependence. Acting out leaves out reality…" (Gaddini, 1982 p.57)

I often wondered if Anna's silence during a spate of missed sessions was a means of inducing me to contact her. Perhaps she was recreating the abandonment she felt with her mother whose lack of interest when she was alive was more painful than her ultimate absence in death. Given Anna's longings and lack of satisfaction in her attachments, I decided to contact her as a way of letting her know that I intended to keep my door open in her presence or absence. This was a perpetual dilemma: should the analyst or shouldn't the analyst repeatedly contact a patient who has missed so many sessions without calling? I had to decide each time whether or not to contact her, wondering whether I was about to duplicate her childhood experience by not calling or support and increase trust by calling. "…Some of us are more active and some of us wait and are willing to do nothing for a period of time." (Ellman, p.189)

Usually, I chose to telephone Anna, understanding that our separations intensified her feelings of isolation and abandonment in an unproductive way. Anna responded once by saying, "I can always depend on you. If I'm a flake, you will contact me." [I noted to myself the word "flake" and it reminded me that on many vacations she enjoyed going skiing with her grandparents.] With some embarrassment, she told me that it made her feel understood when I contacted her after she missed a session. Eventually, I would try to wean her from expecting my calls, but at the time I used them as a way to strengthen her trust in my consistency.

At this time, Anna still had no memories of her mother, but I continued to suggest that this had something to do with her frequent absences. Anna's family never speaks about her mother and Anna feels that this contributes to her repressed memories of her mother. Anna also links her acting out to her mother's absences, in that she is able to shut the door on our work when she absents herself from sessions. In the transference, I become a mother who never forgets her and never allows her to be forgotten.

Even with Anna's disruptions to the analytic frame, the analysis continued and deepened. At one session Anna said: "I had a lot of stress about coming today. I've been sort of frantic. I had to unpack from the photo shoot. (I was reminded of all the packing and unpacking she had to do as a child.) I used to complain about coming to see you in the mornings. Now I feel, that coming at lunchtime is bugging me. Then I don't have time for myself for the day." I wondered with her if she had any thoughts about my upcoming August vacation, which was a month away. Anna was defensive, saying, "For the most part I feel glad that you will be away because it is an inconvenience for me to come in August. We are very busy at work. I feel bad that I missed last Thursday and Friday. I know that I miss coming a little bit. It just feels like it will just be easier to work so I felt relief about that. I keep feeling that you want me to say something that I'm just not feeling. I don't know. I feel nervous about it. I never have time to have lunch with anyone except on Wednesdays. Then when I'm working, I leave for two hours. Then I turn around and come for the next day."

I said to her how she seemed to feel she had no control over things, that the erratic nature of every area of her life—her analysis, her profession and her intimate relationships—produced the feelings she experienced as a child. Anna agreed and went on to say, "Today I don't know if I'll even get to eat or anything. Since I'm coming four times a week, I should be feeling better." My interpretation of this to her was that she felt insufficiently provided for by me, just as she had with her mother. She had felt trapped with a mother who didn't sufficiently feed her; perhaps she felt that I too was starving her. I added that her anger at my not sufficiently feeding her might have something to do with her missing appointments. Anna conceded that this might be true. "…It has been stressed that even when acting out is regarded as a product of resistance, it can also serve the function of communication." (Sandler, et al. p. 142)

After one of my August vacations, three years into the treatment, Anna again expressed her anxiety, disappointment, and anger by saying: "I don't have the money to pay the last bill. I don't want to fall behind. It feels like a mess; a lot of things feel that way." I thought of how she often described her father and stepmother's house as dirty and how she was, in effect, making a mess with me in the transference. She also told me about her rent: "I feel really embarrassed about the rent thing. I can't tell you how far behind I am. I have it written down somewhere."

I knew that Anna was not speaking to me frankly because she owed me "rent." In view of her past, a conflict had been aroused about knowing and not knowing how payment would complicate the treatment. She was chaotic and consistently delinquent with her bills. I had been away for the month and wasn't there to take care of her. She said in a session: "I definitely had stuff to talk about, but I knew I would see you in September. It felt nice to have a break. I have a lot of stress at work and it's hard to leave work and not be like everyone else who eats together. Every single time someone asks me to have lunch they want to know why I can't. It's not that I regret it, but it's nice to have lunch with everyone sometimes." Anna avoided the issue of payment.

Instead of saying that she had been miserable when I was away, Anna used the defense of reversal and said it was nice and even preferable to spending money on her analysis when she could have lunch with her friends. Historically she had a pattern of attempting to exercise control over conversations that could produce conflict. (A notable example was her reluctance to tell her grandparents that she desperately wanted to stay with them; she felt that they had pushed her out the door in sending her to her father's.) Again, she was telling and yet not telling. She was annoyed at my leaving her and went on to describe what she did with those feelings: she doesn't want to come to sessions, or pay me. I wondered if somewhere inside she felt she owed her father money and felt guilty about not giving him any.

At another session, Anna described how she always felt like "a square." "I was always conflicted cause part of me wanted to be normal and have nice clothes. My stepmother brought me clothes from the thrift shop. After I got some of my trust fund, I spent a lot of the money on clothes. When I would visit my grandparents' in California I wanted normal clothes. Their world was what I wanted, but when I was in Seattle I felt more creative and original. My job represents my grandparents' world in California." I spoke to her about how I also might represent her grandparents. She told me how she loves the way I dress and wants to have nice things like I do. I asked her what those would be and she finally began to talk about her mother. (Anna's personal appearance had softened in recent years; although she still wears Wallabees most of the time, she frequently accompanies them with a delicate purse and color coordinated turtleneck; she has also tamed her hair, allowing it to revert to her natural brown color.)

Anna was beginning to remember more and more material about her mother. The images she recollected were disjointed and rarely led to significant insight, but it was an important beginning of her burgeoning memories of her mother; a door was being opened that had been so tightly closed. Predictably, memories of Anna's mother invariably produced a welter of missed sessions. Finally, I was able to connect her erratic attendance to her talking about her mother. Perhaps her connection to me was the safest and strongest when she could preserve me in fantasy rather than have to confront our work.

After many missed sessions, Anna had no difficulty continuing where we had left it; in her mind, we were as linked in absence as we were in session. "…With my mom, it's hard cause I have no memories. I remember feeling that there were things she did that I was in awe of. I remember being in Massachusetts at her mother's house. She was writing at a desk and tapping her fingers like this." [She demonstrated while on the couch, moving her fingers playing an imaginary scale on the piano.] "Another time she was making me breakfast and hid my plate and said a gremlin took it. She was playing a game and I knew it. I also remember a neighbor came for lunch once. My mom was making sandwiches and she asked what kind of bread, white or whole wheat." She went on to say, "There were other times I felt really frustrated with her. We were at a party and I felt really bored. I wanted to leave. Another time we were visiting someone, my mom got so drunk and wasted."

Anna's analysis intensified as she continued to associate around her erratic attendance. As her unpredictable schedule continued, I became a container for the enactment and Anna was slowly able to verbalize her development outside the analysis. She was more and more conscious of the meaning of her inability to maintain any regularity with her appointments. "…I remember being so excited to visit my grandparents. I know my mom resented it. I liked visiting them so much. It made me feel guilty when my mom died because I was getting what I wanted—not really, but it felt that way. I don't remember feeling sad when she died. I did feel sad, but I don't think I really understood it. I don't remember crying or anything. It makes me sad to think of my grandparents having to tell me what happened." I shared my experience of her missed sessions and asked if she was trying to recreate what it felt like to have lived with such uncertainty as a child. She had never been able to count on a consistent adult presence and there had been no constants in her life. She was recreating this with our sessions.

Anna was clearly demonstrating that, "…true acting out may also have advantages" (a) It is a source for the gaining of material; the analyst may be enabled directly to observe the patient's past (supposing the patient does not keep silent about what he is "acting out" outside of his sessions). (b) Acting out increases the demonstrability of the actuality of the material. After having felt the impulse to act out, the patient certainly will no longer be able to believe that certain childhood influences are far away from his present state." (Fenichel, p.202) Anna felt guilt over the recovery of her memories of her mother, she felt it was a betrayal of her grandparents and she was even beginning to have some awareness of the link between such memories and her sporadic attendance.

Anna's insights into herself and her past were now coming in waves. "Sorry about yesterday. I realized I had forgotten. I got depressed that I had forgotten our session again. It felt really overwhelming. Coming here makes my schedule uncomfortable. It reminds me of middle school. I used to play the clarinet. When I went to high school, I hated carrying it. My parents wouldn't let me quit. I hated that I had to continue taking clarinet. It didn't fit in my locker. I had to carry it around. No one else did." This reflected so poignantly Anna's internal state, and the burdens that she had carried as a child. Anna needed me to feel the uncertainty and anxiety that were so crucial to her feelings of displacement.

At a subsequent session, Anna said: "…The whole time I was at my Dad's, I hated it. I didn't like living there and I didn't like my stepmother. She was mean. I felt envious of my friends. They had nice houses and I had to go home to 'boot camp.' I felt trapped. In third or fourth grade, I wanted to run away. My grandparents pretended my living situation was normal, so I decided I couldn't say anything. I convinced myself that it was normal. I do feel that if I tell you that coming to see you is a chore and stressful, you will get angry with me. You worked it out so I could come four times a week so I guess I feel I have no right to think it's a chore…" (She was referring to my financial accommodation, which was the only way she could afford analysis.) Anna was expressing both the negative and the positive transference. It seemed as though therapy felt like 'boot camp' to Anna. Her resistance was implicit in the transference and enactments with me. Her parents wouldn't let her quit the clarinet and now she had committed to an analysis, regardless of her chronic absenteeism.

Anna was now recreating with me in the transference her feeling of isolation. She felt helped by me, but that ultimately, she carried the burden alone. This feeling was exacerbated by her growing insights into her desire for a committed relationship. "Coming here is on my mind so I have to talk about it, but I really don't want to. I feel the burden is all my responsibility to take action so it feels overwhelming. Coming here I have to talk. I know I don't have to. I want to." She went on to say, "If I avoid coming, then I avoid the problems, but at the same time I want to come to figure it out. It feels much more painful and harder than I thought it would."

What followed was a week of missed sessions. Once again, I questioned whether I should allow the enactment to grow or interfere with it? "…While one analyst may see a piece of behavior as acting out, another might regard the same activity as appropriate and adaptive." (Sandler, et al. p.142) "…This is, of course, where Freud came in—clearly concerned that analytic therapists were being drawn into some kind of actual or emotional behavior with the patients rather than remaining neutral. We could say that to some extent all patients do this; they try unconsciously and usually more delicately to draw us into mental or emotional activity, to play on our concern or guilt, to humor us or gratify our assumed expectations. They try to manipulate us to fit in with and act out according to their unconscious demands and phantasies." (Betty Joseph, p.107)

At this point, it would still have been counterproductive to have increased the intensity of the transference experience, which would have also increased Anna's defense. I decided to call her. We talked about how she induces me to take care of her, that I would make a phone call to reassure her that the door is still open. Anna admitted the relief my calls afford her. "A patient may miss a session because of the need to feel 'independent' of the therapist, or to make the therapist 'miss him', like the child hiding under the table who does not answer his mother's frantic calls. Certainly, there is an element of resistance within the unconscious fantasy in this behavior, but to treat it only as such, and to mark it with the negative sign of a reprimand, is surely to obscure the ambiguous communication of the gesture, its positive value as an aspect of intrapsychic individuation in a secret and delicious triumph over the omnipotent mother." (Furlong, p.701)

At the next session, Anna relayed a dream: "I was on a bus. There was a crazy guy. He started walking around and yelling. He had guns in his bag. The bus driver made a fake stop, but the bus didn't stop. I noticed no one was driving the bus and it was going off the road. I went up there." She associated to the dream by saying she has angry, vivid feelings of entrapment. "I definitely have issues coming here. I can't think of what to talk about. It makes me feel trapped. It feels easier to come now that I don't have to come. Not that it's great to come, but I don't have to feel awful about not coming." I thought that the hidden wish Anna was expressing in the dream was that I take care of her and carry her along. However, I decided not to make the interpretation to her at this time. I would drive the bus; she didn't have to feel crazy when I was the parent who took care of her and helped her to act in a socialized way.

Anna went on to say, "Sorry I didn't call. I woke up late, bummed out, and embarrassed to call. I'm in this murky place. I have to come here to figure out solutions. Sometimes it makes me feel more depressed to come and to have to talk and remember things. On Monday and yesterday when I woke up too late to come, I didn't even think, well, oh, just try and go anyway, even if you're late. Getting up and getting ready for work hasn't been easy. At the same time, I'm excited about making changes. It makes me feel good to make good decisions."

After my August vacation this year, Anna's first sessions on my return were substantially different from previous years. Ordinarily she expresses pleasure in my absence, which not only saves her money, but also allows her additional sleep and time for friends. This September, however, she mentioned having missed me and said that she even wanted to see me more. Once again, she then missed her next session.

A week later, she told me of a dream. It was a transference dream in which I had yelled at her for not coming to a session: "How do you think you can continue coming like this? How can you come without ever coming?" Anna associated to the dream saying, "It's amazing that I don't come. I really feel more dedicated to coming now. Yesterday was a slipup. It's weird that I had the dream, since I feel more dedicated to coming. I don't know what to make of it. In the dream, it felt pretty true. I mean, it felt that you had reason to be mad at me, but then again, maybe it's not legitimate. I was with friends and I didn't want them to know what was going on." She felt that the conflicted part of her felt justified for not coming and that the other part of her felt she was doing something she shouldn't do. She went on to say, "It wasn't a defined moment. I wanted to be in my own life. In the dream, I said that I was hanging out with my friends and I didn't give a reason why I didn't come. Even though in the dream, I didn't think it was a real life situation, I could say that I don't want to come when I'm hanging out with my friends. I could say it's important for me to do this. There is nothing wrong with that."

I said that she had made me yell at her in the dream. Anna replied by saying that, "part of me wants to be dedicated to coming and another part doesn't want to have to rush to come. It is important to me to have a little time to relax not to rush. That is kind of a valid desire. The dream was good and I thought oh God, then I called you and you weren't mad at me. That helped me wake up this morning. I woke up early enough not to rush."

I suggested that she might have been angry with me for having abandoned her for the month and that she had slept to avoid these feelings. Anna concurred, saying that she had never thought of it that way, but that it was possible. I wondered with her about the other ways she avoided her feelings, closing the door on painful memories by skipping sessions at times when there is more of a connection to me and to her past. She began to cry and asked why she continued to do this. I said that avoidance had been an adaptive coping mechanism; disassociating and repressing her feelings had helped her to function when she felt most alone.

Several missed sessions followed this one, however Anna was now calling each time to let me know that she intended to skip the session. A week later, dressed in the less bizarre and increasingly gamine style she now favors, Anna returned and said, "The only way I know not to be confused is to withdraw. Even with Leo [her current boyfriend], the only way to deal with him is to shut him out. Because I'm mad—I can't say I'm mad, so I punish him by shutting him out." I suggested that this abrupt closure of the door was a dynamic that played out in our work, that she was never able to be where she wanted to be; doors had opened and closed on her throughout her life and it was a major step that she was now taking control of which door was being closed at which time.

Anna began to cry; her tears have been a new phenomenon, appearing with some regularity since my most recent vacation. While quietly weeping, Anna then connected to her past by relaying a conversation she had just had with her paternal aunt. "When I was little, if I cried, they put me in another room. My Dad was proud of his technique. Everyone criticized my aunt for being so attentive to her kids. Maybe they are spoiling them, but I see them as trying to make her kid feel safe. My Dad was joking that they are too good as parents. I was talking to my aunt who notices that I withdraw when I'm upset. I was shocked she noticed. Then she said it must be really lonely for me to be in the room with other people and to be by myself at the same time. I don't know why I am obsessing about this, but it really affected me." I said that although it was so painful for her to hear about her past, she must have experienced some relief at being noticed and at uncovering pieces of her childhood. Anna continued to cry and ask why she was like this. I said that there was something very positive in her comfort in the room with me, in her willingness to open the door into why she is the way she is.

After all, as Freud (1914) says: "...We have learnt that the patient repeats instead of remembering, and repeats under the conditions of resistance. We may now ask what it is that he in fact repeats or acts out. The answer is that he repeats everything that has already made its way from the sources of the repressed into his manifest personality—his inhibitions symptoms in the course of the treatment. And now we can see that in drawing attention to the compulsion to repeat we have acquired no new fact but only a more comprehensive view. We have only made it clear to ourselves that the patient's state of being ill cannot cease with the beginning of his analysis, and that we must treat his illness, not as an event of the past, but as a present-day force." (p.151)

As Anna opens the door into her past, even she is beginning to see the ways in which she recreates her past in her current relationships. When she began referring to her current boyfriend as "wavy gravy," I asked her to define the term. In her soft-spoken way, she described an undefined relationship with no clear parameters; she was, she explained, having a sexual relationship, but couldn't rely on a Saturday night date. She had been seeing Leo for six months, but wasn't sure if she could consider him her boyfriend because of the "wavy nature" of their relationship. Over a period of sessions, I suggested that she created wavy gravy relationships with all of her important objects, including me. Was she in a relationship? Was she in analysis? I couldn't depend on her presence at the subsequent session, just as she couldn't depend on her boyfriend for Saturday night.

Anna cried and said that she regretted having given her dog, Linus, away. She expressed guilt, but comforted herself with the memory of having provided him with a caring new owner and comfortable home. I said that she had given Linus something that she still craved, a good home and security. Her ambivalence reflected how she felt her parents might have regarded the burden of caring for her. Anna associated by talking about how her mother might have felt about her, that the responsibility might have been too much. I wondered with her about the various doors her mother had struggled to keep open for Anna.

These sessions were particularly uncomfortable for Anna; predictably she would often miss at least one session following any of these explorations. However, she was more and more able to explore the ways in which she recreated her childhood experience of never having the comfort and security of a stable home. She had never told her grandparents how much she wanted to live in their home, just as it had taken years in analysis, with numerous absences, to tell me on my return from vacation how eagerly she anticipated opening the door to my office.

Anna Freud (1968) concurs: "...There seems to me to exist a firm link between the qualitative and quantitative properties of the "forgotten past" and the ways and means by which it is revived in analysis, whether this revival takes the form of mere remembering, or happens in the guise of re-experiencing, re-living, re-enacting, or any other variety of controlled or uncontrolled repetition." (p.168)

As Anna connects her current relationships to her childhood deprivations, memories have surfaced. After her Christmas vacation with her family in Berkeley this year, she returned with extreme anger towards her father and a flood of recollections about her mother. When she was involved in a car accident in early January, she was extremely conscious of her friends having immediate access to their parents. "I remember not knowing what to do because I didn't have anyone to call." Coincidentally, I called her on the evening of her accident; given the nature of our own "wavy gravy" relationship, she had neglected to tell me the extent of her vacation. (By now she always calls to say when she is missing a session, but on this particular occasion I had not heard from her in several days.) Anna cried immediately on hearing my voice and on her return, she mentioned that I am the only one who is always here for her.

In recent sessions, Anna has been peeking through the door into her recollections of her mother. Her regularly irregular schedule of appointments has remained the same, albeit with greater punctuality and phone calls to notify me of her cancellations. She has differentiated between her parental objects, expressing anger towards her father and a new gratitude and understanding of her mother. I suggested that her abrupt move from his house after her high school graduation had triggered his anger and subsequent feeling that she didn't have the freedom to come and go. She responded by saying, "he's made me the bad guy over and over, so I do feel angry over that." Anna was recreating her adolescent experience with me by asserting her freedom with an object she knows will never reject her. In

245

her inability to maintain a consistent analytic schedule, Anna continues to test me; she must repeat the proof of my permanent and positive presence until she is able to reintegrate her traumatic childhood experience and withstand a more comprehensive treatment. Erna Furman poignantly cites her teacher, Anna Freud, as having said, "A mother's job is to be there to be left." In Anna's experience, I am the maternal object who can tolerate her autonomy and her predictably unpredictable abandonments.

When Anna spoke with some pride of an elite nursery school program that she was accepted to because of her mother's persistence, I suggested that she was allowing herself positive memories of her mother. Anna cried throughout this session as we continued the dialogue about her mother. At one point, she spoke of her mother's appearance and the circumstance of her death. This was the most we had ever spoken of her mother. Anna mentioned that her mother had been capable of some things, but not others. "I also remember my Mom took me to the doctor and dentist. My Mom also complained to the school when my kindergarten teacher was mean. That's something my Dad never did." I never felt—feel— important enough and remembered with my Dad and Regina. I can't believe Regina—who never acts like a mom—has the nerve to sign "Mom" on her Christmas card."

The case illustrates so vividly that enactments are a direct result of the compulsion to repeat, and a rich source of understanding, rather than "unacceptable, non-analytic behavior." In Freud's (1914) words, "...What interests us most of all is naturally the relation of this compulsion to repeat to the transference and to resistance. We soon perceive that the transference is itself only a piece of repetition, and that the repetition is transference of the forgotten past not only on to the doctor but also on to all the other aspects of the current situation. We must be prepared to find, therefore, that the patient yields to the compulsion to repeat, which now replaces the impulsion to remember, not only in his personal attitude to his doctor but also in every other activity and relationship which may occupy his life at the time—if, for instance, he falls in love or undertakes a task or starts an enterprise during the treatment. The part played by resistance too is easily recognized." (p.151)

The case of Anna X brings home how important it is to understand what the patient is recreating in any enactment. The analyst comes to understand the patient's actions by allowing treatment to continue and analyzing the enactment without forcing the patient to fit a model of treatment. What is essential is to allow the patient to create the atmosphere in the analytic setting and for the analyst to accept as a communication whatever the patient brings until it can be modified by the analysis. Many analysts would covertly subscribe to this treatment, but the drastic irregularity of the schedule would officially be noted as a poor prognosis.

For Anna, opening and closing doors, coming and not coming, re-created her past in a particularly vivid and challenging way. Anna taught me that the treatment must start with the patient opening the door. The analyst must accompany the patient at the pace set by that patient. Anna still continues to have a very particular pace and I have learned not only to adapt to it, but also to value it as a powerful analytic tool. "A rule which is a rule only for the sake of being a rule inevitably becomes dogmatic, autocratic and sadistic." (Furlong P.700) To date the treatment continues and Anna still misses sessions, but she usually calls to let me know in advance. Anna is developing the capacity for a reflective awareness and she is using her erratic attendance as a means of understanding and opening the doors to her past.

References

Bird, B. (1957). A specific peculiarity of acting out., *J. Amer. Psychoanal. Assn.*, 5:630–647.

Boesky, D. (1982). Acting out: a reconsideration of the concept., *Int. J. Psychoanal.*, 63:39–56.

Brenner, C. (1979) Working alliance, therapeutic alliance, and transference., *J. Amer. Psychoanal. Assn.*, 137–157.

Ellman, S. & Moskowitz M. (1998). *Enactment*. New Jersey: Jason Aronson.

Fenichel, O. (1945). Neurotic acting out., *Psychoanal. Rev.*, 32:197–206.

Freud, A. (1968). Acting-out., *Int. J. Psychoanal.* 49:165–170.

Freud, S. (1914), Remembering, repeating and working-through. *S. E.*, 12,145–156. London: Hogarth Press, 1958.

Furlong, A. (1992). Some technical and theoretical considerations regarding the missed session., *Int. J. Psychoanal.*, 73:700–718.

Furman, E. (1982). Mothers have to be there to be left. *Psychoanal. Study Child.*, 37:15–28.

Gaddini, E. (1982). Acting out in the analytic session., *Int. J. Psychoanal.*, 63:57–64.

Joseph, B. (1993). On transference love: some current observations. In Person, et al, *On Freud's "Observations on Transference-Love"*. New Haven: Yale University Press, pp. 102–113.

Mclaughlin, J.T. (1987). The play of transference: some reflections on enactment in the psychoanalytic situation., *J. Amer. Psychoanal. Assn.*, 35:557–582.

Rangell, L. (1968). A point of view on acting out., *Int. J. Psychoanal.*, 49:195–201.

Smith, H.F. (1997). Resistance, enactment, and interpretation: a self-analytic study., *Psychoanal. Inquiry*, 17:13–30.

Sandler J., Dare C., & Holder A. (1992). *The Patient and the Analyst*. London: Karnac Books.

Stern, D. (1993). *Acting versus remembering in transference love and infantile love. In Person, et al. On Freud's 'Observations on Transference-Love'*. New Haven: Yale University Press, pp.172–185.

Stein, M.H. (1973). Acting out as a character trait: its relation to the transference., *Psychoanal. Study Child.*, 28:347–364.

The Role of Concreteness in Female Genital Pain

by Molly Jones Quinn

Abstract:

C oncreteness is a dynamic which is observed in some women in analytic treatment who suffer genital pain, either chronically or upon contact, and are unable to productively use interpretations about the symbolic meaning of their painful symptom. Problems in early maternal attachment are the basis for difficulty in the formation of primary femininity and female gender role, as well as in the effective consolidation of anal phase tasks which leads to representational thinking. The capacity to think symbolically needs to be developed in treatment before such a patient will be able to explore the primitive fantasies, thoughts, and feelings which have been hidden in this painful symptom with its resulting emotional and sexual disruptions. The analyst whose frustrated interpretative efforts may be based on Freud's ideas about the role of repression in symptom formation needs to make a conceptual shift. Freud's later ideas (1927) about fetishism, based on primitive anxieties fended off by disavowal and splitting, may be more useful in establishing a therapeutic alliance with patients who suffer this particular symptom complex. Illustrations are drawn from clinical material in the treatment of four women whose early resistance to analytic treatment was rooted in rigid, concrete thinking about their genital pain.

Burning or knifelike vulvar pain, either chronically or upon specific contact, has been reported in the histories of an estimated 16% of American women (Harlow and Stewart, 2003). Eliminating obvious organic causes (i.e. inflammation of the Bartholin gland), there is a startling variety of medical explanations and treatments for female genital pain. Inevitably, some women with this debilitating pain syndrome, either as the presenting symptom or as a secondary complaint, are referred for analytically oriented treatment. By the time such a patient reaches the analytic consulting room, she is likely to be ashamed, angry, confused, and highly resistant to psychological interpretations. She may appear depressed, hopeless, rejecting the notion that psychological treatment offers anything useful; she may instead present a facade of cooperative compliance, without being able to authentically express her thoughts and feelings; or she may entertain psychological explanations in a detached, intellectualized manner.

This paper will explore the manifestation of concreteness in the treatment of four women suffering chronic genital pain and postulate that early trauma in the maternal relationship is related to both the painful symptom and their difficulty thinking about it symbolically, with the caveat that not all women with chronic genital pain necessarily fit this constellation.

Some women suffering idiopathic genital pain do not have the capacity for symbolic or representational thinking which is necessary to understand, much less use productively, an interpretation which might link pain to masochism, primary femininity, or female genital anxiety when they embark on analytic treatment. Disturbances in early relationships, such as intense fear of bad objects and fear of loss or inaccessibility of good objects, can create disruption in the woman's capacity for symbol formation. In particular, disturbances in differentiation between self- and object may result in an inability to differentiate between fantasy, emotion,

252

and physical sensation. The result is that the physical body remains the primary venue for expression of conflictual thoughts or feelings and, in particular, of fantasies which must be cut off from awareness. Despite her apparent developmental progress, early disruptions in her attachment to and identification with mother in particular may disturb the growth of a child's ability to perceive and differentiate herself from her primary care giver and inner from outer, as well as her evolving system of defenses against anxiety normally consolidated during the anal phase in preparation for the trials and tasks of Oedipal psychosexual development.

Traditionally analysts have been trained to think about idiopathic physical symptoms in terms of hysterical conversion reactions, psychic leaks in the patient's capacity to repress internal conflicts (Freud, 1905). Therefore, a well-timed and titrated interpretation appropriately drawn from the patient's history should offer relief from the physical symptom, raising the conflict to a mental/emotional sphere for exploration. However, I have observed in my clinical experience with four women suffering chronic and disabling genital pain that these assumptions do not bear fruit. Instead, thinking about the physical symptom as a sign of concrete mental processes and working with patients' primitive defensive processes (disavowal, projection, and splitting) as discussed by Freud in his later work on fetishism (1927) has been more useful. This latter work evolved out of Freud's interest in some children's inability to tolerate knowledge of gender difference, but Bass (1997, 2000) expands its relevance to differentiation at all levels of early development (self/other, location of control, and gender). Resistance to differentiation at any or all of these levels may be expressed in primitive defenses which may remain into adulthood, crippling the development of higher levels of defense and of representational thinking which are usually consolidated as the last step of pre-Oedipal development during the anal phase.

Much has been written (Jones, 1927; Segal, 1957; Bion, 1959; Fonagy, 1991 and 1993; Steiner, 1993; Novick and Novick, 1996; Bass, 2000) about the complex interweaving of psychological tasks involved in the developing capacity for symbolization during the anal phase. Where there has been significant disruption in early object relationships this ability may not develop at all or it may be erratically available, resulting in the fixation of the primitive defensive processes which support concreteness, as well as a masochistic character structure.

Thinking specifically about female psychosexual development, Tyson and Tyson (1990), among others (Chasseuguet-Smirgel, 1970; Torok, 1970; Lax, 1977 and 1992; McDougall, 1988; Bernstein, 1990; Richards, 1992 and 1996; Mayer, 1995; Gilmore, 1998; Chodorow, 2003) connect early object relationships, intense separation anxiety, preoccupation with the body, and fears of bodily injury. The Tysons argue that disruptive genital concerns in girls' development follow, rather than precede the development of primary femininity. When penis envy and/or castration fantasies are exaggerated and accompanied by a sense of inferiority (as inferred in the nature of my patients' symptoms), these can usually be traced to earlier problems in object relations. These connections have been evidenced in my patients, each of whom reported very difficult circumstances affecting her early maternal attachment, unstable per-ceptions of her femininity and female body image, and vivid dreams and fantasies of injury and bodily damage. Perhaps most importantly, Tyson and Tyson note that when the maternal relationship has been of poor quality, the tasks of separation-individuation are disrupted, resulting in a form of hostile dependence such as I experienced in the powerful transferences of three of my patients.

Despite their apparently high levels of professional functioning the four women upon whom I base this discussion showed evidence of disavowal, splitting, and projection, particularly in thinking about their difficulties with sexuality and intimate relationships. Initially in treatment my efforts to speak about the psychological issues represented in their genital symptoms provoked intense anxiety and primitive defensive reactions. Interesting as I found the symbolic meaning of their disabling symptoms, I all too slowly came to realize that the first order of analytic business was work in the therapeutic alliance to help these women articulate their complicated feelings about me and to think about their defensive processes as we observed them together "in the room." The initial task of overcoming the resignation, passivity, and magical expectations with which these patients approached treatment constitutes what Novick and Novick (1998) refer to as "learning to become an analysand." As described in their schema, a patient becomes actively engaged in self-observation and identifies with the potential ego strength available in the analyst's inquiring, neutral position, as opposed to the familiar shamed/blamed position which is their characteristic inclination. Dealing with mistrust and hostile, negative transference is necessary in order to build the capacity of a patient stuck in a concrete mode of expressing feelings, fantasies, and conflicts, especially as these relate to separation and individuation.

A symptom itself, such as chronic genital pain, can in adulthood become a psychic retreat (Steiner, 1993) from anxiety-provoking ideas or situations, perhaps also serving as a fetish which holds a sort of magical power and serves to fend off anxiety about differentiation (self/other, control, and sexual). The symptom concretely expresses "I am a damaged, defective person who can not function as a mature sexual woman," but can also paradoxically become a source of power or 'specialness' which serves to frustrate physicians, lovers, and analysts in its stubborn resistance to insight and change. At the same time the treatment situation may be dismissed as useless, it may serve as a valuable hiding place where there are subtle gratifications. The hidden pleasures in suffering make it particularly resistant to change.

For a concrete patient's perceptual frame to change there may be required an experience which is discordant with expectations, usually an action or enactment within the context of the analyst-patient relationship since this is accessible to exploration (Chused, 1991, McLaughlin and Johan, 1992). It may not be enough for the analyst to refrain from focus on or interpretation of the patient's symptom. Within the transference it is likely that a concrete mode for provoking an enactment or, at least for signaling an expectation, will emerge. For instance, I tried to listen patiently Ms. C regaled me with detailed explanations about how oxyllate crystals caused by acidic foods stabbed into the tender tissue of her vulva causing her unbearable genital pain. My frustration about her resistance to my efforts at engaging her in more psychological thinking about the meaning of her pain caused me (uncharacteristically) to pick up a knitting project during our session. This in turn provoked her outrage about my perceived inattention to her, leading us into the heart of her rage about her mother's abandonment, a complicated situation about which I had heard little at that point. That I did not become defensive when she attacked me, but was open to and curious about her feelings, caught her attention and deepened her engagement with me.

Another technical approach with a concrete, resistant patient serves to draw attention to cracks in the patient's defensive wall, the analyst speaking to contradictions in thought or behavior which can help a patient observe the defensive splits which obfuscate the line between reality and fantasy (Bass, 2000). For instance, my patient Ms. A was telling me about the deep love she shared with a married man, despite its many painful aspects. She maintained that their sexual contact was pleasurable to her regardless of the excruciating physical pain she also experienced in sexual intercourse. When I expressed my confusion about how something so painful could be pleasurable, she began to explore that contradiction, associating it to her very painful early attachments.

She had never questioned her expectation that love and sexual intimacy would be, in fact needed to be, painful.

Discussing the difficulty of engaging highly anxious, concrete patients, Steiner (1993) emphasizes the 'analyst centered' response in which the analyst speaks to the patient's need for the analyst to understand her instead of a 'patient centered' effort in which the analyst strives to give the patient an interpretation. Ms. C at one point heard my words and recoiled on the couch, complaining of an excruciating, stabbing genital pain. I responded by saying she needed for me to understand how much my words and actions could hurt her; these words seemed to both express and contain the intensity of her heavily laden transference experience. Britton (1989) describes his patient's intolerance for evidence of his (the analyst's) own thinking and the technical difficulty of maintaining his own thoughts while communicating to the patient his understanding of the patient's thinking. The work to build a sturdy relationship must endure the pitfalls of overwhelmingly intense emotion which comes with analytic regression. Harsh superego inhibitions and projections, negative transferences, and concrete defensive distortions attack the therapeutic alliance from within and threaten analytic treatment, especially in the early phases.

Clinical Material

Ms. A

The problem of genital pain came up early in Ms. A's treatment when with great difficulty she told me about ending her long term affair with a married man, just prior to her referral for analytic treatment. Their sexual interactions had been excruciatingly painful for her, as had his emotional insensitivity to this issue. Initially, Ms. A showed no awareness of the complicated psychological issues she had enacted in this relationship, nor in her body's rejection of sexual activity. In our first session Ms. A told me that "I am just like my mother in every way, a carbon copy." Her dependence on splitting was immediately evident as she then described her angry feelings about her father's leaving "us," for another woman when Ms. A was 18. It was during the divorce that Ms. A remembered being first aware of anxiety symptoms, especially "splitting" headaches. After settling into analysis she cut off all heterosexual relationships and focused her emotional energy into an intense, vaguely erotic maternal transference, but she was unable to experience any "as if" quality or think about the meaning of her feelings.

Initially I understood this primitive maternal attachment in the transference as a regressive retreat from the dangerously incestuous reenactments to which she had been drawn. However, as I became more aware of her life-long difficulty in falling and staying asleep and heard about reports of her painful early colic, I realized the extent of the infantile misattunement with mother. This was compounded by her report of early, chronic constipation and urinary tract infections, both conditions involving painful, intrusive treatment. This early history resulted in the development of a sadomasochistic character structure which I experienced in her struggles with me over various issues of control, mostly time and money, but including her efforts to avoid defecating in my office bathroom, obviously avoiding her unacceptable wishes, as well.

Early in treatment Ms. A resisted attachment, saying that she had read Brenner's book about analysis and was determined that she was not going to develop a transference where she would be needy or vulnerable. In fact, she had fantasized about being able to read enough about analysis to 'fix myself' before ever engaging with me. For this reason she had delayed following up her internist's referral to me for more than a year. When she finally embarked upon an analysis, she envisioned it as a process of intellectualized discussions without any of the messy feelings she dreaded.

The first year was characterized by florid dream reports of incestuous sex, various ritualized beating scenarios, and repeated 'Nazi' dreams of macabre and deadly violence, but she was unable to connect these dreams to the transference or her inner world. It was only through my focus on her need for me to understand and accept her suffering, as well as on the small conflations of reality demonstrating her disavowal of feelings, that we were gradually able to use words to contain and explore her anxiety about her murderous, destructive wishes.

Ms. A's struggle to refuse differentiation, in terms of being unable to distinguish 'inner from outer,' can be illustrated by an incident during a period of regression in the transference when she was experiencing intense jealousy of others whom she imagined got more of my attention. One day she reported seeing me on the street, holding hands with a little boy (she has a brother, ten years younger) when, in fact, she had apparently seen me with my tall, gray-haired husband.

By the end of her terminated four times weekly 14 year analysis Ms. A no longer suffered genital pain in gynecological care or intercourse. She had not succeeded in marrying or having children, but had developed the capacity to think symbolically about her inner life where her feminine nurturing and masculine "linking" functions (Birkstead-Breen, 1996) joined to create a rich sense of her inner world. Analysis of her primitive rage in the intense negative transference had included her working through of the need to kill off her own feminine and maternal functions (Chodorow, 2003) and a prolonged grieving of the consequent losses. On the other hand her efforts to capture the power represented by her seductive, incestuous fantasies and enactments gave way to a coherent, internalized sense of her own mental capabilities.

Dr. B

Dr. B came into treatment at age 29, while still in medical training. After a failed effort at sustaining sexual intimacy in an early marriage where she experienced vaginal penetration as excruciating, tolerable only in a drugged or dissociated state, Dr. B entered professional training, maintaining emotional stability by ending her marriage and retreating psychologically from all intimate relationships. When she requested psychoanalysis, saying she hoped it would help her to have a "normal life," she felt her sexual problems were related to growing up with violent, abusive parents, a situation corroborated by the empirical evidence of her own early ego deficits and the severe psychopathology she reported in the lives of her four siblings. She suffered frequent and pervasive dissociations during early 5-day-a-week analytic work and was unable to lie down on the couch for several months, saying she 'needed to keep an eye on me.' My early work with her focused on helping her feel accepted and understood, especially in relation to the intense rage which flooded her with anxiety and triggered primitive defense mechanisms (not only dissociation, but also projection, disavowal, and splitting).

Dr. B's sense of feminine vulnerability, as manifested by painful menstrual cramps, as well as chronic genital pain, suggested conflict in her sense of primary femininity, florid castration fantasies, and penis envy, but she could not tolerate any interpretation related to these issues. She simply needed my assurance that I understood the importance to her of my understanding her suffering. Her concrete thinking was best illustrated in her certainty that she needed not only to sleep with a gun to protect herself against intruders, but also to be licensed to carry a concealed weapon at all times. Unable to distinguish between her fantasies, her physical pain, and external reality, Dr. B defended herself against attackers, despite the fact that there was no particular evidence of real world danger. Several years of analytic work were necessary before she could give up her weapon and begin to use words to express her fears about being hurt, the rage engendered by her sense of helplessness in childhood, and her anxiety about her own destructive fantasies.

Core gender identity was a particularly difficult issue for Dr. B and in the first years of analysis she reported experiences of hallucinatory body changes, tall/short, fat/thin, male/female, as well as experiences of merger with me. She reported relationships with male lovers to be traumatically painful (i.e., 'rips me apart') and with female lovers to be traumatic because they morphed into her mother and 'grossed me out.' She described hallucinatory experiences, particularly with female lovers, in which she felt that she had a penis. She preferred lesbian lovers because they did not insist on genital penetration, but she questioned whether she was "actually or defensively" homosexual. She did not attend to gynecological concerns for several years, but after extensive analytic work, she was finally able to resume gynecological care and to have relatively successful intercourse with a male partner. Anxiety about maintaining her sense of separateness (evidenced in the frequent question "Am I OK?"), her ability to take responsibility for choices, and trust in her own considerable inner resources have threatened her analytic gains, especially in her capacity for representational thinking.

Ms.C

Ms. C was referred for psychoanalysis at the age of 32 by her then-boy-friend's analyst because she was unable to have sexual intercourse with the boyfriend. Throughout adolescence Ms. C was closely guarded by her parents, over controlled and vigorously admonished to avoid sexual activity. She became sexually active in her early 20's, at which time her intense genital pain was medically diagnosed as vulvar vestibulitis. She was treated with topical creams, steroid injections, and, finally, two surgical efforts to remove inflamed tissue at the entrance to her vulva, all with minimal

261

benefit. She presented for analytic treatment with 'l'belle indifference,' submitting to a four session weekly analysis with passive compliance. It was not until the transference-countertransference enactment around my knitting that she became actively engaged with me for the first time, though still clinging to concrete thinking about her genital pain and often retreating from me when she became anxious.

During the four years of her interrupted analysis Ms. C developed more capacity for representational thinking about the psychogenic nature of her genital pain, although when she grew anxious she continued to communicate through enactments and other somatic symptoms, long after the chronic genital pain had subsided. One particularly powerful enactment in an analytic session resulted in an attack of intense, stabbing genital pain which Ms. C later associated to the feeling that I had stabbed her with information which was terribly painful, jamming it into her. Then she mused about whether instead it felt like I was trying to scrape something out of her.

The nature of her dreams changed notably during treatment, evolving from primitive expressions of dangerous aggression (dismembered body parts, blood, and terrifying danger, guns, and collisions) to more complex and symbolically laden scenarios. At the same time Ms. C's capacity to think symbolically increased, so that she was able to verbalize fantasies, thoughts, and feelings which had previously been disavowed. The intensity of Ms. C's negative transference was sometimes terrifying to her and she often turned her rage inward, as if to protect me and/or the analysis from destruction. Her projective identification was strong and my countertransferrence, especially rescue fantasies, in the work with Ms. C required constant self scrutiny.

Gradually she was able to recognize her 'poor little match girl' presentation to me as a repetition of a punishing enactment she had repeated innumerable times with the harshly critical, emotionally unavailable early mother, towards whom Ms. C felt deep hatred, as well as love. Her work to move from disavowal, splitting, projection, and introjection (i.e. as illustrated in her history of compartmentalized "secret" and perverse sexual encounters with men while maintaining a virginal social facade) to a better integrated sense of herself and others resulted in a gradual shift from self-defeating compromise formations to more assertive, self-awareness.

Ms. D

27 year old Ms. D was self referred for treatment after her fiancé ended their relationship because of her "sexual problems." Upon inquiry I learned that she found genital penetration painfully impossible because she was "so tight." Physical therapy, biofeedback, and meditation failed to improve her sexual functioning and, before pursuing the surgery recommended by her gynecologist to remove "inflamed" tissue, she decided to see if the problem might be psychological. However, she fled treatment precipitously after two months, leaving a phone message for me saying she was convinced the problems were physical and that she wished to pursue surgery. It appeared to me that her flight was triggered by my observation that she needed me to agree with her that she had an organic problem without any psychological meaning, thus to make me as helpless as she herself felt in the face of her painful disability. However, I did not have the opportunity to learn more about the obvious anxiety my observation aroused in her.

Discussion

Close process monitoring (Gray, 1990), patient-centered interpretations (Steiner, 1993), attention to conflations of reality and fantasy as illuminated by the analytic frame (Bass, 2000), and work to pull enactments into words (Chused, 1992) invited the involvement of my patients' healthy adult egos while avoiding their superegos' resistance. My attention to their desperate need to be understood, to defensive shifts and to small incongruities helped to illuminate the primitive defensive mechanisms employed to avoid dealing with anxiety provoking realities.

Gradually, in three of the four cases, the analysands began to develop awareness of their anxieties about separateness, lack of control, and gender difference, issues which had previously threatened severe narcissistic injury. Building this self-awareness and the capacity to contain it with words lead to greater tolerance for an inquiring analytic ego. Reducing their reliance on projection, disavowal, splitting and externalization as they developed higher level defenses allowed new access to the primitive fantasies, forbidden thoughts, and feelings which had found expression in the genital pain.

Until developmental repair is accomplished, a concrete patient is unable to perceive that the analyst's mind conceptualizes things differently from her own, much less to join in an alliance to learn from those differences, the essence of therapeutic action in psychoanalysis as explicated by Loewald (1960). The process of differentiation (Bass, 2000), ideally con-solidated in the anal phase and necessary to successfully move into the phallic and genital phases of development (Birkstead-Breen, 1996), is also essential to analytic progress. In my experience the patients who manifested their intense intrapsychic deficits and conflicts in a genital pain syndrome were stuck in a very resistant mode of concrete thinking,

264

rooted in preoedipal deficits in such a way as to block further emotional and sexual development.

In each of my four cases patterns of sadomasochism (with the beating fantasy as its essence) were evident, as well as the trials of omnipotent fantasies. Lax (1977) describes a masochistic syndrome in women involving internalization of a negative feminine identification (incorporating mother's devaluing attitudes in turning against the feminine self as unlovable, worthless, and inadequate) while seeking success in male identified pursuits, specifically career aspirations. Lax (1992) proposed a revision to Freud's ideas about beating fantasies, suggesting that in her experience the fantasy of being beaten by mother is far more common and is perhaps even universal in the anal phase of a girl's psychosexual development. All four of my patients reported various manifestations of beating fantasies and two of the women reported fantasies and/or dreams in which I was beating them. The beatings depicted in fantasy were administered by each parent, suggesting that gender role and object choice confusion was an additional dynamic (i.e., "My mother wore the pants in the family."). In some instances the beating by father may serve as a screen for the preoedipal phallic mother, while in others it may hide the ambivalent wish to remain a symbiotic part of the preoedipal mother. In all four of my cases projection of their envious, murderous rage accounted for the unconscious image of mother as ready to punish, even kill, them. The internalized, punishing mother formed the nucleus of the girl's superego, complicated in two of my cases by fathers who apparently openly colluded with the little girl's guilty belief that he preferred her to mother. Such conflicts contribute to splits in the superego which evolve into overt pathology, especially manifesting in inhibition or suppression of sexuality and sadomasochistic enactments in intimate relationships.

As I have indicated, each of these women had done exceptionally well in school and was professionally successful. In itself this would not necessarily signal difficulty with female gender role identity; however, each reported that she had not played with dolls as a child, nor engaged in play which signaled maternal identification. Tyson and Tyson (1990) summarizing their own and others' research (Kortenberg, 1956; McDevitt, 1975 and 1979; Parens et al, 1976;) see the wish for a baby and playing at caregiving as central to female gender identity. Typically feminine nurturing interests such as cooking, gardening, selecting clothing, home-making, and caring for pets held little interest for them, despite the fact that each paid lip service to the wish to bear children. In fact Ms. A and Ms. C both guiltily reported covert, sadistic treatment of pets and children entrusted to them for baby-sitting. Ms. C mocked 'girly-girl' things, as did Dr. B and they both felt intensely competitive with men in their work-place. Perhaps most compelling is the grief each of these women experienced during treatment as she came to realize how her primitive rage had caused her to "kill off" her own maternal functions (Chodorow, 2003).

Because the underlying psychological conflicts and defensive functions were very similar in each of these four cases, despite some differences in early history and symptom manifestation, I believe the genital pain can be conceptualized on a continuum. Of the four women of my sample, Ms. A, representing the mildest (vaginismus), experienced pain only from touching or penetration and without tissue change, at one end of the continuum; Ms. C and Ms. D , with the most severe and chronic pain which was accompanied by tissue inflammation (vulvar vestibulitis) are at the other. In the treatment of Ms. A and Dr. B pathological dependency (Coen, 1992) served as a defense against destructive primitive rage and created a difficult analytic challenge, while in Ms. Cs work the intense aggression was more actively expressed in the negative transference. I believe Ms. D fled psychological treatment because she was too anxious about what would emerge. I have understood the underlying conflicts relating to be frightening, destructive rage and intense fears to be related to differentiation in each case.

Of the four, only Dr. B presented clear, explicit memories of physical and emotional abuse in early childhood (dramatic 'memories' of painful sexual penetration by a faceless man appeared twice while she was in a deeply regressed state). Dr. B experienced genital pain which was located on the continuum between A and C, both in frequency and intensity with occasional references to x-ray evidence of her 'broken pelvis,' which she believed was evidence of some kind of early physical abuse.

Both Ms. C and Ms. D had medical diagnoses of vulvar vestibulitis based on inflammation of the tissue in the vestibule of the vulva. I will not undertake to address the literature exploring the organic processes which may contribute to such genital tissue inflammation. Current research is very much at odds on this subject, but a search on the Internet will reveal metabolic, genetic, and dietary explanations. Coen (1992) offers a more analytically based medical explanation, suggesting that anxiety-induced myoneuralgia, mediated through the autonomic nervous system and leading to regional ischemia and muscle pain, due to alterations in lactic acid metabolism and episodic tetanus, might account for the tissue inflammation.

While two of the patients were specifically referred for sexual dys-function, the complaint of chronic genital pain was central to the mood disorder for which the other two had been referred. The complex array of fantasies, thoughts, and emotions which are expressed in the symptom of chronic genital pain must await exploration until a patient can recognize that her pain means something more than she has previously been able to conceptualize or express in words. Recognition of concreteness as a primitive protective mechanism signals the need to work first on consolidating the patient's capacity for symbolic or representational thinking. Each of the women described above brought into psychoanalytic treatment a conviction that her physical pain and crippled sexuality was organic and that I would fail, just as she herself and other health care providers had already failed.

Conventional work in the transference is particularly difficult with patients whose development has gotten stuck in a metaphoric traffic jam of issues which converge in the anal phase of preoedipal development. Their character structure, by definition, resists help and their difficulty of thinking symbolically makes analytic interpretations meaningless. Early in treatment it is necessary to avoid symbolic interpretations linking the physical symptoms with repressed early fantasies, thoughts, and feelings, drawing instead on Freud's insights late in his career about the possibility of defenses against recognition of gender difference which result in concreteness and its supporting defenses. Careful work in the minefield of transference, especially as unacceptable thoughts and feelings are introduced in analytic enactments, is useful to develop the patient's higher level defenses. Strengthening her ability to use words and to think representationally will increase her capacity to contain the anxieties and conflicts related to sexual differentiation, gender concerns, and relationship in the therapeutic alliance. In conclusion, chronic genital pain and the attendant sexual dysfunction are concrete expressions of difficulties in early psychosocial development which have resulted, among other things, in the disruption of representational thinking and the need to express emotions, thoughts and fantasies concretely.

References

Bass, A. (1997) The problem of "concreteness." *Psychoanalytic Quarterly*, 66:642–82.

Bass, A. (2000). Difference and Disavowal: *The Trauma of Eros*, Stanford, CA: Stanford University Press.

Bernstein, D. (1990) Female genital anxieties, conflicts and typical mastery modes. *International Journal of Psycho-Analysis*, 71:151–165.

Bion, W. (1959) A theory of thinking. In *Second Thoughts*. London: Heinemann Press (1967).

Birkstead-Breen, D. (1996) Phallus, penis and mental space. *International Journal of Psycho-Analysis*, 77:649–657.

Britton, R. (1989) The missing link. In *The Oedipus Complex Today*. London: Karnac Press.

Chasseuguet-Smirgel, J.(English translation 1970) *Female Sexuality*. London: Karnac Books.

Chodorow, N. (2003). "Too late." *Journal of the American Psychoanalytic Association*. 51/4:181–199.

Chused, J. (1991). The evocative power of enactments. *Journal of the American Psychoanalytic Association*, 39:615–639.

Coen, S. (2003) *The Misuse of Persons: Analyzing Pathological Dependency*. Hillsdale, NJ: The Analytic Press.

Fonagy, P. (1991) Thinking about thinking. International *Journal of Psycho-Analysis*, 72: 639–656.

Fonagy, P., et al (1993) The roles of mental representations and mental process in therapeutic action. *The Psychoanalytic Study of the Child*, 48–64.

Freud, S. (1905). Three essays on the theory of sexuality. *Standard Edition* 7:123–243.

Freud, S. (1927). Fetishism. *Standard Edition* 21:152–159.

Gilmore, K. (1998) Cloacal anxiety in female development. *J. Amer. Psychoanal. Assn.* 46/2:443–470.

Gray, P. (1990) The nature of therapeutic action in psychoanalysis. *J. Amer. Psychoanal. Assn.* 38: 1083–1096.

Harlow, B.L., Stewart, E.G. (2003) A population-based assessment of chronic unexplained vulvar pain: have we underestimated the presence of vulvadynia? *Journal of the American Medical Women's Association*, 58, (2): 82–88.

Jones, E. (1927) The early development of female sexuality. *International Journal of Psycho-Analysis*, 8:459–472.

Kestenberg, J (1956). On the development of maternal feelings in early childhood. *The Psychoanalytic Study of the Child*, 11: 257–291.

Lax, R. (1977) The role of externalization in the development of certain aspects of female masochism. *International Journal of Psycho-Analysis*, 58:289–300.

Lax, R. (1992) A variation on Freud's theme in "A Child is Being Beaten"- mother's role: some implications for superego development in women. *Journal of the American Psychoanalytic Association*, 40:455–473.

Loewald, H. (1980) *Papers on Psychoanalysis*. New Haven, CT: Yale University Press.

Mayer, E. (1995) Toward female gender identity. *Journal of the American Psychoanalytic Association*, 43 #1: 17–38.

McDevitt, J. (1975). Separation and object constancy. *Journal of the American Psychoanalytic Association.* 23: 713–743.

McDevitt, J. (1979). The role of internalization in the development of object relations during the separation-individuation phase. *Journal of the American Psychoanalytic Association.* 27: 327–343.

McDougall, J. (1988) Identification, neoneeds, and neosenialities. *International Journal of Psycho-Analysis*, 67: 19–30.

McLaughlin, J. And Johan, M. (1992) Enactments in psychoanalysis. *Journal of the American Psychoanalytic Association*, 40:827–841.

Novick, J. And Novick, K. (1996) *Fearful Symmetry: The Development and Treatment of Sadomasochism*. Northvale, NJ: Jason Aronson, Inc..

Novick, J. and Novick, K. (1998) The alliance and sadomasochism. *Journal of the American Psychoanalytic Association*, 46: #3, 813–847.

Parens, H.; Pollack, L.: Stern, J; and Kramer, L. (1976). On the girl's entry into the Oedipus complex. *Journal of the American Psychoanalytic Association*. 24: 79–107.

Richards, A.K. (1992) The influence of sphincter control and genital sensation on body image and gender identity in women. *The Psychoanalytic Quarterly*, 61:331–349.

Richards, A.K. (1996) Primary femininity and female genital anxiety. *Journal of the American Psychoanalytic Association*.. 44, Supplement, 261–281.

Segal, H. (1957) *Notes on symbol formation. International Journal of Psycho-Analysis*, 38: 391–7.

Steiner, J. (1993) *Psychic Retreats*. New York: Routledge.

Torok, M. (1970) *The significance of penis envy in women. In Female Sexuality*, Ed. *Chasseguet-Smirgel*, J. London: Karnac Books.

Tyson, P. & Tyson, R. (1990) *Psychoanalytic Theories of Development*. New Haven: Yale University Press.

Fear and Loathing on the Couch: The Intersection of Managed Care and Masochism

by Michael L. Krass

The use of managed care insurance benefits to supplement the fee for treatment typically results in breaks in the analytic frame (Langs, 1982) and challenges to maintaining the analytic attitude (Schafer, 1993). Interestingly, despite the large numbers of patients who use their managed mental health care benefits to supplement payment of their fee for psychoanalytically-oriented therapies, very little has been written about the specific ways that such a change in the frame influences the patient, their transference to the analyst and the progress of treatment. The bulk of the focus has been upon whether or not psychoanalytic treatment under such conditions is even feasible, whether it can be considered counter-therapeutic, particularly for certain diagnostic types, such as borderline personality structure (e.g., Gabbard, 1997) and can even be called psycho-analytic (Cummings, 1999; Gray, 1973; Langs, 1982). Langs, for example, makes an emphatic case against the use of third-party payments to supplement the fee, saying that it irreparably compromises the sense of safety that the frame seeks to facilitate in the treatment.

The fear and loathing of the title of this talk refers, in part, to affects and fantasies encountered in relation to managed care insurance companies by both patients and analysts. That is, significant transference and countertransference difficulties are encountered when managed care insurance benefits are involved. Much of the attention that has been given to this issue has been upon the particular challenges such a change in the frame presents in the countertransference with particular attention to the greater likelihood of countertransference enactments (e.g., Edwards, 1997), such as the risks of overidentifying with the patient as a helpless of abuse at the hands of a greedy, envious and unfeeling parent. Less attention has been paid to identifying the variety of ways that the press of reality on the treatment can influence the transference. This paper has as its aim to identify and better understand some of the deleterious effects that this "reality problem" can have on the transference and its availability to interpretation. That is, the feelings and fantasies related to the transference can become quite difficult to bring in to the treatment under such conditions. In addition, this paper will explore the ways that such a transference problem might or might not be able to be mitigated by modifications in technique. I will use a case illustration to clarify the ways that the involvement of managed care insurance might affect the treatment of a patient with masochistic character. Particularly, how using managed care insurance, a variable originating outside the treatment and pushing against and even through the frame of treatment, can engage and exacerbate the patient's masochism. This case will show the ways that the use of managed care insurance resulted in the patient devaluing the analyst. The patient saw the analyst to be as defenseless in the face of sadistic attack as the patient felt herself to be.

The consensus is that managed care makes psychoanalysis difficult—and, as noted, some would say impossible. The outcome of the case that will be presented here suggests that it is manageable [no pun intended] and possible to do. However, there are certain situations and certain conditions relating to who the patient is and what the insurance company does that can make such a treatment exceedingly difficult - to the point that most patients would simply give up. The use of managed care health insurance to supplement the fee for treatment can have a depleting effect on the transference. This effect, in turn, can have serious consequences with respect to the efficacy of the treatment and the patient's sense of hopefulness about themselves and their treatment. Specifically, the active involvement of managed health care insurance in the treatment can result in a significant increase in defenses against experiencing transference feelings of all types in the treatment. Particularly, transference feelings and their related fantasies and conflicts are more likely to be displaced onto the insurance company and those who work for it. (Miller, personal communication). This limits the "as if" quality of the transference to the extent that the patient (and, at times, the analyst) is pulled to express him/herself by way of enactments (Jacobs, 1986) or "enacted symbols" (Steingart, 1995) rather than symbolic language. Enacted symbols, as defined by Steingart, entail "the expression, either consciously or dynamically unconsciously, of a symbolic vehicle that incorporates an urge for action of one sort or another in the psychoanalytic relationship" (p. 135). Such enacted symbols can be seen as, essentially, non-adaptive compromise formations (Brenner, 1982) that are likely** to be difficult to work with in an interpretive way, requiring extra care and attention to discern the symbolic underpinnings and to communicate such meanings back to the patient in a way that can be workable analytically. Needless to say, counter-transference challenges in such situations can be enormous. They can require a great deal of monitoring to keep from, themselves, resulting in the analyst expressing his or herself through enactments or enacted symbols that could then lead to impasse and even premature termination.

Several types of fantasies and feelings that can be evoked when managed care oversight of a treatment takes place. Halpert (1972), for example, has described common fantasies accompanying the decision to use insurance benefits including "the need for control as well as protection against castration and the depletion of body contents." As Halpert points out, insurance is defined as the "protection of loss" (1986, p. 170) and defensive fantasies of using insurance benefits to deflect any variety of calamities are likely to be activated. The patient's decision to use his/her health insurance to pay for part of their psychotherapy fee is also often a way to use reality as a defense. For example, it can be used as a defense against the prohibited wish that the therapeutic relationship might come to resemble the heated exclusivity of an Oedipal relationship. Patients are often afraid that, if it's just the two of us, it's going to be too exciting and too dangerous. The patient can sometimes make use of the inclusion of a "third party" to cool things off in the transference (Miller & Twomey, 2000).

The involvement of an insurance company in the treatment is also often used in the service of a defense against aspects of transference hate that typically arise in relation to payment of the fee. The patient may hope to fend off feelings of resentment, envy, and even persecutory fantasies related to that which the patient is sacrificing and the clinician getting. These can include the belief that the clinician is seeking to exploit the patient for financial gain, a fantasy that emanates from the projection of infantile wishes at all three levels of psychosexual development. Oral-level projections might include the cannibalistic wish to devour the analyst. Anal-level projections might entail the wish to greedily withhold supplies and resources from the analyst. Projections of genital-level fantasies and wishes might include the wish to be more powerful or more generative than the analyst. One can imagine, for example, that the Rat Man's dream of Freud's daughter where in the place of her eyes are pieces of dung (Freud, 1909), would have been much more disguised, if not entirely unremembered had this expression of highly sexualized feelings about money in the transference not been facilitated by his paying a fee directly to his analyst. MORE Had there been an outside payor and decision-maker, these powerful anally-tinged Oedipal feelings of love for, competition with and envy of Freud might not have been expressed in such a clear and poignant manner. When managed care insurance benefits are used, these aspects of the transference may be blunted and more difficult to observe and interpret in the treatment. Thus the chance that the patient will come into contact with the instinctual wishes that form the basis for these projections can be reduced. More that is unconscious is likely to remain so.

Several authors have written specifically about the limiting effect on the transference and the free expression of feelings and fantasies of all types that the involvement of managed care in treatment can have. Alperin (1997) has written about the increasingly common situation where it is contractually required that the insurance company send supplemental payments for fees directly to the clinician. He writes that, in this kind of set up, "the therapeutic dyad is deprived of an excellent opportunity to examine certain conflicts within the relationship" (p. 187). The potential for the insurance company to refuse to authorize continued treatment (thus continued payment of supplements to fees) also can inhibit patients in their being able to freely say whatever comes to mind. As Edwards (1997) writes, such an issue can serve "as an ongoing distraction, interfering with the expression of the patient's endogenously determined thoughts and thereby diminishing the opportunity to gain access to the workings of the patient's mind" (p. 200). There is general consensus that the use of managed care in analysis creates an array of obstacles to the deepening of the transference. Consequently, it may impede the development of a transference neurosis in a way that is available for analytic study.

In the case that follows, a patient in analysis who had decided to use her managed care insurance benefits to supplement all four of her sessions per week was faced with a series of unfavorable decisions regarding the authorization of continued treatment. This reality problem nearly resulted in a premature termination. The impact that this had on interfering with the patient's willingness and ability to focus genuinely loving and hating feelings on me will be discussed.

Case Illustration

Ms. M is an intelligent and articulate 59-year-old divorcee with twin adult sons who lives alone and is employed in a highly secure and utterly drab job with a government contractor. She has twin adult sons with whom she has overly close and, at times enmeshed, yet generally good relationships. Before her marriage, from her late teenage years until just before she was married, she had been an alcoholic. As might be expected, those years were fraught with relationships with other addicts that were terribly destructive and characterized by a sado-masochistic emotional quality (with Ms. M. in the role of the ever-enabling recipient of pain and mistreatment), a number of abortions—one of which nearly killed her, an abandoned career as a writer and a series of dead-end and menial jobs. She is a woman who, by her own report, had been quite a beauty when she was young and, consequently, had been sought after by many potential suitors. She speaks in a breathy, hushed manner suggesting the affectation of a woman used to being seen as sexy by men, giving her a Marilyn Monroe-like coquettishness that clashes with her current appearance. Years of addiction and a hard lifestyle have taken their toll and she has the look of a woman much older than she. This hushed way of speaking also gives the impression that she is holding back or pressing down on a good deal of who she is and what she feels.

Ms. M.'s mother was a very talented writer but appears to have been quite disturbed. This patient was the object of her mother's envy and intense competition for the patient's father's attention and adoration— which he freely gave her until he stopped doing so when she was pre- pubescent and her younger sister was born. Her mother was frankly abusive, frequently slapping her on the face, at home and in public, and regularly shouting at her, calling her names. An early memory she dates at age four entails she and one of her sisters waking up early on Easter morning to joyously peel and devour their Easter eggs, only to have their mother wake up and, horrified by the mess the giggling girls had made, beat them both. In addition to her rivalry with her sisters who appeared to receive much less of their mother's ire, she was rivalrous with several pets upon whom her mother showered unconditional love. This was particularly true of a chicken who was allowed to live in the house and, consequently, as apparently chickens will do if permitted, to excrete wherever it happened to be walking. In adolescence, her mother made wild accusations about Ms. M.'s smutty intentions even though she recalls that, as a young child, her mother relished in telling her about the practice of mothers in certain African tribes who soothe their baby girls by stroking their clitorises. Her father, a middle manager at a steel mill, appears to have been a fairly benevolent though largely absent character who was seen by the patient as entirely unwilling to stand up to his wife when she would have her regular tirades and rants about Ms. M.'s flaws and misdeeds. He would also bend to his wife's will when she scolded the patient and her father for loving each other more than either loved her. He would do this by distancing himself from his adoring and adored daughter.

The patient presented for psychotherapy ostensibly because she had been diagnosed late in life with Bipolar Disorder and her prescribing psychiatrist had recommended therapy after she returned home from a visit with her mother in a highly agitated state; she had been unable to sleep regularly for several weeks and felt generally like she was "going to jump out of [her] skin." She had received my name from a list given to her by her health insurance company. By the time she had called me, it was several months past the crisis and she had recently started a relationship with a man who was already appearing to show sadistic disregard for her feelings and needs, a characteristic that only intensified in the next several years of their relationship. As the psychotherapy progressed, both in content and in frequency, and as she responded quite well to the psychoanalytic psychotherapy that I was providing, I recommended a psychoanalysis. It was also agreed that, as her insurance company offered to potentially authorize an unlimited number of sessions based upon their deeming it to meet their criteria as being "medically necessary," she elected to have all four sessions per week billed to insurance. This she decided despite the risk of eliciting an unfavorable review by doing so.

Under these less than ideal conditions, the psychoanalysis began. She responded reasonably well, despite some initial regression in response to the intensity of the transference elicited by the increased frequency of sessions and use of the couch. For example, she came to the second analytic session announcing that she had "googled" me. In addition, she, at times, protested that I was cold, uptight and mechanistic in my adherence to the session beginning and ending times. She made advances intended to make our time together more personable, mutual, friendly and exciting. She would occasionally comment on my "wonderful" tie or my "beautiful paintings," and even once, during a peak in the defensively erotized transference, she sat up and looked at me to tell me that I was "gorgeous." Despite this. she seemed to appreciate the ways in which my exclusive attention to her and her thoughts, my adherence to the frame of treatment, and my attempts to be respectful to and professional with her established me as a "new object" (Loewald, 1960) for her—even though I seemed sort of boring to her now that she wasn't looking at me.

Her masochistic character, which had been fairly well outlined in the therapy, became crystallized as an area of concern and focus in the analysis. She had internalized her mother's abusiveness and she felt guilty about the extent to which she had felt like she had been an Oedipal victor. This resulted in a compromise entailing a character organization around obsessionally-tinged masochism and oral dependence. This compromise was also supported by her identification with her mother's profound level of unhappiness and unceasing pessimism. A pathological degree of penis envy and an experience of herself as a castrated boy left her feeling inhibited in her capacity to be creative and generative. Instead of enjoying her femaleness, she felt it marked her as defective as her mother had been, in contrast to her father. She also felt that, had she been a boy, she might not have been the subject of so much of her mother's cruelty. Finally, it was proof, she felt, of her mother's power to viciously exact revenge on her for her Oedipal wishes and her competitive feelings.

Tragically, Ms. M.'s masochistic solution has led to a life of painful choices (as well as choices to not make choices) that have served to meet the demands of her powerful sense of unconscious guilt, to identify and maintain an attachment with her mother, to deny her mother's castrated state and to avoid overt competition with her. Following a negative review of the status of the "medical necessity" of her treatment, there was a significant increase in her masochism in the transference and the treatment situation. There was also a significant spike in defensiveness and resistances that seemed at times to be intractable. I wish to focus upon this aspect of the treatment here.

Two years into the analysis, Ms. M. received a rejection letter from the company that sub-contracts with her health insurance company to "manage" the "authorization" of her mental health treatment. This letter was the start of a truly Kafkaesque series of communications with the sub-contractor. This first letter stated that, as the patient had not made sufficient progress in her treatment, three more sessions would be authorized to allow for termination of the treatment. In this letter, the cause for rejection was, in part, based upon their insistence that I had not provided them with enough information to determine that continuation of treatment was justified—I had not documented in enough detail the mental health difficulties we were addressing in the treatment nor had I outlined a behaviorally measurable treatment plan. My narcissism aside, none of this information had ever been requested on the form that the company had been requiring me to use. Essentially, authorization to continue supplementing the fee was declined on the basis that I had not provided information that the insurance company had not yet requested.

The illogical—and, frankly—fairly transparent manner in which this rejection of payment was pursued was also illustrated in the fact that the reviewing psychiatrist's second letter—a response to an appeal the patient had prepared that included a letter from me—confirmed the sub-contractor's decision to refuse continued authorization this time with the opposite rationale: that the patient had made too much progress in the treatment I had been providing to justify continuing to authorize it.

The inconsistencies in the manner in which the insurance company proceeded to refuse continued authorization of the treatment proved to be a veritable magnet for the negative transference. This level of frank disregard for the patient's needs and for the integrity of her treatment proved to be irresistible to the displacements of transference hate, given her masochistic character and childhood history of unpredictably castrating, intrusive and narcissistic mothering.

Needless to say, the session when the patient reported receiving this initial letter from the managed care company was one filled for both of us with great anxiety and anger. Ms. M.'s initial reactions were characterized by rapid shifts between self-sufficient grandiosity and hopeless passivity that included me and the analysis as equally impotent and ineffectual. She first said that she believed she had had a "psychic dream" that had predicted getting the letter. However, she then associated to a friend of her family's as a child, a woman who seems to have been an analyst, with the same initials as me, who, Ms. M. stated, "could've helped when we were young and she didn't help." She added that she had told this family friend that she wanted her to be her mother and this evidently kind woman had explained that, regretfully, that would not be possible. She then proceeded to talk in an idealizing way about the woman, only to add that every gift she had ever given the patient had been either become broken, lost, or had been jealously kept from her by her mother. Here she was telling me about the ways in which I had disappointed her. By not protecting her from her cruel and envious mother appearing here in the form of the insurance company, she was given fresh proof that her positive transferences to me and the analysis and her experiences of me as a new object had been illusory as she felt I had disappointed her. I think she was also warning me about the power of her masochism to spoil the analysis.

She finished this very tense and upsetting (for both of us) session by associating to two classmates from elementary school. One was a boy whose mother had such contempt for him that she dressed him in girl's clothing, did not bathe him despite his being a bed-wetter and slapped him in front of his friends. This association suggested a merging of representations of both of us being rendered helpless and, as a result, humiliated by an envious and hateful mother in front of one another as we sat stewing in our own feeling of being impotently pissed off. The other was a girl who was "so pathetic and her mother so horrible that nobody ever picked on her." I feel that this was a foreshadowing of the level of masochistic surrender that would soon envelope the treatment.

In retrospect, I think my counter-transferences interfered with my making what I see now to be an obvious transference interpretation regarding the family friend and the way the patient was feeling that I had let her down. However, as clear as this transference feature is to me now, I still have doubts about whether the patient, at that moment, would have been able to make use of such an interpretation given her own heightened state of anxiety and her need to displace much of her negative transferential feelings out of the treatment in order to maintain some sense of safety. She was, understandably, frightened and feeling narcissistically vulnerable. The rejections of the authorization request aroused fears about all of the calamities (loss of object, loss of love, castration) (Brenner, 1982; Freud, 1926). As the insurance company had, by its conduct, been very effective at positioning itself to divert such feelings away from me, I was simultaneously idealized and devalued and felt to be needed in a concrete way that she was afraid would not withstand her feeling ambivalent about me.

The second session after she had received the first rejection letter from the managed care company exemplifies the way that this traumatic experience exacerbated her masochism. She had started the session describing in an unusually clear-headed and full-voiced way the steps she was already taken in order to attempt to fight this decision. She seemed energized and focused. From there, the tenor of the session shifted demonstrably. She spoke about a series of self-destructive acts and thoughts she had engaged in over the previous weekend and in her past. She had cut her hair far shorter than she had intended, as she said, she had been "hacking at it" because she had felt "manic-y" and anxious over the weekend break. She described finding herself identifying with and personalizing the insurance company's decision, saying she felt "dehumanized and attacked," that she was someone who "might as well check herself into a hospital" if she was "that sick." I called her attention to the defensive shift, at that point, saying, "Your thoughts go from thinking about fighting back to feeling hopeless. Something about the fighting back scares you." To which she responded, " What if I fight back and lose?" along with thoughts of "what if they're right?" She then described feeling regretful that, before cutting her hair, she had not remembered that "one of the symptoms when I have an anxiety attack is to attack myself." I said to this, "Your thoughts about how the insurance company is right in cutting you off has to do with how, when you have an anxiety attack, you attack yourself, the way you attack yourself here by thinking about giving up the fight."

She then associated to more masochistic and self-punitive imagery: past experiences of mutilating herself, her experience of Irritable Bowel Syndrome as being "like eating your insides up" and to receiving a colonoscopy. She followed this by exhibiting a kind of recovery that she often shows after a regression—and it always surprises me. She stated, near the end of the session, "When I'm being rational my anxiety level drops because I know they're not right. The whole premise of making decisions about paying for therapy without talking to people is wrong and hateful. Maybe part of the anxiety is also anger." She was right about this and it was significant that she was able to direct her attacks at a more appropriate foe than herself. However, her anger at and disappointment with me remained only in the displacement and out of reach of interpretation or comment.

The progress of treatment seemed to be largely maintained, with similar swings between passive spikes in masochism and recoveries involving a greater sense of self care and self-protection. However, when the second letter rejecting her appeal was received and the prospect for winning a reversal in the decision appeared unlikely, she demonstrated a much higher and more problematic level of defensiveness. Her immediate reaction was anger and outrage followed by a consequent distancing from her feelings and from treatment. This intensified in the months ahead.

She associated to being 8 years old and, in the company of the family friend mentioned before, she dissociated while her mother was "viciously angry" at her one moment and sugary sweet toward a small dog that was being walked nearby. She said, "I just disappeared and watched... I was in a tree watching me."

Staying in the displacement, I pointed out the similarity of her being angry and confused about what was happening with the insurance company and then going away in the session with how she had handled her mother's impetuousness and her own sense of injury, fear and anger. She then told me how avoiding getting angry was adaptive as a child, as it was a way to avoid her mother's wrath. She added, "There's a part of me that'd like to say 'OK, I quit, I'm not going to fight anymore.' I guess when I was a kid, I had to do that because I really believed that if I hadn't done something like that, my mother might've killed me." Experiences of Oedipal victory had evoked terrific fears of retribution at her mother's hands, fears that were only encouraged by her mother's actual violence and cruelty.

She experienced the insurance problem as similar—in reality and in fantasy—to her mother's cruelty, petulance and, especially, her vengefulness enraged and terrified Ms. M. She was enraged with and terrified of me, as well as the insurance company, but only the latter was anywhere near the surface of her consciousness. Like her mother's kind friend, I was seen as a passive and largely ineffective witness to her beatings. She dissociated to protect me and to protect herself from what she feared would be a murderous retaliation on my part. She ended the session with an early memory having highly positive affect: she is alone playing in a cardboard box. She stated rather simply: "Nobody's bothering me, I was just playing." A defensive retreat into isolation and self-sufficiency and an idealization of withdrawal were seen as the only safe route in the treatment for her at that point.

Postscript

For many months, she did become fairly disconnected from me, the treatment and herself. Countertransferentially, she became quite boring and I found myself fighting sleep in session after session. The difficulties with the insurance company had resulted in a significant degree of withdrawal and displacement of most transference feelings, fantasies and conflicts outside the treatment. This pattern of monotonal speech, decreased affect and repetitive masochistic complaints was abruptly interrupted when she announced that she was seriously considering retiring early and moving to the North Carolina coast and that she fully intended to do so within six months. She spoke about this plan excitedly and unambivalently for many months, apparently impervious to the loss she would suffer by prematurely terminating her analysis. Having divested the treatment of such a great deal of her positive and negative transferential connectedness and having presented so consistently with compromise formations that were unapproachable in the treatment, her capacity to masochistically defend against the meaningfulness and value of the treatment for her had been strengthened. What had previously been a treatment that was, at times, overbrimming with transference feelings had become a kind of empty vessel for her. The danger situation stimulated by the insurance company's rejections had evoked a severe enough degree of defensiveness that she was more completely able to deny the extent to which the treatment had mattered to her. It was looking like the treatment would end as most of her romantic relationships had or that it would be aborted as several of her babies had been, in a bewildered and resigned sense of defeat combined with massive—almost manic—denial of what was being lost until long after the relationship had ended.

This dire course was diverted in large part, I believe, because the insurance company indicated that, although it would not provide payment for half a year's worth of treatment, it would pay for some of it each subsequent year. This was experienced as a success by the patient and was greeted with great relief. I feel that this resulted in a number of shifts in her feelings, particularly about me: she felt less conscious and unconscious guilt about my not getting paid sufficiently, an amelioration of her sense of me as being like her as a masochistic victim of her mother/insurance company's sadistic attacks, and a reduction of her rage at me for allowing her to be beaten (in both senses of the word) by her mother/insurance company.

Feeling safer and less intruded upon, she became less inclined to defend against the transference feelings and fantasies that are so necessary for an analysis to unfold and deepen and, basically, come to life. She became, as a result, more receptive to some technical changes, when I shifted from the analytic attitude of being non-directive to a more educative and directive approach. Specifically, I utilized any opportunity of her wondering about her pattern of masochistic behavior to highlight for her my sense that there were still quite a number of tasks to complete on her analytic to-do list (Miller, personal communication). In doing so, I tried to clarify the potential for her to achieve significant and defined gains from remaining in her analysis rather than fleeing to an idealized image of freedom and unending warmth. She had been able to deny much of her feeling for and about me as a transference figure. As a result, I saw fit to speak to her more practical side and engage her intellectual defenses and capacities. I also think that, in the sense that Loewald talks about the function of the analyst as being a "new object" as he/she goes about the non-interpreting parts of being an analyst (1960), I implicitly conveyed to her my having remained emotionally connected to and involved with her and her treatment.

Conclusion

With this case of a woman in analysis using managed care health benefits to supplement the fee for the analysis where a managed care company suddenly discontinued authorizing (payment of) the sessions, I have intended to document some of the effects that the use of such insurance benefits can have on a number of aspects of the treatment. Specifically, the way such a reality problem can result in an increase in displacement of the negative transference away from the analyst and onto the insurance company. As was shown, this had occurred to such a great extent that the patient was nearly able to fully deny the value of the treatment for her and the depth of her transference to me. Only by engaging her intellectual and practical resources—coupled by a somewhat favorable decision made by the insurance company—were we able to avert a premature termination. In addition, in this case of a patient with a primarily masochistic character structure and a history of sadistic and unpredictable mothering, the decision made by the insurance company detracted from her capacity to view the analyst as a potentially "new object." I was seen as being just as helpless in the face of sadistic attack she had long seen herself to be. In a sense, I was forced, by virtue of the ways that she understood what the insurance company did, into an enactment of her masochism in relation to her sadistic objects.***

A managed care-type approach to providing insurance benefits for mental health treatment appears to be here to stay, in one form or another. It is not an ideal way to conduct a psychoanalysis. On the other hand, many middle class patients such as Ms. M. would be unable to afford analysis without it. Accounting for the variety of ways that it can affect a treatment may be helpful in better weathering the storms that can blow in when a patient chooses to use such managed care benefits. [At a time when psychoanalysis is struggling with its image as an elitist luxury rather than the treatment of choice for a considerable majority of patients, a systematic study of this topic is in order in order to attempt to mitigate the damage that can be done when such a "third party" is involved.]

References

Alperin, R. M. (1997). Is psychoanalytically oriented psychotherapy compatible with managed care? In Alperin, R. M. & Phillips, D. G. (Eds.) *The impact of managed care on the practice of psychotherapy: innovation, implementation and controversy.* New York: Bruner Mazel.

Brenner, C. (1982). *The mind in conflict.* Connecticut: International Universities Press.

Cummings, R. R. (1999). Psychoanalysis under managed care: The loss of analytic freedom. In Kaley, H., Eagle, M. N. & Wolitzky, D. L. (Eds.) *Psychoanalytic therapy as health care: Effectiveness and economics in the 21st century.* Hillsdale, NJ: The Analytic Press.

Edward, Joyce. (1997). The impact of managed care on the psychoanalytic psychotherapeutic process. In Alperin, R. M. & Phillips, D. G. (Eds.) *The impact of managed care on the practice of psychotherapy: innovation, implementation and controversy.* New York: Bruner Mazel.

Freud, S. (1909) Notes upon a case of obsessional neurosis. *Standard Edition*, 10:155–318. London: Hogarth Press.

Freud, S. (1926). Inhibitions, symptoms and anxiety. *Standard Edition*, 20: 75–174.

Gabbard, G. O. (1997). Borderline personality disorder and rational managed care policy. *Psychoanalytic Inquiry.* Supplement: 17–28.

Gabbard, G. O., Takahashi, T., Davidson, J., Bauman-Bork, M. & Ensroth, K. (1991), A psychodynamic perspective on the clinical impact of review. *American Journal of Psychiatry*, 148:318–323.

Gray, S. H. (1973). Does insurance affect psychoanalytic practice? *Bulletin of the Philadelphia Association of Psychoanalysis*, 21: 101–110.

Halpert, E. (1986). The meanings and effects of insurance in psychotherapy and psychoanalysis. In Krueger, D. W. (Ed.) *The last taboo: money as symbol and reality in psychotherapy and psychoanalysis*. New York: Bruner Mazel.

Kernberg, O. (1985) *Borderline conditions and pathological narcissism*, Northvale, NJ: Jason Aaronson.

Langs, R. (1982). *Psychotherapy: A basic text*. New York: Jason Aaronson.

Loewald, H. W. (1960). On the therapeutic action of psycho-analysis. *International Journal of Psychoanalysis*, 41: 16–33.

McWilliams, N. (1994). *Psychoanalytic Diagnosis: Understanding personality structure in the clinical process*, New York: Guilford Press.

Miller, L. & Twomey, J. E. (2000). Incoherence incognito. *Contemporary Psychoanalysis*, 36-427-456.

Schafer, R. (1983). *The analytic attitude*. New York: Basic Books.

Steingart, I. (1995) *A thing apart: Love and reality in the therapeutic relationship*. Northvale, NJ: Jason Aaronson.

Culture Shock: A Factor in Dissociative Identity Disorder

by Molly M. Jones

The author proposes that 'culture shock' with a traumatic level of emotional intensity and significant losses can force or contribute to identity fragmentation. The thirty year follow up of the treatment of an Alaskan native woman, diagnosed with Multiple Personality Disorder, suggests that her positive and lasting response to intensive treatment is rooted in her strong early attachments. Two additional case summaries with more equivocal results also emphasize the central role of cultural changes in creating intense stressors leading to fragmentation. In conclusion the author argues that prognosis for treatment of severe identity disorders is directly related not only to early psychosocial and neurobiological issues, but also to innate resources and an intense drive toward health.

Culture Shock: A Factor in Dissociative Identity Disorder

Challenging the prevailing assumption that Dissociative Identity Disorder (DID) by definition is caused by parental neglect and abuse in the earliest years of childhood, I propose that this condition can also result from other trauma. These could include the violent assault of one culture upon another, causing an individual psychic structure to shatter, giving way to the most primitive of anxieties and coping mechanisms. Kuhn showed (1962) how scientific paradigms coalesce around data, stabilize for a discreet period of time, then begin to erode in the face of data that do not fit the paradigm. We are presently in a period of realignment in our thinking about dissociation in general, and specifically the causes, treatment, and prognosis for Dissociative Identity Disorder. My thinking about these changes during the span of my 35-year clinical career has been spurred by my recent contact with a former patient; she is a survivor of some radical US government policies in the mid 20 century, a woman the who provided my first encounter with what was at the time called Multiple Personality Disorder.

Over the years it has been my privilege to work with a score of other patients from a wide variety of circumstances who have also relied upon dissociation as a necessary and useful coping mechanism. I will briefly describe my work with that first DID patient and our follow-up conversations 30 years later. I will then speculate about some of the reasons why she was apparently able to use psychotherapy, itself totally alien to her cultural background, to great and lasting benefit. By contrast, I will describe more recent work with two other DID patients in whose lives cultural clashes were contributory, if not causal, to the stress that forced their dissociative adaptations. Of course, the variables in each case are innumerable, but I argue our mental health community has given short shrift to the social or environmental contributions to the stress that may force an individual into rigidly compartmentalized and disorganized self states.

In conclusion, I propose that we augment the linear, even epigenetic, concepts of human development in which many of us were trained to embrace a nuanced possibility: that in earliest childhood all children experience a variety of self states as a part of normal development. Ideally they will develop the capacity to hold conscious awareness of these different aspects of themselves within an over-all cohesive sense that becomes a unified sense of "me."(Bromberg, 2010) However, if we focus on self state shifts rather than on specific content, we may recognize in patients with a variety of diagnoses the moments when their cohesive sense of "me" gives way to raw and unsymbolized emotion, which has been protectively banished from conscious awareness.

Clinical Report Illustrating the Impact of Culture Shock

Paradoxically, challenging cases of Dissociative Identity Disorder usually appear in police stations, hospital emergency rooms, community mental health centers, and university counseling offices that are often staffed by young mental health practitioners. In my experience, they are ill equipped by their training to deal with severe dissociative cases. A busy hospital outpatient mental health clinic was not an ideal analytic environment and, for me, issues of the 'frame' related to fee were irrelevant because all service was free of charge. My office was a tiny room with a desk, office chair, and one recliner. The patient I shall describe intuitively chose to lie prone, facing into the corner and away from me. Bach (2008) in his discussion of 'the unclassical patient' provides a particularly poetic and compelling picture of the condition in which I found Ida, a 19-year-old, beautiful, petite, and apparently psychotic, Yupik/Inupiat Indian woman. "These patients have lost their trust not only in their caretakers, spouses, friends and others, but also in the environment itself as a place of expectable and manageable contingencies. Thus at times such patients may live in a world of inner chaos, subjected to unpredictable expansions or contractions, explosions and fragmentation; hurtling through space at one moment, being smashed against obstacles at another; always in terror of collapsing, of losing their orientation or losing the connection to their bodies, or of falling endlessly into a black hole." (Bach, unpublished manuscript)

When I met Ida she was flagrantly dissociated, lost in a dark chasm between her traditional parental home and the white culture. It had been forced upon her when she was taken at the age of 5, along with the other village children ages 5–18, to a Bureau of Indian Affairs sponsored boarding school far away from her native Alaskan fishing village. (This government policy created a form of cultural genocide in three generations of Native Americans before it was brought to a halt.) The local police brought a drunk and disorderly Ida, cuffed, gagged, and still violently resisting, into the emergency room about 2 AM one Saturday night. The contents of her purse included $2.11, the stub of an airline ticket from Anchorage to Seattle to Albuquerque, and her Indian Health Service ID card. She was given a big shot of thorazine and admitted to the women's ward to 'sleep it off.' A crude sign printed on the back of scrap paper in large block letters was pinned to the curtain drawn around Ida's bed when I arrived the next morning: DANGEROUS PATIENT! DO NOT DISTURB. When I pushed aside the curtain I was startled to see a tiny figure under the sheet, long black hair strewn across the pillow and a face with perfect features looking anything but dangerous as she slept. Peering at her face more closely, I realized she was feigning sleep, so I pulled up a straight backed plastic chair beside the bed. Sure enough, she was curious and peeked at me through slitted lids. When I introduced myself she shouted in a very big voice,

"Get out! Can't you read?!"

"You must have written that sign. Can you tell me why you're so dangerous, Ida?"

296

"What are you ... stupid? Back off! I'll fight with anybody who messes with me! I'm a hellcat! Leave me alone. I need to sleep."

Her bellicose voice was deep and authoritative, in startling contrast to the child-like figure and sweet face.

Summoning my calmest, firm voice I said, "OK. How long do you need? Tell me when to come back."

Taken aback, Ida slowly sat up and looked around in confusion, disoriented by her surroundings. In a startlingly different, soft voice she said, "I feel awful. Please get me some aspirin and let me sleep until... .two more hours?"

And so began an intensive, five-session-a-week treatment, a daunting experience that lasted for two years. Despite what I believed was good graduate school clinical training, I had learned little about the dissociative process I observed in Ida from the very beginning. My confusion and self-doubt was off-set by a clinical supervisor, an old and seasoned classical analyst, who saw Ida as simply a severe neurotic, eminently treatable with conventional psychoanalytic technique at a time when others were caught up in the high drama of 'integrating alters' in cases of Multiple Personality Disorder. My supervisor encouraged me to be to be open, curious, and patient, focusing primarily on helping my patient to find words for her feelings (Vaughan, 1997). It was fortunate for all of us that resources were available for me to see Ida daily; perhaps this structure was fundamental to the success of our work because it provided a consistent external framework at a time when Ida had few internal resources to draw on.

In any case, language was important from the beginning because Ida often spoke in Yupik. As I struggled to remember the words of Ida's 'mother tongue' and she, to learn mine, perhaps we were repairing some of the damage done by the punishing razor strap at the boarding school when she spoke Yupik. In the first few months of our work there were frequent and dramatic changes in her ego or self states during the sessions, as Ida's voice, face, and body conveyed the emotional roller coaster of the self states which contained her intense fear, shame, and rage. Her changes in self state sometimes looked very much like seizures with rigid and jerky posture, trembling, bizarre distortions of facial expression and voice, often accompanied by her complaint of a headache.

As we worked together it was clear to me that Ida was reenacting her chaotic inner world—disorganized and confusing to both of us—as she drew emotionally close, then screamed abuse at me. I sat with her as she revisited the horrors of abuses she had endured. I slowly pieced together the history of her family and her village. They were a nomadic cooperative group of hunter/gatherers who moved from one fishing camp to another in summer, the women and children settling into one community when the cold weather settled in, while the men hunted and brought their kill for the women and children to process. These early attachment figures with their nurturing, permissive child rearing practices offered a stark contrast to the rule-bound, harsh environment at the government boarding school. Although by white standards she had left an impoverished and dysfunctional community, for Ida it represented an orderly life organized around 'the hunt.' Whether in the netting of salmon, the hunting and curing of caribou, or the search for arctic tern eggs and berries, every child and adult had meaningful work.

Despite my intuitive effort to track her emotionally without theoretical baggage, I had been trained to think in terms of Erikson's early developmental tasks. I gathered evidence, bit by bit, of Ida's basic sense of trust and her solid sense of initiative and autonomy. Those had apparently been shattered, but I came to believe that she had successfully negotiated those early developmental challenges in her first relationships to caregivers and community. Testifying to her sense of great advantage, "We never went hungry and we were happy. A lot of kids came to that boarding school from homes where everyone was addicted to drugs and booze. Not me."

At the boarding school Ida's early resistance became increasingly aggressive as she grew stronger and angrier, resulting in more severe punishments. Finally at the age of 12, when three fingers on her left hand were cut off as she tried to resist the closing door of a detention cell, she was transferred to the state mental hospital where she stayed for two years. There she reported being sexually abused by an attendant on a regular basis, and she became pregnant at age 14. She was then sent to a 'home' for unwed mothers run by nuns near Seattle; her baby girl was placed with a family who were soon moving to New Mexico, and she was returned to the original boarding school to finish high school. It was shortly after her graduation that, working as a prostitute in Anchorage, she got the money to fly to New Mexico in hopes of finding her daughter. A day after her arrival there she was brought into the emergency room by the police. Fortunately, Ida had good basic skills and considerable artistic talent, so she found support and success at the Institute for American Indian Arts in Santa Fe. There she lived and built a community to supplement her work with me. When I left Santa Fe two years after beginning treatment with Ida, she was no longer regularly dissociating, had established a circle of reliable friends, and was very productively engaged in her education, intent on earning a B.A. in psychology at a nearby college, as well as her B.F.A. I heard from her occasionally, including one indignant letter after she returned to Anchorage. There she had encountered a Public Health Service doctor who, upon hearing her history, decreed that she was a Multiple Personality. She was furious that he could not recognize the success of the work she had done with me. She thought he was "just a voyeur, fascinated by The Faces of Eve and trying to make me be like her." The motivation to revisit Ida's treatment came with her recent telephone call from Anchorage, saying that she was writing her life story and would like to discuss the details of her treatment more than thirty years ago. She presented herself in that and subsequent conversations as a warm, thoughtful, and articulate Yupik woman who treasures her 'mother tongue' and all it represents. She is working to develop a grammar and written representation of this heretofore oral tradition. At the same time, she is determined to write her life story in English. Ida works to build support for the growing role of the many native groups in Alaska who have used the legal system of the dominant white culture to take back their children's schools, while at the same time fighting the social and economic deterioration caused by alcohol and drugs. Ida has spoken recently with me about her own struggle with alcohol abuse, which troubled her after her return to Alaska, as did the dual diagnoses of fibromyalgia and rheumatoid arthritis that have badly crippled her. She reports that she is now completely abstinent, but on medical disability after holding several responsible administrative jobs in state government. After her father's death her mother moved from their native village to join Ida in Anchorage. "I still get mad, but I have lots of tools now. I'm not helpless, even in a wheel chair. I don't have to be crazy anymore." Unlike many of her peers, Ida had parents who had withstood the white culture's assaults relatively well. Her mother's village escaped the 'boarding school epidemic' and her father was quite successful in coping at a Catholic mission school near his home, attending through the eighth grade. They were able to provide a relatively stable environment, secure early attachment, and strong cultural values for their children. Ida's memories, although undoubtedly idealized, are of a strong, kind father, head fisherman in the village which she called by an English name 35 years ago and now calls Nunam Iqua. He encouraged her competitive spirit in hunting eggs and berries, typical tasks assigned the youngest children. And her warm and humorous mother patiently taught her children to process fish and meat, as well as to preserve hides to make clothing. Among the horrors stored in her dissociated, split off self

300

fragments and recreated in the transference/countertransference dynamics early in analytic treatment, Ida also had vivid early childhood aspects of herself in warm relationships with the family—dogs, as well as parents and siblings. She sometimes described very poetically such things as the various sounds of the tin runners of the family dogsled, sound quality determined by the types of snow.

Unfortunately, my treatment of Ida was interrupted at the end of two years. Our work was far from finished and she did not have on-going access to analytically- informed treatment. I believe her continuing difficulty with rheumatoid arthritis and fibromyalgia were significantly affected by the boarding school and mental hospital traumas (Krystal, 1988). Although her early attachments were secure, these were cut off before the consolidations of the genital/Oedipal phases of her development, and she later suffered painful abuse at the hands of many men. Ida has had on-going difficulty establishing a mature, loving adult sexual relationship. She has apparently functioned in intimate relationships primarily at a preoedipal psychosocial level, as evidenced by her struggle against the misuse of alcohol and dependent, child-like relationships with men. Two Additional Cases Illustrating Versions of Culture Shock In contrast to Ida's dramatic story of 'culture shock,' I will briefly describe two other DID treatments which occurred in my private practice in Washington, DC in recent years. Here situations in which cultural clashes engendered by race, education, and socio/economic factors have exacerbated the automatically triggered dissociative processes which had been developed early in life. Although I have treated several other severely dissociative patients as well, the outcome of their treatment has not been particularly successful. I believe this was because their natural resources and early attachment experiences offered too little with which to build trust, ego strength, and object constancy.

I met Tina, a 24-year-old beginning medical school student, when I replaced a colleague as co-therapist in a long-term weekly psychotherapy group of eight people who had been meeting together for several years. Of course the group members resisted my entry into their group, seeming to view me as "the wicked step mother." In the first meeting Tina, in particular, was very hostile toward me. When I walked into the second group meeting I observed Tina sitting cross-legged, running toy cars up and down the wooden arms of her chair, making loud car noises. I sat down next to her and, addressing her by name, asked about her cars. She said, "My name is Tommy and I don't like you. Go away!" Later, outside on the steps, I spoke to Tina/Tommy about how angry and sad she must be about losing Dr. P, who had been her individual therapist, as well as the group co-therapist. This conversation established a connection between us which gradually led to Tina's asking me to take over her individual treatment. (Interestingly, my co-therapist in the group said, "It never occurred to me Tina was a Multiple Personality. I've always thought of her as a borderline and just put up with her shenanigans!") Tina was fourth born into the family of impoverished, rural Virginia parents, both of whom had been severely abused as children. Split off parts of her personality bore ample evidence of the helplessness and rage resulting from both physical abuse and at least sexual over-stimulation, probably molestation. Her appealing appearance and manner, as well as her superior intellect enabled Tina to make her way successfully through the educational system, so that she earned significant scholarships for college and graduate school. However, her peer relations and responses to affectively-laden situations caused her to have poor peer relations and to feel ill at ease around others. Apparently the stresses of medical school competition and the loss of her therapist had precipitated intense feelings at the time I entered the group, creating a chaotic dysregulation of her self states. The transference/countertransference dynamics in this treatment were very stormy, often

302

confusing. There were rapid and dramatic changes in her voice and physical demeanor; it was often clear that she had no recollection the following day of an explosive session. However, our relationship somehow survived the hatred and destructiveness she enacted dramatically with me in the early years of treatment. (There was a period when she insisted that she had to carry a licensed, concealed weapon to her sessions with me because 'it's a dangerous neighborhood.") Despite the dangers in 'our neighborhood,' which I understood to be the environment we together created in the consulting room, she successfully finished her medical and specialty training, established a stable intimate relationship with an appropriate man, and now enjoys a hospital-based professional practice. The fact that she has assumed care for her widowed and crippled mother suggests to me that Tina has somehow managed to pull together significant feelings of attachment, first to her therapists, then her sexual partner, and now, finally, to her mother.

Gwen, congenitally blind and black, came to me at age 22 through the Office of Student Services at a local university. In our first interview Gwen appeared very agitated. I learned that her mother, who died of a drug overdose when Gwen was 14, had five children in rural Georgia, before Gwen was born. Gwen said she did not know her father, but had mostly grown up with Uncle John, who in fact was not her uncle, but one of her mother's boyfriends and father of her younger sister. Talking about him, Gwen's agitation increased; suddenly her back arched, her sightless eyes rolled up in her head as she threw her head back and began to moan, a scene which clearly mimicked an orgasmic experience. She was confused and disoriented, unable to reconnect with me for several minutes. Then she began to speak in a high, child-like voice about playing in the church, not wanting to cause trouble.

At the next session a very business-like Gwen discussed the medical situation that caused her blindness and created her current challenges. This pragmatic adult self state was the part of her which most often prevailed in her 'outside' life, talking about courses, readers, and exams. But during the first two years of treatment Gwen 'switched' frequently in our sessions, and I came to anticipate the topics which would trigger the dissociation. Together we were able to contain these episodes, I often speaking to her anxiety and helping her to find words for the intense feelings. She began to noticeably stabilize and maintain a cohesive presentation in the third year of her treatment. In the fifth year of treatment she graduated from a local university and was seeking employment when she was suddenly stricken by a deadly pulmonary embolism. Again, I speculate that her native intelligence and attractive physical presentation enabled Gwen to get enough of her early needs met to provide the emotional building blocks necessary to create a relatively stable identity. This allowed her to make a place for herself in the white world, an academic environment remarkably different from the chaotic, impoverished world of her childhood. And this occurred despite the dramatic roller coaster of emotions and self states in which she had primarily lived.

Research Reports on the Adult Development of Dissociation

There are reports (Lambert, 2008) of abusive treatment of minority groups by the dominant cultures all over the world, particularly the Aborigines in Australia, the Muslims in Kosovo and Chechnya, and in the tribal minorities of many African countries. One of the most compelling discussions of identity diffusion appears in the anecdotal research reports by Erikson (1946). In his treatment of traumatized veterans returning from World War II, Erikson came to realize that manifestation of identity is a life-long process, which can be severely damaged through adult trauma.

Erikson reported widespread loss in the ego's synthesizing capacity and a fracturing of an individual's sense of personal identity. In addition, Erikson noted amnesia, 'pseudologia,' and confusion related to partial loss of time- binding and spatial orientation. He used the diagnosis of 'severe identity discussion,' today manifested widely in the PTSD reported by veterans returning from wars in Iraq and Afghanistan. Soldiers there have experienced massive assaults on their assumptions about the world in which they find themselves—the capabilities and habits acquired by men as members of society.

In a well-controlled research project, Morgan et al ((2001) has reported on their study of dissociative states in general infantry and Special Forces soldiers in response to survival training, a process that involved a nineteen day period of semi-starvation, sleep deprivation, lack of control over personal hygiene, external control of the environment, social contact, and communication. The researchers used the Clinician-Administered Dissociative States Scale to assess dissociative symptoms before and after training. Findings confirmed a substantial increase in dissociative symptoms after training. Especially interesting was the fact that 'fearing for one's life' based on an interpretation of past trauma predisposed soldiers to dissociation significantly evolving from especially trying events in survival training.

Discussion

In this age of globalization, I frequently remind myself about the subtle influences of the cultures in which my patients had spent their early lives. I believe environmental, as well as intrapsychic and interpersonal childhood influences, often reappear in the transference/countertransference dynamics of the analytic treatment. Bearing cultural background in mind helps me to understand some of the challenging clashes which develop in my consulting room, particularly around issues of time and money that are usually tied to cultural values. Understanding the cultural context for these enactments shapes my responses.

I agree with Bromberg's emphasis on nonlinear dynamics in our thinking about severely dissociative patients. He raises not only technical questions about the traditional analytic focus on repression, conflict, and defense, but also takes into account the possibility of domains of dissociated experience that have weak, if any, links to the experience of 'me.' The self states created by the trauma of the ego's being overwhelmed, perhaps only in 'normal' developmental confrontations, will inevitably be reenacted in the analytic couple. These enactments create the potential for what Bromberg terms 'change moments,' when the old conditions are not repeated. Instead, the analyst feels a shift in her patient's state of mind and is able to help her develop language for the confusion, shame, and fear that comes with the loss of a cohesive sense of 'me.' The analyst acknowledges unsymbolized experience, which has been isolated away from conscious awareness.

In addition to patients who have fully developed Dissociative Identity Disorder, I have come to recognize dissociative episodes in some other patients, as well. I believe an area for further research is the incidence of dissociation in a much wider array of people than we previously thought;

thus far, only Morgan and his colleagues have found a method to study and confirm this hypothesis. Although many patients have not been exposed to overt traumas, simply the process of growing up inevitably creates moments of traumatic overload, and adults experience trauma of many kinds. Some of these individuals can benefit greatly from psychological treatment which helps them to gain access to previously unrecognized aspects of themselves.

I have no doubt that 'good enough' parenting, which leads to positive early attachment experiences, enhances a person's ability to internalize a new, healing relationship. That enables her to access and safely regulate a broader range of emotional experience. Neuroscientists confirm (Bromberg, 2003; Solms and Turnbull, 2002; Vaughan, 1997), that dissociative patterns learned early in life will remain available later as defensive tools in the face of excessive stress. Some individuals may experience the vertical splits of dissociation only infrequently. Many will never come into the health care system because they are generally high functioning, but are subject to the characterological features which produce occasional dissociations.

I propose that the time has come to 'normalize' our concept of dissociation as just one of the numerous mental processes, hypnoid in nature, which can be used in defensive maneuvers. They are pathological only as determined by the frequency, intensity, and chronicity of the dissociative episodes. Perhaps psychoanalysts and neuroscientists will work together to further our understanding of the dynamics that produce this puzzling process. This should enable us in the consulting room to recognize dissociation and assist our patients to build more effective bridges between these islands within themselves.

References

Bach, S. (2008). *Psychoanalytic technique and the unclassical patient revisited.* Unpublished paper.

Bromberg, P.M. (1994) "Speak! That I May See You!": some reflections on dissociation, reality, and psychoanalytic listening. *Psychoanalytic Dialogues*, 4:517–547.

Bromberg, P.M. Something Wicked This Way Comes: trauma, dissociation, and conflict: the space where psychoanalysis, cognitive science, and neuroscience overlap. *Psychoanalytic Psychology*, 20:5589–574.

Bromberg, P.M. (2008) Shrinking the tsunami: affect regulation, dissociation, and the shadow of the flood. *Contemporary Psychoanalysis*, 44:329–350.

Bromberg, P.M. (2010), Minding the dissociative gap. *Contemporary Psychoanalysis*, 46:19–31.

Davies, J.M. and Frawley, M.G. (1994). *Treating the Adult Survivor of Childhood Sexual Abuse: A Psychoanalytic Perspective*, New York: Basic Books.

Erikson, E.H. (1946). Ego development and historical change-clinical notes. Psychoanal. Study of the Child, 2: 359–396.

Erikson, E.H. (1950) *Childhood and Society*, New York: W.W. Norton & Co.

Erikson, E. H. (1956) The problem of ego identity. *J. Amer. Psychoanal. Assn.* 4:56–121.

Krystal, H. (1988) *Integration & Self Healing: Affect, Trauma, Alexithymia.* Hillsdale, NJ: The Analytic Press.

Kuhn, S.T. (1962) *The Structure of Scientific Revolutions.* University of Chicago Press.

Lambert, C. (2008) Trails of Tears, and Hope in *Harvard Magazine*, Cambridge. March/April 2008.

Lowenstein, R.J. and Ross, D.R. (1992). Multiple personality and psychoanalysis: an introduction. *Psychoanalytic. Inquiry.* 12: 3–48.

Meissner, W.W. (2008) The role of language in the development of the self: language acquisition. *Psychoanalytic Psychology.* 25/1:26–46.

Morgan, C., et al (2001) Symptoms of dissociation in humans experiencing acute, uncontrollable stress: a prospective investigation. *The American Journal of Psychiatry*, 158(8), 1239–1247.

Solms, M. And Turnbull, O. (2002) *The Brain and The Inner World.* New York: Other Press.

Thigpen, C.H. and Cleckley, H.M. (1957) *The Three Faces of Eve*, New York: Seeder and Warburg Publishers.

Vaughan, S.C. (1997), *The Talking Cure.* New Haven: Yale University Press.

Treating the Subject: Toward Common Ground in Psychoanalysis and Ethnography

by Christian J. Churchill

I. Introduction

F antasy is the gift of consciousness. Human beings have the expansive
capacity to project themselves into the lives of others, forward into
the future, and backward to interpret the past. Novelists, playwrights, and
poets have always toiled in this material. The social sciences, however, are
new to the scene dwelling closest to philosophy among older attempts to
grasp what it means to wonder. Within the social sciences, ethnography
and psychoanalysis stand out as two approaches to human behavior and
thought which while closely related have received little consideration as
to where they meet on both an applied and theoretical level. This paper
makes that link introducing the concept of psycho-interactionism as a
means to join psychoanalysis and symbolic interactionism, a key theoretical
approach to interpreting empirical field data in ethnographic research.

By psycho-interactionism, or psycho-interactionist ethnography, I mean an approach to field data which incorporates both an understanding of symbolic interactionism's explanation of the mechanics of everyday social behavior and psychoanalysis's identification of the unconscious mind and its conflicts as the source of human motivation. Sociologists know there are understood rules-in-use in all interactive situations (Mead 1967 [1934]; Blumer 1998 [1969]; Goffman 1959). They also know that society produces and is simultaneously a product of those rules. But what gets us beyond this apparent tautology? How can we grasp what drives one social actor to observe or ignore, obey or violate, understand or misinterpret rules-in-use as they navigate the ambiguities of everyday life? The answer is: a theory of motivation. Sociology largely lacks this. A clear sociological statement on the topic is C. Wright Mills's "Situated Actions and Vocabularies of Motive" (1963[1940]), but even there motivation is addressed as an ultimate mystery. This paper is an effort to preserve in ethnography what symbolic interactionism does so well—interpreting everyday interaction—and add to it a depth approach to social behavior using the insights psychoanalysis offers the field observer.

The word "treating" in the title of the paper is meant in two ways. From an ethnographic perspective, I use it to mean the manner in which the field researcher collects, frames, and interprets—i.e. treats—data gathered through observation of a group of people. In his or her approach to social data, the ethnographer will often try to bracket whatever desire s/he may have to help those being studied, at least for the duration of the study. Of course, circumstances may compel assistance, and research subjects can also benefit by simply going through the process of being studied. But in its ideal form, ethnography is a means to understand, not to heal.

By contrast, I use the word treat from the psychoanalytic perspective of wanting to expand the ego capacity of the patient, i.e. the subject. In Freud's words, the psychoanalyst seeks to achieve the following: "Where id was, there ego shall be. It is a work of culture..." (1986[1933], p.80). The clinician seeks to treat the subject with the objective of making his or her life better, or more bearable, by increasing the patient's self-mastery at multiple levels of consciousness. The analyst's chief goal is to attend to human suffering; a secondary goal is gathering data for research. And psychoanalysis proceeds from a theory of motivation which postulates that inner conflicts and outer behavior originate in unconscious processes.

Psychoanalysis and ethnography meet in this territory of difference. In ethnography, the term participant-observation is used to describe the manner in which the researcher occupies a liminal space between involvement and analysis. As most ethnographers explain, acquiring meaningful field data requires one's subjects know one well enough to convey crucial (often hidden) aspects of their collective lives but see one as distant enough so as to trust the researcher not to use that information for personal aims. The ethnographer must be both proximate and removed. In psychoanalysis, the equivalent term is "evenly suspended attention." That is, the psychoanalyst is listening and present, but simultaneously s/he has no personal stake in the subject's inner turmoil beyond the goal of helping the subject gain mastery. Though this indicates standing at a remove from the subject, the psychoanalyst is very much on the scene. While the clinician does not operate in the daily social spheres of the subject, because of the frequency of sessions (three to five per week) the clinician does become an active, known (and unknown) presence in the subject's consciousness (and unconsciousness). Like the ethnographer who must seem both engaged and removed from the action of the group s/he studies, the psychoanalyst can only achieve his or her professional goal if the subject senses both that s/he is attentive to the subject's fears and needs but will not be personally wounded or elated by receiving the material the subject presents to him or her.

Neither ethnographer nor psychoanalyst, of course, can achieve an exact balance of presence and distance. In a positive (though not positivistic) sense, the range of action in which practitioners in the two fields fail to achieve this ideal is where the best work can often occur. Yet only psychoanalysts have an intellectual language for this: they call it transference and counter transference. In ethnography, no generally accepted equivalent term has emerged. Rather than add a new term, the transference/counter transference dynamic seems to serve well for ethnography too. Unlike in psychoanalysis, though, in ethnography one rarely has rigorous training in how to deal with this process.

Generally, but especially with regard to key informants, we could speak of ethnographic transference as the state in which the subject perceives a relationship with the ethnographer and sees him or her as a significant other in the same group that the ethnographer is studying. Only when this tension is achieved—i.e. the ethnographer is accepted as belonging all while s/he stands apart—can meaningful data be acquired that transforms the ethnographer's perspective from that of displaced scientist to located co-perceiver of the action at hand. Notice, though, that the purpose of ethnographic transference is first understanding the field situation; transformation may occur, but it is not intentional and usually figures only secondarily into analysis of the field setting. By contrast, the fundamental purpose of transference in psychoanalysis is transformation of the patient followed secondarily by intellectual understanding. The ethnographer uses the transference from self to group to give a balanced written treatment of the subjects in the field. The psychoanalyst uses the transference, meanwhile, to provide a curative treatment of the patient on the couch.

The power of the concept of transference from the time Freud first noticed it (1986[1905]) is that in reality it happens constantly in every situation in which one person relates to another. Human beings transfer onto one another impressions and attitudes which originate in earlier experience and which are brought to the surface by others who for one reason or another prompt us to reconnect with those earlier impressions and attitudes. (Importantly, this concept emerges in psychoanalysis at the same moment in Western thought [c. 1900] that George Herbert Mead in sociology arrives at the concept of the Generalized Other, arguably a close cousin of Freud's notion of the transference object [Mead 1967(1934)].) Psychoanalysts and other mental health clinicians merely witness one of transference's most acute manifestations in handling the key personal crises their patients bring to them. But often in ethnography, subjects project onto the researcher attitudes of fear, trust, confidentiality, and so on that seem to have their origins more properly in the subject's prior life experiences.

To cope with transference, psychoanalysts themselves are required to undergo analysis as part of their training. If one is analyzed, one will know more precisely where one's own countertransferential feelings toward the patient originate. But neither sociology nor anthropology graduate programs mandate a similar mechanism by which the student would be compelled to know what it feels like to be ethnographed, for want of a better term, and thereby handle his or her subjects' data more deftly (Churchill 2005). While there may be no viable means other than rudimentary exercises to incorporate this perspective into ethnographic training prior to fieldwork, its absence may provide a clue to the ambivalence often felt by neophyte ethnographers as they approach their task.

Ethnography and psychoanalysis share a commitment to digging for interpretive meanings their subjects give to key events and objects in their lives. In both fields, discovery of the meanings the subject attributes to objects (personal and social, animate and inanimate) and of the actions and fantasies which those meanings trigger is regarded as the fulcrum upon which a treatment tilts to success or failure. Moreover, each field requires the practitioner possess the capacity to empathically inhabit the position of the subject while not being subsumed into it.

II. Common Ground

In one of the most significant theoretical influences upon contemporary ethnography, symbolic interactionism, we find hostility to psychoanalysis, especially in the work of its founder Herbert Blumer (Blumer 1998 [1969]; Manning 2005). Following Mead, Blumer argues that the sociologist is interested chiefly in how people define social objects. This idea is in keeping with Durkheim's definition of social facts (Durkheim 1982 [1895], pp. 50–9) as well as Mills's article "Situated Actions and Vocabularies of Motive" (1963 [1940]). Throughout Blumer's essay "The Methodological Position of Symbolic Interactionism" (1998 [1969], pp. 1–60), he asserts that the empirical obligation of symbolic interactionism is to come to terms with what appears before the observer's eyes rather than with unconscious drives and conflicts. Blumer claims the psychoanalytic assumption of the unconscious mind is in contradiction to the empirically rooted tenets of symbolic interactionism. Moreover, Blumer finds the emphasis in psychoanalysis upon inner dynamics to be antagonistic to the symbolic interactionist's search for the collaborative meaning-making process between social actors. For Blumer, the Freudian notion that inner dynamics are the key factor in the formation of meaning is the fatal flaw of the psychoanalytic approach:

> One should recognize what is true, namely, that the diverse array of participants occupying different positions in the network engage in their actions at those points on the basis of using given sets of meanings. A network or an institution does not

316

function automatically because of some inner dynamics or system requirements; it functions because people at different points do something, and what they do is a result of how they define the situation in which they are called on to act. (1998 [1969], p. 19) [emphasis added]

Ethnographers have given little or no attention to this dispute, even when they are influenced by both Freud and Blumer. One reads ethnographies finding much from both psychoanalysis and symbolic interactionism in their methodological and interpretive approaches but little that strives to resolve the theoretical standoff between the two approaches. In attempting to define a middle ground in this disputed territory, while we are unlikely to settle the difference, we may light a path to enhance field research.

In Kurt Wolff's essay, "Surrender and the Community Study: The Study of Loma," he argues that a key aspect of successful ethnography is to surrender one's sense of mastery (1960, p. 262), to give up the idea that one can fully understand the field setting in a completely rational manner. For Wolff, achieving the surrender of mastery allows one to more fully "catch" the meaning and content of the field situation. Wolff implies the ethnographer should develop the ability to fantasize about the field setting in much the same way social actors fantasize about the meanings of the events and objects they share in common. His method for surrendering in order to the catch these meanings is divided into five parts (1960, p. 236–40). First, one must become totally involved in the field, opening oneself to the possibility of anything happening. This total involvement, he argues, resembles the phenomenon of being in love. As between the beloved and the lover where there is a surrender and openness to all the possibilities of the other, so too in the ethnographer must there be an infinite curiosity. Wolff adds that one must suspend one's ego and not allow bias or self-consciousness to infiltrate the data gathering process.

Second, and extending the metaphor of fieldwork-as-love, the ethnographer must suspend his or her received notions, giving up prior attitudes and prejudices. While this may lead to confusion, out of that confusion patterns emerge. Third, the ethnographer sees pertinence in everything s/he finds in the field dismissing no feature or event no matter how seemingly minor or irrelevant. Fourth, the ethnographer must identify with the field setting yet also stand apart from it. While Wolff makes no reference to Mead, this concept is close to Mead's idea that within the person, the self is an object to itself, at once contained within the person and standing outside the person looking back with a critical gaze. The ethnographer is that Meadian self, subsumed in the field setting and standing outside it looking back critically. Finally, Wolff argues that in opening the self fully to the field experience, as beloved to lover, there exists the risk of being hurt—one is, after all, human and not merely a mechanical data gathering instrument.

While Wolff's model provides a humanistic and practical modality for ethnographic work, his theory mirrors the psychoanalytic approach to clinical work. The psychoanalyst is open to all possibilities in each new patient, suspends judgment, finds everything the patient says and does relevant, empathically identifies with the patient while maintaining distance, and, in his or her humanity, is at some risk for being hurt. The advantage the psychoanalyst has over the ethnographer is s/he has been analyzed and knows through that experience how to deal with the transference and counter transference dynamics raised in the consulting room. Following Wolff's model, the ethnographer should also be aware of those dynamics, must surrender the self to them, and fully enter that vortex of feeling and experience.

In reading and doing ethnography, one sees that the weakness of symbolic interactionist theory is in its reluctance to inspect and explore the affective, emotion saturated world of people and the communities they

318

inhabit. Yet no ethnographer is doing his or her job unless s/he attends to the mechanics of everyday life that symbolic interactionism so eloquently explicates. This joining place where ethnography, symbolic interactionism, and psychoanalysis meet deserves a name.

III. The Case for Psycho-Interactionism

Transferences are assumed to mediate the relationship between researcher and subjects. Symbolic interaction, traditionally viewed by sociologists in terms of its cultural and behavioral dimensions, can be interpreted as a complex exchange of unconscious fantasies. Similarly, it is possible to analyze symbolic acts of both researcher and subjects as compromise formations which embody hidden desires and defenses.... [F]ieldwork is, in part, the discovery of the self through the detour of the other. Jennifer C. Hunt (1989, p. 26, 42)

If there is any value to this [ethnographic] practice [of becoming a native] I have not discovered it. Still, it may be a stage through which novice researchers must pass—just as some adolescents get pimples and some graduate students attack the pet notions of their professors. Perhaps, illusion though it is, the conviction that a fieldworker is "in" may serve as a crutch and comfort during the initial period when he must sometimes live in an almost total social limbo. Later, when he becomes more genuinely "involved," he can dispense with illusions and accept the fact that he is and will always remain a non-native. Rosalie H. Wax (1988 [1971], p. 192)

In neither ethnography nor psychoanalysis must the practitioner become completely a resident native of the place s/he examines. As anthropologist Clifford Geertz puts it, "Ethnographic findings are not privileged, just particular: another country heard from" (1988 [1973], p. 53). Like Madame Olenska in Edith Wharton's novel The Age of Innocence, ethnographers long for a place which they know is close yet permanently distant even as they seek to speak its language, engage its customs, and thereby know the subject they seek to treat. To Newland Archer, the lover who beseeches Olenska to get away to a place where the condemnation of others who disapprove of their relationship will not torment them, she knowingly replies, " 'Oh, my dear—where is that country? Have you ever been there? ... I know so many who've tried to find it; and, believe me, they all got out by mistake at wayside stations: at places like Boulogne, or Pisa, or Monte Carlo—and it wasn't at all different from the old world they'd left, but only rather smaller and dingier and more promiscuous'" (1987 [1920], p. 290). The romantic tension between Olenska and Archer resembles the ethnographer's and psychoanalyst's need and desire to know the subject. One yearns to know Geertz's "other country heard from" better by immersion in it, but one also knows that to immerse oneself fully into that place may derail the pursuit of the Wolff's "catch." For the "catch" is a product not of full relationality but rather of bracketed connection lubricated with empathy and orchestrated by technique. Practitioners in each discipline should heed Olenska's warning. She fears her love for Archer and his for her because she knows the forces of their culture would respond to their open union by forcing them into exile. As clinicians and ethnographers, we know that total immersion in our subjects and its loss of perspective is likewise a ticket to intellectual and professional exile.

My proposed psycho-interactionist approach embraces this conflicted stance. Through it we view the subject as driven by what we can see and hear—i.e. the empirical country of consciousness we occupy together—and by what we cannot see and hear—i.e. "another country" of the unconscious mind and of the conscious thoughts not revealed. This other country extends away from the researcher and clinician like spokes from the hub of a wheel. Ethnographers and psychoanalysts follow those spokes, but like the darkness beyond the stars in an astronomer's telescope, this distance is infinite. Seeing the unknowable darkness requires we be humble in our search and toil within our limitations.

Both ethnographers and psychoanalysts speak to the anxieties of such limitations on technique and knowing. In each field, the practitioner is concerned with language and how it is simultaneously our chief means of communication yet inherently ambiguous (Churchill 2005). As Joyce McDougall explains, "Psychoanalysis as a science is centered on meaning (and in particular on the meaning of relationships); its unyielding logic is the logic of language" (1989, p. 101). McDougall makes this observation to contrast psychoanalysis with neurobiological approaches to mental illness. In sociology, we could use the same terms to contrast quantitative survey research and other hyper-positivist approaches with ethnography.

Extending the link between psychoanalysis and ethnography, Jacob Arlow compares the clinician to a participant observer:

Fundamentally, the function of the psychoanalytic situation is to further several important technical goals. Foremost among these is to ensure that what emerges into the patient's consciousness is as far as possible endogenously determined, i.e., that the thoughts, fantasies, feelings, etc., that the patient perceives represent derivatives of the persistent pressure of his unconscious conflicts. The analyst as participant-observer is in a position to study the interplay between impulse and defense, between moral pressures and aspirations, together with considerations of the realistic consequences of action.... In effect, the analyst may be viewed

321

as presiding over an operational field, observing and eventually influencing a dynamically unstable equilibrium (1979, pp. 193–4).[1]

The ethnographer also presides over an operational field developing an eye and an ear for the depth soundings of the community s/he studies. The ethnographer, like the psychoanalyst, wants to know what cannot be seen but must be satisfied to use what is offered by the subject as a clue to what might be found. This is similar to Mills's thesis in "Situated Actions and Vocabularies of Motive" that we must toil in the observed situation and in the accounts of motivation offered by our subjects in order to determine what propels them into the context where we encounter them. There is a connection here also to Freud's notion that every dream has a "navel" which, in the patient's retelling of the dream during analysis, remains obscured yet is the key to determining the origin of the content of the dream (1986 [1900], p. 111 footnote 1 & p. 525). The psychoanalytic clinician and the ethnographic observer both want to get to that hidden locale. The knowledge that it is ultimately hidden proves no barrier for searching because it is a given that the search is the thing to be found.

In George Orwell's novel 1984, the navel at the core of Winston Smith's dreams is a wall beyond which something terrible that he dreads dwells. O'Brien, Winston's tormentor, discerns through hidden observation and torture that rats, Winston's greatest fear, are what lie beyond that wall. The reader knows, however, that the rats are only significant because Winston associates them to the forces that annihilated his mother when he was a boy (1984 [1949]). As ethnographers and psychoanalysts, we ally ourselves with the reader's position vis-à-vis 1984 and look for the meaningful associations people make to the dreamlike contents of their

---

1 In writing about the "operational field," Arlow echoes Herbert Blumer's definition of symbolic interactionism.

waking states. But we reject, of course, the manipulative approach of O'Brien who only gets at the navel of the dream to force the subject into a prostrate, dependent position in the service of external power rather than inner realization.

Both Freud and Mills point to key features of a psycho-interactionist perspective: to know based on what we see and hear, to realize we cannot know more than what our subjects allude to via their actions and accounts, to seek through what we observe that which cannot be observed, and to utilize this knowing for the purpose of enhanced human understanding rather than manipulation and control. Psychoanalysis and ethnography are joined in this way as epistemologies of liberation.

The tool which allows this interpretation to happen is the mind of the observer filtering and sorting data sent to it from the mind of the observed (Churchill 2005). "The 'instrument' of the psychoanalyst is his mind, so that in the interview we investigate how the interviewee behaves with others, without losing sight of the fact that we ourselves are that other to whom that person has to relate" (Etchegoyen 1991, p. 46). In her essay "Fiction and Social Science" (1983), ethnographer Susan Krieger makes a similar point in describing how fiction and social science each seek to model the world. Similarly, psychoanalyst and patient both seek to grasp the model of the self which predominates in the patient's unconscious. In a later article, "Beyond 'Subjectivity': The Use of the Self in Social Science" (1985), Krieger plumbs more psychoanalytically germane territory arguing that in ethnography, distance between subject and observer is not fully possible or desirable and that, in embracing the frequent discomfort and destabilization which proximity brings, we may get to know the other's reality better.

We see others as we know ourselves. If the understanding of self is limited and unyielding to change, the understanding of the other is as well. If the understanding of the self is harsh, uncaring and not generous to all the possibilities for being a person, the understanding of the other will show this.... We need to link our statements about those we study with statements about ourselves, for in reality neither stands alone (1985, pp. 320–1). [emphasis added]

This is similar to what the psychoanalyst tries to confront via his or her training analysis where through understanding of one's own unconscious conflicts one may better attend to those of one's patients (Hunt 1989, pp. 57–80). Krieger offers a kind of self-interrogation for ethnographers which she calls "a case-analytic technique" (1985, pp. 312–20) to get the ethnographer to the point which training analysis gets the psychoanalytic candidate, but common to both is the paradoxical command to know thyself both before and through knowing the other.

Through Krieger, we can see psychoanalysis and ethnography as ways to grasp the subjects' fictionalized reality in order to obtain a clearer grasp of the real. Surprisingly, this same process exists at the core of Mead's and Blumer's theories. For them, the key to understanding social reality is understanding that the reality of social phenomena is entirely determined by the perceptions and then conversations about these perceptions (i.e. symbols and interactions) that occur between social actors. In other words, people are constantly writing personalized fictions of their reality based on their perceptions. A psycho-interactionist ethnographer would investigate that writing process by assuming that forces not immediately visible or audible are the driving factors behind this process. Strict symbolic interactionism, on the other hand, requires we stick to what is seen and heard rather than "inner dynamics or system requirements" (Blumer 1998 [1969] p.19). The "third ear" utilized in psychoanalysis, however, shows that what is heard is not always what is "said."

To what degree, then, if any does the diagnostic aspect of treating the subject in psychoanalysis carry over into ethnography? On one level, it is irrelevant to worry about diagnosis in the Diagnostic and Statistical Manual's (DSM) sense of the term.[2] The need for precise diagnostic terminology is an artifact of the mental health professions which have largely determined that to treat human suffering adequately, and to be compensated for it, it is necessary to have a rationalized (albeit imperfect) nosological system with which to conceptualize and name psychological complexes and symptoms. On a heuristic level, though, diagnosis is an approach which closely links psychoanalysis and ethnography. While he does not mention psychoanalysis, in the "Statement on Method" appendix to his ethnography Sidewalk, Mitchell Duneier calls his approach to the field "diagnostic ethnography":

A colleague of mine who teaches courses in the philosophy of science, Erik Olen Wright, calls my approach "diagnostic ethnography," and I agree with that characterization. I begin observation by gaining an appreciation of the "symptoms" that characterize my "patient." Once I have gained a knowledge of these symptoms, I return to the field, aided by new diagnostic tools—such as photographs—and try to "understand" these symptoms (which is an amalgam of "explain" and "interpret" and "render meaningful"). I also read in more general literature, seeking ideas that will illuminate my case (1999, p. 342).

---

2   To challenge the diagnostic paradigm of the DSM, several psychoanalytic associations created the Psychodynamic Diagnostic Manual (PDM) published in May 2006. It is possible that with the recent licensing of psychoanalysis as its own profession in several states, health insurance providers may begin accepting PDM diagnostic criteria in lieu of traditional DSM criteria. It is worth mentioning, though, that the DSM was begun by a psychiatrist who underwent Reichian psychoanalysis in his early training (Spiegel 2005).

As well as closely paralleling what the analyst does in the room with a patient, Duneier's "diagnostic ethnography" fits precisely with psycho-interactionism. The psycho-interactionist ethnographer does not stop at what s/he sees but follows the "symptoms" presented in the field as closely to their source as possible.[3] While the terminology utilized in ethnographic diagnosis cannot and should not be codified so exactly as DSM or psychoanalytic diagnoses are, the approach to identifying the problem is similar.

In his book Freud and American Sociology (2005), Philip Manning gives a far reaching and historically detailed account of the relationship between symbolic interactionism and psychoanalysis since the start of the twentieth century, long before the term "symbolic interactionism" was introduced by Blumer. Though more complete in its treatment of sociology than of psychoanalysis and lacking a full review of what Freud's structural theory offers to sociology (Fellman 2005), Manning's book provides a useful contribution to the intellectual history of the two fields. In his final chapter, Manning speaks to how and where psychoanalysis and ethnography meet. Pointing out that since 1988 certification and licensure in psychoanalysis has become available for people with graduate training outside the traditional mental health disciplines of psychiatry, psychology, and social work, Manning suggests sociologists pursue clinical training (Manning 2005, p. 131), and he uses the examples of Jeffery Prager, Nancy Chodorow, and Neil Smelser to explore this possibility.

While there is a case to be made for both anthropologists and sociologists to train as psychoanalysts, I do not think that is necessary in order for ethnographers to utilize a psycho-interactionist approach to the field. In fact, Manning conveys Prager, Chodorow, and Smelser's deep ambivalence

---

3   Duneier refers in the same essay to this process as an "extended place method" (1999, p. 345)

regarding the degree to which clinical psychoanalytic practice has helped them in their sociological work and thinking. Hunt also addresses this issue and clearly assesses the logistical, economic, and characterological reasons why sociologists may in general be hard pressed to be trained as analysts or even simply enter analytic treatment (1989, p. 83).

The tenets of the psycho-interactionist approach are simple enough for an insightful ethnographer to put to use. In fact, the main tenet is to embrace what many ethnographers have been saying and doing but not codifying for nearly a century. One must attend to the unseen and the unheard as much as to the empirically obvious if one is to treat one's subject with intellectual honesty. This paper, then, merely seeks to close the gap between symbolic interactionism and psychoanalytic theory which seems artificial on its face and which has been being bridged without being named for some time now. Rather than continuing along the lines of the antagonism expressed by the progenitors of symbolic interactionism toward psychoanalysis, ethnographers would do well to dig deeper into the natural affinities which exist between the two approaches.

IV. Implementation

Hunt's psychoanalytic model for interpreting researcher-subject inter-subjectivity in ethnography (1989, pp. 49–80) illuminates an often confusing dynamic for anyone who has spent time in the field. Her exploration of her own work in an urban police department is a lucid, witty, and instructive window onto the anxieties ethnographers often face.[4] She

---

4   She writes of herself: "That the police represented forbidden objects of sexual desire was revealed in dreams and slips of the tongue. For example, I recall one conversation with female officers concerning the professional attributes of an attractive male member of the squad. I agreed with the policewomen's assessment of their colleague and tried to say a

demonstrates how researchers can make use of those anxieties once they understand them. One of her main concerns is in determining what about a given field setting the researcher associates to his or her own background. For in determining this we may know better why we choose a field setting and, in turn, why we respond to subjects in that setting as we do. Three examples from my own field experience come to mind.

As an undergraduate in 1990 researching communes for my senior thesis in sociology, I found myself powerfully drawn to rural "hippie" and religious outposts in the northeastern US. In my several months of fieldwork for that project, I was internally drawn to and repelled by what I found. I alternately romanticized and severely critiqued the people I met. As I reflect now upon that work, the first image that comes to mind is a memory from the early 1970s of sitting at the foot of my parents' seemingly immense bookcases when I was in grade school and flipping through the pages of their Whole Earth Catalogue, a counter culture touchstone of the time. My parents then also lived an overtly "hippie" lifestyle.

In 1993, after graduating from college, I worked with my undergraduate sociology mentor on a field study of a US Job Corps center in New England. While there was much at the field setting to critique, my reflections now on the work reach further back to another mentor of mine from summer camp when I was an adolescent. This earlier mentor taught part time at a Job Corps center in upstate New York. He was intensely critical of its policies and the impact the place had on the lives of the young people who passed through its doors. This mentor died prematurely in the early 1990s of Lou Gherig's disease, a painful loss for me.

---

few words in his favor. Much to the women's amusement and my chagrin, the intended sentence 'Jim's a good cop' came out instead 'Jim's a good cock.' In those words, I revealed my sexual interest in a category of men who were forbidden as a result of their status as research subjects. In that way, they resembled incestuous objects" (1989, p. 40).

In the summer of 2000, I was one of several field interviewers for a Brandeis University project exploring the sociology of interfaith marriages in Jewish-Christian couples with children.[5] We traveled to several major US cities and interviewed many men and women in their homes and offices. The stories of these families were inspiring, amusing, and sometimes heartbreaking. This research, however, prompted associations to my past. The first is of the choir director in the Lutheran church which my family attended during much of my youth. During a rehearsal one day, the director was discussing the idea of salvation and who would be included. I asked him if my Jewish aunt would be saved. He quickly replied she would go to hell. I was horrified. My second memory is of stories my paternal grandfather told and the pictures he showed me when I was a child of the Nazi concentration camp at which he was among the Allied liberators at the close of World War II. The horror of seeing images of the emaciated people and hearing descriptions of the atrocities he saw evidence of there made a vivid impact on my mind at the time.

At nearly the same time in my youth, two other incidents shaped me. In one, my mother reacted to history lessons I was given at grade school on the Holocaust by angrily complaining to my teacher because she felt the reality of it was too gruesome for a child to bear. In the second, my mother intercepted a letter from the Aryan youth movement inviting me to join. She was furious they had tried to recruit me and made a big show of demanding the post office block any mail from them being delivered to our home again. I believe these incidents marked the start of my path to secular humanism. But they no doubt had some unconscious bearing on my choice to participate in the interfaith marriage research project and on

---

5   The result of this research is a book written by the principal investigator, Sylvia Barack Fishman, *Double or Nothing?: Jewish Families and Mixed Marriage* (Brandeis 2004).

my behavior while conducting interviews and my interpretations in writing field notes and during conferences with my fellow field investigators.

Surely there is more I could say about my associations to each of these brief examples. I provide them merely to illustrate Hunt's assertion (well supported by her with theory and data) that the researcher has significant transference experiences and opportunities to project the personal onto the subject in any field setting. My intention for psycho-interactionism is to expand this frame for inspection of all field data. That is, to move from the researcher-subject dynamic to the subject-subject dynamics which are the primary focus of ethnography. Again from Hunt but taking the idea further we want to remember that the "emphasis on consciousness and intentionality represents both the strength and weakness of the symbolic interactionist approach" (1989, p. 19).

Think now of a rudimentary example. Two people are shopping for groceries in a supermarket. They aim for the meat case. One gets there first and blocks access of the other to the food. The blocked shopper asks the blocker to move. The blocker ignores (maybe does not hear) the request. Rather than ask the blocker again, the blocked moves the blocker's cart with a slight hint of irritation. An awkward exchange of apologies accompanied by half smiles follows and the shoppers are on their way again.

The symbolic interactionist approach allows us to interpret the mechanics of this encounter by asking about the meanings typically given by these shoppers to their carts, to their right-of-way assumptions, to their definition of manners, to the social and economic context in which the store exists, to the expectations these people have of shopping at this time of day as opposed to earlier or later, and to the ethnic appearance and gender identity of each actor. All of these are useful and necessary routes of inquiry and would be sufficient for a capable, persuasive analysis. But as Erving Goffman states at the conclusion of The Presentation of Self in

Everyday Life, "here the language and mask of the stage will be dropped. Scaffolds, after all, are to build other things with, and should be erected with an eye to taking them down" (p. 254). In other words, the symbolic interactionist platforms for interpretation I list above are merely bars and bolts on the scaffolding of the supermarket interaction. Meanwhile, we could also ask what are the actors' feelings and fantasies about meat, about their weight and blood pressure, about their assumptions regarding the presumed culinary habits of each other's ethnic group, about what it means to shop for food, about whether they are shopping for themselves or a family, about the lack of appreciation of their families for their time spent shopping, or about the dream one of them had the night before which resonates with the present dilemma? Still more, in what ways if at all does each actor project these feelings and fantasies onto and into the other? When we ask these questions, we begin to see the materials from which is built the house that Goffman's symbolic interactionist scaffolding first framed.

To begin this deeper search requires a qualitative inquiry which goes beyond the shared meanings and collaboratively created definitions of social objects which Mead and Blumer address and into the origins of the subjects' affective response to these things. The ethnographer is not a psychoanalyst and will not be able to fully penetrate the depth of meaning the subject associates to and in turn acts upon in the field setting. But a psycho-interactive approach would open the door to these possibilities. Yet unlike clinical technique which must follow some standard protocols, each ethnographer is free to discover his or her own method. In fact, that process of methodological innovation and discovery is the life blood of ethnographic work. So while it is not my task here to devise a prescribed method for psycho-interactive inquiry, I am comfortable suggesting that it would make sense to include in one's approach questions as to the subject's and one's own dreams and fantasies. Once recorded, these then become the stuff of the "situated actions" and "vocabularies of motive" described by Mills (1963 [1940]).

In the psychotherapeutic setting, there are immediate routes to this work. For example, a psychotherapy patient and I had the following exchange during a session several weeks into the treatment:

Patient: I'm feeling overwhelmed. So much debt—the mortgage, food, credit cards.
Me: You're spending more than you can pay for.
Patient: Yea—you know, on lots of senseless stuff.
Me: Senseless.

By repeating the word "senseless," I invited the patient to respond to the meanings he attributed to it and, more significantly, the unconscious associations and fantasies attached to it. The session then shifted into a painful and introspective exploration of the patient's relationship with his wife, where it was going, how it started, whether it would last, and if it did not last what will happen to their children. My technique in the therapeutic setting is to listen for indications of meaning in word choice, tone of voice, and physical posture and to utilize those to prompt the patient to work deeper. Ethnographically, I work in a similar way, but a chief difference is that I am more (though never completely) a co-conversationist when I do participant observation and when I conduct an ethnographic interview. As an ethnographer, I still search for the feeling prompts in the subject's comments and attitude, but there is no expectation that the subject is participating in order to heal. The problem for the psycho-interactionist ethnographer, then, is to move the subject to that more substantive location in the context of only one or two interviews or field encounters, depending on the structure of the study, without inferring that it is a therapeutic experience.

In therapy, there is time to build a relationship in which clinician can ally with the patient and his or her unconscious in order to edge incrementally into that deeper space of the self. In ethnography one must accept the necessary limitations which the single (or multiple) interview places on this quest. But this changes radically when through participant observation the ethnographer is on the scene regularly, building deep trust, and thus is in more naturalistic conversation with subjects who have already become used to the researcher. Here the route to deeper material is opened. Now the ethnographer becomes a closer equivalent to the psychoanalyst qua participant observer described earlier by Arlow (1979).

From 1994–1999, I conducted extensive participant observation, document analysis, and interviews at three telefundraising companies in a major metropolitan area of the northeastern US. This research began casually. My sociological curiosity was sparked while I was a new graduate student trying to pay my bills by working in an industry about which I had conflicted feelings. Then, as I moved toward my dissertation and was simultaneously promoted to management positions at these companies, I formalized my exploration. I did not conduct this research from an explicitly psycho-interactive perspective, nor did I consciously use symbolic interactionism. Rather I wrote down what I saw and analyzed what I gathered using basic qualitative techniques and attitudes. If I were to start the research anew now, I could employ an explicitly psycho-interactionist approach, but even as I still work with this data, I apply psycho-interactionist perspectives in reverse to already gathered data. Some of the things that emerge in the telefundraising field setting for which one would want to dig below the surface of the subjects' impressions are: the fantasies evoked by asking the disembodied voices of strangers over the telephone for donations to causes for which one may have at best indifferent feelings; the associations callers have to the constant rejection they receive over the telephone each calling shift; the meanings and fantasies projected onto the lottery tickets frequently strewn across call center floors at the end of shifts; the unconscious meanings of the telephone and of money to the workers; cigarette breaks; bathrooms for workers filled with organic and manufactured debris; candy left on the grimy desk of a worker by a manager to reward acquisition of a large donation on a credit card. In this last example, the symbolic interactionist might discover the meanings attributed to the gum drop by caller and manager and thereby interpret it correctly and insightfully in that context. But what happens when the psycho-interactionist ethnographer thinks to follow the mention of the gum drop in an interview with questions about the fantasies of what it means to feed and be fed? Then we begin to sink our field anchors into deeper waters where untold riches lay waiting to be discovered.

While symbolic interactionism provides many ways to mine the riches of these social encounters, *adding* a psycho-interactionist lens deepens the exploration. It opens unanticipated doors in much the same way patients experience a change in the transition from being treated in once a week behavioral therapy to multiple sessions per week of psychoanalysis. The work is harder and sometimes deeply frustrating, but the depths of discovery and rewards in personal transformation are often incomparable.

V. Conclusion: Wild Analysis?

In our culture of ready-made products and prepackaged experiences (Hochschild 2003; Churchill 2002, 2004), people are not always prepared, either temperamentally or economically, to patiently search for the origins of their troubles. The ever increasing commodification and commercialization of everyday life and the saturation of our minds by marketing and propaganda may dull the senses to the value and pleasures of exploring ambiguity in the empirical world. This exploration of ambiguity, though, sits at the center of ethnography and psychoanalysis. It may be for this reason that these two approaches to understanding human behavior and alleviating its troubles receive scant institutional support today. But what may be even more responsible for the marginalization of ethnography and psychoanalysis is their common founding in the notion that to understand human behavior requires one be humble first and realize how much understanding evades our grasp and remains ineffable.

A core premise of social science is that human behavior can only be understood in context. If part of that context is the unconscious mind and the dynamic relationship between it and the people and places it encounters, then we can understand neither the naturalistic observations nor the interview data captured by ethnographers without at least acknowledging the role of the unconscious and trying to incorporate it into the methods we use to gather data. From this perspective, symbolic interactionism, if used on its own, falls short of the mark as a tool for field investigation.

Yet in exploring ways to formulate and employ a psycho-interactionist ethnography, we must be very clear in differentiating it from clinical psychoanalysis or psychotherapy. Without this clear separation, we risk engaging, at least partly, in what Freud called "wild analysis" (1986[1910]). Freud wrote his paper on "'Wild' Psycho-Analysis" in reaction to a woman who consulted him on the advice of her physician. The physician apparently told her in an offhand way that the anxiety she experienced after divorcing her husband could be alleviated by reconciling with him and then resuming sexual intercourse, seeking intercourse by engaging in an affair, or masturbation. Freud was evidently furious at the physician after the woman told him that the physician claimed his advice was in line with the new insights of psychoanalysis. The bulk of the essay contains Freud's argument for why psychoanalysis should not be practiced in this "wild" way but rather only after the practitioner undergoes years of training and personal analysis. Similarly, Freud states that one cannot gain therapeutic benefit by reading in or listening to lectures on psychoanalysis, for these activities "have as much influence on the symptoms of nervous illness as a distribution of menu-cards in a time of famine has upon hunger" (1986 [1910], p. 225).

Put another way, ethnographers using a psycho-interactionist (or any other technique) should never operate under the false assumption that they are providing therapy—even when they are also trained as therapists or, as may occur, a research subject proclaims the therapeutic benefits of having been given the chance in an interview to think deeply about some aspect of his or her lifeworld. Hunt similarly warns, "In view of the many complexities of doing applied psychoanalysis, researchers will inevitably make mistakes and be tempted to indulge in 'wild analysis'" (1989, p. 84).

The sources of alienation in modern industrial societies are myriad. The means to heal alienation are few and require much work to extract their curative powers. Ethnography is a method for explaining how the social world functions and, in so doing, it offers a route to better living through reconnection and greater understanding. Psychoanalysis does this too, but differently. If each discipline operates separately yet also finds ways to contribute to the other, then these areas of social science praxis will have proven of some worth, even as the world may seem not to listen.

References

Arlow, J.A. (1979). The genesis of interpretation. *Journal of the American Psychoanalytic Association*, 27, 193–205.

Blumer, H. (1998 [1969]). *Symbolic interactionism: Perspective and method.* Berkeley: University of California Press.

Churchill (2005). Ethnography as translation. *Qualitative Sociology*, 28, 3–24.

Churchill (2004). Collective dissociation in mass society. *Humanity and Society*, 28, 384–402.

Churchill (2002). The scrim of concern. *International Journal of Politics, Culture and Society*, 15, 485–497.

Duneier, M. (1999). *Sidewalk.* New York: Farrar, Straus, and Giroux.

Durkheim, E. (1982 [1895]). *The rules of sociological method.* New York: Free Press.

Etchegoyen, H. (1991). *The evolution of psychoanalytic technique.* London: Karnac Books.

Fellman, G. (in press). Review of Freud and American sociology by Philip Manning. *Contemporary Sociology.*

Fishman, S.B. (2004). *Double or nothing?: Jewish families and mixed marriage.* Lebanon, NH: Brandeis University Press.

Freud, S. (1986[1900]). The interpretation of dreams. In J. Strachey et al (Ed. & trans.) *The standard edition of the complete psychological works of Sigmund Freud*, Vols. IV & V. London: Hogarth Press.

Freud, S. (1986[1905]). Fragment of an analysis of a case of hysteria. In J. Strachey et al (Ed. & trans.) *The standard edition of the complete psychological works of Sigmund Freud*, Vol. VII (pp. 3–122). London: Hogarth Press.

Freud, S. (1986[1910]). 'Wild' psycho-analysis. In J. Strachey et al (Ed. & trans.) *The standard edition of the complete psychological works of Sigmund Freud*, Vol. XI (pp. 219–227). London: Hogarth Press.

Freud, S. (1986[1933]). Lecture XXXI: The dissection of the psychical personality. In J. Strachey et al (Ed. & trans.) *The standard edition of the complete psychological works of Sigmund Freud*, Vol. XXII (pp. 57–80). London: Hogarth Press.

Geertz, C. (1988[1973]). Thick description: Toward an interpretive theory of culture. In R.M. Emerson (Ed.), *Contemporary field research: A collection of readings* (pp. 37–59). Prospect Heights, IL: Waveland Press.

Goffman, E. (1959). *The presentation of self in everyday life*. New York: Anchor.

Hochschild, A.R. (2003). The commodity frontier. In *The commercialization of intimate life* (pp. 30–44). Berkeley: University of California Press.

Hunt, J.C. (1989). *Psychoanalytic aspects of fieldwork*. (Sage University Paper Series on Qualitative Methods, Vol. 18). Beverly Hills, CA: Sage.

Krieger, S. (1983). *The mirror dance: Identity in a women's community*. Philadelphia: Temple University Press.

Krieger, S. (1985). Beyond 'subjectivity': The use of the self in social science. *Qualitative Sociology*, 8, 309–324.

Manning, P. (2005). *Freud and American sociology*. Malden, MA: Polity Press.

McDougall, J. (1989). *Theaters of the body: A psychoanalytic approach to psychosomatic illness*. New York: W. W. Norton & Company.

Mead, G.H. (1967 [1934]). *Mind, self, and society: From the standpoint of a social behaviorist*. Chicago: University of Chicago Press.

Mills, C.W. (1963[1940]). Situated actions and vocabularies of motive. In I.L. Horowitz (Ed.), *Power, politics, and people: The collected essays of C. Wright Mills* (pp. 439–452). New York: Oxford University Press.

Orwell, G. (1984[1949]). *1984*. New York: Signet.

Spiegel, A. (2005) The dictionary of disorder. *The New Yorker*, Jan. 3.

Wax, R.H. (1988[1971]). The ambiguities of fieldwork. In R.M. Emerson (Ed.), *Contemporary field research: A collection of readings* (pp. 191–202). Prospect Heights, IL: Waveland Press.

Wharton, E. (1987[1920]). *The age of innocence*. New York: Colllier.

Wolff, Kurt H. (1964). Surrender and community study: The study of Loma. In A.J. Vidich, J. Bensman, and M. R. Stein (Eds.), *Reflections on Community Studies* (pp. 233–263). New York: Harper & Row.

The Rules of Disengagement
The Interaction of Brain and Mind in the Analytic Treatment of Children and Adults with Asperger's Syndrome.

by Michael Krass

"I love technology. But I love you even more. But I still love technology, now and forever." Kip to his new bride in *Napoleon Dynamite*

Analytic treatment of people with Asperger's syndrome (AS) entails understanding that AS is a neurologically-based disorder that affects psychological growth throughout childhood. The neurological deficits that are present in people with AS can be expected to have a great deal of impact on interactions between the infant and the mothering object that involve unconscious processes that are instrumental to the infant's emotional development. Thus, patients with AS, as they present in analytic therapy or analysis, struggle with difficulties deriving from neurological deficits that impact many aspects of psychological and interpersonal functioning. But they also present with unconscious conflicts, fantasies, defenses and problems with identification and internalization that are interwoven into their more hard-wired challenges. This has implications for technique in analytic therapy and analysis with people with AS. It involves a great deal of flexibility on the part of the analyst in order to shift attention between neurological deficit and psychic conflict.

By looking at the ways neurological deficits may interfere with and alter the infant's crucial interactions with his mother during neurologically sensitive periods (e.g., Schore, 2002), this paper will show ways that the person with Asperger's embodies a highly complex interaction between deficit and conflict, nature and nurture, brain and mind. The paper will include examples from the analytic play therapy of Ian, a child with AS, and from the analysis of Eleanor, an adult with AS, to illustrate ways to distinguish between emotional challenges that are caused by neurological structure from those that derive from inner conflict. The inner conflict these patients demonstrate is, at times, related to the losses, severe isolation and loneliness resulting from the AS patient's idiosyncratic interpersonal manner, sensory sensitivities and difficulties with emotional closeness. In other instances, the inner conflict they demonstrate is related to childhood trauma not directly related to having AS, but is nonetheless influenced by the particular ways that the child with AS tries to take in and metabolize such impingements.

The case material presented will also demonstrate technical approaches that integrate an appreciation for the neurological basis of the patient's perceptual, cognitive and social difficulties with an understanding of unconscious fantasy, the process of internalizing parenting objects, compromise formation development and the role of defenses. In addition, the paper will illustrate the ways internal and external traumas and conflicts play out in the transference/countertransference field in work with patients with AS. I will look at this duality in the context of transference feelings and fantasies that arise with these patients, and of countertransference, particularly as it arises in the face of seemingly impenetrable protective mechanisms.

Neurocognitive Research Into Asperger's Syndrome

Neurobiological research on AS and autistic spectrum disorders (ASDs), in general, overwhelmingly support the hypothesis that these disorders are neurological in etiology. Structurally and functionally, the brains of people with ASDs are different from those without ASDs (e.g., Mundy, 2003). Such research has suggested that people with ASDs are neurologically impaired, for example, in the capacity to read faces (Weeks & Hobson, 1987; Welchew, et al., 2005) and voices (Ting Wang, et al., 2007), to infer others' internal motivations (e.g., Baron-Cohen, Leslie & Frith 1985; Happe, F., et al., 1996), to prefer human faces to other types of animate and inanimate stimuli (CIT), to attend to emotionally-arousing stimuli (Corden, Chilvers & Skuse, 2008), the tendency to look at other people's eyes (CIT) and the tendency to initiate episodes of joint attention (Mundy, et al., 1986).

Neurocognitive research is beginning to identify those neurological features in AS and ASDs that are present at birth and those which arise over the course of development. For example, Lee and Yerys and their colleagues (2009) found that neurological abnormalities that were not evident in young children with ASD were apparent in adults with ASD. In addition, Yerys and his colleagues' research (2007) suggests that executive functioning deficits that typically accompany ASDs are secondary to the autism. Thanks to studies such as these, we are beginning to get a clearer picture of that with which the person with ASD (including AS) is born and that which develops over the course of development, likely as a result of the interaction of these neurological features with pivotal developmental steps involving complex unconscious processes.

Psychoanalytic Perspectives of AS

An understanding of child development that integrates neurological structure and unconscious processes helps to identify the developmental processes that contribute to AS. This perspective makes it possible to deduce that many of those features of AS that psychoanalytic and neurological researches suggest are secondary to the primary neurological deficiencies of AS come about because of failures in the Asperger infant's capacity to use the mother in many important ways. For example, it is quite possible that many of the cognitive difficulties (i.e., difficulties forming a theory of mind, attention deficits, executive functioning deficits) that people with AS are faced with derive from the inability of the Asperger child to benefit from essential maternal functions such as mirroring/reflecting, containing and digesting the primitive emotional states of infancy and early childhood. Psychoanalytic perspectives of child development, particularly those that focus on psychological process occurring at the earliest phases of life, shed much light on the difficulties that the infant and young child with AS faces as he tries to derive benefit from his parenting environment.

Psychoanalytic writers such as Tustin, Meltzer and Alvarez have a number of hypotheses based upon their observations of their patients who were diagnosed with autism or who exhibited autistic characteristics. They identify psychological functions meant to either express or protect against horrific anxieties that they see as endemic to people with autism. They argue that such anxieties arise because of difficulties that the infant or young child with autism has with making constructive use of emotional and cognitive interactions with his or her maternal object. Deficits in social perception and cognition interfere with the development of a fundamental sense of one's body as whole and connected.

Tustin, for example, (e.g., 1971, 1989) has described the many ways autistic people try to shield themselves from outside stimulation as "autistic objects" and "autistic shapes." These are psychological constructs that people on the autism spectrum use to manage their fears of losing body parts, of becoming unable to process the stimulation that results from interpersonal contact and of being unable to bear considering the terrifying consequences that people with autism often associate with separation.

Mitrani: the Needs of the Autistic Patient in Analysis

Mitrani's (1992, 1993) writings on analytic work with patient with autism or autistic features illuminates many aspects of the analytic process with such patients. She stresses the importance for the analyst to tolerate the intense disappointment and loneliness that their patients on the autism spectrum express. She writes with great sensitivity that this is necessary "so that we may be better equipped to weave, out of the threads of our own experience, a blanket of understanding which may adequately hold and warm them" (1993, p. 552). Mitrani recognizes that people with ASDs have suffered tremendous isolation and are profoundly aware of all of the enriching inter and intra-personal experiences that they have missed out on from their earliest years. To me, although she does not say this outright, such comments reflect an implicit understanding of the extent to which people with ASDs are aware that a piece of brain function is literally missing and that its being gone compromises many essential aspects of emotional development throughout the lifespan. Thus it is necessary to sit with pervasive feelings of loss and hopelessness, to resist interpretations based implicitly on hope before the patient has had the opportunity to have their disappointment recognized and felt, before the patient has sufficiently mourned the loss of what they never had, and that prevented them from obtaining that which they might never be able to have. The analyst must sustain the pressures of feeling with the patient the crushing letdown of past losses and failings, current ones, especially those taking place in the immediate transference field, and future limitations that are realistic to be expected.

Mitrani speaks to an essential point that has been little explored or discussed in either the neurocognitive or psychoanalytic literature on ASD's. Specifically, her comments illustrate the difficulties that infants and young children on the autism spectrum have in their capacity to receive containment from mothering objects or to relate to their mothers in such a way as to develop a sense of unique subjectivity of self and other. Along these lines, it is to be expected that the mothering object of an infant who cannot take in the mother's containing function is likely to experience a great deal of pressure to despair and that this, in turn, would interfere with her capacity to sustain her capacity to contain, digest, mediate and translate her infant's inchoate experiences, her good-enoughness.

Mitrani (1993) also contributes to our attempts to hone the analytic instrument we use in working with patients on the autism spectrum. She is sensitive to hearing when such patients are able to gain access to and to reveal their pained longings to be unfettered by their autism, by their tendency to erect protective barriers between themselves and others and their difficulty reading and assessing the signs other people give that indicate connectedness. From this, she emphasizes the importance of recognizing "their desperate appeals for our help in finding a way out of the autistic tomb—this numbness which incarcerates them" (p. 557). As with any series of dualities between a closed and open attitude towards one's inner life (Novick & Novick, 2003) she adds the continuum of "triumphant pleasure of manic flight from depressive anxiety" to pained awareness of the autistic patient's isolation from themselves and from others (p. 556). Here, she is talking about patients with essentially neurotic character structures for whom autistic defenses evolve from deficiencies in their facilitating environments. Nonetheless, it is my sense that what she describes could just as accurately fit the patient with AS who is burdened with handicaps in their capacity to tolerate sensory stimulation from within and without and in their capacity to perceive and convey interpersonal communications. The intensity of the defensive swings one often encounters with such patients—between grandiose sense of contemptuous superiority to feelings of total and complete worthlessness—suggests to me the totality of the deficits and their impact on the development of an inner emotional life, as well as the patients' desperation in trying to obtain a sense of human connectedness and a stable identity. In this way, Mitrani has added to the analyst's toolbox with which to work with people with AS. Her insights help analysts who work with patients with AS to, as Polmear (2004) puts it, "be ready to catch the wish to make contact, or to recognize the need for the retreats" (p. 99).

A Brief Example of the Unconscious Grandiose Defense in AS

This back and forth was very blatantly illustrated by an adolescent boy I saw in therapy because he had been becoming explosive and threatening his mother with violence when she attempted to set limits on his computer role-playing game time. In one of our earlier sessions, he said without any irony, "I may be one of the most—if not the most intelligent person on the planet. On the other hand, that may not be true because I am also arrogant."

Several months into his treatment, he tried to choke a boy who made an insulting racial comment to my patient (who was White) and he was suspended from school. For several months he was stricken with an almost paralyzing depressive self-hatred. He spoke in session after session about his feeling stunned by his violent behavior and his feeling helpless in his capacity to make sense of it or to try to prevent similar episodes in the future. He earnestly tried to engage me in trying to sort out just what had happened and we worked terribly hard together to try to do so. He felt powerless to prevent such an outburst in the future as he recognized that he had "just flipped" when the other boy had insulted him. During those sessions his sense of frailty and vulnerability was astounding. It was as if he had virtually no defenses to speak of. His previously expressed sense of invincibility was replaced by a recognition of his impaired ability to sufficiently regulate himself, that is, to be able to conduct himself as a civilized person. This example illustrates the ways that people with AS generally lack higher level defenses and ego functions and the ways that they typically utilize more primitive defenses—especially grandiosity. They often do so in a way that, although inhibiting emotional development, safeguards a very fragile inner structure. It also shows the importance for the therapist or analyst to be sensitive to those moments when the protective barrier is lowered or the shell is cracked, as the case may be, and of recognizing the great deal of care and caution that is necessary, particularly with respect to self-esteem, in working with patients with AS. Such sensitivity to narcissistic vulnerability is important both during the seemingly endless periods of defensive distancing and self-aggrandizement and the far less frequent times where the AS patient's defensive fortress—and the inner contents it protects and gives shape to—collapses.

Winnicott's Model of Emotional Development and Neurological Deficit in AS

In the attempt to pinpoint those places in development where the infant with AS hits obstacles to reaching higher stages of emotional maturity, it is necessary to look at the developmental processes early in life that are most instrumental to emotional and cognitive growth. Winnicott's (1971) understanding of the infant's interaction with the mothering object in the development of the earliest forms of the self as separate from the object offers some clues. Specifically, his model suggests ways that the infant-mother bond shapes emotional and cognitive development of the child born with the primary features of AS. Particularly, his understanding of the infant's development from object relating to object usage is particularly useful in elucidating those processes that we can infer go wrong in such situations.

According to Winnicott, the infant initially relates to the mothering object—not as separate from the self, but, rather, as a "bundle of projections" (p. 88). The process of maturing from object relating to object usage relies upon the good enough mother of the facilitating environment. He says that this process, the "most difficult thing, perhaps, in human development" (p.89), entails the infant destroying the internalized mothering object and the mothering object surviving this destruction. In so doing, the infant forms the earliest conceptions of himself as separate from his mother and, likewise, of his mother as a separate being with her own subjectivity.

Winnicott writes that what distinguishes object usage from object relating is "the subject's placing of the object outside the area of the subject's omnipotent control" (p. 89, italics added). This clearly applies to AS. The infant who is born with deficiencies in his or her capacity to relate to other people and those observable aspects that convey interior experience to others will be hampered in transitioning from object relating to object usage. It is very difficult for this infant to attend to those interpersonal cues that communicate that the mother has survived the child's destructive attacks—that the internalized mothering object was destroyed and the real mother was able to put herself back together and be a mother again. Thus, the infant with AS is prone to believe both that his aggression is annihilative and that his mothering object is unable to withstand his aggressive attacks. Unlike in ideal development, the infant with AS does not have the opportunity to learn to know his mothering object as a psychologically separate other. Therefore, he cannot know his mother as an object who is felt to be able to withstand the infant's developmentally appropriate aggressive attacks and is therefore able to prove she is not under the child's omnipotent control. This has serious ramifications for the child's capacity to internalize a strong and steady regulating parental object that can help the child to manage his affects and impulses as well as help him to protect himself from external danger –both real and projected (cf; Sherkow, 2004).

Unconscious Processes Entailed in Some Common Features of AS

This section examines some common features of AS from the perspective of the interaction between neurological deficits and unconscious conflict. In this section, I will look at the meanings and psychological functions of the protective shell (Tustin, 1990) as created by verbal ruminations and preoccupations, repetitive comments or activities and obsessive dissection of focused areas of interest. I will also look at some of the unconscious meanings of the hostility toward others that is evident in some people with AS, with an eye toward understanding ways that neurological deficit

350

creates a psychological situation wherein the patient with AS might be prone to rely upon these types of mechanisms.

The Protective Shell

Thomas was a plump 12-year-old boy with dark piercing eyes and an open, naïve face who was on the upper end of the autism spectrum who I treated while he was attending a special education school where I was employed as a school psychologist. Thomas would, in a very automatic way, imitate several other children in his class. His teachers admonished him to stop and punished him frequently for imitating these other students, both of them severely impaired boys, during class time. However, he continued to do so in a way that appeared to all who observed him to be willful and stubborn. Nonetheless, it was my sense that he was doing this without malice. Rather, his mimicry was a way to adapt to a variety of difficult internal and external realities that he lacked the inner resources to handle otherwise. It was a way to manage his feelings of emotional overload, on one hand, and a way to express certain feelings and feeling states that, because of his autistic difficulties using verbal language in a spontaneous way, he was unable to convey. It also reflected his idiosyncratic way of articulating his fantasies about his own sense of being neurologically impaired. It reflected a wish to be more passive with regard to his intense wishes and to not be held accountable for them. He was also reluctant to stop aping his classmates during class because the anger and punishments it evoked from his teachers perpetuated a sado-masochistic relationship with them. This was, it turned out, a re-creation of what I eventually learned was a frankly abusive one he had with his mother and step-father who would, for example, make Thomas copy texts from the Bible for hours for the most minor infractions. His teachers implored me to use my therapy sessions with him to help him to learn to stop imitating the other students. Understandably, they were concerned about the effect this was having on the children he imitated, that they felt teased, even harassed.

I decided to work with him around this on two levels: to simultaneously address his capacity to control and regulate himself and to explore the meanings of this behavior that had become so disruptive. While walking with me from his classroom to the play therapy room, I would reward him for limiting his imitative behaviors, giving him warnings and levying consequences in a non-emotive manner so as to distinguish myself in this role from the more playful and receptive person that I wanted him to see me as while we were in the office. Once in the therapy room, I would change my demeanor and, after we would process his feelings about his earning or not earning the reward, I would fall silent to make it clear that I was waiting for whatever it was that he wanted to say or do. During these sessions he would go in and out of periods of talking and acting like one of the other two students. To his great delight, I would talk to him as if he were the other child, using the other child's name. This allowed him to express his profound degree of unmet dependency needs, often shown by holding both of my hands or both of his arms around my arm in an effusive bear hug (probably a sensorally-motivated act as much as a dynamically-motivated one). It also led to his beginning to talk to me, in his own quite disjointed and perseverative way, about the terrifying, humiliating and enraging reality of his physically abusive step-father. In this way we were able to address a variety of concerns with which he was struggling. With this approach, we were able to address the variety of meanings of his off-putting and repetitive behavior. By limiting this behavior in a way that reduced the extent it could be used to elicit sado-masochistic responses from his peers and teachers, we were able to make use of it, so to speak, to create a transitional space between us within which he could safely explore his inner life. Thus we were able to break through the emotional bottleneck that arose from the intersection of the trauma of the abuse, his neurological tendency to use language in a perseverative and emotionally and interpersonally walled-off way, and impairments in his capacity to recognize, process and reflect on his inner life.

A number of writers (e.g., Alvarez & Reid, 1999; Bromfield, 2000; Grotstein, 2001; Klauber, 2004; Meltzer, 1975; Mitrani, 1991; Rhode, 2004) suggest that much of the isolative behavior of the autistic spectrum child is defensive, meant to reduce exposure to contact with others that are felt to be primarily impingements—at best annoying, at worst excruciating and terrifying. Klauber (2004), for example, writes about the ways that repetitive verbalizations and preoccupations can serve as both a defense against intense fears and panic as well as a kind of mental paralysis that functions as an overly relied upon way to stop time and eliminate contact with others. Mitrani, looking at the unconscious mechanisms at play when someone erects a wall of words or of intellectualized thinking, suggests that the intellect can be used to "create a second skin as a container for unbearable experiences" (1991 p. 15). In describing an adult patient of hers who utilized this kind of defense, she writes that these "ruminations were not really thoughts connected to experiences of loss, but rather that these were an agglomeration of words that provided a cocoon of sensation within which she could wrap her precarious self for protection against the awareness of loss" (p. 15, italics added). Polmear (2004) stresses the dual and somewhat paradoxical role of such protective mechanisms: to both keep in frightening aggressive urges and to keep out other people with their potential to destroy one's very sense of being by establishing oneself as separate. Alvarez (1999, 2004) has also considered the meanings of the protective shell. She believes that these activities serve multiple psychological purposes. They assist in self-regulation of affects and impulses, they provide a way to create a feeling of sameness and regularity which helps fend off fears of becoming overwhelmed by sensory stimulation and unpredictability, they are used for attention-getting and as simply a way to annoy others in order to create interpersonal distance. Stressing the adaptive and non-pathological aspects of these types of repetitive verbal patterns, Shapiro (2000) suggests that the way people on the autism spectrum use words and the intellect perseveratively reflects progressive needs to, for example, master one's impulses and anxiety-fraught interpersonal exchanges, to take pleasure in the familiarity and sensory impact of patterns and repetition and to obtain gratification from adults' encouragement. Thus, there is a range of ways to understand the psychological and developmental function of the verbal rigidity that is often seen in such people. However, there is some consensus that these behaviors have adaptive, regressive and defensive functions and that these meanings likely shift and change from one to the other depending on their context.

This corresponds with my experience. I have observed that the casing that a person with AS can construct around themselves with words, noises, activity or silence, as well as more concretely by physically isolating themselves, is, like any other product of the mind, a compromise formation serving multiple and ever-shifting purposes involving all aspects of the mind and its relation to objects. Particularly, I would emphasize the way that this protective shell creates distance from the object, as the object is seen as dangerous in so many ways. The object can arouse intense and poorly contained wishes and longing that the person with AS may have great difficulty making cognitive sense of. The object, if it is separate from the self, can think, feel and act in ways that can be quite disconcerting to the person with AS. As a separate entity, the object would be able to create intense anxiety by, for example, creating sensory agitation, impinging on tightly clung-to patterns and scripts designed to provide both cognitive-perceptual order as well as emotional predictability, and, most importantly, by having the potential to leave. In Winnicott's terms, the person with AS, because of the ways their neurological deficits interfered with their early relations, typically has had much difficulty using the object. The person with AS feels he must maintain utter control over the object because he cannot tolerate the separation entailed in relinquishing the control.

With the tightly woven sheet of words or sounds or behaviors, repetitive and meaningful only on the surface but lacking apparent unconscious resonance, the person with AS demonstrates the inextricably intertwined relationship between neurology and psychology, between what is apparently hard-wired from early on in life and what derives from conflict-laden attempts to manage anxieties at all levels of psychosexual development. To say that the Asbergian stream of repetitive preoccupations is just a defense, or just an attempt to maintain inner cohesion, or just a way to create distance from both external and internal objects, or just a symptom of neurological deficit, as perseveration can be with brain damaged individuals, would be to oversimplify what appears to be as highly complex and multiply determined as any product of the mind.

The following clinical example illustrates the way a child with AS uses the protective shell compulsively to keep others as well as contact with himself at bay. It also shows some of the ways a clinician can address this to help the child with AS to relinquish his protective seal in order to allow an opening in which other people, feelings and self-knowledge can enter.

Ian is a boy with AS who I saw from age 8 to 11 to address his frequent tantrums and violent outbursts at home and his occasionally peculiar behavior (e.g., spending recess picking up bits of trash to take home in his pocket, covering the walls and floors of his bathroom with his father's shaving cream). A sweet-dispositioned boy with a goofy sense of humor, Ian spent a good portion of the first few months of his therapy fantasizing about becoming a robot so that he could be easily re-wired to behave better. Despite being a bright boy with a vivid imagination, he could not attend to his schoolwork. He found it understimulating and he was unable to screen out sounds, smells and proprioceptive sensations that impinged on him while he is trying to concentrate. In session, he often repeated disjointed observations and exclamations in a way that Brown (2009) has described as "association-starved." These comments had the surface appearance of having meaning, as they were colorful, filled with what appeared to be drive derivatives (e.g., cheerfully-expressed thoughts about blowing up his school with an atomic bomb), yet they were repetitive and I had great difficulty staying with him. Often, I had to pull myself back out of a pleasantly disconnected reverie having no obvious connection to his play. When I spoke, I often found myself responding either with reflective observations or interpretations that felt as superficial and stereotyped as his did.

The following process material shows one approach I used to address the ways in which he had been actively trying to obfuscate meaning and to avoid real feelings. When, at the start of his session, he went through his typical routine of rooting through the toy cabinet and making perky but disconnected comments or associations, I felt pressure to follow my script of playing the straight man. I resisted this which allowed me to be more aware that he was trying to control me. I simply asked him, "What are you doing now?" He answered, smiling with a vacant look in his eyes, "Not much. Just random stuff." Seeing my first opportunity to underline for him his active involvement in fending me off, I said, "You're trying to be random." I added, "I think that doing random things is a way to not talk about anything 'important.'" He agreed without hesitation—a confirmation as well as, I felt, an unthinking deflection of my interpretation. Later in the session, he tied black yarn to the handle of the toy cabinet and wrapped it back and forth through the office, from one side of the room to the other. It looked to me to be a kind of web that we were both ensnared in. When he finished this project, he tugged on the end of the yarn until, sliding slowly around chair and table legs, the yarn barely pulled the door open. He said, "It's the lazy person's way of opening a door. " Seeing an obvious discrepancy, I protested: "Lazy? It seems harder to do it this way, yet you say you're being lazy. You think you're lazy because you do things differently. But maybe you work harder than everyone else to do things everyone else can do really easily." I decided to address his attention and executive function difficulties by connecting this with his inability to complete his homework, saying, "You have to do all kinds of difficult things to do something that's probably easy." He absently agreed, then started talking to me, for the first time this session, making eye contact. He told me about the "best" museum he had ever been to that had a contraption that made a bubble around his whole body. I told him I could understand why he liked the bubble contraption so much, that I thought that was what the "random stuff" was, "a bubble that you put yourself in that keeps me out." He stopped moving around and stared at me wide-eyed. He invited me to imagine big fat Jabba the Hutt trying to do jumping jacks—that he would be straining but hardly moving. I continued along this line of thought, saying that this is what he thinks he looks like to everyone else, that he is trying very hard but it looks like he's not trying hard at all. He heartily agreed and added emphatically, "And everyone thinks I'm lazy!" I said, "For you, the fact you're so smart and so much is so hard for you feels random to you—it doesn't make any sense to you." He responded quickly, "No, it doesn't! It should be easy but it isn't and it doesn't make any sense." I said, "It sounds pretty random." He almost yelled back, "It is!" Unlike practically every previous session where he watched the clock and sometimes left early or found excuses to invite his mother in to the office, he tried to stay past the end of the session.

I found the opportunity to link up his autistic defensive maneuver of making everything "random" and nonsensical to a range of feelings related to his deficits: that he cannot complete work that he should be able to do easily, that he is different than other children, that he is seen as

357

a bad student when he is, in fact, working harder than most and mostly, that he feels he lives in a world of nonsense and random cause and effect relationships. As this is a once weekly therapy, I did not address his fear of letting himself feel closer to me, fear, I imagine, that I will find him to be just as random as he and others find him to be.

Aggression Toward Others

Some of the children and adults with AS with whom I have worked convey a deep hostility for most other people. This subgroup of patients appear most alive when they are verbally flailing at what they see are the inconsistencies, hypocrisies and emotional vulnerability evident in the behaviors and attitudes of others. Guided in their understanding of all things, animate and inanimate alike, by rationality and pattern-like consistency, some patients with AS express disgust and condescending exasperation with the typically idiosyncratic and erratic ways that most people behave. Polmear (2004) addresses this by talking about her adult Asperger patients' verbal assaults on her. She describes these attacks as serving to communicate to the analyst their unceasingly persecutory day to day experience. Polmear also suggests that these attacks are felt to be survival techniques meant to create distance from the analyst who is seen as having annihilative potential.

In my work with patients who demonstrate this particular quality, the fiercest attacks on me come after I have interpreted incorrectly, too deeply or I have hit upon feelings of hopelessness connected to a sense of being broken. At such times, these patients feel that I have abandoned them. They feel that I have either left them without any hope of connecting with humanity or I have pointed at their missing parts with cold, cruel remove without any offer of help. I wonder if such a sentiment reflects terrible fears that the emotional skin is neither sufficiently strong to keep inside and outside reasonably separate nor sufficiently porous to allow a freer flow between the self and the object (Anzieu, 1993; Bick, 1968).

Technically speaking, I have found it to be of little or no value to identify or interpret the sadistic aspects of the aggression in the AS patient's hostile attacks on the analyst. The result of such an approach is that the patient feels both overwhelmed with guilt and shame and a sinking sense of being, once again, now and forever, misunderstood. With children and adults alike, it is more constructive to try to silently withstand the volley of insults that some patients with AS shoot over at the analyst until they are ready to hear about the primitive fears that they are trying to allay by creating distance between us or by making me less consequential.

Two Clinical Moments

As I have tried to show, attuned analytic work with people with AS requires an appreciation of the back and forth flow that they exhibit in treatment between concerns related to neurological deficits and images of their selves that are infused with unconscious fantasy and psychic conflict. The following two clinical moments with Eleanor, a woman in analysis who has many characteristics of AS, illustrate the ways it is necessary for the analyst working with the patient with AS to stay alert to the need to work one's way from a non-Asperger way of thinking to an Aspergian mindset. In that mindset, the analyst is often less than a part object, more of an inanimate function. It also illustrates that, for the analyst to try to be anything more assaults the patient with a sense of herself as an alien who will never find her way home.

Clues that Eleanor had features of AS included her physical presentation, the quality of her voice and her avoidance of eye contact with me. She dressed in an unadorned way: no makeup, no hairstyles and wearing plain unobtrusive clothes, explaining that she preferred to buy clothes from thrift stores because they had already been used and, thus, were not jarring to her the way new clothes were. In fact, on the rare occasion that she bought new clothes, she would leave them in her closet for several months before wearing them so that she had time to get used to them. Her voice, too, had the lack of color and expressiveness that is typical of some people on the autism spectrum. Her face was virtually unchanging. She usually looked unhappy, rarely smiled and said very little with her eyes. As I got to know her, she revealed more about herself that suggested that there was an underlying autistic structure. She was nearly phobic of change, becoming upset when she heard that the parents of a friend renovated their house and distressed when the car she thought I drove was parked in a different spot than usual—so much so that she moved to the other side of the sidewalk as she walked past it. Her extreme sensitivities to smells, colors, temperature and, in general, the layout of the physical world around her often took priority over her interest in people. For example, she had a great deal of trouble breaking up with a man who was who regularly berated her because she adored the suburban rambler he owned. Apart from the defensive aspects of her focus on the house, she was enamored with the parsimony of its layout and the aesthetic balance she felt was evident in its bland yard.

In one of Eleanor's session, she started out by telling me that the lobby of my building smelled "like a wet dog" and that the office had its own "bad" smell. Despite her so directly expressing negative transferential feelings, I had learned that, with her, it was best to sit back and wait to see the meanings that arose rather than to even ask about such comments. As if to confirm my intuition not to comment on her aggression toward me (and perhaps to comment on my having mistakenly highlighted her hostility toward me in the past—much to her dismay and consternation), she then associated to feeling that, when her best friend treats her as if she is "tough," she responds by acting mean. She said that she gets so mean that, had she been born a dog, she would have been put to sleep. She associated to her friend's mother putting down her friend's dog after it playfully bit a child. She then associated to watching, as a young teenager, her own dog get killed by a horse that kicked it, feeling all along that she was to blame because she thought the dog could help corral the horse. After I asked her to tell me more, she realized that the dog actually took several weeks to die and that her mother never brought the dog to the veterinarian to see if it could be helped.

I had chosen to not address her toughness with and her meanness toward me. I had implicitly acknowledged it as a protective mechanism rather than the expression of contempt that it, on the surface, appeared to be. This choice was rewarded by her presenting a less autistic form of defense. This, I interpreted, saying that she had protected her mother by blaming herself. She started to cry—perhaps the first time in the two years I had seen her up to that point—and to speak in an intensely affective way that was highly unusual for her about how much she missed her dog and how, for all these years, she had felt that her letting her dog get kicked was proof of her defect, of her lack of human qualities.

At a later point in the analysis, Eleanor faced a self-imposed crisis in her life and her analysis with me. She was trying to decide whether she was going to return to the country she was raised in, where her mother lived, in order to start a graduate program in an entirely new career. The more she spoke about it, the clearer it became that she did not want to change her career. She was doing very well in her professional work for the first time in her life but she was devaluing this and devaluing her reluctance to make such a radical change in her life. As often happened with her, a session where she explored painful and complex feelings about her childhood and where I was able to help her connect those feelings with a contemporary issue was followed by several sessions of intense resistance, including canceling Wednesday's session and arriving to Thursday's and Friday's sessions over twenty minutes late. In Friday's session, she started out in silence. When I asked about this, she said that, no matter how things sound when she thinks them, as soon she says them out loud they sound trivial, "like it wasn't worth being said." Thinking about her lateness and figuring that she was protecting me by framing things in terms of her deficiency, I tried to re-frame this in terms of her feeling that I was not conveying a sense to her that I felt what she was saying was important. She thought about this for a few moments and then said, "Most of the time you don't say anything and, when you do talk, it usually doesn't have anything to do with what I'm talking about." This struck me as a clear example of the negative transference that I felt was operative in her intensified resistance of the past few days. She explained that I had been mistaken when I had made a direct interpretation of what I felt was resistance several sessions previously and my being wrong led her to feel hopeless, that she is "not very good at communicating" and that she is "incomprehensible." She had felt that I had not been understanding her lately, but feared that this was because, as we were getting at deeper parts of her, she was becoming more "nonsensical."

I felt that Eleanor was trying to veil her disappointment with me and I felt guilty. I thought to myself about what was true about what she was saying. Had I lost my way with her? Was she clearer, more comprehensible to me when I was seeing her, as I had for the first six months of her treatment, in face-to-face therapy? Did this mean that I was harming her by seeing her in analysis instead of therapy? I decided to address what I thought was her attempt to protect me and I shared my opinion that she had only been questioning her ability but was not including the option of considering my ability to understand. She continued to disagree with me and then said, in an uncharacteristically pained and plaintive way, "Generally, I'm not being understood by anyone, anywhere. So I'm not inclined to think it's your fault." The change in her demeanor, the atypical degree of emotionality she conveyed in her voice signaled to me that she was trying to tell me that I was wrong in saying she was trying to protect me. She was telling me that, by virtue of her analytic work, she was developing a painful recognition that she keeps herself from being understood by others and then resents them for not understanding her. Implied in this was that the many withering attacks she made on me and my therapeutic skills in the past represented an attempt to avoid facing her severe deficits. Of course, by my insisting that she was defending against her disappointment with me, I was also proving my own point—that I was having difficulty understanding her and difficulty appreciating the dead end aspects of her, those qualities that, because of her deficits, were erected around her like concrete block walls and were not likely to change very much.

I shared with Eleanor my impression that her feeling this way, that she was unable to make herself understood properly, was related to a session at the beginning of the week. In that session, she had recollected a childhood feeling—one that she was unable to reclaim as an adult —that her life and the material objects around her were "substantial." I suggested that she was wondering if changing her homeland and changing her career would solve that problem. That, even though she clearly did not want to start this new career, the decision was fraught because it felt to her like her "life is at stake." She agreed immediately with this and said that she was convincing herself that she did not want to make these changes because she has such a deep fear of change. Thinking about her intense reaction to the earlier session where she conveyed a level of openness that had been uncommon previously in the analysis, I told her that I thought that her fear of feelings was an even more serious fear for her. I said, "It's playing out here, coming later and later to the sessions, not wanting to come on Wednesday—it's because on Tuesday, feelings came up that were painful and confusing. So you question the analysis and me and you question the words that come out of your mouth." She responded to this interpretation with the first dream she had told me in over four months. It was a nightmare that had important transference implications and demonstrated her sense of her brokenness—not a brokenness resulting from unconscious guilt or from persecutory attacks, but a sense of her mind as structurally compromised. The dream went as follows: "A huge shed filled with water. It was dark and me and this guy were trying to cover up the water with these huge slabs of wood and it was incredibly dangerous because one of them was tilted. And the whole idea was this woman's idea—and she wasn't even there." She added, bluntly, "That's my life." She felt I was complicit in trying to cover over the way that she is unable to contain and regulate her feelings. She felt that her being broken ("tilted") made her dangerous, as she was unable to hold in the overflowing feelings that were likely poorly modulated, poorly metabolized. The huge slabs of wood clearly represented her autistic defenses, defenses she still very much needed at this point. She saw me here in a more benevolent way than she had in the past, collaborating with her in a manner that she had not been able to dare to let herself imagine before. However, she felt that she and I were perhaps not in the driver's seat. Rather, "this woman," her mother, a neglectful, childish and eccentric woman (herself, I'd wondered, having some autistic features), was the more powerful one.

Summary

In this paper, I used examples from the play therapy with a child and the psychoanalysis of an adult with AS to illustrate the challenge and the importance of the interplay between neurological deficit and psychic conflict in working with people with AS. Our understanding of AS is still, in my view, rudimentary. Psychoanalytic treatments have a great deal to offer those with AS. However, it is incumbent upon those of us who treat people with AS to sustain an appreciation of all aspects of AS including those that derive directly from neurological differences, those that derive from the interaction of atypical neurological functioning on processes essential to psychological development, and those that derive from sub-optimal emotional environments (that is, parenting that was not good enough). One purpose of this paper is to raise interest in thinking about the intricate ways that neurological deficits affecting social perception and social cognition interact with the types of interpersonal infant-mother experiences that Winnicott has identified as essential for the child's formation of a separate sense of self and a sense of the other as separate and as having its own subjectivity. Highlighting the multi-level processes that likely occur in AS helps us to approach analytic treatment of children and adults with AS with greater empathic sensitivity to, patience for and understanding of that which can and that which cannot be changed.

References

Alvarez, A. (1993). Making the thought thinkable: On introjection and projection. *Psychoanalytic Inquiry*, 13:103–122.

Álvarez, A. (2004). Issues in assessment: Asperger's syndrome and personality. In M. Rhode & T. Klauber (Ed.), *The Many Faces of Asperger's Syndrome* (pp. 113–128). New York: Karnac.

Anzieu, D. (1993). Autistic phenomena and the skin ego. *Psychoanalytic Inquiry*, 13:42–48.

Baron-Cohen, S., Leslie, A. & Frith, U. (1985) Does the autistic child have a "theory of mind"? *Cognition*, 21:37–46.

Baron-Cohen, S., Ring, H., Wheelwright, S., Bullmore, E., Brammer, M. Simmons, A., & Williams, S. (1999). Social intelligence in the normal and autistic brain: an fMRI study. *European Journal of Neuroscience*, 11, 1891–1898.

Bick, E. (1968). The experience of the skin in early object-relations. *The International Journal of Psychoanalysis*, 49:484–486.

Bion, W.R. (1962). *Learning from experience*. New York: Jason Aronson.

Bromfield, R. (1989). Psychodynamic play therapy with a high-functioning autistic child. *Psychoanalytic Psychology*, 6:439–453.

Bromfield, R. (2000). It's the tortoise race: Long-term psychodynamic psychotherapy with a high-functioning autistic adolescent. *Psychoanalytic Inquiry*, 20:732–745.

Brown, L. (2009). Bion's ego psychology: implications for an intersubjective view of psychic structure. *The Psychoanalytic Quarterly*, 78(1): 27–56.

Corden, B, Chilvers, R., Skuse, D. (2006). Avoidance of emotionally arousing stimuli predicts social-perceptual impairment in Asperger's syndrome. *Neuropsychologia*, 46(1): 137–147.

Grotstein, J. (2001). Some reflections on the psychoanalytic theory of motivation: toward a theory of entelechy. *Psychoanalytic Inquiry*, 21:572–588.

Happe, F., Ehlers, S., Fletcher, P., Frith, U., Johansson, M., Gillberg, C., Dolan, R. Frackowiak, R., & Frith, C. (1996). "Theory of mind" in the brain: Evidence from a PET scan study of Asperger syndrome. *Clinical Neuroscience and Neuropathology*, 8(1):1970150201.

Haznedar, M. Buchsbaum, M., Wei, T., Hof, P., Cartwright, C., Bienstock, C. & Hollander, E. (2000). Limbic circuitry in patients with autism spectrum disorders studied with positron emissiontomography and magnetic resonance imaging. *American Journal of Psychiatry*, 157, 1994–2001.

Klauber, T. (2004). A child psychotherapist's commentary on Hans Asperger's 1944 paper, "'Autistic Psychopathy' in Childhood." In M. Rhode & T. Klauber (Ed.), *The Many Faces of Asperger's Syndrome* (pp. 54–69). New York: Karnac.

Lee, A. & Hobson, R. P. (1998). On developing self-concepts: A controlled study of children and adolescents with autism. *The Journal of Child Psychology and Psychiatry and Allied Disciplines*, 39:1131–1144.

Meltzer, D. (1975). Adhesive identifications. *Contemporary Psychoanalysis*, 11:289–310.

Mitrani, J. (1991). *Framework for the Imaginary: Clinical explorations in primitive states of being*. London: Rowman & Littlefield.

Mundy, P., Sigman, M., Ungerer, J. & Sherman, T. (1986). Defining the social deficits of autism: The contribution of nonverbal communication measures. *Journal of Child Psychology and Psychiatry*, 27:657–669.

Mundy, P. (2003). Annotation: the neural basis of social impairments in autism: the role of the dorsal medial-frontal cortex and anterior cingulate system. *Journal of Child Psychology and Psychiatry*, 44(6): 793–809.

Novick, K.K. & Novick, J. (2003). Two systems of self-regulation and the differential application of psychoanalytic technique. *American Journal of Psychoanalysis*, 63(1):1–20.

Polmear, (2004). Finding the bridge: psychoanalytic work with Asperger's syndrome adults. In M. Rhode & T. Klauber (Ed.), *The Many Faces of Asperger's Syndrome* (pp. 70–85). New York: Karnac.

Rhode. M. (2004). What does it feel like: Two first-person accounts by adults with Asperger's syndrome. In M. Rhode & T. Klauber (Ed.), *The Many Faces of Asperger's Syndrome* (pp. 70–85). New York: Karnac.

Shapiro, T. (2000). Autism and the psychoanalyst. *Psychoanalytic Inquiry*, 20:648–659.

Sherkow, S. (2004). Further reflections on the "watched" play state and role of "watched play" in analytic work. *The Psychoanalytic Study of the Child*, 59:55–73.

Shore, A. (2002). Dysregulation of the right brain: a fundamental mechanism of traumatic attachment and the psychopathogenesis of posttraumatic stress disorder. *Australian and New Zealand Journal of Psychiatry*, 36:9–30.

Ting Wang, A., Lee, S. S., Sigman, M., Dapretto, M. (2007). Reading affect in the face and voice: Neural correlates of interpreting communicative intent in children and adolescents with autism spectrum disorders. *Archives of General Psychiatry*, 64(6):698–708.

Tustin, F. (1981). *Autistic States in Children*. London: Routledge & Kegan Paul.

Tustin, F. (1988). Psychotherapy with children who cannot play. *International Review of Psycho-Analysis*, 15: 93–106.

Weeks, S. J. & Hobson, R. P. (1987). The salience of facial expression for autistic children. *Journal of Child Psychology and Psychiatry*, 28:137–152.

Welchew, D., Ashwin, C., Berkoud, K., Salvador, R., Suckling, J., Baron-Cohen, S., Bullmore, E. (2005). Functional disconnectivity of the medial temporal lobe in Asperger's syndrome. *Biological Psychiatry*, 57(9): 991–998.

Winnicott, D. W. (1971). The use of an object and relating through identifications. In *Playing and Reality*. London: Tavistock Publications.

Psychoanalysis in Cyberspace

by Debra A. Neumann

Abstract

The internet is playing an ever increasing role in society, and not surprisingly in psychoanalytic practice as well. In spite of political and theoretical disputes regarding its status, internet analysis is currently emerging as a frontier of contemporary analytic practice. How do the cultures of psychoanalysis and of the internet interact and interpenetrate each other when the internet is used as a medium in providing a pioneering form of psychoanalytic treatment.? Is a psychoanalytic process possible in cyberspace? This paper will describe some of the factors that must be considered in establishing and maintaining a psychoanalytic setting or frame when using internet videoconferencing for treatment, and the nature of some of the issues that emerge for patient and analyst when practicing psychoanalysis or psychoanalytic psychotherapy using internet videoconferencing technology.

Psychoanalysis in Cyberspace

While growing up on the Nebraska prairie, I often dreamed of riding my horse across the endless plains; of dressing up as Davy Crockett or Annie

371

Oakley and participating in an Old West re-enactments during my town's annual Frontier Days celebration. I read and re-read Willa Cather's amazing novel "Oh Pioneers!" So it is no wonder that as a candidate and aspiring analyst, I would be drawn to the frontier of psychoanalysis, in this case a pioneering effort to bring psychoanalytic education to distant lands.[6]

I first learned of an opportunity to be involved in such an effort in 2008 from a colleague and my interest was piqued when I learned that although many American mental health practitioners reject psychoanalysis, in China there is a hunger to learn about psychoanalytic theory and treatment. And yet there were very few analysts in China who could provide training or treatment. This colleague pointed me to the China American Psychoanalytic Alliance (CAPA), a nonprofit organization incorporated in 2006 whose mission is to develop and promote mental health services in China by training Chinese mental health professionals in psychoanalytically-oriented psychotherapy using the internet for instruction and supervision. In addition to using internet videoconferencing for instruction and supervision, CAPA strongly encourages its students in China (all of whom are mental health professionals) to undergo psychoanalytically oriented psychotherapy or psychoanalysis during their training by means of Skype internet videoconferencing.

I was intrigued by the notion of conducting analysis via the internet, especially so perhaps since in my pre-analytic life I had researched the use of computer technology to provide psychotherapy (Neumann, 1985). In one such attempt, a computer program called Eliza provided Rogerian responses when a client typed in a statement concerning a problem they were having.

---

6 Gabbard (2001) has drawn a parallel between the frontier of the American West and the position of cyberspace vis a vis analytic practice.

Although I found the intention of attempts to make psychotherapy more accessible to the American public by using such software laudable, the actualization left much to be desired. Out of curiosity about the new application of internet videoconferencing technology to training and providing treatment, and in appreciation for the Chinese interest in analysis, I decided to explore at first-hand this new venture. To my surprise, I learned that there was a waiting list of Chinese students requesting internet psychoanalytic treatment. I volunteered to take on a patient and, in consultation with supervisors, I began seeing a Chinese patient 3 times a week using Skype internet videoconferencing technology. After 1 year, this treatment increased in frequency and depth and now entails a 4 times weekly analysis using the couch.

My journey has enlightened me as to the possibilities and also some of the difficulties posed by this type of psychoanalytic treatment. In this paper, I will describe and discuss some of the things I have learned, along with the implications for future use of internet technology in psychoanalysis.

How do the cultures of psychoanalysis and of the internet interact and affect each other when the internet is used as a medium in providing a pioneering form of psychoanalytic treatment? Is the psychoanalytic task possible in cyberspace? Tuckett (2005) describes psychoanalytic treatment as requiring 3 analytic capacities or tasks:(1) the creation of an external and internal setting in which to sense the relevant psychoanalytic data (e.g., affects, unconscious meanings); (2) the ability to conceive what is sensed, and (3) the capacity to offer interpretations based on these, as well as to sense and to conceive the effects of these interpretations. Specifically, this paper will describe some of the factors that must be considered in establishing and maintaining a psychoanalytic setting or frame when using internet videoconferencing for treatment.

Prior to my exposition on 'frame issues' I will provide a brief overview of the nature of some of the issues that emerge for patient and analyst when practicing using internet videoconferencing technology. These concern the way in which using the internet as a vehicle for treatment affects the mutual interpenetration of conscious and unconscious material that is received, experienced and processed by both patient and analyst. Using the internet for treatment impacts the types of transference/countertransference, types of defenses, the nature of unconscious material such as dreams, associations and resistances or blocks that emerge and is a giant area for future exploration. For purposes of my exposition in this paper, I will describe in the few paragraphs that follow several important considerations that the use of the internet for analysis brings to the fore and which must be held in mind. I list these in no particular order but rather to give a flavor of these issues.

In practicing internet psychoanalytic treatment, we must constantly ask ourselves how the qualities of cyberspace itself impact the analytic work. What type of space is cyberspace and what kind of analytic contact and process is possible there? Virtual reality possesses qualities that in some ways are remarkably similar to the potential space of the therapeutic relationship (Fischbein, 2010; Malater, 2007; Lingiardi, 2008). It can function as transitional space. Cyberspace can be a place of liberation from the confines of the self . It may serve as a play space for identity exploration and development free from social sanctions. It can be used as a ground for trial action, and for increased self-definition.

By the same token, virtual reality can create or foster resistances to dealing with everyday reality. It can boost the abilities of individuals to split off their own virtual actions from behaviors and actions in the physical realm. Virtual reality can establish a sense of an altered state, free of conventional rules of time, place and logic. It can engender a sense of freedom and omnipotence, the loss of self boundaries and a pull to regression and merger.

Cyberspace can function as a venue for disavowal and as a psychic retreat. Lingiardi (2008) gives an example of a patient for whom this was the case, and shows how analytic work was transformative for this patient. It can be pseudo helpful, comforting, animated. There is often no fear of reprisal or judgment. There are a myriad of functions cyberspace may serve for the analytic couple (Malater, 2007). What are the meanings to both analyst and patient of working via the internet? What are one's associations to and experiences with this form of technology? Is it used for browsing sexually explicit sites, for assuming an alias identity, for engaging others in factitious relationships, or for purchasing pirated fashions or music? What is the meaning of screens and of seeing and being seen on-line? Will using the internet for treatment evoke voyeuristic, exhibitionistic fantasies in either party, and can these fantasies be contained and used for the benefit of the patient? Lingiardi (2008) mentions that internet treatment may evoke intrusion anxiety in analysts. Peering through a glass screen and viewing a two-dimensional patient on a couch in the patient's residence may bring up many very early and here-to-fore unanalyzed impulses. How does the use of the internet affect the analyst's capacity to foster a treatment alliance or to experience reverie? What kind of enactments between patient and analyst are likely to occur?

What will the effect of the internet be on individuals of specific diagnostic groups? Are people more likely to evidence perversion during internet treatment? How will the impact differ for a schizoid person? Is internet treatment suitable for an individual with vulnerability to fragmentation or is this treatment only suitable for relatively intact, neurotic individuals?

My experience with using the internet to provide psychoanalytically oriented treatment echoes the experience of many of my CAPA colleagues.

(cf. Rosen, 2011). In our psychoanalytic researches, we have found that, when used within clearly defined parameters, internet videoconferencing technology allows sufficient contact and engagement between patient and analyst to provide effective and ethical psychoanalytic treatment. [7]

Prerequisites

There are several essential prerequisites for undertaking an internet psychoanalysis. First, each member of the dyad, patient and analyst, must have at their disposal sufficiently powerful technology to support this type of treatment. The memory available on one's hard drive must be sufficient (2GB is what I have found necessary) and one's broadband connection must be as fast as possible (a fiber optic or high speed DSL connection is required). If memory and connection speed is not adequate on either side of the couch, the video feedback is apt to degenerate into pixels, the audio become indecipherable and the likelihood of dropped calls is high. In my informal survey of CAPA colleagues, there was complete agreement that the quality of the internet connection directly correlates with analysts/ therapists sense that a significant analytic process can develop via the internet. However, when the call quality is poor, the too Criteria for effective

---

7   Criteria for effective and ethical treatment have been articulated by the IPA (March, 2007). They include the capacity to foster and sustain an analytic process over time. An analytic process is one in which unconscious activity, mechanisms and motivations including the transference, countertransference, unconscious affects, and latent unconscious themes can be recognized and followed and formulations can be made to guide interventions. Progress and impasses and developmental aspects can be monitored. Ethical principles related to the practice of psychoanalysis, and in accord with the profession of the practitioner, and laws related to the particular locale of both analyst and patient are followed. Our phenomenological studies indicate potential positive benefits for patients. In the next stage, empirical research will be conducted to validate our findings.

and ethical treatment have been articulated by the IPA (March, 2 2007). They include the capacity to foster and sustain an analytic process over time. An analytic process is one in which unconscious activity, mechanisms and motivations including the transference, countertransference, unconscious affects, and latent unconscious themes can be recognized and followed and formulations can be made to guide interventions. Progress and impasses and developmental aspects can be monitored. Ethical principles related to the practice of psychoanalysis, and in accord with the profession of the practitioner, and laws related to the particular locale of both analyst and patient are followed. Our phenomenological studies indicate potential positive benefits for patients. In the next stage, empirical research will be conducted to validate our findings. frequent queries by analyst or patient "What?" "What?" "Can you see me? Can you hear me?" is highly disruptive to both patient and analyst.

A second prerequisite, when treatment is provided in a language that is non-native for at least one of the participants, is that both analyst and patient have adequate fluency in the language in which the analysis is conducted. When fluency is absent, much time is spent searching for words either in one's mind or in a dictionary. This can result in a choppiness to the flow of sessions which hinders the development of an adequate interior space for unconscious processing. (However, a colleague has shared her experience that her patient's lack of fluency in English has served to slow the process down in a way she has found helpful, as it has focused both herself and her patient on clarifying what is intended, rather than proceeding on the assumption that what is intended is known and shared.)[8]

---

8   Criteria for effective and ethical treatment have been articulated by the IPA (March, 2007). They include the capacity to foster and sustain an analytic process over time. An analytic process is one in which unconscious activity, mechanisms and motivations including the transference, countertransference, unconscious affects, and latent unconscious themes can be recognized and followed and formulations can be made to guide interventions. Progress and impasses and developmental aspects can be monitored.

The third prerequisite relates to the need to provide ethical treatment. Considerations here include mandates of the professional associations of the analyst, the licensure laws regarding internet practice of the jurisdictions in which both patient and analyst live, and provisions for patient confidentiality. It is also necessary to be able to meet mandated reporting requirements, to provide local backup and emergency coverage, and to reduce the potential for harm. (For example, Sabin (2010) finds that psychoanalysis itself is subversive and suggests that providing it to individuals living in countries governed by totalitarian political regimes may bring increased and unwarranted risk to the patients.)

Ways of meeting the requirement to provide ethical treatment vary by profession of the therapist/analyst and by location. A full discussion of the various issues surrounding this topic is beyond the scope of this paper. In the work done by CAPA, much attention has been given to matters regarding meeting legal and ethical requirements when treating patients in China. These are described in the CAPA Ethics and Confidentiality Statement and in a handbook prepared for all CAPA members (Buckner, 2011). Ethical issues are discussed regularly in on-line list-serve forums, at winter and spring APsaA discussion groups, and among board members.

The Psychoanalytic Frame—Past to Present

In this section I will describe factors involved in the creation of an external and internal treatment setting in which psychoanalytic data can emerge,

---

Ethical principles related to the practice of psychoanalysis, and in accord with the profession of the practitioner, and laws related to the particular locale of both analyst and patient are followed. Our phenomenological studies indicate potential positive benefits for patients. In the next stage, empirical research will be conducted to validate our findings.

be detected and responded to. I will address the question, "does internet treatment provide sufficient conditions for the analyst and the patient to establish a stable analytic frame?" There are multiple conceptualizations of an appropriate analytic frame, and this notion is tied to one's theoretical orientation. To begin, I will provide a brief historical overview of psychoanalytic thought related to the concept of frame.

Freud (1913), in "On Beginning the Treatment", made recommendations about the opening phase of treatment and the need to establish rules for its conduct, using chess as an analogy. Freud's recommendations included arrangements about time and money—his practice of leasing frequent and regular hours (six appointments per week) to his patients and expecting payment for these hours, whether or not the patient attended, the need to establish a fair fee schedule, the use of the couch, the use of free association, and following the lead of the patient as to content.

Over the course of time, these recommendations solidified into the traditional or classical conception of "the frame," which comprises fixed conditions that purport to create a therapeutic structure with clear boundaries. The frame is to be outlined in the first session(s) by the analyst as a series of clearly articulated policies, or rules. Typical elements of the classical frame include regularly scheduled appointments of a fixed length (the 45–50 minute 'hour') and frequent sessions that are held at a permanent place. The patient is to lie on a couch with the analyst sitting behind the patient.[9] Sessions are to be paid for on a regular basis,

---

9　In discussing the somewhat arbitrary nature of many elements of the classical frame, 4 Wallerstein (2009) describes several ways that the frame has changed in response to socio-cultural factors. For example, Freud's original recommended frequency of six visits per week was appropriate to the culture of 19th century Vienna, where the typical work week was six days. When psychoanalysis was imported to England and the US, the recommended frequency was reduced to five days to adapt to the 5-day work week of these cultures. After World War II, there was a huge demand for training analyses by returning wartime psychiatrists in the United States. Training analysts had insufficient hours available to meet this demand, but by reducing the frequency for analytic treatment

communication is limited to the verbal level, the patient's role is to say whatever comes to mind, and the analyst's role is to listen, formulate and interpret the resistance and transference. It is the analyst's responsibility to maintain the frame and hold it as constant as possible. The analyst's role is to set the frame, the patient's role is to adapt to it.

The rationale offered for holding firmly to an established frame is that it provides a clear structure within which patients can become absorbed in their internal reality and the analytic process can emerge. Bleger (1967) demarcates two components of psychoanalytic treatment: the first is the process, which is studied, analyzed and interpreted and the second is the frame, by which Bleger refers to "everything else", e.g., the constants within which the process takes place. From a classical viewpoint, the frame is usually in the background and must be kept stable so that the process can be studied and the transference-countertransference and resistance can emerge fully. Prospective analysands must be able to tolerate the conditions of the classical frame. Winnicott suggested a modification to this notion of the frame. At the 19th International Congress of Psychoanalysis in Geneva in 1955, he spoke of the analyst's need to adapt the frame to the developmental needs of the patient. Winnicott (1955) referred to the frame as the psychoanalytic setting, and included in it all aspects of the management of the treatment carried out by the analyst. He pointed out that with patients who have deficits in ego development, as well as with regressed patients, management of the setting moves to the foreground, and it becomes a more important element in the treatment than interpretation of the transference.

While Winnicott's views differ significantly from the classical position, they share with it the common feature that the frame is set and

---

from five to four sessions weekly, the demand could be met. Currently, in most countries, frequency requirements for analytic treatment have been reduced further to three sessions per week.

maintained by the analyst. For the classical analyst, a patient must adapt to the analyst's frame, and if this cannot be done, the patient is deemed unsuitable for treatment. For Winnicott, the analyst sets the frame, based on empathic attunement with the ego needs of the patient. Presumably, if the analyst is not able to adapt the frame to the patient's needs, the analyst is unsuitable to treat the patient. In both cases, the frame is viewed as a consistent, invariable structure established and maintained by the analyst that supports the treatment. More recently, analysts from the intersubjective/relational school have challenged traditional views about the nature of the frame. Bass (2007) views the frame as co- created by analyst and patient in an endeavor to establish the conditions which will make the therapy process tolerable or even possible for the patient. The frame contains elements brought both by the analyst and by the patient and reflects aspects of both of their lives and their relationship. The frame is not viewed as a series of relatively inflexible rules, but rather as a set of preferences unique to each patient-analyst pair and subject to revision throughout the course of treatment with each patient. The frame changes over time as the patient, analyst, and their relationship changes. The frame is thus viewed as an evolving system of shifting arrangements. Bromberg (2007) amplifies this notion with his self-state perspective, in which in each treatment there are many frames and many framers (i.e., various frames are used by various self-states of patient and analyst.)

The relational, as well as the classical and developmental views seem united in agreement that the frame (or frames) function to guarantee that patient and analyst can become absorbed in a timeless experience of internal space—an analytic couple can enter the intense inner dimension of a psychoanalytic treatment. A central aspect of analytic treatment is that conditions must be established to provide analyst and patient the possibility to immerse themselves in the unconscious realm of psychic reality, regardless of their physical location in space or time. The external frame serves the internal psychic function of demarcating a realm of a different kind of reality from consensually validated 'normal' external reality. This protected inner realm can then become a potential space for analytic work—a space in which the patient can regress as needed and in which unconscious dynamics can emerge in clear relief.

Various aspects of this internal aspect of the frame have been highlighted. For some, such as Bleger (1967), a stable external frame facilitates the development of a symbiosis, representing an early state of merger with a mothering parent figure. Within a stable frame, the patient will be able to regress and bring into the treatment the most primitive, most non-differentiated aspects of the self. The frame thus delineates a potential magical realm, where the omnipotent, infantile self of the patient can emerge. To use the felicitous phrase of a patient of Francis Tustin (1986), the external frame provides an internal "rhythm of safety" for both analyst and analysand. The establishment of this type of frame allows the patient to feel secure and is a precondition for the development of dependence on a good object via internalization of the functions of the analyst. The patient feels safe and can use the analyst as needed.

Modell (1988) amplified Bleger's ideas. He differentiated the type of transference engendered by the frame from that of the classical 'transference neurosis'. He calls the transference derived from the reliable, relatively constant psychoanalytic setting as the 'dependent/containing transference'. Modell believes that this type of transference is continually present, that it symbolically actualizes developmental conflicts and that its presence enhances and strengthens mutative interpretations.

Arlow and Brenner (1990), extend the internal function of the external frame by pointing out that the frame does not necessarily serve a symbiotic function, but rather can ground the treatment in the adult world of contractual relationships. Chasseguet-Smirgel (1992) terms the situation evoked by the frame as an archaic matrix of the oedipal complex. While, on the one hand, the frame guarantees the establishment of an enclave in which the patient is able to abandon himself to narcissistic regression, on the other hand, the frame presents the patient with a reality oriented 'paternal function', opposing the wish to return to prenatal existence.

The Psychoanalytic Frame—Present to Future

This overview of the literature on the frame indicates that irrespective of theoretical differences, there is widespread agreement that the establishment of a frame is necessary in order for an analytic, therapeutic process to occur. The question is posed, can this type of frame be provided when using internet videoconferencing technology to conduct analysis or analytic therapy?

Some would state that this is not possible. For example, Curtis (2007) characterizes internet treatment as conducted in an autistic space —a space which she views as limited to two-dimensional information and 'artificial intelligence'. Curtis refers to Bion's concept of an analytic setting and process as one in which a patient learns from experience "within the context of two minds in the same time and space emotionally containing each other." In her view, when using the internet, two minds are not in the same time and space, emotional containment cannot occur, and it is not possible to detect and manage the analytic process.

Taken concretely, in the world of internet treatment at a distance, analyst and patient are not meeting "in the same time and space." After all, there is a 12 hour time difference between my office in Chevy Chase, Maryland and Mainland China. It is 9 a.m. my time here in the states and 9 p.m. Beijing time[10] when I meet my patient. The same also applies to how "in the same space" is defined. If we think on a less concrete, less

---

10 The entire vast country of mainland China comprises a single time zone, "Beijing time."

reductionistic level, it is possible to extend traditional thoughts about what constitutes time and space to a more interior realm—the world of the unconscious mind—my patient and I do in fact interact in a setting outside the limits of physical space and linear time.

Following this view, during the analytic hour patient and analyst are in the same time and space during the session, and that time and space may or may not coincide with the physical location of either party. At the boundaries of the session, this is clearly not the case. For example, it is jarring to me when at the end of a session, at nearly 10 p.m.in China, my patient closes the hour saying, "Good Night" or when in an unthinking morning moment I greet her with "Good Morning" at the start. In these situations, we are compelled to acknowledge the obvious distance between us represented by the difference in time, which during our emergence in the unconscious realm during the hour has disappeared. Sand (2007) has referred to doing psychoanalysis in cyberspace as requiring the development of a 'consensual hallucination'. My experience has been that clearly this is possible in the unconscious realm, where analyst and patient, whether in the same geographic location or separated by thousands of miles, are in the same time and space.

The third element that Curtis finds lacking when using the internet for treatment relates to her view that emotional containment cannot be provided during internet treatment. In this regard the possibility of frequent dropped calls and pixelated screens does make containment exceedingly difficult. On an internal level, a dropped call maybe akin to a fragmentation of relationship, a Bionian 'catastrophe'—an attack on linking. In a conventional in-office treatment, one would rely on elements of an invariant or co-constructed frame, on the reliability and consistency of the analyst to contain and control a regression or a crisis.

However, as I stated in the section on prerequisites for treatment, above, the technology used by both patient and analyst must be adequate, and if it is, this disruption can be manageable. A treatment can tolerate disruptions, such as a UPS delivery knocking at the door in mid-session, so long as they are infrequent and the disruptive effect on the patient attended to.

Some think that it is not possible for an on-line analyst to detect and manage the analytic process. Others feel that we internet analysts need to compensate for the fragile nature of the technological distance and disrupted connection by extra efforts to solidify the relational connection and to modify a traditional frame, such as by direct statements conveying warmth and acceptance, by sending gifts, by scheduling sessions during patient's time away or during our own. While it is true that using the internet to provide treatment does pose a significant challenge to both patient and analyst in sensing an emotional presence, certain ways of constructing the setting make it more likely that containment is possible, for example arranging seating so that the analyst has a profile view of the patient on the couch and the patient can easily turn to view the analyst when feeling insecure. Many of us who have provided psychoanalytic treatment to Chinese patients using the internet agree that it is possible, given the appropriate patient-analyst match, to create an analytic frame that provides a rhythm of safety and emotional containment sufficient to allow an analytic process to develop.

The Future

This paper has articulated issues for contemporary psychoanalysis that have resulted from the encounter of the culture of psychoanalysis with the culture of virtual reality. The history of psychoanalysis has been marked by controversies over the introduction of changes to the prevailing paradigm, as psychoanalysis has changed and evolved in response to encounters with new frontiers. According to Merriam-Webster (2007), the word frontier can be used to denote two types of boundary. It can indicate both a line of division between different or opposed things, and a new field for exploration and development. Offering psychotherapy and psychoanalysis via the internet expands and redefines the boundary of analytic experience. Does this practice break new ground in a constructive and creative way or transgress?

Some analysts feel cyberspace and psychoanalysis are cultures that are opposed to one another and reject the idea of internet psychoanalysis. Some view it as a self-focused attempt to exploit others for financial or other forms of gain. Others object to it as a violation of the basic rules and boundaries of psychoanalysis. Internet analysis is considered an oxymoron, or worse yet, a heresy. Some opponents find that the technology itself is not adequate to encompass an analytic process. They condemn the use of the internet for psychoanalysis, largely basing their arguments on the incompatibility of an intimate personal encounter with the distance imposed by internet contact and find the use of internet technology incomprehensible. I have addressed some of these concerns above, and here want to specifically address two others.

First, there is a historical precedent within psychoanalysis for the use of new technology. Berger (2005) points out that Freud used the technology of his day—he used the postal service in his analysis of Lil Hans. Freud also introduced a new psychoanalytic application for existing technology in his use of the couch.

Over the decades, analysts have adapted their practice to changes brought by new technology. For example, most contemporary analysts use the digital clock to keep time. Other examples of technological applications that have brought changes to psychoanalytic practice are the telephone, cell phone, answering machine, voice mail, even the electric light. When adapting new technology to their clinical work, analysts have needed to analyze the meanings of this. For example, Berger (2007) illustrates the way in which using digital clocks has changed our relationship to the structure of the session by fostering for analyst and patient alike a sense of exactitude we otherwise would not have.

Second, political considerations play a prominent role in the rejection of the idea of internet psychoanalysis. The use of the internet to conduct psychoanalysis is a highly charged political issue that is being debated intensely in both the APsaA and IPA. As an example, Scharff (2010) gives an overview of a discussion group at the IPA conference in Chicago. The organizers of the panel and the speakers presented the view that psychoanalysis must both adapt to the current social reality of a global economy and make use of information technology to meet the needs and demands of those in rural areas where psychoanalysis would not otherwise be available, the needs of business executives and the like who wish an analysis but travel too frequently to commit to meeting 4 or 5 times weekly, and to meet the desires of young adults who have grown up with the new technology. Opponents argued that psychoanalysis is chasing after technology as an alternative to in-depth person-to- person work and that telephone analysis/internet analysis is not analysis.

The panelists countered that use of information technology does not preclude attention to the analytic dyad, and depth work. Affective attunement, unconscious communication, an appreciation of resistance, work with the transference/ countertransference are all part of Skype analysis. They add that psychoanalysis has been responding to cultural developments from the beginning and this responsiveness has led to new and valued pathways of understanding. Proponents conclude that the 21st century has brought a transformation in our understanding of the mind, which transcends specific cultures and that a new international culture of psychoanalysis is required to meet the challenges of the 21st century.

Internet analysis also is likely to have a large impact on psychoanalytic training. For example, the internet is supplanting the telephone in being used for analysis for candidates who live at some distance from their analysts, provided a certain number of hours are completed in the same physical location.[11] The IPA is currently establishing a psychoanalytic training program in China, although very few qualified analysts reside there. Chinese candidates are permitted an internet training/personal analysis after completing a specified number of hours of in person treatment.[12] At present a consensus seems to have emerged, at least within the IPA, that internet psychoanalysis is acceptable as a form of treatment for some candidates. Internet analyses are not at this time acceptable as control cases in most training institutes. APsaA and IPA institutes in the USA currently require that for control cases, the treatment must occur 4 times weekly in person on the couch.[13]

In this paper, I have addressed considerations raised for the future of psychoanalysis in light of the development of the possibility to use the internet for psychoanalysis. Such a possibility evokes anxiety and fears among many. One worry is that what is most basic to psychoanalysis will be undermined by the use of the internet.

Current discourse within some circles around aspects of psychoanalytic culture such as the frame are comprised of concepts and practices that limit our ability to think beyond traditional forms of culture. Paradoxically, a theory and therapy that has been described as subversive to cultural

---

11 An example is the training program of the International Psychoanalytic Training Institute, located in Chevy Chase, Maryland and drawing candidates from more remote areas such as Panama.

12 Elise Snyder, M.D., personal communication.

13 The meaning of 'in person' in a virtual world remains to be fully thought out. To view internet video encounters as not occurring 'in person' is problematic. Internet psychoanalysis poses analysts and analytic institutions with a need to re-think our current notions of the nature of time, space/locale, human beings and of what constitutes a personal relationship.

status quo and convention (Thompson, 2002, p. 82) is at present being used in some camps to oppose innovation.

Curtis (2007, p.135) writes that the internet and cyberspace contribute vital and importantly to our theoretical discourse about the nature of analysis, but have nothing to offer psychoanalytic praxis. I hope that in this paper I have encouraged you to question this statement, and to be open to internet applications in psychoanalysis which are making the profound contribution of psychoanalytic thought and practice available on a global level.

References

Arlow, J.A. & Brenner, C. (1990). The psychoanalytic process. *Psychoanalytic Quarterly*, 59, 678–692.

Bass, A. (2007). When the frame doesn't fit the picture. *Psychoanalytic Dialogues*, 17, 1–27.

Berger, N. (2005). New medium, new messages, new meanings: Communication and interaction in child treatment in an age of technology. *Journal of Infant, Child and Adolescent Psychotherapy*, 4, 218–229.

Bleger, J. (1967). Psychoanalysis of the psychoanalytic frame. *International Journal of Psychoanalysis*, 48, 511–519.

Bromberg, P. (2007) The analytic moment doesn't fit analytic "technique": Commentary on Tony Bass's "When the frame doesn't fit the picture". *Psychoanalytic Dialogues*, 17, 909–921.

Buckner, L. (Ed.) (2011, May 31) *China American Psychoanalytic Alliance Handbook*. Retrieved June 25, 2011 from http://groups.yahoo.com/groups/CAPATREAT/files

Chasseguet-Smirgel, J. (1992). Some thoughts on the psychoanalytic situation. *Journal of the American Psychoanalytic Association*, 40, 3-25.

Curtis, A.E. (2007). The claustrum: Sequestration of cyberspace. *The Psychoanalytic Review*, 94, 99–139.

Fischbein, S.V. (2010). Psychoanalysis and virtual reality. *International Journal of Psychoanalysis*, 91, 985–988.

Freud, S. (1958). On Beginning the Treatment (Further Recommendations on the Technique of Psycho-Analysis I). In J. Strachey (Ed. & Trans.), *The standard edition of the complete psychological works of Sigmund Freud*, (Volume 12, pp. 121–144.) London: Hogarth Press. (Original work published 1932–36)

Gabbard, G. O. (2001). Cyberpassion: E-rotic transference on the internet. *Psychoanalytic Quarterly*, 70, 719–737.

International Psychoanalytical Association. (2007, March) Equivalency procedures for assessing individual applicants for IPA membership or for recognition as IPA child and adolescent analysts trained in non-IPA organisations. Retrieved June 25, 2011 from http://www.ipa.org.uk/eng/about-ipa/ipa-procedural-code.

Lingiardi, V. (2008). Playing with unreality: transference and computer. *International Journal of Psychoanalysis*, 89, 111–126.

Malater, E. (2007). Caught in the web: Patient, therapist, e-mail and the internet. *Psychoanalytic Review*, 94, 151–168.

Merriam-Webster's collegiate dictionary (11th ed.). (2007). Springfield, MA: Merriam-Webster.

Modell, A. H. (1988). The centrality of the psychoanalytic setting and the changing aims of treatment. *Psychoanalytic Quarterly*, 57, 577–596.

Neumann, D.A. (1985). A psychotherapeutic computer application: Modification of technological competence. *Behavioral Research Methods, Instruments, & Computers*, 18, 135–140.

Parker, I. (2007). Psychoanalytic cyberspace, beyond psychology. *Psychoanalytic Review*, 94, 63–82.

Rosen, C. (2010, March 5). Can You Hear Me? Can You See Me?: Conducting a Skype Internet Analysis in Chinese. [Electronic version] Paper presented at Symposium 2011:

Our Practice Today, Treatment and Transformation, Mount Sinai Medical Center, New York City. Retrieved March 29, 2011 from htpp://internationalpsychoanalysis.net/wp-content/uploads/2011/03/CaroleRosenpaper.pdf

Sabin, J. (2010, October 12). Health Care Organizational Ethics: Psychoanalysis in China. Retrieved June 25, 2011 from http://

healthcareorganizationalethics.blogspot.com/2010/10/psychoanalysis-in-china.html

Sand, S. (2007). Future considerations; Interactive identities and the interactive self. *Psychoanalytic Review*, 94, 83–97.

Scharff, J. (2010). Telephone analysis. *International Journal of Psychoanalysis*, 91, 989–992.

Thompson, M.G. (2002). The Ethic of Honesty: The Moral Dimension to Psychoanalysis. *Fort Da*, 8, 72–83

Tustin, F. (1986). *Autistic barriers in neurotic patients*. New Haven & London: Yale University Press.

Wallerstein, R. (2009). Defining psychoanalysis: A review and a commentary. *Psychoanalytic Dialogues*, 19, 675–690.

Winnicott, D.W. (1955). Metapsychological and clinical aspects of regression within the psychoanalytical set-up. *International Journal of Psychoanalysis*, 36, 16–26.

The Dilemma of Separation in Female Development and the Relevance of the Persephone Myth

by Marie Murphy

C ontemporary psychoanalytic thinking about the strivings implicit in separation-individuation issues in female development has been hampered by a rigidly orthodox adherence to the Oedipus Complex as universally related to both males and females. This approach to a triangulation phase sets up an interesting and troubling dilemma when theory is juxtaposed to the reality of what is seen in clinical practice with many female patients. My own observation is that the bedrock phenomenon of the universal Oedipus Complex, with its emphasis on castration fears, power, fate, rage, murder, and violence, does not fully or adequately reflect the deeper tensions and conflicts at play in female development, particularly around a girl's separating from her primary object.

The Oedipus Complex, as the central conflict in the human psyche and as a cornerstone of psychoanalytic thinking, demands some reconsideration in light of clinical work with many female patients. Freud initially assumed a relative parallel process in the triangular situations of males and females—"As you can see, I have only described the relation of a boy to his father and mother. Things happen in just the same way with little girls, with the necessary changes: an affectionate attachment to her father, a need to get rid of her mother as superfluous and to take her place…" (Freud, 1916, p. 333). Freud theorized that for a girl to turn her attentions to her father, she must refocus her original sexuality in three ways: in sexual organ, aim, and object: "She must abandon pleasures from the 'masculine' clitoris…; she must give up a phallic, active masculine orientation for a more passive feminine one; and finally, she must renounce her original sexual object, the mother, and turn her attentions to the father instead" (Kulish and Holtzman, 2008, p. 9).

Freud later altered his views based on his clinical observations. He then postulated that it was fear of the loss of love more than castration fears that seemed so apparent in the development of little girls; yet, these observations still obscured a critical motivating factor for girls in their development, which is that there would be a wish to remain attached in some way to the very person that the little girl must separate from. Instead, Freud "…dismissed condescendingly the importance of his own observation and described the situation in language that implied the superego of girls was inferior to, or weaker than, that of boys" (Kulish and Holtzman, 2008, p. 10). Freud relegated a little girl's fears about the loss of her mother or the loss of her mother's love to the status of a pre-oedipal anxiety. In Freud's "The New Introductory Lectures on Psychoanalysis" (1933), he wrote that "…the girl remains indefinitely mired in the Oedipus phase. Her attachment to her mother is dissolved only by hostility toward her—hostility arising, in part, from the fact that the girl continues to hold the mother responsible for her lack of a penis" (Kulish and Holtzman, 2008, p. 11). In Freud's "Femininity", he addressed more specifically the question of what brings a daughter's attachment to her mother to an end:

"This step in development does not involve a simple change of object. The turning away from the mother is accompanied by hostility; the attachment to the mother ends in hate. A hate of that kind may become very striking and last all through life ..." (Freud, 1933, p. 121).

Freud laid the groundwork about the Oedipus Complex's universality for male and female development. His views were elaborated by other writers such as Karl Abraham, who emphasized the castration complex as central to female development and Otto Fenichel, who agreed with Freud's emphasis on the importance of pre-oedipal influences, such as the girl's enduring ties to her mother, but he felt that the mother's failure to provide her daughter with a penis was the decisive disappointment that leads to a girl's entry into the oedipal phase. (Kulish and Holtzman, 2008) Freud welcomed contributions from some of his female colleagues, such as Lampl-de Groot and Marie Bonaparte, who explained aspects of female development through an exploration of a pre-oedipal phase but at the same time closely adhered to Freud's basic model for the oedipal situation itself. (Holtzman and Kulish, 2000) Even Hans Loewald, who spotlighted the significance of the maternal caretaking of the infant, "...elaborated dramatically on the impossibility of growing up without killing off one's parents. Within genuine creativity was utter destruction" (Balsam, 2010, pp. 511–512). Freud's adherence to a phallocentric interpretation of the Oedipus Complex continued to hold female development hostage to a masculine norm.

Karen Horney differed from Freud in that she held that penis envy and feelings of inferiority had cultural determinants: "Women have adapted themselves to the wishes of men and felt as if their adaptation were their true nature" (Horney, 1926, p. 326). She saw penis envy as a defensive reaction to oedipal disappointment—inevitable but also transitory. (Kulish and Holtzman, 2008)

Melanie Klein offered important contributions to the evolving theories of female development. She believed that the Oedipus Complex originated much earlier in development as a consequence of frustration at the breast and was influenced by introjective and projective processes. She said that it was frustration at the breast and crucially the weaning process that made the infant turn to the father's penis and become aware of a triangular situation. (Britton, 1989) Klein, ever the Freudian, did not differentiate early development between girls and boys: "In my view infants of both sexes experience genital desires directed towards their mother and father, and they have unconscious knowledge of the vagina as well as of the penis ... Under the sway of fantasy life and of conflicting emotions, the child at every stage of libidinal organization introjects his objects—primarily his parents ..." (Britton, 1989, p. 78). Yet Klein's thinking illuminated ideas about the unique interiority of the female and the unconscious knowledge of an important internal space where the girl's emotions and phantasy life are built around her own and her mother's world of internal objects. The little girl's phantasies and emotions embrace a grateful although ambivalent relationship to the breast and to the penis as the source of good gifts. (Spillius et al., 2011) Klein's views expanded the possibilities that phantasies and projections in early oedipal dynamics color the girl's triangular conflicts. This emphasis "...provided a corrective to a developmental perspective skewed by its phallic preoccupation and its linear sequencing" (Kulish and Holtzman, 2008, p. 14).

Notwithstanding the reality that there are many complex patterns of anxieties, fantasies, defenses and object relationships that make up the oedipal phase for girls and for boys, the aspects that I wish to focus on are the dilemmas around separation issues that are implicit in the triangular situation confronting girls. Boys certainly have separation issues—"...both boys and girls have to deal with the developmental tasks of loosening infantile ties to internal parental objects and integrating disparate parental imagos...." (Holtzman and Kulish, 2000, p. 1418)—but girls entering this triangular stage in their development face separation issues with a particular intensity and in different and nuanced ways.

If triangulation and separation for girls is not simply a mirror reflection of what happens in boys, then what formulation might offer a deeper understanding of the unique dynamics at work in female development? An important idea about the difference between the triangular situations of little girls and little boys that is an undercurrent running through a myriad of psychoanalytic writings is "....the importance to the girl of her relationship to her mother, and its role in the development, shape, and resolution of her 'oedipal' situation" (Holtzman and Kulish, 2000, p. 1414). It is this central relationship with the mother and the importance of issues of separation from the mother in triangular conflicts that is a critical and a differentiating element in understanding the deeper dimensions of female development. I would like to illustrate this by combining Holtzman and Kulish's creative use of the Persephone myth—called the Persephone Complex—and a clinical example from my analytic work.

My patient, Ms. E., reports this dream:

I'm walking along the shore, no safe place to walk. There's water on the right. I'm in a swimsuit and barefoot. I'm walking in a calculated way because there were not enough safe spots to walk. Looking down there were remnants of balloons, condoms, even dead animals. There were a lot of people. I was approaching an open field covered with a smooth coat of grass. It was exciting to see. I came closer, evidently I was not supposed to get close to the field, or linger there too long. I ventured into the field. There was a small fence protecting a garden—such a welcome sight. I walked up to the few small plants that were on the inside of the fence. I was very curious and I had a strong desire to touch, smell and look at a tomato plant up close. I felt overpowered not to stay there. I was beginning to experience this small plant. Maybe it was my brother who pointed out that my exploration was not acceptable. He said: "C'mon we're not supposed to be here." I believe I got back in the Honda with Mom.

The sense of something dangerous and forbidden is captured in this rich dream material. The patient, a young female artist, age 31, chooses to focus her associations in the analytic hour on the enclosed garden imagery in the dream and the feeling of the allure of the tomato plant. She describes the intensity of the wish to touch and smell the tomato plant and how hard it is to hold herself back from picking it and eating it. I understand this curiosity as a sensory signal of the patient's repressed eroticism. She describes her sense of "danger" in the dream and her feeling that she was doing something "bad". Yet at the same time she felt pulled towards it as if it were a gravitational force field—a force field of a critical superego scanning her as her curiosity swells. Ms. E. recalls feeling reluctant to leave the little garden and get back into the car with her mother.

We could view this material from many perspectives in attempting to understand something of this woman's struggle with her identity and conflicts around her developing sexuality and separation from her mother and transferentially from me. She notes in the dream that "...there are not enough safe spots to walk...". We can also view this as a seduction scene with Ms. E. being tantalized by the world outside the mother-daughter dyad as she comes to know the pleasures of sexuality with assuming the adult female role. Thus unfolds this young woman's "oedipal" conflict.

In attempting to grapple with this conflict, some uniquely female challenges in development around the oedipal phase emerge that may not be adequately represented in the more phallocentric myth of Oedipus Rex. Instead, the myth of Demeter and Persephone may be better suited to the nuances that are particular to female development with its emphasis on the critical importance of the mother-daughter bond, the identifications implicit in this, and the conflicts around a daughter's paradoxical wish to maintain a relationship with mother while separating and individuating.

The ancient myth of Demeter and Persephone has many variations. The one that I find most interesting is the classical Greek version that typifies the devoted bond between a mother and her daughter—in this case, Demeter, the goddess of the harvest and her beautiful daughter Kore, meaning "maiden" (who becomes Persephone in the Underworld). In the myth Demeter is presented as a totally devoted mother who is always attentive and is determined to keep Kore within her sight. One day, as Kore is dancing in the fields with her mother and other maidens, she wanders off and is attracted to a beautiful narcissus flower. As she picks it, the earth splits open and Hades, the god of the Underworld, appears and abducts Kore in his chariot, taking her screaming into his world. Demeter is unaware of what has happened and becomes frantic as she searches the earth for Kore. The catastrophe of the loss of her daughter causes Demeter to become transformed. She loses her youth and vitality and becomes a retaliatory figure that punishes the earth with famine and destruction in the wake of her grief at not finding her beloved daughter. When Demeter learns that Kore is now Queen of the Underworld and is now called Persephone, she threatens to further devastate the earth with more famine unless Zeus gains the release of Persephone from his own brother, Hades. Zeus sends Hermes to Hades and arranges for Persephone's return until it is discovered that Persephone has eaten several pomegranate seeds, the food of the dead, and therefore must remain in the Underworld. The ensuing negotiation allows Persephone to return to her mother for two thirds of the year, although she must be with Hades for one third of the year. The earth is fertile and in bloom when Persephone is with her mother and turns barren when she is with Hades. While this myth accounts for the seasons of the year, it certainly suggests much more in terms of the intricacies of the mother-daughter relationship and the painfulness of separation from the mother as well as the painfulness of separation for the mother. It also speaks of the anxieties related to an entry into adult heterosexuality, and the eventual rapprochement between a mother and daughter.

The Persephone myth highlights the deep bond of loyalty between a mother and daughter and the intensity of feelings around separating and reuniting. It focuses on the subtle element in female development that the daughter is caught in a bind where she may wish to be loyal to the very same person that she must identify and compete with, and ultimately separate from. This underscores the tremendous difficulty of a daughter's leaving the mother and the impact of this on the daughter's sense of self. When Persephone is returned to her mother, she has eaten the pomegranate seeds, "forbidden fruit", and is no longer a virgin. She has become Hades' Queen and is bound to him. Although Persephone initially refuses to eat anything in the Underworld because she is so unhappy without her mother, she eventually becomes very hungry and eats a few pomegranate seeds. In so doing she takes in a different kind of knowledge of herself, one that is not a reflection of the gleam in her mother's eye. In a sense, she becomes "impregnated" with the blood red pomegranate seeds of sexuality and moves towards a more separate sense of self from her mother. Thus Persephone, in leaving the protected world under the control of Demeter, "tastes" the knowledge of another realm that creates a breach in the symbiotic bond with her mother, and that breach begins to define them as separate people. According to this version of the myth, the breach in the symbiotic bond occurs in a passive way, as Persephone is abducted against her will and is tricked into eating pomegranate seeds. This version of the myth seems to align with Freud's primal fantasy of the sexual seduction of the child which leaves the child innocent of any sexual desire and intention. Kore as Persephone finds herself as a woman transformed to the dynamics of the "nether world", which encompasses sexuality and innocence. However because this transformation into a woman is "against her will", it protects her childlike desire to remain innocent at all costs—to remain the ideal little girl/maiden. This version allows Persephone to disavow her own desire, believing that she has been tricked into recognizing her sexuality and protecting her from her own direct competitive feelings with her mother.

This version might suggest that female autonomy is achieved only against one's will and could undermine the significance of a daughter's own sense of agency in becoming differentiated from her mother. However, it does underscore the struggle in achieving autonomy and the importance of a strong and forceful "interference" (such as the notion of the nom du pere of Lacan) to rupture the undifferentiated relationship between mother and daughter. It is noteworthy that in other versions of this myth, Persephone is not just abducted, but is seen as a more active agent of her curiosity, investigating the narcissus flower and then finding herself in the Underworld. Her fascination and attraction to the narcissus flower reveals Kore's infatuation with her own allure and beauty and a hunger to possess the deep eroticism that is the domain of Goethe's "eternal feminine". Moreover, in these other versions of the myth, Persephone is not tricked into eating the pomegranate seeds but freely explores and tastes them and is attracted to Hades. In those versions, the pomegranate seeds are the blood red seeds of full sexual maturity and intention. So there are conflicting stories in portraying the sense of agency and human intentionality in a daughter's freeing herself from the symbiotic bond with the mother.

I don't know if Demeter would have continued to grow old in her grief and ravage the earth in search of her beloved daughter if she knew that Persephone had been curious and wandered into the Underworld of her own volition while attracted by a beautiful flower. This sets up a potential conflict for both mother and daughter in how to engage in the process of separation without destroying the relationship that has been a primary preoccupation of mother and an essential source of life for the daughter. We might imagine that for the young Persephone, the threat of merger with her mother creates ongoing anxieties as well as pleasures, but that she might fear her mother's resentment, envy, and retaliation if she were to become more curious and sexual. In addition, the young daughter might fear her own hatred towards her mother if she were to fully realize her mother's need for control and possession of her. For the daughter to have a private life that includes an intimate relationship with a man, even in the Underworld, could potentially enrage her mother. The guilt emanating from these fears might create a myriad of self-sabotaging and self-inhibiting behaviors for the young daughter. Above all, it could impair the possibility of the development of a real and mature relationship between mother and daughter. What unfolds then is an interlocking tension of rejection, envy, and self-sabotage where both mother and daughter are embroiled in a relationship that becomes self-defeating for each at different times. To explore this separation primarily through the lens of murder, castration and the violence of the Oedipus Rex myth limits the understanding of the complexity of the problem of parental love and parental possessiveness in female development.

Turning once again to my patient, Ms. E is a present day Persephone who struggles with finding her autonomy in a world where her anxiety and guilt about her sexuality can shut down her thinking and feeling. For her, differentiation from her mother holds excitement, a threat of abandonment, and a phantasy of annihilation.

Ms. E. walks on eggshells in her fragile relationship with her mother: "…I'm walking in a calculated way because there were not enough safe spots to walk…". In her dream, she must navigate amidst remnants of symbolically provocative and erotic objects such as balloons (breasts), condoms (interrupted sexual potency), and dead animals (dead objects or dead babies) as they are "washed up" onto shore from her unconscious. These are indeed not "safe spots" to walk. In addition, her curiosity and "…strong desire to touch, smell and look at a tomato plant up close…" reveals a sensory connection to the feel and smell of her genitals. She both wishes and fears that her mother would recognize her separateness as a sexual woman along with her desire to still be close to her mother. Ms. E.'s brother's warning to her that "…exploring was not good…" and to get back into the Honda ignites the conflict around whether she can safely return to the Honda, the containment of mother, or perhaps the return is a potential entrapment in the mechanical world of the mother's possession.

Ms. E.'s history reveals a family culture of impingement and fused relational dynamics under the guise of "care and devotion". There is also a family culture where feelings are swept under the carpet—"You just didn't talk about certain things"—and where her role in the family is to bring sunshine to her very depressed mother. Her mother always called her "my sunshine". This legacy was imposed by the maternal grandmother whose depressive presence in Ms. E.'s home was quite pronounced. The bond between mother and grandmother was intense and preoccupying for Ms. E.'s mother. Ms. E.'s grandmother was raped by a man whom she knew and her mother is the child born of that rape. This event was held as such a family secret that her mother did not learn about the rape until after the grandmother's death. Her grandmother had never married and nothing was ever said about a "father". Likewise, in Ms. E.'s analysis, very little was introduced about her father. Ms. E.'s mother still actively grieves her mother's death, even though it occurred 12 years ago. She continues to display the silk funeral flowers prominently in the family home and keeps the grandmother's furniture in her garage. There is a "Demeter" feel to

403

this continued unmourned preoccupation with the grandmother, who in a very real sense is still "alive".

Ms. E.'s mother and grandmother created countless prohibitions around sexuality, bodily sensations, pleasure, and the dangers of leaving home. Ms. E. feels anxiety about both her body and her sexuality from these injunctions and from the prohibitions of her religious background that fuel the primitive constitution of her superego. Her grandmother would admonish her to never allow an "impure thought" in her mind and taught her several religious mantras to protect her from these intrusions and bodily sensations. Despite these impingements, Ms. E. committed the multiple unforgivable sins of leaving home for college, studying art abroad, marrying someone outside of her religion, and having a baby. These are all punishable offenses for choosing life outside the maternal crypt, and indeed they are Ms. E.'s pomegranate seeds of separation.

Not surprisingly, Ms. E experiences difficulty engaging in sexual intimacies with her husband—her thoughts are often racing and sometimes her mother's voice intrudes to make sexual enjoyment impossible. Their form of birth control has been to interrupt coitus and Ms. E. finds orgasm impossible. This certainly has been reenacted in the transference with me, when Ms. E. can feel too close or intimate and must interrupt and redirect us or she will just "pull out". Her mother pervades her thoughts and she often refers to "my mind" as "my mom". She experiences tremendous guilt if she begins to feel pleasure. At times, she can numb herself and join her mother in moments of symbiotic union and then refuse to allow happiness in her life for fear of its inevitable punishment. She then gets angry at herself for "giving in" to this conflict.

Yet Ms. E. continues to be curious and "wander" into her internal world and has begun to open up more areas of potential excitement, pleasure, and growth for herself. She and her husband recently decided to move back to the metropolitan area rather than return to the Midwest to be closer to her family. She wishes to continue our analytic work (she had been commuting 90 minutes each way to sessions four times a week), and finish her graduate work in art which she had abandoned after the first year--perhaps because it was too exciting.

Ms. E.'s work as an artist ebbs and flows depending on whether she retreats into the parasitic crypt with her mother and grandmother (and her mother's vampiric and narcissistic need to feed from the life of her daughter) or whether she can manage to honor the generativity and fertility of her own life. This area of her professional life has been impacted like Persephone with the pomegranate seeds and she wonders if she can tolerate the expansion of knowledge and the fullness of the sexual world in her work. She struggles with whether she must second guess her every brush stroke or whether she can allow herself the sexual experience of paint and canvas. Sometimes when the paintings "come up too quickly" and are pleasurable and exciting, she has cut off her work for months. When she shuts her work down, this may become a way for Ms. E. to dedifferentiate herself and rejoin a merged state with her mother. She wonders if she is allowed to enjoy more accomplishment and self-satisfaction than her mother. Here the oedipal dynamic comes alive as she grapples with being an oedipal victor over mother awaiting a harsh retaliation. But this is not the whole story. A question Ms. E. and I often struggle with revolves around whether there is a way to take pleasure in her work and in her world with her husband and baby, and at the same time maintain a meaningful relationship with her mother that does not involve envy, rejection, and a self-criticism for being "too greedy".

Ms. E. reported another dream one week later:

I was running, my body was drained and withered. It was dusk. I was running behind a parking garage of some sort—massive concrete shelves to my left. There were small pockets of grass containing an attractive tree. I thought that maybe this was supposed to distract me from all the lifeless concrete that was around. The tree was so green. I was drawn to the tree.

Like the opening dream of this paper, this more recent dream material again offers the image of something alluring, erotic, and dangerous. The tree is out of context with the concrete surroundings. Ms. E.'s associations question whether the tree was a distraction or a trick, or whether it was just something beautiful in the middle of the expanse of barren concrete that appeared so dead to her. She wonders if there can be generativity as represented in the dream by the pockets of grass and a tree—perhaps symbols of vagina and penis in the creative intercourse of a primal fantasy. I felt that this might also be a commentary on the hope she feels in the analytic relationship that the treatment can break up the dead concrete world and pay homage to some life developing around her in the pockets of grass. But such generativity also frightens her because it is surrounded by lifeless concrete. Ms. E. worries that disavowing the concrete parking garage world of her mother—the hardness of the mother's internal container—means that she will be the lonely tree whose roots ultimately will be strangled by all the concrete because they can't continue to expand and grow in this environment. She identifies with the tree as being alone and at the mercy of the "concrete" mother around her that threatens to "kill" her because "I would be too alive". Here we see the theme of the oedipal murder acknowledged. We explore whether Ms. E. is both the tree and the concrete parking garage wishing to protect herself from retribution by inhibiting her own aliveness and growth with self-defeating behaviors. Abandonment and annihilation seem inevitable in the concrete world of her unconscious. In the transference, she can also see me at times as a "concrete" mother who can envy her aliveness.

The vacillation between who is the concrete garage and who is the tree opens up for analytic scrutiny the inevitable dilemmas involved in psychic integration in female development. As Dahl writes: "The process of psychic integration of the tie to the mother as an aspect of the self is never fully complete. The hallmark of adult female psychic organization lies in the daughter's capacity to permit continuing reverberations within herself of the representations of the tie to the mother, in her ongoing intrapsychic dialogue with her mother" (Dahl, 1995, pp. 201–202).

The versions of the Persephone myth pose an interesting dilemma— can a life outside of mother, a world of sexuality and knowledge, only be achieved with a "seasonal" pattern because they cannot coexist with an ongoing life with mother. It seems absurd to imagine that Ms. E. can be with her mother two thirds of the year and only have one third of the year to enjoy the riches of her own sexually alive world. The questions abound. Does the threat of envy and rejection destroy aliveness for mother and daughter in different ways? Is there no way to integrate a woman's life so that the mother of symbiosis can also be the mother who supports the daughter's "harvesting" of her own sexuality and full mature life? Can Ms. E. pick the alluring tomato plant of the first dream and bring it with her into the Honda with her mother? Can a woman be both loyal to her mother while she must identify and compete with her? Ms. E. is burdened by the idea that sexuality, especially with a forbidden male, is aggressively opposed by the mother: "Sexuality is seen as belonging to the mother and not to the girl. This perception produces the striking need in the girl to compartmentalize intrapsychic representations of a sexual and nonsexual self. We view this compartmentalization primarily as defensive, in the interest of sustaining the tie to the mother… Thus passions and sexuality are relegated to a secret part of the self, separate from the mother" (Holtzman and Kulish, 2000, p. 1431). Ms. E.'s life when in the "Underworld" is alive and is filled with her husband, baby, her painting, and the analysis—safe from the perceived impinging eye of her mother.

Psychic integration for Ms. E. requires her to recognize the splits in her self-representations. One split is the Kore as maiden/little girl and the other is the world-upsetting Persephone, who needs to descend into the Underworld to be fully and sexually alive. Ms. E. at times resists exploring these depths and the blood red seeds of sexuality, but this is to avoid the guilt that haunts her. The fact that Ms. E. questions and struggles with this conflict suggests that someone (an "interference") offered her enough love investment (eros) that she could imagine and wish to free herself, somewhat, from the gravitational force field of the mother and grandmother's incestuous and suffocating love without losing a meaningful relationship with these maternal figures.

References

Balsam, R. (2010). Where Has Oedipus Gone? A Turn of the Century Contemplation. *Psychoanalytic Inquiry*, 30: 511–519.

Britton, R., Feldman, M., O'Shaughnessy, E. (1989). *The Oedipus Complex Today*. London: Karnac Books.

Dahl, E. Kirsten. (1995). Daughters and Mothers: Aspects of the Representational World During Adolescence. *The Psychoanalytic Study of the Child*, 50: 187–204.

Freud, S. (1916). The Development of the Libido and the Sexual Organizations. *Standard Edition*, 16, 320–338.

Freud, S. (1933). Femininity. *Standard Edition*, 22, 112–135.

Fairfield, S. (1994). The Kore Complex: The Myths and Some Unconscious Fantasies. *International Journal of Psychoanalysis*. 75: 243–263.

Horney, K. (1926). The Flight from Womanhood: The Masculinity Complex in women, as Viewed by Men and by Women. *International Journal of Psychoanalysis*, 7: 324–339.

Holtzman, D. and Kulish, N. (2000). The Feminization of the Female Oedipal Complex, Part I: Reconsideration of the Significance of Separation Issues. *Journal of the American Psychoanalytic Association*, 48: 1413–1437.

Kulish, N. and Holtzman, D. (1998). Persephone, the Loss of Virginity and the Female Oedipus Complex. *International Journal of Psychoanalysis*, 79: 57–71.

Kulish, N. and Holtzman, D. (2008). *A Story of Her Own*. New York: Jason Aronson.

Spillius, E., Milton, J., Garvey, P., Couve, C., Steiner, D. (2011). *The New Dictionary of Kleinian Thought*. New York: Routledge.

Bisexuality and Its Vicissitudes: A Psychoanalytic Exploration

by Roman Yumatov

In his letter to Wilhelm Fliess (written on March 15, 1898), Sigmund Freud asserts: "I do not in the least underestimate bisexuality... I expect it to provide all further enlightenment" (as cited in Masson, 1985, p. 323). However, despite Freud's emphasis on bisexuality, this subject remains largely underdeveloped and often misunderstood (Bryan, 1930; Elise, 1998, 2000; Grossman, 2001; Khan, 1974; Layton, 2000). Nevertheless, its significance cannot be overstated, especially considering the fundamental role that sexuality in general—and bisexuality in particular—plays in psychoanalysis. Additionally, the major shift of focus—from sexuality to relational issues (as if these were separate from one another)—that has been taking place in the post-Freudian psychoanalysis seems to obscure the prospect of elucidation of bisexuality. In fact, many analysts (e.g., Chodorow, 1992; Elise, 1998; Fonagy, as cited in Heenen-Wolff, 2011; Green, 1995; Kernberg, as cited in Grossman, 2001; Young-Bruehl, 2001) have recently emphasized the need for further investigation of sexuality, along with a number of others (e.g., Gamelgaard, as cited in Brook, 1998; Heenen-Wolff, 2011; Stimmel, 1996), who have urged for a careful reconsideration of Freud's original ideas, as they may still be applicable to the current theorization of (bi)sexuality.

Moreover, once the history of the psychoanalytic attitudes toward homosexuality is taken into account (see the previous essay in this book), the subject of bisexuality becomes of paramount importance, as recognized by Freud over one hundred years ago. Therefore, I contend that a more rigorous psychoanalytic examination of bisexuality would provide invaluable insights into the two cornerstones of psychoanalysis—namely, sexuality and gender—and, thus, would be of immense usefulness to anyone interested in the dynamic, unconscious aspects of these phenomena.

Accordingly, this paper represents an attempt at a critical exploration of the psychoanalytic conceptualization of bisexuality and its various vicissitudes. Because the hypotheses related to gender are highly inter-twined with those that pertain to sexuality, I will discuss both of these dimensions, but will also try to focus on bisexuality as a mode of object-choice. Furthermore, I shall note that my inquiry centers upon bisexuality among men; however, many of the ideas discussed herein may be applicable to women as well.

Third, I will highlight and examine a number of con I will, first, perform a critical, comparative appraisal of a multitude of the psychoanalytic perspectives on bisexuality, traced historically—from the initial views of Freud to those of the contemporary analysts. I shall do so in order to demonstrate the evolution and the diversity of these viewpoints. Second, I will discuss relevant findings from non-psychodynamic areas of research (such as biology, psychology, sociology and anthropology), in their connection to the temporary controversies that pertain to this theorization. Finally, I will attempt to show that, overall, Freud's original conceptualization of bisexuality is not only supported by a number of studies conducted outside of the psychodynamic framework, but is also still relevant and useful today.

412

Sigmund Freud

Psychoanalytic conception of bisexuality dates back to the correspondence of Sigmund Freud with Wilhelm Fliess (see Masson, 1985). Fliess, who was, perhaps, Freud's closest friend at the time, proposed that bisexuality is a universal phenomenon based upon certain biological influences. While Freud strongly agreed with the idea of the universality of bisexuality among humans, he appeared to be skeptical with regard to the purely biological explanation. As such, in Three Essays on the Theory of Sexuality, Freud (1905a) stated: "There is neither need nor justification for replacing the psychological problem by the anatomical one" (p. 142). In this and, especially, later works (e.g., Freud, 1913, 1923b, 1933, 1937), he would consistently (and increasingly) argue in favor of the significance of bisexuality in the mental life of an individual. Nonetheless, Freud's conceptualization of bisexuality is connected to three different, though interrelated, dimensions.

First, he spoke of the innate bisexuality (e.g., Freud, 1908, 1928, 1931), or constitutional bisexuality (e.g., Freud, 1923b, 1925a, 1928), thus, to a degree, admitting to the biological basis of it. At the same time, as mentioned above, he also emphasized the psychological corollaries of such biological disposition (Gann, as cited in Brook, 1998; Stimmel, 1996; Young-Bruehl, 2001). Moreover, on many occasions, Freud referred to the notions of activity and passivity that he seemingly associated with masculinity and femininity, respectively (the latter of which are nowadays conceptualized as gender); I shall discuss this terminology further below. Thus, Freud, well ahead of his time, was able to conceive of bisexuality as a multi–dimensional phenomenon—namely, as psychic bisexuality (i.e., gender) and a form of object-choice (i.e., sexual orientation), both of which may be related to the biological predisposition to bisexuality (as originally proposed by Fliess). It may appear as though Freud (1912, 1924) may have overly emphasized the idea that "anatomy is destiny". However, it is important to be mindful of the fact that he did not presume that one's biological sex is connected, in any straightforward manner, to one's gender or sexuality (Gann, as cited in Brook, 1998). As regards the former, in the footnote added ten years after the original publication of the Three Essays, Freud (1905a), affirms:

It is essential to understand clearly that the concepts of 'masculine' and 'feminine' (…) are among the most confused that occur in science. (…) in human beings pure masculinity or femininity is not to be found either in a psychological or a biological sense. (p. 219) Additionally, with regard to the bisexual object-choice, toward the end of his life and career, in Analysis Terminable and Interminable, Freud (1937) asserted: It is well known that at all periods there have been, as there still are, people who can take as their sexual objects members of their own sex as well as of the opposite one, without the one trend interfering with the other. We call such people bisexuals, and we accept their existence without feeling much surprise about it. We have come to learn, however, that every human being is bisexual in this sense and that his libido is distributed, either in a manifest or a latent fashion, over objects of both sexes. (pp. 243–244) Thus, as Smith (2002) highlights, Freud's clinical observations and ensuing theories of bisexuality demonstrate the recognition of the "complexity that is celebrated today but rarely attributed to Freud" (p. 551). Therefore, Smith contends that Freud may, in actuality, be seen as a post-modern theorist. Similarly, Young-Bruehl (2001) refers to Freud as "a great appreciator of the complexity and variability of human sexuality" (p. 183). I shall return to these points below. At the same time, one of the problems with Freud's conception of bisexuality was his assumption that it "comes to the fore much more clearly in women than in men" (Freud, 1931, p. 228). Horney (1932), for instance, did not share this conviction and instead preferred "to leave it an open question" (p. 359).

Ferraro (2001), on the other hand, emphasized the psychoanalytic finding that "the fantasy use of the anus" among boys plays "the fundamental role of the receptive disposition towards the father's penis" (p. 494; see also Fast, 1990). This suggestion would certainly agree with Freud's (e.g., 1905a, 1909, 1918, 1933) own observation that boys, as well as girls, tend to equate the process of defecation with childbirth and, consequently, their feces with children (who, in this phantasy, can be conceived through the receptive anal intercourse with the father). Besides, it can be suggested that the ability of a male to reach orgasm exclusively by means of the stimulation of his prostate (e.g., Ladas, Whipple, & Perry, 1982) serves as an additional factor that may be contributing to his predisposition to bisexuality. Nevertheless, it appears that Freud's original conceptualization of human bisexuality and its three different, but interrelated, domains— biological, psychosocial (gender) and psychosexual (sexual orientation)— is, overall, significant. In support of this statement, I shall now review some of the relevant research that has been conducted outside of the psychodynamic framework.

Non-Psychodynamic Research

Biological Domain: Constitutional, or Innate, Bisexuality

Both Money (1990) and Young-Bruehl (2001) note that contemporary biologists tend to refer to the concept of sexual bipotentiality, which, however, in its essence, is practically identical to what Freud designated as constitutional, or innate, bisexuality. In his appraisal of the biological findings related to bisexuality, Money (1990) emphasizes the discovery that the development of a human fetus initially (i.e., during the first trimester) occurs in the form of a female organism (see also Drescher,

415

2007; Guttman, 1955). He also highlights the fact that "the male and female hormones are bisexual hormones, for they are shared by both sexes, though in different ratios" (Money, 1990, p. 402; see also Young-Bruehl, 2001). Nonetheless, Money (1990) underlines that "there is no overall correlation between (…) hormonal levels (…) and sexual orientation" (p. 402). Additionally, he maintains that the "total (…) evidence points to the conclusion that neuroanatomical structures destined to become either male or female are initially bipotential" (Money, 1990, p. 405). Thus, it appears that a number of findings in genetics, endocrinology, and neuroscience provide empirical support for Freud's assumption of the constitutional, or innate, bisexuality (see also Stimmel, 1996).

At the same time, akin to Money (and Freud), Young-Bruehl (2001) rightfully stresses that "the subdomains making up biological sex do not (…) determine gender identity and object choice" (p. 195); she further adds that "usually, if not always, biological factors are overridden by gender development, including sex assignment and a person's history of object choices and experiences" (p. 195; see also Nunberg, 1947). She also underscores the fact that human "sexual drive is least tied to biological functions, specifically reproduction" (Young-Bruehl, p. 195), which is in agreement with Freud's (1916–1917) assertion that, in humans, "sexual" often has "nothing to do with reproduction" (p. 321). With this in mind, I shall now review some of the fairly recent findings in the various disciplines of social science, as regard the psychosocial and psychosexual dimensions of bisexuality. Psychosocial Domain: Psychic Bisexuality (Gender) Psychologists Bem and Lewis (1975) found that the individuals, who are rather androgynous (i.e., more flexible in accessing personality features traditionally described as masculine or feminine), are generally better adjusted socially and, overall, manifest a higher level of psychological well-being than rigidly masculine or rigidly feminine persons. Indeed, the concept of androgyny may be viewed as an extension of Freud's notion of psychic bisexuality (e.g., Money, 1990). Additionally, as Greenson (1968) pointed out and the American Psychiatric Association (2000) affirmed over thirty years afterward, transvestic fetishism is the mental disorder prevalent almost exclusively among males, the vast majority of whom self–identify as heterosexuals (Drescher, 2007). Furthermore, very recently Escoffier (2011) indicated that the so-called "she/male" pornography is geared predominantly toward (presumably) heterosexual men. While these findings may demonstrate the dissatisfaction of males with the masculine gender role that they are generally expected to perform within various sociocultural contexts, it can also be argued that such conflict is related to the universal psychic bisexuality, as initially described by Freud. Moreover, as regards Escoffier's (2011) conclusion in particular, Freud's (e.g., 1905a, 1933) conception of the phallic mother springs to mind; however, as Stimmel (1996) argues, since "one of the most powerful wishes (…) is (…) to be female and male at once (…) the phallic woman is not only a defense against castration anxiety (…) but also a straightforward representation of an ideal" (p. 203; see also Weissman, 1962).

Psychosexual Domain: Bisexual Object-Choice (Sexual Orientation)

Further, Kinsey and his colleagues (Kinsey, Pomeroy, Martin, & Gebhard, 1954) conducted, perhaps, the most groundbreaking empirical study of human sexuality to-date (Friedman & Downey, 2010; Lewes, 1988; Young-Bruehl, 2001). While it was largely ignored by the psychoanalytic community at the time (Lewes, 1988), it provided critical data pertinent to both actual sexual experiences and, more importantly, sexual fantasies of males. Amongst its many crucial findings, it revealed that nearly half of the American men (from adolescence onward) have had at least one homosexual experience that resulted in an orgasm. Besides, it was indicated that this number might, in actuality, be underestimated, due to the widespread presence of bisexual fantasies among men (Kinsey et al., 1954). Moreover, this study was replicated on several occasions in both Europe and the United States, and the results obtained were similar to those found in the original research (Lewes, 1988). Therefore, it appears that both bisexual behavior and sexual fantasies of bisexual nature are rather ubiquitous, as Freud suggested.

Similarly to the discoveries of Kinsey et al. (1954) and around the same time, in 1951, anthropologists Ford and Beach (as cited in Friedman, 1986), in their major cross-cultural research, concluded that the potential for bisexual behavior is universal and that the extremes (i.e., exclusive heterosexuality or exclusive homosexuality) are quite rare. In addition, the social-anthropological studies outlined by Stoller and Herdt (1982), as well as Lidz and Lidz (1986), showed the existence of societies outside of the Western civilization, where certain forms of bisexuality are practiced in a ritualized manner, on a cultural level. Recently, in 2010, Adams, Anderson, and Rivers (as cited in Ripley, Anderson, McCormack, Adams, & Pitts, 2011) revealed that, in the United Kingdom, almost 90% of White male students, who self-identified as heterosexuals, have kissed another man. In my view, all of these findings lend further empirical support for Freud's assumption of the universal bisexual nature of human sexuality.

Nevertheless, while Freud's conceptualization of bisexuality has remained largely prevalent in psychoanalysis (Gann, as cited in Brook, 1998; Smith, 2002; Stimmel, 1996; Young-Bruehl, 2001), it is important to note that it was also elaborated by a number of his followers, as well as repudiated by some of the revisionists of his original theorization. Therefore, I shall now focus on these particular post-Freudian developments.

Post-Freudian Perspectives

The Freudians

Sandor Ferenczi, one of Freud's first followers, claimed his support for the theory of universal human bisexuality. At the same time, however, Ferenczi (1952a, 1952b) also seemed to have reservations, concerning the way it was conceptualized by Freud (mostly, due to the biological influences cited by Fliess) and therefore suggested the term ambisexuality instead. He contended that this revision would accentuate "the child's psychical capacity for bestowing his erotism, originally objectless, on either the male or the female sex, or on both" (Ferenczi, 1952a, p. 184, footnote). Thus, as Stimmel (1996) highlights, Ferenczi was mainly interested in the fluid nature of sexuality, which differs from the focus on the biological determinants of bisexuality (that was central for Fliess). Further, Otto Fenichel also shared Freud's conviction in the universality of bisexuality and therefore affirmed that "a certain amount of sexual feeling toward one's own sex remains in everyone" (as cited in Lewes, 1988, p. 63). Furthermore, akin to Freud, he believed in the biological roots of the bisexual disposition among humans and agreed with the concepts of activity and passivity, as well as with the idea that the possibility of the bisexual object–choice is universal (as cited in Lewes, 1988). Additionally, a number of other Freudian analysts proposed a variety of hypotheses on the subject. As such, Patry (1928) published the study of a male, who presented with the case of (what nowadays would be classified as) gender dysphoria. However, Patry (1928) characterized bisexuality as "a qualitative anomaly" and elaborated that "its abnormal manifestation in the psychical sphere is likely (...) due to (...) vivid identification with a child of the opposite sex, or development of an exaggerated erotic attachment to both parents or their substitutes" (p. 438). Bryan (1930), on the other hand, emphasized "the unconscious resistances to bisexuality (...) from which even psychoanalysts are not

419

immune" (p. 151) and underlined the problem of fusing and substituting the elucidation of bisexuality with that of homosexuality (see also Khan, 1974; Roughton, as cited in Grossman, 2001; Young-Bruehl, 2001). In addition, he offered some conjectures on the matter of the biological basis of human bisexuality.

Further, both Nunberg (1947) and Bird (1958) examined the relationship between circumcision and bisexuality. In doing so, they suggested that, for a boy, foreskin might symbolize female genitalia and that, in different cases, circumcision might reinforce either masculine or feminine identification.

Moreover, Guttman (1955) proposed that the analysis of the deeper layers of the unconscious would increasingly bring up bisexual symbolism (see also Young-Bruehl, 2001). Additionally, he argued that the justification for the notions of activity and passivity is not as straightforward as it may appear to be. Furthermore, Weiss (1958) asserted that bisexuality, essentially, manifested a narcissistic ego structure. On this note, I shall now address the ego-psychological conceptualization of bisexuality (or lack thereof).

Ego-Psychology

Basically, it appears that there are two (equally extreme) positions that the ego-psychology assumes on the subject: that is, several prominent representatives of this school openly deny and disavow any notion of human bisexuality, while others seem to confuse bisexuality with homosexuality and therefore, as it is common within this framework (Lewes, 1988), view it as a type of psychopathology (see also the previous essay in this book).

As regards the former group, American ego-psychologist Rado is generally credited as the proverbial pioneer, who repudiated—or, at least, attempted to repudiate—Freud's postulate of universal bisexuality (Drescher, 2007; Lewes, 1988; Stensson, 1992a). Indeed, Rado (1940) was unequivocal in proclaiming that "there is no such thing as bisexuality" (p. 463). As a number of his colleagues, who shared the allegiance to the ego-psychological paradigm, he took the stand in favor of biological determinism (of a much more reductionist kind than that, which Freud is frequently accused of) and, as such, believed that bisexuality could only manifest itself in those human beings, who displayed so-called complete hermaphroditism, which to-date has not been known to exist (which Bryan [1930] noted 10 years prior to Rado's publication). Furthermore, because Rado (1940) presumed the primacy and supremacy of the reproductive system and (what he referred to as) "the orgasm reflex", he generalized these assumptions onto the mental sphere of human functioning, thereby making exactly the same mistake, for which he criticized Freud. He further speculated that the masculine or feminine quality of one's fantasies might be clearly discerned only insofar as these fantasies were connected to the genitalia and to the processes of conception, pregnancy or childbirth. Thus, Rado (1940) concluded that "the basic problem (…) is to determine the factors that cause the individual to apply aberrant forms of stimulation to his standard genital equipment" (p. 466). This formulation implies that the heterosexual intercourse, engaged into for the purpose of reproduction, is the only form of healthy sexual behavior. This conclusion may appear to be drawn from Freud's work, but such inference would, in actuality, be inaccurate, due to the fact that Freud consistently admitted the existence of not only a variety of sexualities (i.e., object-choices), but also the diversity of sexual practices (i.e., sexual aims), without, however, necessarily attempting to pathologize the former or the latter. Nonetheless, many other prominent ego-psychologists at the time accepted Rado's supposed repudiation of Freud's concept of universal bisexuality and subsequently

421

based their own theorization upon this questionable refutation (e.g., Kardiner, 1978; Person & Ovesey, 1983; see also Stensson, 1992a).

On the other hand, Weissman (1962) appeared to be in disagreement with this trend and, as such, published the paper in effort to address the subject of bisexuality among males. However, he mostly tended to fuse bisexuality with homosexuality, and, moreover, since within the framework of ego-psychology, the latter was viewed as pathological (for a detailed examination of this issue, see the previous essay in this book), it becomes difficult to value his contribution. Nevertheless, Weissman (1962) attempted to discern between (what he designated as) "normal male bisexuality" and "overt male bisexuality". Regarding the former, he proposed that "the overt sexual behaviour is mainly heterosexual, but the unconscious wishes are to be in the mother's feminine role in the sexual relationship with the father" (Weissman, 1962, p. 163). In relation to the "overt male bisexuality", Weissman (1962) suggested that it "can be understood as a regressive defence against unconscious heterosexual oedipal conflict, or an acting out of the entire content of the oedipal conflict" (p. 163). He further linked these ideas to the concepts of perversion (including fetishism) and narcissism, as well as the notion of "pseudoheterosexuality", which demonstrates his pathologizing stance on the subject. Additionally, Weissman (1962) raised the question of the early Oedipal versus Oedipal identifications and longings, which is one of the most important issues in the post-Freudian psychoanalysis—especially, concerning the subject of bisexuality. Accordingly, I will address this controversial matter in-detail below. Meanwhile, as the elucidation of the early Oedipal development is one of the key goals of the object-relations paradigm, to it I shall now turn.

Object-Relations School and Melanie Klein

Unfortunately, object-relations school is mostly lacking in the theorization of bisexuality—specifically, as regards the dimension of object-choice (Kernberg, as cited in Grossman, 2001). In fact, it appears that Donald Winnicott was its only prominent representative, who had addressed this subject explicitly; however, he was largely concerned with psychic bisexuality. Winnicott (1971) emphasized the need for psychoanalysis in general—and, perhaps, for the object-relations theories in particular—to "allow for both a male and a female element in boys and men and girls and women", as "these elements may be split off from each other to a high degree" (p. 77). In line with the Freudian tradition, Winnicott (1971) suggested that this would require "both a study of the clinical effects of this type of dissociation and an examination of the distilled male and female elements themselves" (p. 79). What are, then, these "artificially dissected male and female elements" (Winnicott, 1971, p. 84; emphasis added) that he refers to? According to Winnicott (1971), "object-relating backed by instinct drive" is associated with the male element, whereas "the characteristic of the female element in the context of object-relating is identity, giving the child the basis for being, and then, later on, a basis for a sense of self" (p. 84). In essence, for Winnicott (1971), "the male element does while the female element (in males and females) is" (p. 81). Thus, it appears that, besides agreeing with Freud's postulate of universal bisexuality (as well as his theory of instinctual drives), Winnicott presented an additional hypothesis in relation to the dimension of psychic bisexuality that provided the starting point for a number of analysts, upon which they based some of their elaborations on the subject.

As such, while emphasizing the need for the elucidation of "bisexual love" (mostly, due to the frequent confusion of it with latent homosexuality), Khan (1974) proposed that the former is "almost exclusively an ego-experience,

423

that is, the ego's way of relating to and cherishing an object of the same gender identity" (p. 143). He argued that, because "in such relationships the id-energy is neutralized and turned to use in the ego's passionate interest in the object", the result of "the climax of such cathexis of the object is ego-orgasm" (Khan, 1974, p. 143). Therefore, Khan contended that one's affective attachment to the persons of the same sex is devoid of sexual desire. Khan, thereby, was referring to the close friendships that men often form with each other. However, unlike Freud (e.g., 1911, 1916–1917, 1922), he viewed such relationships not as a means of sublimation of homosexual desires, but, rather, as a desexualized mode of relating to the objects of the same sex (an idea that can certainly be questioned).

Further, both Elise (1998) and Ferraro (2001) invoke the metaphor of the nursing couple (i.e., Winnicott's [1971] mother–infant dyad) as the primary site of the universal bisexual identifications in children. Elise (1998) elaborates: The mother penetrates the infant with her nipple and her stream of milky fluid. Additionally, the mother's (…) hands and fingers are on, around, and into all of the infant's orifices (…). The mother lays the infant on its back and does 'everything' to the infant's body, including, with the infant's legs up and apart, opening up and exposing the genital area. These are the earliest forms of penetration and receptive excitement. (p. 362) Additionally, Ferraro (2001), in highlighting the oscillating nature of multiple identifications (i.e., with both mother and father), argues: The reconstruction of the individual's fundamental bisexuality reveals a composite formation whose elements are, on the one hand, the primal bisexuality (…) underlain by a primary relationship that has supplied a sufficiency of female elements (Winnicott's being), and, on the other, the play of identifications with the parental couple resulting from the bisexual disposition of the drive. (p. 496)

On this note, I shall now turn to Melanie Klein (1932) and her original concept of the combined parent figure. According to my research, it appears that Klein, actually, never referred to bisexuality per se in any of her published works. Nonetheless, her idea of the combined parent figure (Klein, 1932, 1952, 1957, 1961) has been assumed to pertain to this subject by many of the contemporary analysts (e.g., Aron, 1995; Christiansen, 1996; Elise, 1998, 2000; Fogel, 2006; Hurwood, 2009; Stimmel, 1996). Klein (1932) asserted that, in this primitive phantasy, an infant perceives both of the parents combined "as a hostile entity" (p. 191), "engaged in dangerous copulation" (p. 333); she further elaborated: If, side by side with the imago of the combined parents, imagos of the single father and mother, especially the 'good' mother, are sufficiently strongly operative, the boy's growing relationship to objects and adaptation to reality will have the result that his phantasies about his father's penis inside his mother will lose their power, and his hatred, already less in itself, will be more strongly directed to his real object. (p. 334) Thus, she affirms that, by means of this development (i.e., the differentiation of the threatening figure of combined parents into the non-threatening and separate images of mother and father), the boy's erotic desires become directed at the mother, while his aggressive wishes become directed at the father, thereby establishing the early version of the (positive) Oedipus complex.

While it may appear as though this conceptualization is rooted in the (heteronormative) assumption that the boy's homosexual, or homoerotic, longings in general, as well as his negative Oedipus complex in particular, may represent a disturbance in psychosexual development, Aron (1995) contends that Klein's model of the combined parent figure may, in actuality, be "seen as a valuable and constructive organizing structure" (p. 197; see also Stimmel, 1996). He suggests that, as a child progresses from this primitive (early Oedipal) phantasy to the more mature (Oedipal) primal scene (Freud, 1918; see also Schuster, 1969; Stensson, 1992b), he is also advancing from the paranoid-schizoid to the depressive ideation, by means of which "the internal imago of the combined parent figure becomes transformed into the image of [the] parents as separate whole-objects in a mutually gratifying interaction with each other" (Aron, 1995, p. 211). Moreover, Aron (1995) argues that the "notion of the combined parent figure is useful precisely because it does not privilege heterosexual intercourse but rather allows for, and even suggests, all sorts of sexual and aggressive arrangements: heterosexual and homosexual combinations and also nongenital sexuality" (p. 213). He justifies this argument by asserting that, during the early Oedipal developmental period, children are not yet aware of the anatomical differences between the sexes. Furthermore, Aron (1995) highlights the integrative role of bisexuality, rooted in the identifications with both parents: With the internalization of the combined parents and the transformation of this imago into the primal scene, which occurs with the shift from the paranoid-schizoid to the depressive position, the individual consolidates a sense of self as bigendered, a self that is constituted by different, opposing, and contradictory self-representations, all of which exist in dynamic interaction with each other. (p. 219)

On the same note, in her theorizing on psychic bisexuality, Sweetnam (1996) also invokes Klein's conceptualization of the paranoid-schizoid (Klein, 1946) and depressive (Klein, 1935) positions. In doing so, she affirms that, in the paranoid-schizoid position, "the relationship between masculinity and femininity is (...) experienced in terms of part, rather than whole, objects" (Sweetnam, 1996, p. 450). Furthermore, Sweetnam (1996) asserts that, in this mode, "gender is (...) experienced as a given" (p. 451). Conversely, she points out that "the depressive position normatively integrates the relationship between masculinity and femininity and provides fluidity and access to change" (Sweetnam, 1996, p. 457). In this regard, Elise (2001) suggests that "the culture at large has not yet reached the depressive position" (p. 525, footnote). Most importantly, however, both Aron and Sweetnam highlight the need for psychoanalysis to recognize the value of both splitting and integration in relation to the universal human bisexuality. Moreover, both of them, along with Kernberg (as cited in Grossman, 2001), emphasize the necessity for the analysts to consistently reflect upon the significance of their counter-transferential responses to their analysands', as well as their own, (psychic) bisexuality (see also Blechner, 1998; Roughton, 2001; Smith, 2002).

Additionally, capitalizing on the work of Klein and Freud, Kernberg (1991) points out that the identifications with both parents are universal. Furthermore, in agreement with Meltzer (1973/2008), he asserts that all types of sexuality, including those generally referred to as normal, demonstrate the polymorphously perverse (Freud, 1905a, 1916–1917, 1925a) features. It appears that a number of other psychoanalysts also share this view (e.g., Blechner, 1998; Elise, 2000; Heenen-Wolff, 2011). I will return to the controversies pertaining to the universality of multiple identifications, the early Oedipal versus Oedipal basis of bisexuality and the problem of splitting and integration (as regards bisexuality) below. In the meantime, I shall focus on some of the notable contributions made by the contemporary analysts.

Contemporary Psychoanalysis

The hypotheses that I will discuss herein do not represent an exhaustive appraisal of the contemporary psychoanalytic conceptualization of bisexuality. Nonetheless, according to my research, they epitomize some of the principal lines of thought in the recent theorizing on the subject. I must reiterate, however, that, since the aspects of bisexuality pertaining to gender and those pertinent to object-choice remain highly intertwined in psychoanalysis, I will be addressing both of these dimensions.

Kubie: Drive to Become Both Sexes

Kubie (1974) affirmed that the drive to become both sexes is rather universal among both males and females. He described it as the "unconscious drive [the aim of which] is not to give up the gender to which one was born but to supplement or complement it by developing side by side with it the opposite gender, thereby ending up as both" (Kubie, 1974, pp. 356–357). He further asserted that "the assumption whether tacit or overt that any human being can ever want to be only one sex to the exclusion of the other is psychoanalytically naïve and runs counter to all analytic experience" (Kubie, 1974, p. 360). Additionally, while Kubie (1974) strongly believed that, "both for the little boy and the little girl one of the deepest tendencies (…) is to attempt to identify with and to become both parents" (p. 370), he was also convinced that the "implication is that conflicting gender identities, misidentifications, false identifications, and irreconcilable identifications give rise to unattainable and irreconcilable drives and wishes which, in turn, become fresh sources of neurotic conflict which on occasion may lead to psychotic disorganization" (p. 408).

As Aron (1995) points out, the positioning of the drive to become both sexes as "one of the most self-destroying" (Kubie, 1974, p. 353) is rather unfortunate. As such, Aron (1995) argues that the wish "'to have it all,' to fulfill symbolically the phantasy of being both sexes, can be used constructively and needs to be appreciated as a valuable human motive" (p. 197; see also Roughton, as cited in Grossman, 2001; Stimmel, 1996). In support of this argument, Aron (1995) turns to his reconsideration of Klein's concept of the combined parent figure, as discussed above. Furthermore, building upon Kubie's theorization, Aron (1995) highlights the "desire to have both sexes" (p. 196), along with Sweetnam (as cited in Elise, 1998), who also emphasizes the wish for the reciprocal emotional and sexual intimacy with both men and women. It is peculiar, however, that, in his theorizing, Kubie (1974) does not refer to Freud whatsoever, even when admitting that the drive to become both sexes may function on the conscious, pre-conscious or unconscious levels (or any combination thereof) and may be connected to any of the stages of psychosexual development, as conceived by Freud.

Fast: Differentiation Model

Further, Fast (1990) proposed the differentiation model, in which she distinguished the three phases in maturation of psychic bisexuality among children: undifferentiated period, recognition of sex differences, and differentiation proper. As regards the undifferentiated period (occurring during the first 18 to 24 months after birth, according to her research), Fast (1990) postulated that children tend to be "over-inclusive", that is, they consistently "include representations of experience with both men and women as they occur in the intimacies of daily life" (p. 108). Nevertheless, Fast indicated that such representations are not perceived in terms of gender at that time. On the same note, she asserted that "children's primary identifications with both (...) parents provide a developmental base for the bisexuality Freud observed clinically" (Fast, 1990, p. 108; emphasis added). Further, Fast (1990) affirmed that, beginning at 1.5 to 2 years of age, children grow increasingly aware of the anatomical differences between the sexes and that, subsequently, "this awareness requires the recognition of limit, that characteristics of other-sex persons (...) cannot be their own" (pp. 109–110). Additionally, in what may be viewed as an agreement with Kubie (1974), Fast (1990) argued that the "denial of sex difference in both boys and girls is expressed in notions of being bisexually complete" (p. 111). Furthermore, concerning the stage of differentiation proper (coinciding with the Oedipal period), in agreement with Freud, Fast (1990) suggested that, at this time, children of both sexes begin to view themselves and others through the prism of gender and that, consequently, "boys are likely to identify their penises as male, their anuses as female" (p. 112).

In relation to Fast's conceptualization, Aron (1995) raised the issue of discerning the dimension of psychic bisexuality from that of the bisexual object-choice (see also Roughton, as cited in Grossman, 2001). Indeed, this remains as one of the key problems in the psychoanalytic theorizing on the subject, as I also aim to show herein. Also, Fast (1990), actually, appears to be somewhat echoing Greenson's (1968) idea of "dis-identifying from mother", although, in her conceptualization, it is rather the renunciation of the early "over-inclusive" identifications that ought to take place in order for the normal (normative?) development of gender to occur (Aron, 1995; Benjamin, 1996). Layton (2000) describes this situation as "the child's last stand before giving in to the culturally required splitting that produces dominant femininity and masculinity" (p. 55), while also calling attention to "the pathologizing suggestion in the very term overinclusiveness" (p. 44, footnote). In similar fashion, Elise (2000) suggests that "gender identity might better be referred to as either inclusive (flexible and integrated) or underinclusive-exclusive (rigid normative splitting into 'feminine' and 'masculine')" (p. 65; emphasis added). On the other hand, in agreement with, and elaborating upon, Fast's conceptualization of psychic bisexuality, Diamond (1997) deems the renunciation of the early "over-inclusive" identifications as a " 'necessary' loss" (p. 451), because, in his view, it provides the basis needed for the maturation of "boys to men" (hence, the title of his article). Additionally, he later argued that "a securely rooted male identity is largely built upon a boy's identification with his mother's unconscious attitudes toward his maleness" (Diamond, 2004, p. 367). Furthermore, in agreement with Butler (1995), whose ideas will be discussed shortly, Diamond (2004) affirms that "boys experience greater prohibitions against early homoerotic attachments and homosexuality than do girls" (p. 370); he also adds that, "due to heightened shame associated with homoeroticism (…), boys become increasingly inhibited (…) around paternal erotic desires" (p. 370). Moreover, Diamond (2004) points out that a boy is not only subjected to the loss of the attachment to his mother, as well as the loss of the (homoerotic) attachment to his father, but, most significantly, he is consistently "forced to repudiate, renounce or deny what he has lost" (p. 370). On this note, I shall now discuss some of the novel ideas proposed by several contemporary analysts in relation to the (bi)sexual object-choice.

Chodorow: (Hetero)Sexuality as a Compromise Formation

Largely in agreement with Freud (e.g., 1905a), Chodorow (1992), amongst many others (e.g., Butler, 1995; Drescher, 2002; Elise, 1998; Heenen-Wolff, 2011; Layton, 2000; Money, 1990; Young-Bruehl, 2001), highlights the observation that, both socioculturally and psychoanalytically, heterosexuality has been taken for granted. Additionally, also in agreement with Freud (e.g., 1938), she emphasizes the fact that the notion of normalcy—particularly, in its association with heterosexuality—carries no clear meaning, "other than [in] the statistical or normative sense" (Chodorow, 1992, p. 269). As did Freud (1905a), when he asserted that "the exclusive sexual interest felt by men for women is (…) a problem that needs elucidating" (p. 144, footnote), Chodorow (1992) also contends that, although "many psychoanalysts probably think (…) that heterosexuality is innate or natural" (p. 271), heterosexuality should be examined more critically. Moreover, Chodorow (1992) takes the psychoanalytic discussion of the nature of object-choices one step further by proposing that exclusive heterosexuality (as well as exclusive homosexuality) may be viewed as a compromise formation (cf. Freud, 1901, 1923a, 1925a)—that is, a compromise between one's innate bisexual nature (both in the biological and psychological sense) and the demands of the society and culture.

Furthermore, she invokes Kernberg in stating that the "definitions of mature love require not heterosexual object choice but instead a coming to

431

terms with and sublimating both homosexual and heterosexual, preoedipal and oedipal, identifications" (Chodorow, 1992, p. 283). Chodorow (as cited in Grossman, 2001) also later noted that, "although everyone identifies with (…) mother and father, the nature of that identification will always be an individual matter" (p. 1368; emphasis added). Additionally, she asserted that, "if we find [only] one form of object choice or gender identity in one person, we are in an arena of conflict and repression or splitting" (Chodorow, as cited in Grossman, 2001, p. 1367). I shall return to the idea of multiple (Oedipal and early Oedipal) identifications, as well as the notion of splitting (as regards bisexuality) below, in the discussion of these particular contemporary controversies.

Butler: Melancholic Identification

On a different note, turning to the fundamental conceptualization outlined by Freud (1917) in Mourning and Melancholia, Butler (1995) suggested that the seemingly singular identification (i.e., identification with only one of the parents) manifests a melancholic identification. Capitalizing on Freud's (1917) ideas further, she proposed that such "melancholic identification permits the loss of the object in the external world precisely because it provides a way to preserve the object as part of the ego itself and, hence, to avert the (…) complete loss" (Butler, 1995, p. 167). In applying this conception to the dimensions of bisexuality that pertain to both gender identity and, particularly, sexual orientation, Butler (1995) asserted the following: The positions of 'masculine' and 'feminine' (…) are established in part through prohibitions that demand the loss of certain sexual attachments and demand as well that those losses not be avowed and not be grieved. If the assumption of femininity and the assumption of masculinity proceed through the accomplishment of always tenuous heterosexuality, we might understand the force of this accomplishment as the mandating of the abandonment of homosexual attachments or, perhaps more trenchantly, the preemption of the possibility of homosexual attachment (...) that produces a domain of homosexuality understood as unlivable passion and ungrievable loss. (p. 168)

Thereby, Butler emphasized several ideas simultaneously: first, that the notions of gender are regularly and implicitly connected to those of sexuality (which is, in itself, problematic); second, that, generally, boys must not only abandon their primary identification with the mother, but are also required (by the parents) to renounce any homosexual, or homoerotic, attachment to their fathers; and, third, that, more often than not, boys must also disavow and deny these losses (due to the enforcement of heteronormativity that many parents tend to perform, whether consciously or not). Thus, Butler (1995) affirms that "heterosexuality is cultivated through prohibitions (...) of (...) homosexual attachments, thereby forcing the loss of those attachments" (p. 169). It is noteworthy that, according to Butler (1995), "becoming a 'man' (...) requires not only a repudiation of femininity, but also a repudiation (...) of sexual desire" (p. 169) toward other men. Moreover, Butler (1995) asserts that "the loss of homosexual objects and aims (not simply this person of the same gender, but any person of that same gender) will be foreclosed from the start" (p. 171); she explains: "I use the word 'foreclosed' to suggest that this is a preemptive loss, a mourning for unlived possibilities" (p. 171; emphasis added). In other words, she elaborates that "the man who insists on the coherence of his heterosexuality will claim that he never loved another man and thus never lost another man" (Butler, 1995, p. 172; emphasis added; see also Elise, 1998). Finally, as regard the widespread heterosexist—or, at best, heteronormative—sociocultural attitudes, she contends: "When the prohibition against homosexuality is culturally pervasive, then the 'loss' of homosexual love is precipitated through a prohibition that is repeated and ritualized throughout the culture" (Butler, 1995, p. 172; emphasis added; see also Friedman & Downey, 2010; Layton, 2000).

In light of this conceptualization, Elise (2000) proposed that Butler's (1995) hypothesis "can be expanded to include the loss entailed in recognizing that one cannot be the other sex" (p. 65, footnote). In similar fashion, Diamond (1997) asserted that the "repudiation of one's earliest sex and gender 'inappropriate' identifications with both the preoedipal mother and father is largely responsible for men's unconscious gender ossification in the form of either gender confusion or rigid certainty" (p. 456). Moreover, Diamond (2004) later described such repudiation as a "painful narcissistic mortification" (p. 362) and affirmed that the struggle pertinent to the "gendered nature of the masculine ego ideal (…) requires that the little boy adapt to a significant disruption and loss in relation to his mother" (p. 370). On a different note, Blechner (1998), in his reading of Butler (1995), suggested that, due to "the strongest taboo in [Western] culture" (p. 607)—that is, in his view, the taboo against homosexuality— "the relations between heterosexual men (…) are twisted (…), because it creates anxiety whenever men want to have intimate exchanges with other men" (p. 607). In this regard, Ferenczi's (1952b) earlier assertion comes to mind—namely, that the "present–day men (…) [show] signs of resistance as reaction–formations, as defence symptoms erected against affection for the same sex" (p. 315) and that, consequently, "the men of today are (…) obsessively heterosexual as the result of this affective displacement" (pp. 315–316). While these ideas may be disputed by some, in my opinion (and as research shows), they may still be applicable to the current sociocultural context in many parts of today's world.

Young-Bruehl: Choice of a Bisexual Object

Further, akin to Butler (1995), Young-Bruehl (2001) stated that "all human beings are in mourning for roads not taken" (p. 185). At the same time, she affirmed that "bisexuals (…) are in less conflict, [because they] do not repress as relentlessly, as do heterosexuals or homosexuals" (Young-Bruehl,

434

2001, p. 184). While the latter assumption can be questioned, in my view, Young-Bruehl (2001) justly noted that, in the psychoanalytic discussion of object-choice, "the emphasis has always fallen on the choice, not the object" (p. 203; emphasis added). Therefore, she proposed that "the sex, gender, and type of object choice of the chosen object (in reality and in the choser's [sic] mind) must be accounted for" (Young-Bruehl, 2001, p. 203). Accordingly, drawing upon her clinical experience, Young-Bruehl (2001) suggested four different types of objects that can be chosen: the object based upon part-objects, the split object, the doubled object and the layered, or "manifest-and-latent", object. In regard to the first type, she states that it is the object that originates in the infant's perception of part-objects (e.g., the breast). Young-Bruehl (2001) elaborates: "When a child is capable of whole-object choice, the part-object can stand for the whole and define how the whole is experienced" (p. 205); she also adds that, "if the part-object is sexed or gendered, so too—in some way will the whole object be" (p. 205). She further notes that "this mode of object choice operates in everyone, but some people are dominated by it, particularly those who incline to perversions" (Young-Bruehl, 2001, p. 205). It is important, however, that she does not consider homo- or bisexuality as being perverse.

As regard the second and the third types, Young-Bruehl (2001) maintains that one may utilize split or double objects, onto which one would project "separated desires and needs and sometimes separated sides of an ambivalence, a hate and a love, once felt toward a single object" (p. 205). For instance, she cites that "it is not unusual for a man to love a woman who is chaste and a man who is sensual, as is often the case in the so-called married bisexuality or Latin bisexuality" (Young-Bruehl, 2001, p. 205); I shall discuss these types of bisexuality below. Finally, concerning the fourth type, Young-Bruehl (2001) indicates that an individual can "relate to the same object on both conscious and unconscious channels" (p. 206), which, in her view, represents "a layering situation" (p. 206). She provides an example of "a woman [who] might love a man consciously for his masculine qualities while she simultaneously loves this man unconsciously for his feminine qualities" (Young-Bruehl, 2001, p. 206).

Additionally, Young-Bruehl (2001) emphasizes the "object's felt capacity to satisfy narcissistic needs and anaclitic dependency needs, or (...) sensual needs and affectional needs" (p. 206). In this regard, Young-Bruehl (2001) underlines that, "in patriarchal societies, where women do the primary child-rearing, dependency and affectional needs tend to be associated originally with maternal objects" (p. 206); thus, she concludes that "the primary anaclitic or dependency object is usually someone chosen on the model of the woman who has fed us, and a later version is chosen on the model of the man who has protected us" (p. 206). Furthermore, Young-Bruehl (2001) highlights that "one of the key stories that will emerge (...), to be reconstructed and (...) experienced by my patients and me in the analytic transference is the story of how the patient's objects got to be bisexual" (p. 207); most importantly, she adds that "a patient's desired object will always be bisexual" (p. 208; emphasis added; see also Smith, 2002). On this note, concluding the review of the psychoanalytic theorization of bisexuality, I shall now turn to the examination of some of the controversies pertinent to this theorizing.

Contemporary Controversies

Considering the appraisal of the psychoanalytic conceptualization of bisexuality undertaken above, it becomes evident that there exist numerous issues that pertain to this complex subject. While recognizing that I am unable to discuss all of them extensively, I have identified the following questions that, in my view, appear to be some of the most controversial:

1. Is bisexuality a mode of object-choice in its own right, distinct from homosexuality?
2. Is bisexuality rooted in the early Oedipal or Oedipal development?
3. Is bisexuality connected to the splitting or integration of the mind?
4. Are the notions of activity and passivity satisfactory or does psychoanalysis need other descriptive categories?
5. Does bisexuality manifest psychopathology or mental health? And (being mindful of the lack in the elucidation of heterosexuality), what can be said concerning the psychoanalysis of bisexual individuals?
6. Finally, what sociocultural and historical factors should be taken into account, as regards the psychoanalytic conceptualization of bisexuality?

Accordingly, I will now address each of these controversial issues.

Is bisexuality a mode of object-choice in its own right, distinct from homosexuality? In other words, this question may also be posed as follows: Does bisexuality exist? As my research shows, it fuels the debate both in and outside of psychoanalysis (for some of the notable non-psychodynamic contributions to this subject, see: Blumstein & Schwartz, 1976; Cerny & Janssen, 2011; Goo, 2008; Guidry, 1999; MacDowall, 2009; Rieger, Chivers, & Bailey, 2005; Rosenthal, Sylva, Safron, & Bailey, 2012; Rust, 2002; Vernallis, 1999). As mentioned above, a number of analysts (e.g., Bryan, 1930; Khan, 1974; Roughton, as cited in Grossman, 2001; Young-Bruehl, 2001) pointed out the frequent confusion of bisexuality with homosexuality. Consequently, these analysts, amongst others (e.g., Brook, 1998; Elise, 1998, 2000; Grossman, 2001; Layton, 2000), also advocated for the investigation of bisexuality as a distinct type of object-choice.

Importantly, Bryan (1930) noted the resistances that psychoanalysts themselves seem to demonstrate in regard to bisexuality. More than 80 years later, this notion appears to remain valid, because, as my research suggests, psychoanalytic literature is still lacking in addressing bisexuality as a mode of object-choice. Further, Khan (1974) viewed "bisexual love" as "an authentic and necessary human experience, which can become distorted through repressions and reaction-formations as much as heterosexual love" (p. 143), which differs from the hypothesis proposed by Young-Bruehl (2001) that heterosexual and homosexual persons experience more conflict than bisexual individuals, because the latter "do not repress as relentlessly" (p. 184). On this note, Valedon (as cited in Brook, 1998), in agreement with Freud's original ideas, argued that, through the process of resolution of the Oedipus complex, bisexual object-choice might become either repressed or suppressed (and, subsequently, remain latent, in the context of manifest hetero- or homosexuality), or it can develop into the manifest, or overt, bisexuality. Additionally, also in agreement with Freud, he asserted that the desire for father's love is as universal and vital among boys, as it is in girls, and therefore should not be disregarded (due to the mistaken—yet, widespread—assumptions guided by the ideas of heteronormativity). Furthermore, because the psychoanalytic conceptualization of bisexuality was, for the most part, previously based on the pathologizing view of homosexuality (Grossman, 2001; Lewes, 1988), the former was also deemed a manifestation of narcissism (and the corresponding unconscious delusion of omnipotence) or a result of the overwhelming castration anxiety (Aron, 1995; Layton, 2000; Stimmel, 1996). As my research shows, it appears that nowadays such views are largely obsolete. On the same note, however, as a number of analysts (e.g., Bemporad, 1999; Friedman & Downey, 2010; Roughton, 2001) and non-psychodynamic researchers (e.g., Guidry, 1999; Rust, 2002) suggest, it is also possible that, for some adults, bisexuality may, in fact, be a transitional phenomenon, that is, the position assumed before coming to terms with either homo- or heterosexuality.

438

Nevertheless, in my opinion, psychoanalysts should, first and foremost, be mindful of the fluid character of human sexuality (Bemporad, 1999; Ferenczi, 1952a, 1952b; Friedman & Downey, 2010; Layton, 2000; Stimmel, 1996). Moreover, they must remember Freud's (1937) observation that some "people (…) can take as their sexual objects members of their own sex as well as of the opposite one, without the one trend interfering with the other" (pp. 243–244; emphasis added). At the same time, this does not imply that psychoanalysis should pay no attention to the elucidation of bisexuality—to the contrary, I argue that it is the subject (especially, in the context of the psychoanalytic theorization of object-choice) that needs to be investigated more thoroughly.

Is bisexuality rooted in the early Oedipal or Oedipal development? As regards the answer to this question (as is the case with many others), the psychoanalytic field appears to be somewhat split. As such, there are analysts, who argued in favor of the Oedipal basis of bisexual identifications (e.g., Guttman, 1955; Nunberg, 1947; Patry, 1928; Schuster, 1969), while there are also those, who seem to privilege the early Oedipal level as the ultimate root of bisexuality (e.g., Elise, 1998; Ferraro, 2001; Lane & Goeltz, 1998; Stensson, 1992b). At the same time, as my research demonstrates, many of the contemporary psychoanalysts (e.g., Aron, 1995; Fast, 1990; Hartman & Gibbard, 1973; Kernberg, 1991; Kubie, 1974; Weissman, 1962; Young-Bruehl, 2001) appear to be unanimous in acknowledging that both of these periods play an important role in the development of psychic bisexuality, as well as in the possibility of the establishment of bisexual object-choice. Furthermore, a vast number of the contemporary analysts (e.g., Aron, 1995; Bassin, as cited in Layton, 2000; Chodorow, as cited in Grossman, 2001; Christiansen, 1996; Fast, 1990; Ferraro, 2001; Kernberg, as cited in Grossman, 2001; Stimmel, 1996) emphasize the idea that one's identifications are never singular—in other words, that all children identify with both of their parents. On this note, I argue that it is also important to take into account Freud's original conceptualization of the complete Oedipus complex (see also Heenen-Wolff, 2011). In The Ego and the Id, Freud (1923b) stated:

Complete Oedipus complex, which is twofold, positive and negative, (…) is due to the bisexuality originally present in children: that is to say, a boy has not merely an ambivalent attitude towards his father and an affectionate object-choice towards his mother, but at the same time he also (…) displays an affectionate (…) attitude to his father and a corresponding jealousy and hostility towards his mother. (p. 33) Here, Freud (1923b) is also referring to "the earliest object-choices and identifications" (p. 33) and, in doing so, he appears to be hinting at the plausibility of identifications being both Oedipal and early Oedipal. Besides, if one carefully considers his subsequent assertion that "the ambivalence displayed in the relations to the parents should be attributed entirely to bisexuality and (…) not (…) [to] identification in consequence of rivalry" (Freud, 1923b, p. 33; see also Freud, 1925b), it may be suggested that Freud was contemplating the ubiquitous nature of identifications with both parents, which is currently viewed as a given by many psychoanalysts.

Additionally, as Klein regularly designated her contributions as being largely in line with the Freudian tradition, it may be hypothesized that her concept of the combined parent figure, as discussed above, also emphasizes the universal (although, in her original view, primitive) nature of multiple identifications. Moreover, as many of the contemporary analysts contend, this concept represents a useful model for the purpose of elucidation of the intricacies of psychic bisexuality and of the bisexual object-choice (e.g., Aron, 1995; Elise, 1998; Hurwood, 2009; Kernberg, 1991; Stimmel, 1996).

Thus, it appears that these two phenomena have important determinants in both Oedipal and early Oedipal periods of development (as Freud and Klein had shown in their corresponding conceptualizations). It is difficult to determine with certainty, however, which of these two levels plays the ultimate role. Additionally, as regards the contemporary theorizing on the subject, I believe that a vital advance has been made in recognizing the universality of (bisexual) identifications with both parental figures (I use these words instead of the word "parents" in order to accommodate for the non-traditional family constellations, such as those that include samesex, intersex, transsexual or transgendered partners and/or caregivers). Is bisexuality connected to the splitting or integration of the mind? As illustrated above, in psychoanalysis, bisexuality has been consistently conceptualized in relation to various binaries or dichotomies, such as: activity/ passivity, masculinity/femininity, maleness/femaleness, heterosexuality/ homosexuality and so forth. In my view, such polarization reflects not only the splitting that is seemingly inherent in the notion of bisexuality itself, but it also—and, perhaps, more importantly—corresponds to the splitting of gender binaries that is common within the sociocultural discourse. In fact, as mentioned above, many of the contemporary analysts suggested a number of ideas with regard to such splitting. For instance, Elise (1998) alludes to the splitting between the "sexed body" and the "gendered psyche", as well as the ability to be penetrated juxtaposed with the ability to penetrate, the latter of which, according to her, is "not inherently male but (...) comes to be seen as such" (p. 363; for further discussion, see p. 72 below). Layton (2000), on the other hand, argues against "the splitting that is inherent to the very definitions of masculinity and femininity" (p. 44), due to her observation that these are "cultural constructs defined psychically in relation to each other [that] do not exist apart" (p. 48). However, in response to Layton's (2000) grievances, Elise (2000) asserts that the "splitting into two polarized sexual categories is ubiquitous, not only because of patriarchy (...), but also because of the tremendous psychological task for the child to comprehend cognitively and emotionally the fact of two sexes" (p. 63; emphasis added; see also Benjamin, 1996). Most importantly, in my view, Elise (2000) affirms that such "splitting in [Western] culture is inevitable—and this entanglement in binaries is what [psychoanalysts] work with as a clinical reality" (p. 63; emphasis added). Furthermore, she asserts that "some attributes are experienced as gendered, and clinicians have to deal with this psychic reality in [their] patients notwithstanding how, as feminists, we might wish it were" (Elise, 2000, p. 63).

On a different note, Chodorow (as cited in Grossman, 2001) suggested that any rigid certainty, expressed by an analysand in relation to his/ her gender identity or object-choice, is likely to manifest splitting (cf. Winnicott's [1971] ideas regarding the dissociation between the male and female elements, as discussed above). Additionally, Young-Bruehl (2001) proposed that some objects could be chosen on the basis of splitting (viz., the splitting of the affective longings and erotic desires or the splitting of the ambivalent feelings that used to be directed at a single object). On the other hand, many of the contemporary analysts also emphasize the integrative role of bisexuality in mental functioning (e.g., Aron, 1995; Benjamin, 1996; Chodorow, as cited in Grossman, 2001; Elise, 1998, 2000; Ferraro, 2001; Hurwood, 2009; Khan, 1974; Stimmel, 1996). For instance, invoking Britton, Ogden asserts that "the triangulation that is the outcome of a satisfactory Oedipal transitional relationship represents a restructuring of the individual's fundamental bisexuality in such a way that femininity need not be a flight from, or denial of, masculinity (and vice versa)" (as cited in Ferraro, 2001, pp. 495–496; emphasis added). Additionally, while agreeing with the notion of the ubiquitous sociocultural splitting of masculinity and femininity, both Aron (1995) and Sweetnam (1996) acknowledge the positive influence derived from the integration of psychic bisexuality and, at the same time, they highlight the organizing function of such splitting, as it allows children the opportunity for the elucidation of the perplexing differences between the sexes (see also Elise, 2000).

Thus, it can be concluded that bisexuality pertains to both splitting and integration of the mind. However, in light of the contemporary theorizing reviewed above, it is also my opinion that psychoanalysts must be mindful of the negative connotation that is generally attributed to the concept of splitting and, when appropriate, they must recognize its positive (i.e., structuring) role as well. Are the notions of activity and passivity satisfactory or does psychoanalysis need other descriptive categories?

It is evident that, throughout most of its history, psychoanalysis operated in terms of activity and passivity, as regards its theorization of psychic bisexuality and object-choice (e.g., Bird, 1958; Brook, 1998; Bryan, 1930; Guttman, 1955; Nunberg, 1947; Patry, 1928; Tyson, 1982; Weissman, 1962). In fact, Freud (1905a) himself originated this conceptualization, when he proposed that "the opposing masculinity and femininity which are combined in bisexuality [represent] a contrast which often has to be replaced in psycho-analysis by that between activity and passivity" (p. 160). Needless to say, this conception has been one of the most controversial and, as such, was to dissatisfaction of many—from the general (and, especially, feminist-minded) critics of psychoanalysis to a number of analysts themselves (e.g., Aron, 1995; Chodorow, as cited in Grossman, 2001; Elise, 1998, 2000; Ferraro, 2001; Gann, as cited in Brook, 1998; Guttman, 1955; Kernberg, 1991; Kubie, 1974; Layton, 2000; Smith, 2002; Stimmel, 1996). Nonetheless, it is curious that Freud's own discontent concerning this theorizing has been overlooked, if not ignored, as he also stated that "we find masculinity vanishing into activity and femininity into passivity, and that does not tell us enough" (Freud, 1920, p. 171; emphasis added), and reiterated this problem again 10 years later: "For psychology the contrast between the sexes fades away into one between activity and passivity, in which we far too readily identify activity with maleness and passivity with femaleness" (Freud, 1930, p. 105, footnote; emphasis added; see also Freud, 1933, pp. 114–115). Thus, I, first of all, contend that it is crucial for those, who pursue the task of criticizing this particular area of psychoanalytic theory, to recognize Freud's own dissatisfaction with it. At the same time, I would also like to highlight some of the contemporary contributions to this controversial issue. First, Elise (1998, 2000) proposed that, instead of the categories of active and passive, the notions of "penetrating" and "penetrated" be used (see also Aron, 1995). As discussed briefly above, she argued that the infant's first experience of penetration is that, which is performed by the mother (by means of her nipples, fingers, etc.). Thus, Elise (1998) asserted that penetration, in itself, is not an inherently male ability, but, rather, it has been commonly—and, she argues, mistakenly—perceived as such within the widespread sociocultural and psychoanalytic discourses. On a different note, due to her utter disdain for the idea that one's biological sex may somehow be connected to one's gender, Layton (2000) suggested that "it would be a significant terminological advance were psychoanalysts to call identifications with male and female parents paternal and maternal rather than masculine and feminine" (p. 55, footnote). Further, Ferraro (2001), capitalizing mainly on Winnicott's (e.g., 1971) theory of infant development, recommended that the notions of activity and passivity be replaced by those of "omnipotence" and "impotence", which, as Ferraro contends, are more accurate.

Thus, while I certainly agree with Freud (and contemporary analysts), in that psychoanalysis is in need of other, more nuanced, descriptive categories, I would like to point out, however, that, in my opinion, the revised terms (e.g., as proposed by the three analysts just mentioned) still remain dichotomous and therefore pertain to the exact splitting that they, in part, aim to contest (cf. Layton, 2000). Moreover, in agreement with Aron (1995), I would suggest that psychoanalysts should recognize the importance of such dichotomous splitting (regardless of the terminology used to described it) as a fact of psychic reality (Elise, 2000), while also taking into account the vital task of the integration of these split-off (gendered) parts of the mind. Perhaps, this would allow psychoanalysis the opportunity to move closer toward the depressive position in its understanding of both psychic bisexuality and bisexual object-choice.

Does bisexuality manifest psychopathology or mental health? And, being mindful of the lack in the elucidation of heterosexuality, what can be said concerning the psychoanalysis of bisexual individuals? The view that bisexuality is a manifestation of psychopathology is grounded, mostly, in the discourses of monosexuality, which share the assumption that one's affective wishes and erotic desires can only be directed at either, but not both, of the sexes and, furthermore, that the mature object-choice must be heterosexual (Layton, 2000; Money, 1990; Roughton, as cited in Grossman, 2001; Young-Bruehl, 2001). Owing to the latter notion in particular, bisexuality has been viewed as psychopathological, to some degree or other, by many analysts (e.g., Bryan, 1930; Fast, 1990; Guttman, 1955; Kubie, 1974; Lane & Goeltz, 1998; Patry, 1928; Stensson, 1992a, 1992b; Weiss, 1958; Weissman, 1962). However, a vast number of the contemporary psychoanalysts of diverse theoretical adherences (e.g., Elise, 1998; Friedman & Downey, 2010; Grossman, 2001; Heenen-Wolff, 2011; Layton, 2000; Roughton, 2001; Smith, 2002; Stimmel, 1996; Valedon, as cited in Brook, 1998; Young-Bruehl, 2001) tend to agree that the conception of bisexuality as rooted in the narcissistic wish for omnipotence (derived from the object-relations perspectives) or as a failure in the resolution of the castration and Oedipus complexes (inferred from Freud's and his followers' conceptualizations) is misguided and therefore no longer satisfactory.

On the other hand, Kernberg (as cited in Grossman, 2001), while noting the psychoanalytic history of pathologizing of homosexuality (see also Lewes, 1988, as well as the previous essay in this book), suggested that, to answer "the question of whether bisexual orientation is considered a lifestyle or a psychopathology, (...) would require examination of the overall structure and organization of the personality and the maturity of object relationships" (p. 1372). At the same time, he affirmed that his clinical observations point to the connection between (what he refers to as) "habitual bisexual behavior" among men and their "significant narcissistic character pathology" (Kernberg, as cited in Grossman, 2001, p. 1364). In response to Kernberg, Roughton (2001) stated that his own extensive analytic experience does not support this finding. Roughton (2001) also thoughtfully pointed out that "countless numbers of men seek self-repair through sexualizing their narcissistic needs with women, but [psychoanalysts] do not then impugn heterosexuality as the problem" (pp. 1198–1199). Further, Roughton (2001) suggested that "an evaluation of the role of sexuality in the life of a bisexual man should be based on the quality and meaning of the sexuality and personal relationships", as opposed to "the varying gender of the partners or the initial difficulty in deciding what he wants" (p. 1207). Thus, he concluded that "knowing a person's sexual orientation tells us nothing about his psychological health and maturity, his character, his inner conflicts, his object relationships, or his integrity" (Roughton, 2001, p. 1212). At the same time, while not attempting to pathologize the bisexual choice of an object, Roughton (2001) indicated that, in some men, heterosexual trends (within the larger context of their bisexuality) may represent the defense against homosexual desires and vice versa (see also Bemporad, 1999; Smith, 2002), which, as he noted, can also occur among gay and heterosexual men. Therefore, he asserted that, instead of attempting to "cure" a patient from his/her non–heterosexual tendencies (thereby risking to instill a false self in him/her, due to the mistaken heterosexist assumptions), analysts must observe the fundamental principle of technical neutrality (see also Mitchell, 1981) and be mindful of their own counter-transferential attitudes, as regards the latent and manifest, as well as psychic and/or practiced, bisexuality in their analysands. Incidentally, Kernberg (as cited in Grossman, 2001) agrees with both of these recommendations (see also Aron, 1995; Blechner, 1998; Smith, 2002; Sweetnam, 1996).

In similar fashion, in their recent article (notably, the only published source I was able to locate that specifically addresses the psychoanalytic psychotherapy of bisexual men), Friedman and Downey (2010) argue that "bisexuality itself is not inherently psychopathological and bisexual men do not necessarily seek, or should seek, psychotherapy" (p. 182; emphasis added). Further, in response to Erikson's (e.g., 1956) idea that bisexuality manifests "identity diffusion", Friedman and Downey (2010), drawing upon their clinical experience, contend that "there is no reason to think that bisexuality itself 'causes' weakened ego identity" (p. 184). They also underscore their finding that many patients with borderline psychopathology tend to associate this mental illness with their bisexual orientation. However, Friedman and Downey caution analysts against making the same connection, as they affirm that the mentally disordered state is not, in itself, caused by one's (bisexual) choice of an object, as Roughton (2001) also argued. Additionally, regarding the psychotherapy of bisexual men, in agreement with both Kernberg (as cited in Grossman, 2001) and Roughton (2001), Friedman and Downey (2010) insist that "the goal should be to assess the history and meaning of the patient's erotic experiences and his reactions to them" (p. 191); they conclude their paper by recommending that "therapists (…) avoid simple reductionistic formulas, and help their patients explore an area of life that is potentially rich with meaning and significance" (p. 195). Further, in her re-evaluation of Freud's original conceptualization, Heenen-Wolff (2011) very recently—and, in my view, justly—observed that, as regards "maintaining a manifest bisexual orientation as an adult, Freud does not say (…) that it is structurally more pathological than another drive destiny" (p. 1216; see also Ferraro, 2001; Smith, 2002). Additionally, in line with Freud's theorizing, she pointed out that "the unconscious (and the id's urge) is and remains bisexual" (Heenen-Wolff, 2011, p. 1217; emphasis added; see also Stimmel, 1996). Moreover, Heenen-Wolff (2011) emphasized that "the heterosexual genital constellation is but one of the forms which infantile sexuality may arrive at, the 'polymorphic perverse' elements always remaining alive and active" (p. 1218; emphasis added); she further added that "the Oedipus complex is organized bisexually and (...) it remains a potential challenge for life" (p. 1218). On the same note, as mentioned above, both Meltzer (1973/2008) and Kernberg (1991) earlier highlighted the polymorphously perverse tendencies present in all sexualities, including those positioned as normal (see also Blechner, 1998; Elise, 2000), which, incidentally, is in agreement with Freud's (1914) assertion that "being in love (...) has the power to remove repressions and re-instate perversions" (p. 100). Thus, I argue that any current theorization of bisexuality, including—and especially—that, which pertains to the psychoanalysis and psychoanalytic psychotherapy of bisexual individuals, must take into account the problem of heterosexuality—that is, the lack in elucidation of the nature of heterosexual object-choice that many analysts (e.g., Chodorow, 1992; Drescher, 2002; Elise, 1998; Heenen-Wolff, 2011; Layton, 2000; Money, 1990; Young-Bruehl, 2001), beginning with Freud (e.g., 1905a), had emphasized. Furthermore, in agreement with Roughton (2001), as well as Friedman and Downey (2010), I would like to underline my view that any given object-choice is not implicitly associated with psychopathology. Additionally, as many psychoanalysts point out, it is also my opinion that the key task of any analysis is the exploration of numerous dimensions of the analysand's experience, rather than the attempt to subdue him/her to the conventional understanding of normalcy (or morality): that is, in the words of Kernberg (as cited in Grossman, 2001), "we are trying to help patients achieve greater autonomy, not adaptivity" (p. 1369; emphasis added). On this note, I shall now discuss some of the historical and sociocultural concerns that may be relevant to the psychoanalytic theorizing on bisexuality. What sociocultural and historical factors should be taken into account, as regards the psychoanalytic conceptualization of bisexuality?

While it is not my main goal in this paper to examine the social, cultural or historical factors that may pertain to the psychoanalytic theorization of bisexuality, I believe it is important to address several of them. First, as a number of analysts (e.g., Friedman & Downey, 2010; Guttman, 1955; Nunberg, 1947; Weissman, 1962; Young-Bruehl, 2001), beginning with Freud (e.g., 1905b), highlight, male bisexuality was a rather common phenomenon in the sophisticated civilization that was Ancient Greece; not to mention the allusions to bisexual heroes present in myths, including the religious myths (e.g., Hartman & Gibbard, 1973; Money, 1990; Nunberg, 1947). This must serve as a reminder for psychoanalysts to be mindful of the sociocultural influences that, at any given time and place in history, may be reflected in their theoretical constructions. Undoubtedly, these influences also include the current, post-modern fads and trends—such as those that substitute the (psycho)analytical investigation of sexual and gender differences with the obliteration of said differences—mostly, masquerading as progressive political and activist agenda, which, in actuality, is being fiercely promoted by the ruthless capitalist forces of globalization. Second, non-psychodynamic research shows that, even nowadays, male bisexuality is as widespread as it is covert: that is, there exist many various types of bisexual behavior among men that generally remain hidden from the public view (e.g., Blumstein & Schwartz, 1976; Carrier, 1985; Ford & Beach, as cited in Friedman, 1986; Guidry, 1999; Kinsey et al., 1954; Ripley, et al., 2011; Rust, 2002). For instance, consider the current discourse of Latin male bisexuality, which refers to the notion (common in the Latin-American cultures) that a man does not "lose" his masculinity per se in the homosexual intercourse with another man, as long as he remains in the penetrating position (e.g., Carrier, 1985; Friedman, 1986; Munoz-Laboy, 2008, 2009; Young-Bruehl, 2001). As another example, consider the so-called married bisexuality, which, according to Young-Bruehl (2001) and many of the non-psychodynamic researchers (e.g., Blumstein & Schwartz, 1976; Goo, 2008; Guidry, 1999; Rust, 2002; Vernallis, 1999), is virtually customary in the cultures that prohibit non-heterosexual forms of sexual behavior among males: in such cultures, it is commonly accepted, but not openly admitted or discussed, that married men can and do have homosexual encounters, as long as they take place in secrecy. Additionally, as Weissman (1962), Isay (1986) and Valedon (as cited in Brook, 1998) pointed out, the so-called situational bisexuality is also quite frequent among males, as it often occurs, when the availability of the other-sex partner(s) is constrained (e.g., in the military or penitentiary settings).

Third, a number of analysts (e.g., Blechner, 1998; Diamond, 2004; Elise, 1998; Friedman & Downey, 2010; Layton, 2000; Roughton, as cited in Grossman, 2001; Smith, 2002; Young-Bruehl, 2001) emphasize the taboo, stigma and marginalization of homosexuality that are still widespread nowadays, even in the Western world. Many of them cite this reality in relation to the bisexual individuals, who are not only frequently ostracized by the heterosexual people, but are also often excluded from gay communities, due to the presumptions that their bisexual orientation is either a mere disguise for homosexuality or a desire to experiment with the latter, which is inappropriate for a "true" heterosexual (see also Blumstein & Schwartz, 1976; Goo, 2008; Guidry, 1999; Rust, 2002; Vernallis, 1999).

On the same note, Roughton (as cited in Grossman, 2001) raises some thought-provoking questions in regard to both sociocultural and psychoanalytic views of bisexuality, such as, for instance: "If it were not for the taboo against homosexuality, would everyone be capable of enjoying sex with both men and women?" (pp. 1365–1366; see also Friedman & Downey, 2010); or: "With the decreasing stigma toward homosexuality, will bisexuality increase in the younger generation?" (p. 1366; see also Ripley, et al., 2011). Similarly, Smith (2002) wonders about what psychoanalysts might find, "if [they] were to look for evidence of a universal [intrapsychic] predisposition to bisexuality" among "younger children" (p. 556). In my view, such questions should be taken into account, as regards the psychoanalytic inquiry into bisexuality (though, I must admit, addressing them is beyond the limit of scope of the present paper). Thus, I believe that it is vital for psychoanalysts to be mindful of the sociocultural and historical discourses pertinent to bisexuality, so as not to let the common heteronormative or heterosexist (or even homophobic) presumptions interfere with their sound clinical judgment (as Roughton [2001] thoughtfully contends). Most importantly, however, as I have argued throughout this paper, psychoanalysts must undertake a more rigorous examination of the bisexual object-choice—especially, considering its widespread nature, which, incidentally, Freud was aware of over a century ago.

Summary and Conclusion

I have taken you through the laborious, though not exhaustive (and, hopefully, not exhausting), exploration of the psychoanalytic conceptualization of bisexuality and its vicissitudes, many of which were discussed: innate or constitutional, bisexuality, psychic bisexuality (i.e., gender), bisexual object-choice, and homosexuality. Thereby, one of my aims was to show that the confusion pertaining to such wide distribution of terminology related to the concept of bisexuality is one of the problems in the psychoanalytic theorizing on this subject, insofar as these different dimensions frequently overlapped, colluded are conflated with, and substituted with one another. Consequently, it is my opinion that the concept of psychic bisexuality should be examined independently from that of the bisexual object-choice. Additionally, my research suggests that bisexuality as an object-choice should be investigated as a unique phenomenon, distinct from homosexuality. Nonetheless, I also argued that, while bisexuality, among some individuals, might represent an object-choice in its own right, in others, it may manifest a defense against either homosexual or heterosexual tendencies. Further, I demonstrated that both psychic bisexuality and bisexual choice of an object might have their determinants in both early Oedipal and Oedipal periods of development, as they appear to be connected to multiple identifications (i.e., bisexual identifications with both parental figures). I also suggested that bisexuality might pertain to both splitting and integration of the mind. However, I contended that such splitting (especially, with regard to psychic bisexuality) might be a useful organizing structure—particularly, among younger children, who face the difficult task of comprehending the complexity of the differences between the sexes. On the same note, while recognizing that psychoanalysis is in need of better descriptive categories than those of activity and passivity, I also indicated that the splitting inherent in these

452

categories corresponds to the intrapsychic reality that analysts generally work with—and therefore must not disavow or disallow—in their clinical encounters with the analysands of both sexes (however passionate they might feel about the post-modern idea[1] of obliteration/amalgamation of gender and sexual differences). Additionally, I argued that no object-choice is implicitly associated with psychopathology. Consequently, I also suggest that it would be beneficial to enquire into bisexuality in the non-clinical population. Moreover, taking into account the post-Freudian history of pathologizing of homosexuality, I maintain that psychoanalysts (amongst other mental health professionals) should approach both the study of bisexuality and psychotherapy of bisexual men (and women) in a careful and unbiased manner, as did Freud.

On this note, I also showed that Freud's original views on bisexuality are not only supported by the empirical findings in various non-psycho-dynamic disciplines, but are still largely relevant today, if their evolution and implications are considered fully (and not selectively) and if they are re-evaluated carefully (and not tendentiously). In fact, it appears that many of the post-modern theorists, who tend to accuse Freud of being immensely biologically deterministic, are themselves assuming an equally extreme position—namely, that of the sociocultural determinism (not to mention that of, at times, misguided activism), while virtually disregarding the vital importance of both biological and intrapsychic forces present in all human beings. This being said, I do recognize that our knowledge of the ways, in which the vicissitudes of bisexuality may oscillate, is more complex and nuanced nowadays than it was in Freud's time. Moreover, as demonstrated in this paper, I value many of the post-Freudian contributions to the elucidation of this intricate phenomenon. Nevertheless, it is also my position that the fundamental unconscious drives and their corresponding desires are universal among humans and, as such, not susceptible to acquiescent change over time, because they tend to internally withstand many of the fluctuating external influences (such as those of society and culture).

Finally, as I had suggested in the previous essay, psychoanalytic views on homosexuality appear to have been undergoing a transformation—namely, from the initial ambiguity inherent in Freud's conceptualization, through the paranoid-schizoid ideation evident in the revisionists' theorizing, to a more depressive stance of the contemporary analysts and, thus, reparation. Therein, I argued that the ambiguity of Freud's theories, while being central to the overall psychoanalytic conception of the human mind, can also provoke the defensive reactions that derive their paranoid-schizoid character from the intolerance of such ambiguity. As regards bisexuality, my research clearly shows that it is one of the most ambiguous topics in psychoanalysis (as well as in other disciplines). However, in my view, a rigorous investigation of bisexuality can provide invaluable insights, as regard the two key areas of interest in psychoanalysis—that is, gender and sexuality. Moreover, in my opinion, further examination of bisexuality would also allow psychoanalysis (and maybe the culture as well) to move forward, in the direction of the depressive position. After all, as Smith (2002)—largely in agreement with Freud—stated, isn't it accurate that "all of us are bisexual, but some are more bisexual than others?" (p. 556)

References

American Psychiatric Association. (2000). *Diagnostic and statistical manual of mental disorders: DSM-IV-TR* (4th ed., text rev.). Washington, DC: Author.

Aron, L. (1995). The internalized primal scene. *Psychoanalytic Dialogues*, 5, 195–237.

Bem, S. L., & Lewis, S. A. (1975). Sex role adaptability: One consequence of psychological androgyny. *Journal of Personality and Social Psychology*, 31(4), 634–643. doi: 10.1037/h0077098

Bemporad, J. R. (1999). Epigenesis and sexual orientation: A report of five bisexual males. The Journal of the American Academy of Psychoanalysis and Dynamic Psychiatry, 27, 221–237. Benjamin, J. (1996). In defense of gender ambiguity. Gender and Psychoanalysis, 1, 27–43. Bird, B. (1958). A study of the bisexual meaning of the foreskin. *Journal of the American Psychoanalytic Association*, 6, 287–304.

Blechner, M. J. (1998). Maleness and masculinity. Contemporary Psychoanalysis, 34, 597–613. Blumstein, P. W., & Schwartz, P. (1976). Bisexuality in men. *Urban Life*, 5(3), 339– 358.

Brook, A. (Ed.). (1998). Castration as an organiser of bisexuality: Chaired by Erik Gann, San Francisco. *The International Journal of Psycho-Analysis*, 79, 380– 383.

Bryan, D. (1930). Bisexuality. The International Journal of Psycho-Analysis, 11, 150–166. Butler, J. (1995). Melancholy gender—Refused identification. *Psychoanalytic Dialogues*, 5, 165–180.

Carrier, J. M. (1985). Mexican male bisexuality. Journal of Homosexuality, 11(1–2), 75–86. doi: 10.1300/J082v11n01_07

Cerny, J. A., & Janssen, E. (2011). Patterns of sexual arousal in homosexual, bisexual, and heterosexual men. *Archives of Sexual Behavior*, 40(4), 687–697. doi: 10.1007/s10508–011–9746–0

Chodorow, N. J. (1992). Heterosexuality as a compromise formation: Reflections on the psychoanalytic theory of sexual development. *Psychoanalysis and Contemporary Thought*, 15, 267–304.

Christiansen, A. (1996). Masculinity and its vicissitudes: Reflections on some gaps in the psychoanalytic theory of male identity formation. The Psychoanalytic Review, 83, 97–124. Diamond, M. J. (1997). Boys to men: The maturing of masculine gender identity through paternal watchful protectiveness. *Gender and Psychoanalysis*, 2, 443– 468.

Diamond, M. J. (2004). The shaping of masculinity: Revisioning boys turning away from their mothers to construct male gender identity. *The International Journal of Psycho-Analysis*, 85, 359–380.

Drescher, J. (2002). Causes and becauses: On etiological theories of homosexuality. *The Annual of Psychoanalysis*, 30, 57–68.

Drescher, J. (2007). From bisexuality to intersexuality: Rethinking gender categories. *Contemporary Psychoanalysis*, 43, 204–228.

Elise, D. (1998). Gender repertoire: Body, mind, and bisexuality. Psychoanalytic Dialogues, 8, 353–371.

Elise, D. (2000). "Bye-bye" to bisexuality? Response to Lynne Layton. *Studies in Gender and Sexuality*, 1, 61–68.

Elise, D. (2001). Unlawful entry: Male fears of psychic penetration. *Psychoanalytic Dialogues*, 11, 499–531.

Erikson, E. H. (1956). The problem of ego identity. *Journal of the American Psychoanalytic Association*, 4, 56–121.

Escoffier, J. (2011). Imagining the she/male: Pornography and the transsexualization of the heterosexual male. *Studies in Gender and Sexuality*, 12(4), 268–281.

Fast, I. (1990). Aspects of early gender development: Toward a reformulation. *Psychoanalytic Psychology*, 7S, 105–117.

Ferenczi, S. (1952a). Chapter V: On the part played by homosexuality in the pathogenesis of paranoia. In E. Jones (Ed. and Trans.), First contributions to psycho–analysis. *The International Psycho-Analytical Library*, 45, 154–184. London, UK: The Hogarth Press and The Institute of Psycho–Analysis.

Ferenczi, S. (1952b). Chapter XII: The nosology of male homosexuality (homoerotism). In E. Jones (Ed. and Trans.), First contributions to psycho-analysis. *The International Psycho-Analytical Library*, 45, 296–318. London, UK: The Hogarth Press and The Institute of Psycho-Analysis.

Ferraro, F. (2001). Vicissitudes of bisexuality. In P. Slotkin (Trans.). *The International Journal of Psycho-Analysis*, 82, 485–499.

Fogel, G. I. (2006). Riddles of masculinity: Gender, bisexuality, and thirdness. *Journal of the American Psychoanalytic Association*, 54, 1139–1163.

Freud, S. (1901). The psychopathology of everyday life: Forgetting, slips of the tongue, bungled actions, superstitions and errors. In J. Strachey (Ed. and Trans.), *The standard edition of the complete psychological works of Sigmund Freud*, Vol. VI, vii–296. London, UK: The Hogarth Press and The Institute of Psycho-Analysis.

Freud, S. (1905a). Three essays on the theory of sexuality. In J. Strachey (Ed. and Trans.), *The standard edition of the complete psychological works of Sigmund Freud*, Vol. VII, 123–246. London, UK: The Hogarth Press and The Institute of Psycho-Analysis.

Freud, S. (1905b). Fragment of an analysis of a case of hysteria. In J. Strachey (Ed. and Trans.), *The standard edition of the complete psychological works of Sigmund Freud*, Vol. VII, 1–122. London, UK: The Hogarth Press and The Institute of Psycho-Analysis.

Freud, S. (1908). Hysterical phantasies and their relation to bisexuality. In J. Strachey (Ed. and Trans.), *The standard edition of the complete psychological works of Sigmund Freud*, Vol. IX, 155–166. London, UK: The Hogarth Press and The Institute of Psycho-Analysis.

Freud, S. (1909). Analysis of a phobia in a five-year-old boy. In J. Strachey (Ed. and Trans.), *The standard edition of the complete psychological works of Sigmund Freud*, Vol. X, 1–150. London, UK: The Hogarth Press and The Institute of Psycho-Analysis.

Freud, S. (1911). Psycho–analytic notes on an autobiographical account of a case of paranoia. In J. Strachey (Ed. and Trans.), *The standard edition of the complete psychological works of Sigmund Freud*, Vol. XII, 1–82. London, UK: The Hogarth Press and The Institute of Psycho-Analysis.

Freud, S. (1912). On the universal tendency to debasement in the sphere of love (Contributions to the psychology of love II). In J. Strachey (Ed. and Trans.), *The standard edition of the complete psychological works of Sigmund Freud*, Vol. XI, 177–190. London, UK: The Hogarth Press and The Institute of Psycho-Analysis.

Freud, S. (1913). The claims of psycho-analysis to scientific interest. In J. Strachey (Ed. and Trans.), *The standard edition of the complete psychological works of Sigmund Freud*, Vol. XIII, 163–190. London, UK: The Hogarth Press and The Institute of Psycho-Analysis.

Freud, S. (1914). On narcissism: An introduction. In J. Strachey (Ed. and Trans.), *The standard edition of the complete psychological works of Sigmund Freud*, Vol. XIV, 67–102. London, UK: The Hogarth Press and The Institute of Psycho-Analysis.

Freud, S. (1916–1917). Introductory lectures on psycho-analysis. In J. Strachey (Ed. and Trans.), *The standard edition of the complete psychological works of Sigmund Freud*, Vols. XI–XVI, 1–463. London,

UK: The Hogarth Press and The Institute of Psycho-Analysis. Freud, S. (1917).

Mourning and melancholia. In J. Strachey (Ed. and Trans.), *The standard edition of the complete psychological works of Sigmund Freud*, Vol. XIV, 237–258. London, UK: The Hogarth Press and The Institute of Psycho– Analysis.

Freud, S. (1918). From the history of an infantile neurosis. In J. Strachey (Ed. and Trans.), *The standard edition of the complete psychological works of Sigmund Freud*, Vol. XVII, 1–124. London, UK: The Hogarth Press and The Institute of Psycho-Analysis.

Freud, S. (1920). The psychogenesis of a case of homosexuality in a woman. In J. Strachey (Ed. and Trans.), *The standard edition of the complete psychological works of Sigmund Freud*, Vol. XVIII, 145–172. London, UK: The Hogarth Press and The Institute of Psycho-Analysis.

Freud, S. (1922). Some neurotic mechanisms in jealousy, paranoia and homosexuality. In J. Strachey (Ed. and Trans.), *The standard edition of the complete psychological works of Sigmund Freud*, Vol. XVIII, 221–232. London, UK: The Hogarth Press and The Institute of Psycho-Analysis.

Freud, S. (1923a). Two encyclopaedia articles. In J. Strachey (Ed. and Trans.), *The standard edition of the complete psychological works of Sigmund Freud*, Vol. XVIII, 233–260. London, UK: The Hogarth Press and The Institute of Psycho-Analysis.

Freud, S. (1923b). The ego and the id. In J. Strachey (Ed. and Trans.), *The standard edition of the complete psychological works of Sigmund Freud*, Vol. XIX, 1–66. London, UK: The Hogarth Press and The Institute of Psycho-Analysis.

Freud, S. (1924). The dissolution of the Oedipus complex. In J. Strachey (Ed. and Trans.), *The standard edition of the complete psychological works of Sigmund Freud*, Vol. XIX, 171–180. London, UK: The Hogarth Press and The Institute of Psycho-Analysis.

Freud, S. (1925a). An autobiographical study. In J. Strachey (Ed. and Trans.), *The standard edition of the complete psychological works of Sigmund Freud*, Vol. XX, 1–74. London, UK: The Hogarth Press and The Institute of Psycho-Analysis.

Freud, S. (1925b). Some psychical consequences of the anatomical distinction between the sexes. In J. Strachey (Ed. and Trans.), *The standard edition of the complete psychological works of Sigmund Freud*, Vol. XIX, 241–258. London, UK: The Hogarth Press and The Institute of Psycho-Analysis.

Freud, S. (1928). Dostoevsky and parricide. In J. Strachey (Ed. and Trans.), *The standard edition of the complete psychological works of Sigmund Freud*, Vol. XXI, 173–194. London, UK: The Hogarth Press and The Institute of Psycho-Analysis.

Freud, S. (1930). Civilization and its discontents. In J. Strachey (Ed. and Trans.), *The standard edition of the complete psychological works of Sigmund Freud*, Vol. XXI, 57–146. London, UK: The Hogarth Press and The Institute of Psycho-Analysis.

Freud, S. (1931). Female sexuality. In J. Strachey (Ed. and Trans.), *The standard edition of the complete psychological works of Sigmund Freud*, Vol. XXI, 221– 244. London, UK: The Hogarth Press and The Institute of Psycho-Analysis.

Freud, S. (1933). New introductory lectures on psycho–analysis. In J. Strachey (Ed. and Trans.), *The standard edition of the complete psychological works of Sigmund Freud*, Vol. XXII, 1–182. London, UK: The Hogarth Press and The Institute of Psycho-Analysis.

Freud, S. (1937). Analysis terminable and interminable. In J. Strachey (Ed. and Trans.), *The standard edition of the complete psychological works of Sigmund Freud*, Vol. XXIII, 209–254. London, UK: The Hogarth Press and The Institute of Psycho-Analysis.

Freud, S. (1938). An outline of psycho–analysis. In J. Strachey (Ed. and Trans.), *The standard edition of the complete psychological works of Sigmund Freud*, Vol. XXIII, 139–208. London, UK: The Hogarth Press and The Institute of Psycho-Analysis.

Friedman, R. C., & Downey, J. I. (2010). Psychotherapy of bisexual men. *The Journal of the American Academy of Psychoanalysis and Dynamic Psychiatry*, 82 38(1), 181–197.

Friedman, R. M. (1986). The psychoanalytic model of male homosexuality: A historical and theoretical critique. *The Psychoanalytic Review*, 73D, 79–115. Goo, U.

(2008). Concepts of bisexuality. *Journal of Bisexuality*, 8(1–2), 9–23. doi: 10.1080/15299710802142127 Green, A. (1995). Has sexuality anything to do with psychoanalysis? *The International Journal of Psycho-Analysis*, 76, 871–883.

Greenson, R. R. (1968). Dis–identifying from mother: Its special importance for the boy. *The International Journal of Psycho-Analysis*, 49, 370–374.

Grossman, G. (Ed). (2001). Contemporary views of bisexuality in clinical work. *Journal of the American Psychoanalytic Association*, 49, 1361–1377.

Guidry, L. L. (1999). Clinical intervention with bisexuals: A contextualized understanding. *Professional Psychology: Research and Practice*, 30(1), 22–26.

Guttman, S. A. (1955). Bisexuality in symbolism. *Journal of the American Psychoanalytic Association*, 3, 280–284.

Hartman, J. J., & Gibbard, G. S. (1973). Bisexual fantasy and group process. *Contemporary Psychoanalysis*, 9, 303–322.

Heenen-Wolff, S. (2011). Infantile bisexuality and the 'complete oedipal complex:' Freudian views on heterosexuality and homosexuality. In S. Jaron (Trans). *The International Journal of Psycho-Analysis*, 92, 1209–1220. doi: 10.1111/j. 1745–8315.2011.00436.x

461

Horney, K. (1932). Observations on a specific difference in the dread felt by men and by women respectively for the opposite sex. *The International Journal of Psycho-Analysis*, 13, 348–360.

Hurwood, J. (2009). Psychic and mental bisexuality in the development of a sense of self and mind. *British Journal of Psychotherapy*, 25(4), 520–532. doi: 10.1111/ j.1752–0118.2009.01146.x

Isay, R. A. (1986). The development of sexual identity in homosexual men. *The Psychoanalytic Study of the Child*, 41, 467–489.

Kardiner, A. (1978). The social distress syndrome of our time, part 2. The Journal of the American Academy of Psychoanalysis and Dynamic Psychiatry, 6, 215–

Kernberg, O. (1991). Sadomasochism, sexual excitement, and perversion. *Journal of the American Psychoanalytic Association*, 39, 333–362.

Khan, M. R. (1974). Ego-orgasm in bisexual love. *The International Review of Psycho-Analysis*, 1, 143–149.

Kinsey, A. C., Pomeroy W. B., Martin C. E., & Gebhard, P. (1954). *Sexual behavior in the human male*. Philadelphia, PA: W. B. Saunders.

Klein, M. (1932). *The psycho–analysis of children*. The International Psycho–Analytical Library, 22, 1–379. London, UK: The Hogarth Press and The Institute of Psycho-Analysis.

Klein, M. (1935). A contribution to the psychogenesis of manic-depressive states. In *Love, guilt and reparation and other works, 1921–1945*, 262–289. London, UK: Vintage Books and The Melanie Klein Trust.

Klein, M. (1946). Notes on some schizoid mechanisms. In M. M. R. Khan (Ed.), *Envy and gratitude and other works, 1946–1963*. The International Psycho-Analytical Library, 104, 1–24. London, UK: The Hogarth Press and The Institute of Psycho-Analysis.

Klein, M. (1952). The origins of transference. In M. M. R. Khan (Ed.), *Envy and gratitude and other works, 1946–1963*. The International

Psycho-Analytical Library, 104, 48–56. London, UK: The Hogarth Press and The Institute of Psycho-Analysis.

Klein, M. (1957). Envy and gratitude. In M. M. R. Khan (Ed.), *Envy and gratitude and other works, 1946–1963.* The International Psycho-Analytical Library, 104, 176–235. London, UK: The Hogarth Press and The Institute of Psycho-Analysis.

Klein, M. (1961). *Narrative of a child analysis: The conduct of the psycho-analysis of children as seen in the treatment of a ten year old boy*, 1–496. London, UK: 84 Vintage Books and The Melanie Klein Trust.

Kubie, L. S. (1974). The drive to become both sexes. *The Psychoanalytic Quarterly*, 43, 349–426.

Ladas, A. K., Whipple, B., & Perry, J. D. (1982). *The g-spot and other discoveries about human sexuality.* New York: Holt, Rinehart, and Winston.

Lane, R. C., & Goeltz, W. B. (1998). Identity confusion, bisexuality, and flight from the mother. *Clinical Psychology Review*, 18(3), 259–272.

Layton, L. B. (2000). The psychopolitics of bisexuality. *Studies in Gender and Sexuality*, 1, 41–60.

Lewes, K. (1988). Psychoanalytic theory of male homosexuality. New York, NY: Simon and Schuster. Lidz, T., & Lidz, R. W. (1986). Turning women things into men: Masculinization in Papua New Guinea. *The Psychoanalytic Review*, 73D, 117–135.

MacDowall, L. (2009). Historicising contemporary bisexuality. *Journal of Bisexuality*, 9(1), 3–15. doi: 10.1080/15299710802659989

Masson, J. M. (Ed.). (1985). *The complete letters of Sigmund Freud to Wilhelm Fliess, 1887–1904.* Cambridge, MA: Harvard University Press. Meltzer, D. (2008). Sexual states of mind (4th ed.). London, UK: Karnac Books Ltd. (Original work published 1973)

Mitchell, S. A. (1981). The psychoanalytic treatment of homosexuality: Some technical considerations. *The International Review of Psycho-Analysis*, 8, 63–80.

Money, J. (1990). Androgyne becomes bisexual in sexological theory: Plato to Freud and neuroscience. *The Journal of the American Academy of Psychoanalysis and Dynamic Psychiatry*, 18, 392–413.

Munoz-Laboy, M. A. (2008). Familism and sexual regulation among bisexual Latino men. *Archives of Sexual Behavior*, 37, 773–782. doi: 10.1007/s10508–008–9360–y

Munoz-Laboy, M. A. (2009). Negotiating bisexual desire and familism: The case of 85 Latino/a bisexual young men and women in New York City. *Culture, Health and Sexuality*, 11(3), 331–344. doi:10.1080/13691050802710634

Nunberg, H. (1947). Circumcision and problems of bisexuality. *The International Journal of Psycho-Analysis*, 28, 145–179.

Patry, F. L. (1928). Theories of bisexuality with report of a case. *The Psychoanalytic Review*, 15, 417–439.

Person, E. S., & Ovesey, L. (1983). Psychoanalytic theories of gender identity. The Journal of the American Academy of Psychoanalysis and Dynamic Psychiatry, 11, 203–226.

Rado, S. (1940). A critical examination of the concept of bisexuality. *Psychosomatic Medicine*, 2(4), 459–467.

Rieger, G., Chivers, M. L., & Bailey, J. M. (2005). *Sexual arousal patterns of bisexual men. Psychological Science*, 16(8), 579–584. doi: 10.1111/j.1467–9280.2005.01578.x

Ripley, M., Anderson, E., McCormack, M., Adams, A., & Pitts, R. (Eds.). (2011). The decreasing significance of stigma in the lives of bisexual men: Keynote address, Bisexual Research Convention, London. *Journal of Bisexuality*, 11(2), 195–206. doi: 10.1080/15299716.2011.571985

Rosenthal, A. M., Sylva, D., Safron, A., & Bailey, J. M. (2012). The male bisexuality debate revisited: Some bisexual men have bisexual arousal patterns. *Archives of Sexual Behavior*, 41, 135–147. doi: 10.1007/s10508-011-9881-7

Roughton, R. E. (2001). Four men in treatment: An evolving perspective on homosexuality and bisexuality, 1965 to 2000. Journal of the American Psychoanalytic Association, 49, 1187–1217. Rust, P. (2002). Bisexuality: The state of the union. *Annual Review of Sex Research*, 13, 180–240.

Schuster, D. B. (1969). Bisexuality and body as phallus. *The Psychoanalytic Quarterly*, 38, 72–80.

Smith, H. F. (2002). On psychic bisexuality. *The Psychoanalytic Quarterly*, 71, 549–558.

Stensson, J. (1992a). Male and female themes in the psychoanalytic process: On the notion of bisexuality. *International Forum of Psychoanalysis*, 1, 5–10.

Stensson, J. (1992b). Sexual identity and choice of sexual object: From bisexuality to implicate order. *International Forum of Psychoanalysis*, 1, 93–97.

Stimmel, B. (1996). From "nothing" to "something" to "everything:" Bisexuality and metaphors of the mind. *Journal of the American Psychoanalytic Association*, 44S, 191–214.

Stoller, R. J., & Herdt, G. H. (1982). The development of masculinity: A cross– cultural contribution. *Journal of the American Psychoanalytic Association*, 30, 29–59.

Sweetnam, A. (1996). The changing contexts of gender: Between fixed and fluid experience. *Psychoanalytic Dialogues*, 6, 437–459.

Tyson, P. (1982). A developmental line of gender identity, gender role, and choice of love object. *Journal of the American Psychoanalytic Association*, 30, 61–86.

Vernallis, K. (1999). Bisexual monogamy: Twice the temptation but half the fun? *Journal of Social Philosophy*, 30(3), 347–368.

Weiss, E. (1958). Bisexuality and ego structure. *The International Journal of Psycho-Analysis*, 39, 91–97.

Weissman, P. (1962). Structural considerations in overt male bisexuality. *The International Journal of Psycho-Analysis*, 43, 159–168.

Winnicott, D. W. (1971). *Playing and reality*. London, UK: Tavistock Publications.

Young-Bruehl, E. (2001). Are human beings "by nature" bisexual? *Studies in Gender and Sexuality*, 2, 179–213.

Psychosomatic Illness in a Claustro-Agoraphobic Patient

by Susan Finkelstein

"Take a man who is released and suddenly compelled to...look up toward the light; and who, moreover, in doing all this is in pain, and because he is dazzled, is unable to make out those things whose shadows he saw before. What do you suppose he'd say if someone were to tell him that before he saw silly nothings, while now, because he is somewhat nearer to what *is* and more turned toward beings, he sees more correctly...?... Don't you suppose he'd be at a loss and believe that what was seen before is truer than what is now shown?"

~ Bloom, Allan David, The Republic of Plato, New York, Basic Books: 1991, stanza 515d, p194

In one of the most powerful images of Western literature, Plato describes a group of people who have spent their lives imprisoned in a cave, chained so that they face the back wall. All they can see are shadows cast on the wall by a fire behind them. These shadows are the only reality these people know; they have come to understand them as the only reality there is. Plato then imagines what would happen if a prisoner should escape from the cave and so become witness to another reality previously unknown to and unimagined by him. The Parable of the Cave vividly depicts the anxiety of living with uncertainty—uncertainty about safety and danger, about knowledge and ignorance, about where we stop and the rest of the world begins.

These are universal human concerns. In the more than two thousand years since the Republic, many other thinkers have shared Plato's interest in how we learn to integrate internal experience with the "realities" of the outside world. Certainly that is a task that has long fascinated psychoanalysts. Contemporary Kleinians especially have paid close attention to the ambiguous appeal of Plato's cave, that fantasied space in which we are protected from the dangers of freedom and autonomy, but trapped in the privacy of our own minds.

Confusions between "inside" and "outside" confront us all as infants. When all goes well, we first make use of them and then resolve them by means of the dynamic that Melanie Klein (1946, p. 8) called projective identification. Projective identification is a normal ego function and defense mechanism. It is necessary for psychological growth and development, both as the preverbal baby's way of communicating its needs to its mother and as a process instrumental in the development of empathy.

Ideally, an infant's cries, smiles, struggles, and bodily productions alert his mother to what he is feeling by evoking in her—Klein would say projecting into her—experiences similar to his own (Klein 1946, p. 8-9). The mother receives these nonverbal communications and takes them in. She interprets her baby's emotional and physical states and acts on them appropriately, eventually offering them back to the baby in a contained, detoxified, and assimilated form. Bion, in A Theory of Thinking, called this process reverie; he was referring to the mother's ability to experience her infant both consciously, through thinking, and unconsciously, through a process akin to dreaming (1962b, p. 116).

468

By her words and her actions, the mother demonstrates to the baby what kind of a problem he has, and what can be done about it, probably talking to her baby throughout the process in a soothing language. The baby receives her ministrations, he feels her calm, and eventually he comes to understand her words. The process is repeated over and over again, and in time he internalizes it, eventually learning to accomplish the mother's empathic functioning himself—specifically, to identify emotional and physical states of mind (his and hers), to distinguish among them, and to communicate them, whether to himself or to someone else.

This primary dynamic, when it works correctly, allows the infant to develop experience of his own mind and of the mind of another. Through this conjoint awareness he begins to separate himself from his objects and also to distinguish internal phenomena like unhappiness from phenomena that exist outside himself. Even when soothing is not immediately available, the fortunate baby comes to expect that his problems will eventually be addressed, and so he learns to tolerate frustration. Successful projective identification mitigates the baby's aloneness and helplessness. It allows him to develop trust in his objects, and eventually in himself.

When a mother for whatever reason is not receptive to her child's projections, the infant cannot develop this dual awareness. Even an emotionally competent mother may fail to understand her child's communications or to soothe him adequately, if he is constitutionally endowed with unusual aggression or envy, or if his reactions fall far outside her own experience. Sometimes a mother is unskilled in handling emotions and so cannot read, process, or metabolize even normal physiological or psychological states. If she has been emotionally wounded herself, she may be incapable of empathic reception of the baby's communications.

In these cases the baby is left alone with his distress and without recourse. He is trapped in an emotional state that Bion in Learning from Experience (1962a,1984) calls without-ness (p. 97), where his communications avail him nothing, where confidence and trust cannot develop, and where inside and outside, self and other, are never differentiated. The more the interpersonal aspect of the infant-mother dyad is attenuated, the more the baby's intrapsychic dependence on it, and on projective identification that increases as he grows ever more frantic for a response. Klein (1946) called this pathological state "excessive projective identification," and she explained it like this: "The projection of good feelings and good parts of the self into the mother is essential for the infant's ability to develop good object relations and to integrate his ego. However, if this projective process is carried out excessively, good parts of the personality are felt to be lost, and in this way the mother becomes the ego-ideal; this process too results in weakening and impoverishing the ego" (p. 9).

Worse, the wretched state of a baby left alone with the inchoate fears and miseries that Bion (1962a,1984) calls nameless dread (p. 96) is likely to be exacerbated by the anxiety, frustration, guilt, or despair of the mother who can't soothe him. Projective identification works both ways, and her projections of her own feelings conflate with his unprocessed fears. He internalizes them as he would internalize "good-enough" responses, and they increase his burden of discomfort. The questions of whose feelings are whose and whose body those feelings belong to are never elucidated. All this further inhibits the baby's cognitive, and emotional growth, and his sense of dependency upon an object—an unresponsive object—intensifies.

Failures in projective identification have severe developmental consequences. They deny the baby necessary opportunities to learn to recognize, tolerate, and symbolize feelings and to develop me/not-me distinctions (D.W. Winnicott, 1951). Donald Meltzer (1966, p. 339), a Kleinian analyst interested in the way individuals navigate their internal and external object worlds, writes that a baby who experiences such failure may grow into a kind of pseudo-mature adult--that is, mature intellectually but immature in emotional development.

He may continue to feel so dependent on his mother that he clings to her as though he were living like a newborn kangaroo in its mother's pouch—the marsupial space, as Henri Rey (1994, p. 265) calls it. In this experience of encapsulation within the mother's body, distinctions between self and other, inside and outside, psychic reality and external reality need not (indeed, cannot) be reliably made. The resulting illusion of omnipotence, omniscience, and self-reliance affords a sense of safety, and relieves the fear of separation from the needed object.

It also presents a sharp quandary, however, that Rey has named the claustro-agoraphobic dilemma (Ibid., 1994, p. 221). On the one hand, the individual eventually comes to desire more freedom and wishes to escape the object that constrains him. Yet emergence from the safety of his familiar confinement feels dangerous, especially the threat of losing the object on whom he depends. Mervin Glasser (1979, p. 164) described the dilemma in his patient, whose core problem Glasser saw as a lack of differentiation between self and other, wished to get inside his mother's body, to be enveloped by his object. "[H]e gave characteristically concrete expression to his longings for 'envelopment' in imagining himself crawling up the birth canal and snuggling up inside the womb. But this gradually became supplanted by annihilatory fears expressed in terms of 'getting stuck inside.'" Glasser tells us that even very early in a once-a-week psychotherapy those feelings came into the transference as the patient compared his feeling stifled and engulfed by the sessions with "a description of a chicken in an egg, wanting to burst out of its confining suffocating shell."

Plato's chained cave-dwellers, however, have no access to relational experiences that can expand their one-dimensional, narcissistic, and omnipotent view of the world. They are not even aware of how limited

471

their worldview is. So it often is with people who grow up without the reciprocal interpersonal and intrapsychic explorations of successful projective identification. They remain trapped within their own experience or within the experience of mothers who, unable to cope effectively with anxiety themselves, convey back to their children raw, undigested, and frightening emotion. Such children have little chance to develop emotional skills or to learn themselves as both subject and object. Without the context of an empathic and enlightening adult as an auxiliary ego, they remain at the mercy of overwhelming feelings, both physical and emotional. Indeed, the physical and emotional are poorly enough distinguished that they may manifest themselves together as bodily preoccupations. The seductive but frightening fantasy of entrapment in the body of the mother is only one of these. In fact, Klein described unconscious fantasy in bodily terms, the way she thought the baby concretely felt and imagined its objects. "The baby, having incorporated his parents, feel them to be live people inside his body in the concrete way in which deep unconscious phantasies are experienced—they are, in his mind, 'internal' or 'inner objects' as I have termed them" (1940, p. 345).

Through the process of oral incorporation, the child may further misequate that idea with ideas about his own body parts, as he experiences them. And if he is desperate enough and sufficiently frustrated in his efforts to communicate with *outside objects*, he may attempt to communicate projectively and introjectively with the internal objects that he now unconsciously represents as living within himself. When specific bodily organs come to concretely (that is, in a non-mentalized way) represent incorporated object relationships, they lend themselves to psychosomatic projections and introjections, thus opening the door to psychosomatic symptomatology.

I will demonstrate these concepts at work in the case of a patient who frantically enacted the claustro-agoraphobic dilemma in her psychosomatic symptoms and her object relationships. A long analytic process provided the remedial "learning from experience" that had been frustrated by problems in the infant/mother dyad. This allowed the patient a chance to emerge from the claustro-agoraphobic space into increasing emotional autonomy and freedom.

Ms. A and her Internal Objects

Ms. A began a four-session-weekly psychoanalysis at the age of 48, citing psychosomatic symptoms and relationship difficulties and complaining that she felt imprisoned in her mind and in her body. She was a highly intelligent and successful professional, respected at work and in her community, but she suffered from irritable bowel syndrome, migraines, and intractable skin eruptions. She also had a longstanding eating disorder. She was childless by choice, twice married and twice divorced; when I met her she was once again engaged to be married but had been dating another man without her fiancé's knowledge. Fears that she was suffocating or having a heart attack had brought her to the emergency room on several occasions. The staff there started her on an SSRI for depression and anxiety. When this failed to help, the private psychopharmacologist who was supervising her medication referred her to me for psychoanalysis.

From the very beginning it was so hard to make contact with Ms. A that I often felt as if we were enacting a covert game of "catch me if you can." It took us a long time even to establish an initial appointment. On the date we finally managed to set for her first visit, she arrived very late and reported having had a massive anxiety attack while driving to my office and looking for a parking space.

These early complications were our first hints of Ms. A's conflicts about entering the concrete representation of the maternal body-mind that we called "my office" and that included my analytic attention as well. I wondered out loud whether her wish to find freedom in analysis might be engaging a fear of entrapment (in this case, the concrete parking of one's car) in an unknown and scary space. This early interpretation was intended to give her a sense of how internal affective states can be conceptualized as separate from their bodily—in this case panicky—manifestations.

Her language was rich and colorful. She told me that "the bottom" had fallen out recently, and I soon learned that she meant this both literally and figuratively. Her lover had abandoned her for another woman, and since then she had been living with floods of diarrhea. It became clear that through two marriages and her current engagement she had always had at least one secret liaison on the side. And she had never, she told me, been left; it had always been she who had precipitated the end of relationships. Now she felt abandoned and out of control. Her fiancé was pressing her to marry him, but without a lover as an escape hatch, the prospect of that decision terrified Ms. A. She felt that she would be trapped if she committed herself and lost and alone if she left. It was this crisis in her love life that precipitated the panics that brought her to the emergency room.

Thus was I alerted to Ms. A's reliance on the defense of splitting objects, which was clearly protecting her from a fear of depending too much on any single person. What I observed in her was a fear of "falling into bits"; I realized that I would have to approach the analysis slowly and carefully so as to not to precipitate any further ego fragmentation.

Ms. A told me that she had been in two previous psychotherapies before but that they had proven "ineffective." Just as she always eventually left imperfect men, so she left these two imperfect therapists who had, she said, failed to ameliorate the psychosomatic symptoms that had plagued her intermittently since college (particularly at times of separation from a relationship or commitment to one). They had also failed to repair the imperfections of the men in her life, which she magically sought to do. It appeared to me that she had come to me not so much on her own behalf but on behalf of her internal world, which was filled with broken objects. She was seeking cure not for herself but for a desperately sought idealized other, which—as she would iterate and reiterate in the beginning of the analysis—she had never quite been able to find. Indeed, for a very long time in her analysis Ms. A spoke much more of the persons with whom she felt enmeshed than about her own self. She could tell me so little about herself that I had to depend on my own countertransference experience for information about what she felt (Pick, 1985).

I knew, of course, that any attempts at repair were destined to fail until Ms. A had a better understanding of what exactly she was trying to fix and what kind of fixing was needed. As it turned out, she was using her external relationships with men to protect her from the primitive and punishing superego of her unconscious introjected relationship with her mother. She needed to learn from this new psychoanalysis that there was an internal relationship that would have to be put right.

As the initial consultation proceeded, I saw more and more of Ms. A's primitive and paranoid anxieties, both about being trapped by other people's doings and about the dangers of autonomous action of her own. She seemed to be deeply uncomfortable in her own skin (one of her main psychosomatic foci). She told me that she broke out in hives when she was anxious and that often she found another person's touch intolerable. Even the soft contact of silk or cotton burned her. Her skin seemed to function for her as a (too-) fragile barrier between inside and outside experience (Bick, 1968). She alternated between periods of intense eye contact (which I experienced in the countertransference as penetration), and periods of hiding her face with her long hair (by which means, I thought, she protected herself from feeling penetrated by me). She was a strikingly attractive woman, tall and slender, who seemed in my office to melt into her surroundings, becoming one with them. She elicited in me, and probably in others, a feeling that she did not wish to be seen.

Before she left that first day, Ms. A reported a dream from the night before. If the first dream is indeed a tell-tale sign to the analyst of a patient's organization of mind and capacity to conceptualize others, this one was very revealing.

"I was in a long corridor, with many apartments. I felt trapped inside, lost. I felt panic, was sweating, fell to the ground crying. I did not know where I was or why I was inside this hallway. I could not find my way out. Finally, some elderly man heard me crying and asked me into his office. I think he was a doctor. But he had me wait until I fell asleep."

She had been late to the hour, and we didn't have much time to work on the dream together. But it did give me some sense of who she was, and it confirmed my belief that she was very anxious about her whereabouts, and specifically about the issue of "inside" vs "outside." It clearly laid out the claustro-agoraphobic dilemma of being trapped, unable to trust either offers of help or the possibility of freedom. She had to wait—crying, panicky, and alone. This was the opposite side of "catch me if you can," the dream of a person who felt lost and in desperate need of being found.

I told her that I thought she doubted my capacity to find her and was fearful about what she might find if I did. I added that our meeting—both her coming to my office and then her having to leave it--seemed to be both exciting and scary and probably accounted for her alarm in the dream. I also pointed out that her reaction to these confusing emotions was the defense of mindlessness: in sleep she spared herself the pain of conflict.

Thus the analysis began. Our "catch me if you can" engagement did not end with the successful negotiation of a first visit; on the contrary, it was the focus of our work for years. We made a series of appointments that first day that should have taken care of several weeks of meetings. But Ms. A phoned me frequently and anxiously with requests that I confirm her hours or change her appointment times. I quickly learned the rules of the game: If I did not return her call, she would feel like she was breaking apart inside, and "break out" in hives; if I did, I would not be able to reach her. Either way, I lived in uncertainty about whether she would be there or not. I held firm to the analytic frame, which, in this period of confusion and uncertainty, had the merit of being real.

When she did arrive on an appointed day, she was often late, and the lateness encapsulated a characteristic claustro-agoraphobic anxiety—she felt trapped whether she was coming or going. As Rey (1994, p. 26) says, "There is nowhere for the claustro-agoraphobic." I interpreted her lateness as an omnipotent effort to control me and so evade her fears of being controlled by me—that is, either taken over or abandoned. I pointed out how heavily she relied on this kind of magical thinking to manage her anxiety, but it was months before we could really talk about it, so afraid was she of her dependency on me.

Ms. A made appointments and canceled them so often that every once in a while I lost track and made a mistake about one of her comings or goings. As I came to understand this through my own countertransference (my guilt at being unable to contain Ms. A, and my anger at her for evoking such feelings of helplessness in me), I interpreted it, first to myself and then to her, as an enactment—a projective identification of her feeling of having been "dropped" in childhood by a mother who took no responsibility for her behavior and felt no guilt about it. I began to speak with Ms. A about this internal object, once external but now with an inner presence too, who had failed her and was continuing to fail her, and about its meaning in the here and now between us.

Early History and Psychosomatic Symptoms

Very slowly I learned something of her history, of which she talked little. She started out with a rather idealized version of her early life in an affluent family in a Midwestern city. Her parents were professionals; she attended private schools and had her choice of excellent colleges.

Material benefits were lavishly provided, and so were "enriching" activities after school and during weekends. Family dinners centered around her and her younger sister's achievements du jour, but discussion of feelings was avoided. This began to account for the "inside" fragility of ego structure that I encountered in the analysis.

Her parents' constant busy-ness gave me a new perspective on the constant time changes she requested—perhaps she needed them in her compulsion to repeat her infantile experience in her adult life. I began to understand the pressure I experienced in the countertransference as that of a child's importunate requests for attention. Her passive-aggressive behavior around our appointments became understandable as we understood the intrusiveness of her mother's scheduling, and the conflict between her need to "comply" and her wish to resist and maintain her autonomy.

Ms. A felt alone and unseen by her parents. Her psychosomatic symptoms represented painful but unmentalized feelings of neglect, disappointment and aggression that she did not otherwise know how to express and an interactive experience of being simultaneously ignored and intruded upon. Ms. A began literally to feel that emotional pain in her own body. To cope with her aloneness, she would read in bed at night, using her imagination to get away from "home"—by which she meant (literally) her parents' house, and (metaphorically) her own increasingly painful self and body.

During this early period we worked steadily on distinguishing her affective states, first from her physical symptoms then from the eating habits with which she contained her phobic anxieties, and finally from her fantasies of the internalized objects inhabiting her—exactly as happens in the normal projective and introjective identifications of a well-functioning infant/mother dyad. As we settled down to the work, it became clear that Ms. A feared that her mother would be damaged if she separated from her—that neither she nor her mother could cope without the other. Ms. A was eventually able to articulate a belief that she would be free to live her own life only if she could repair the depressed and broken mother within. Previous attempts at therapy had failed, we discovered, because while she had always brought the husband-lover to treatment, she had never brought this painful identification with her mother. I learned later that Ms. A's mother had suffered from a severe postpartum depression and that Ms. A had internalized her mother's fear of breaking down again. Her attempts to repair her husbands and lovers through analysis represented an unconscious wish to repair the fantasied harm she had done to her mother by leaving home—even, perhaps, by being born. The eating disorder that emerged when she left home for college was her means of surviving the resulting separation anxiety and fear of breakdown.

Slowly we located and delineated the damaged mother that Ms. A projected into her own body (particularly her head and her gut, where she meted out constant punishment in the form of migraine headaches and bowel disturbances), and Ms. A's identifications with her. She also projected the damaged mother into the men she sought in unconscious replacement of the mother she had needed. "Marriage" to a mother/husband was another way of keeping her internal mother alive through the fantasy of omnipotent control.

Much of what I learned during this time came nonverbally—in the unconscious enactments between us, in the missed hours, in her acting out and acting in, and in what she showed me through her body.

Countertransference conveyed to me my patient's childhood sense of being simultaneously left out and intrusively scrutinized.

As she settled down to the work of analysis, the pain of headache became a demonstration of how hard it was for her to hold a conflict in her mind. In the beginning, in fact, she spoke mostly with her body, which was the sole way available to her of expressing unsymbolized emotional pain. But the stress of my interpretations, the anxiety of a new "committed" relationship, the excitement of the broken sessions (who was "dropping" or cheating on whom?) were experienced not as conflicts about separateness and autonomy, knowing and being known, safety and danger, but as physical symptoms. She felt the experience of being critically scrutinized by her mother, for example, as the penetrating pain behind the eyes characteristic of migraine. She could not experience conflict directly, but her "splitting" headaches were a concrete unconscious representation of the "lost" part of her mind, the part she had never been helped to engage with, including her unconscious aggression and cruelty and her fears of them.

Her headaches were primitive retreats and sado-masochistic enactments. At first we used them to explore her experience of a mother who took no responsibility for her inability to respond to her daughter's needs, but as time went on, we were able to consider Ms. A's own superego, whose cruelty undermined her capacity to bear normal experiences of guilt and responsibility. Instead, she split off her primitive need for punishment and either projected it into others or reintrojected it into her own body organs (Sloate 2010). As we worked on these issues she slowly became better able to tolerate awareness of her internal experience, instead of somatizing into her head or other bodily organs. Psychic knowledge and awareness became less terrifying, and the fear of breakdown faded.

She was a good dreamer, which was another source of material for us during the time when it was so difficult for her to talk about herself. At first she simply reported dreams but over the course of her analysis she came to understand them as communications to her and to me. She became able to "work" on them—not only as concrete thoughts or images but also as symbolic representations of her conscious and unconscious fantasies and conflict. These consisted of keeping me hanging when she missed appointments, disparaging me, dealing with her conflicts and issues somatically by IBS and expulsing them instead of talking to me—in short, for attempting to destroy the analysis and enjoying her triumph over me.

As the analysis advanced, Ms. A became more aware not only of her conscious feelings but also of her unconscious experiences of identification. Concurrently she became more able to distinguish her own self from these internal "others." She also began to be able to think about the mutual influences she and her important others had on each other, both in their real life circumstances and in her unconscious fantasies.

Her mother, for example, who had in fact been both unavailable to her and obsessively preoccupied with her, lived on in Ms. A's unconscious as a body within which she desperately sought refuge but also as an invading and occupying force that took her own body over. These conflicts too Ms. A defended against by converting them into physical symptoms—the "splitting" of migraine; the "holding it in" vs "letting it out" of IBS, the erotic flushing of her skin vs the oversensitivity that made it untouchable. The physical symptoms distracted her, keeping out of her awareness the rage that threatened, the breakdown she feared, and the damage she thought she had done to the internal objects who supported her illusory sense of self-reliance and control.

In short, Ms. A had learned to use what Klein (1946, p. 9) and then, especially, Bion (1954, pp. 38–39; and 1959, pp. 102–103) called excessive projective identification as her most trusted defense against psychic distress. Her headaches and bowel problems were projections into her own body of the danger she felt from other people or from her own projected desires, concrete somatic manifestations of their wishes to force their way into her or her fearsome wishes to do the same to them. Now, however, in the analysis, she could project her feelings onto me, and for the first time it became possible for another person to experience them consciously and unconsciously, identify them, interpret them back to her, and help her address them.

To Eat or To Be Eaten

The analytic office, like a cave, is often assumed to be a location of safety. Not all patients experience it as such, however. To people like Ms. A, locked into fragile narcissistic defenses that depend on their invisibility, curiosity is dangerous. As I noted that first day, Ms. A was terrified of being "seen" by anyone, including herself, and the hair that she kept over her eyes was scant protection. She experienced the analyst and the analytic situation as an invasion, a claustro-agoraphobic bombardment. To explore her "inside space"—even to acknowledge that she had an inside space and reveal it to me or to herself—challenged the absolute secrecy that she depended on for security, even while it kept her trapped in her aloneness.

As we entered the third year of Ms. A's analysis, we continued to struggle with her anxiety over the analytic situation itself. In the self/other confusion, she made little distinction between the anxiety of furious entrapment in her mother's body and the anxiety that her mother was furiously entrapped in hers. She generalized this claustro-agoraphobic confusion to the analysis and to all her other relationships. For instance, she oscillated between the claustrophobic terror of my attention and the agoraphobic terror of being forgotten over weekends and holidays. She could tolerate separations during the week, when she was able to imagine controlling and possessing me. But during the long weekend break, when the fantasy and defense of omnipotent control broke down,

482

her "breakdown" fears surged. She experienced my absence over weekends as an expulsion, and she missed innumerable sessions out of the need to expel me in turn. Furthermore, all this projective fragmentation left her internal experience profoundly impoverished.

When her manic defenses of omnipotence and omniscience failed, her introjected objects inflicted punishment in the organs that she identified with them, and somatic symptoms occurred. We identified her skin as the organ that exposed sexual excitement through her blushes. This function was enacted in the transference as Ms. A tried to seduce me into caring for her body by showing me her rashes and her blushes, or challenging me not to be turned on sexually. But during this middle period of the analysis (the third through sixth years) we paid special attention to her gut, which as we shall see, in Ms. A, represented her mother, who had failed to feed her properly and whom the baby Ms. A had tortured for this failure.

Up until then, Ms. A had described her mother in idealized terms, and herself, too; she was an achieving adult who left home after college to pursue a successful career path of her own. She was not consciously aware of how guilty she felt at having left her mother behind, at having surpassed her intellectually and academically, and at having "replaced" her with the husband she married early in life. Nor was she aware of her rage at her mother's combination of unavailability and control, which we ultimately learned to have arisen originally in the context of her severe depression after Ms. A's birth. Ms. A's lack of internal separation from this defensively idealized mother and her guilt with regard to her still showed mostly in her somatizing; during the period I will be describing, she was both maintaining her mother in her gut and evacuating her continuously out of it. At first we had focused on the infantile wish and accompanying anxiety to retreat into the mother, both as a means of union with her and as a place of safety. But now, as the analysis progressed, we began to focus more on separation issues.

Ms. A had dreamt about leaving home for years. But when she finally did set off for college, she had a very hard time with the separation. That was when her "official" eating disorder started. This included a phobia about eating meat equated with flesh in her mind and also, more destructively, fears about eating in public places, including restaurants and even the school cafeteria. She lost weight and enjoyed becoming thinner and more angular. But her fears impaired her social life and increased her sense of being alone.

Still, she chose to eat at home for two reasons. She could choose the food there—a liquid diet of vegetable and fruit cleanses, or vegetable foods pureed in a food processor—and so relieve her fears about unknown origins and possible contaminants and about others watching her eat.

These habits endured through her adulthood, yet she never thought about their meaning—in fact, she resisted thinking about them at all—until the middle of her analysis. By then a certain amount of trust had been established between us, and another seminal dream led us into the central quandary both of her food problems and of her claustro-agoraphobic dilemma.

I was hooked up to a dialysis machine. I had Type 2 diabetes. There were tubes cleansing my blood, but actually they were putting sugar into my blood. An old kindly nurse was just watching, a male nurse, and reassuring me that this was normal.

In her associations, the nurse, in the guise of feeding her, was actually poisoning her with sugar, exactly the kind of "bad" food she had always been afraid would sneak its way onto her plate. There was a corresponding unconscious fantasy that I was poisoning her with the bad thoughts I sneaked into her mind. The supportive nurse was not to be trusted. He represented what we were just beginning to understand as her unconscious rage for having been pulled away from the maternal breast and weaned too early. Thus the tube (umbilicus) that was purportedly cleansing (feeding) her blood was instead poisoning her. Thus in this middle phase of the analysis, the food phobias appeared directly in the transference.

As the analysis progressed, Ms. A had slowly begun to risk curiosity and learning, and this new courage enriched our exploration of her eating issues. Ms. A also learned that her mother had become depressed when her infant daughter failed to gain weight at the breast and then angry about her failure as a feeding mother. Furthermore, her mother told her, she had been hard to wean from the bottle, not relinquishing it until age four.

Throughout much of the analysis, Ms. A didn't relate her thoughts or associations to me. She simply was; I felt things. I would convey to her what I felt and what I thought it meant, and by this means she slowly became able to recognize her internal experience and put it into words. She also slowly became able to distinguish what she was feeling from what I was doing. In the countertransference, I often found myself feeling unworthy and devalued and as though she were triumphing over me by her insistence on being a self-feeder and her superior rejection of my skills. We began to be able to think and talk about her experience of being dropped in a more direct and reflective way. Her many missed hours became missed "feeding sessions," and we began to delineate and detoxify her unprocessed hatred and envy of her mother and her wishes and fears about cannibalizing and evacuating her. In the seventh year, when Ms. A was age 55, we moved into a new phase of the analysis. Ms. A could see now that her concern about "bad" food represented a lack of trust in her objects, both internal and external. She became increasingly able to recognize and understand her attacking self. As Freud said in Mourning and Melancholia, "the ego wants to incorporate this object into itself and, in accordance with the oral or cannibalistic phase of libidinal development in which it is, it wants to do so by devouring it" (1917, p. 249).

The dialysis dream revealed Ms. A's wish to be fed "baby food," which she had hidden from herself by the omnipotent control she exercised over her food as she measured, pureed, and ate it. But she clung to it regardless, because it expressed both her caring—after all, she was preparing baby food—and her contempt, because it didn't taste very good for the baby in her. This represented a conflict about being fed by her mother and her feelings about having to rely on herself to be her own self-feeder. She was pureeing her destructive feelings along with her vegetables but also continuing to eat as if she were being fed with a bottle, protesting the loss of the feeding breast removed prematurely (in her unconscious fantasy).

In the seventh year, too, along with the development of insight and metaphorical thinking, Ms. A was developing a new capacity for empathy. Through the back and forth of analysis, she eventually came to appreciate the plight of her "outside" mother, the one suffering from post-partum depression, who had felt like a failure in her efforts to nurture her infant. We saw too that Ms. A had introjectively identified with this "madness" as a sadistic internal object that fed her punitive superego, her bowel symptoms, and her claustro-agoraphobic dilemma. She had clung "insanely" to absolute autonomy throughout her adult life, desperately avoiding dependence on anyone else for comfort. She had considered everyone, especially me in the transference as unworthy and dishonest. But her new ego capacities for insight and symbolic thought, and her diminished dependence on omnipotent defenses, gave her a new ability to understand her own self-experience as well as her impact on others. Her harsh superego softened sufficiently for her to begin tolerating her aggression without resorting to endless fantasies of punishment. (Sloate, 2015). Ms. A's continued associations to the dialysis dream revealed that her tie to me through the umbilical cord along with her wishes to tie me up and excitedly control me and especially my thinking, connected us in an erotic and sadomasochistic manner. This was yet another indication of the dilemma of attachment: who was tying up whom? As Henri Rey liked to ask (Steiner 1995, p. 148) " What part of the subject, situated where in

486

space and time, is doing what to what part of the object, situated where in space and time and with what motivations and with what consequences for the subject and object?"

With this dream work, the connection between physical and psychological bondage came challengingly forward. Her claustro-agoraphobic confusion had begun to shift from an insoluble dilemma that had to be expressed physically to an unconscious conflict that could be thought and talked about: Who was the suffering victim and who the torturer? This question had long haunted the analysis, and it engages us to this day.

Psychic Dilemma vs Psychic Conflict

As Ms. A came to know and tolerate her furious fantasies, she was less haunted by her punitive, persecuting "super" ego, which was, as Bion (1962a, 1984) said, "a super-ego that has hardly any characteristics of the super-ego as understood in psycho-analysis: it is a 'super' ego"(p. 97). Her fears that she had damaged herself and others abated; consequently, she was less overwhelmed by frightening feelings of aloneness.

Earlier dreams of dilapidated houses turned into dreams of homes that in their turn evolved into more solid and less isolated structures—two-family houses, row houses, houses on roads and paths that unconsciously demonstrated the shift in Ms. A's internal psychic representations from a one-person model to a two-person experience. And as her psychosomatic symptoms resolved, allowing her greater physical freedom, the dream content shifted again, to internal landscapes, which could be enriched—arranged, decorated—by the power of her own mind and hands. This was a great advance from the days of her earlier destructive wishes when she had no sense of her own creativity and could only enviously wish to destroy mine. Her dreams continued to evolve as her physical symptoms diminished, and she could increasingly link what went on in her mind with its manifestations in her body, which pointed to a shift in her capacity to move from concrete to symbolic thinking.

Building a bridge with me, especially one that connected her loving and hateful feelings, was an act of integration, and she could feel this. True integration of body and mind still terrified her, as it meant giving up her manic defenses, which were heavily dependent on splitting, dissociation, paranoia, and excessive projection; she would have to learn to contain these feelings within her own self and tolerate them there. She was also terrified of recognizing, tolerating, and mourning the real losses in her life, as well as examining the damage she imagined doing and believed she had done to her internal objects. We proceeded with this work gradually, giving her time to learn to accept and grieve and seeking to avoid a defensive retreat to psychosomatic symptomatology. That was the cave that had protected her since her college days and perhaps before. It was an uncomfortable cave, carved as it was out of psychosomatic defenses and omnipotent but brittle fantasies. But it had kept at bay, or at least out of consciousness, the persecutory tortures she feared from others (and from herself). It had also protected her from getting lost in a cave even more terrifying—the conjoint fears of separation from and merger with/invasion of her mother.

Despite these anxieties, Ms. A continued to pursue the analysis. She did so ambivalently, as she did all relationships, and she still threatened from time to time to abort it with premature termination.

Ms. A had broken off her engagement to her fiancé early on in her analysis, but in time, she met a man whom she was able to commit to marrying, and the analysis took another step forward. A crisis of continuing her analysis or moving out of state erupted with a renewal of her partially worked through psychosomatic symptoms. Ms. A could see herself now as separate from her objects—neither living inside them, nor housing them within herself—and that gave us our first opportunity to work in the analysis with the realistic risks of commitment and the ever-present possibilities of separation and loss.

Over time, Ms. A was able to locate the lost child she had once been, and to hold this part of her within her mind. Our analysis of her omnipotence and the work we had done with her harsh and punitive superego lessened her fears of damaging others or being damaged by them, and this enabled her to relinquish the ferocious need for control that she had previously brought to relationships. This included her relationships with her mother's—the internal one and the external one—with both of whom she was able to form new and better connections.

Her own "self voices" of health ultimately prevailed over the critical and retributive internal voices that had previously populated her, and she escaped from her prison to reclaim her autonomous self through the process of what Bion (1957) calls the reversal of projective identification (pp. 51, 61)—that is, the retrieval of the parts of the self and its objects that have previously been projected into the other. Thus her fragmented self, so long depleted by projection, was progressively enriched.

Lost and Found

Analysis progresses, as Money-Kyrle (1968, p. 694) has said, from somatic states of unsymbolized experience, to concrete representation through words, to dreams, and ultimately to verbal thought and symbolization. Projective identification is one important means to that end. It is a baby's first step not only to affect management but also to solid identifications that can support the self-confidence and empathy necessary to take on the real world without the excessive pain and "dazzlement" that Plato describes. Despite her professional success, Ms. A in the early years of her analysis was a woman who feared reality—both the external reality of the world and the psychic reality of her own experience. She lived unreflectively in the fear that she would fall to pieces if her thoughts and feelings were to become known, even to herself. Rather than tackling the risky actualities of self-knowledge and relationship, she engaged in a struggle with the classical but illusory claustro-agoraphobic alternatives: experiencing any supposedly "safe" structure as too restrictive and any freer existence as insufficiently safe. She hated the dilemma, but she was afraid to challenge it, and afraid of the cannibalistic rage that it evoked in her. Early failures in projective identification had left her with little reliable capacity for self-object differentiation, and the ferocious fantasies to which her confusion gave rise left her as fearful for her own survival as for that of her objects. As Glasser (1979, p. 164) said of his patient, "The object in which he desires to be enveloped is always felt as having the opposing attributes of offering fulfillment and protection on the one hand, but of being engulfing and obliterative on the other."

Patients seek our help ostensibly to fix themselves. Often, however, they are really looking to repair the objects—in adults, usually internal objects—without which they do not know how to function. "The patient does not know how to do it, cannot do it; he or she seeks help with regard to those objects without a conscious realization of what he or she is looking for" (Rey 1994, p. 229). The presence of competent and reliable objects, both real and internalized, provide crucial support for robust emotional growth and a confident life outside of the confines of the cave. Ms. A came to analysis with a broken internal maternal object that could neither support her out of its own resources nor encourage her to separate and so discover resources of her own. The construction of resilient internal objects is one of the tasks of the analytic dyad.

Ms. A clung to her frustrated desire for the right kind of mothering by existing, in defiance of reality, as if she and her mother occupied one space—whose space and whose ownership of it, was not always clear. But the resulting superimposition became overwhelmingly frightening. Her poor self-object differentiation meant that her unconscious destructive fantasies endangered herself as much as their ostensible object, her mother. And her internal mother was no more able to provide the ego modeling she needed than the real "outside" mother had been. She remained a frustrating and enraging object, unable either to provide nurturing or to model growth, separation, and true autonomy. At first Ms. A could attempt only magical repairs that left her feeling unreal; she couldn't even imagine solid interpersonal relationships that could be imperfect and yet allow for meaningful reparation.

The psychosomatic defensive structure was Ms. A's cave. It channeled thoughts and feelings into physical sensation, distracting her from unwelcome knowledge and protecting her with illusions of omnipotence from the awareness of her own vulnerability. It kept her, and anyone else, from seeing her desire, her anger, her envy, or her fear. But it also imprisoned her in solitude and precluded emotional growth. It threw her back on her own inadequate resources and required her to turn away from people and experiences that might have expanded them. Like Plato's cave-dwellers, she saw only shadows, but she lived in terror about what the light might show her. Her unbearable fear of attention—as we learned later, of being discovered in her orgies of destructive mastication—extended to the analytic situation. To be watched by me, listened to by me, even smelled by me meant to be taken in, imprisoned. Turning away from the cave wall, looking toward the opening, and taking the risk of seeing and being seen is no small step for Ms. A and the other psychosomatic patients chained in such caves.

For Ms. A, the cave was the place where she could hide from the threat of her own superego—called by Mason (1983, p.143) "the internal watcher [who] cannot be defied." In the dark, she felt the pain of its punishments, but she did not have to confront it face to face and acknowledge the torturer as herself.

When she ventured into the real world, Ms. A depended on an arsenal of erotic and somatic defenses; she controlled her feelings by controlling her body and her lovers. When those defenses failed, she projected or reintrojected conflict into concrete psychosomatic symptomatology. All of this was in the service of helping her tolerate the claustro-agoraphobic dilemma as she experienced it—the choice between enforced merger and dependency and enforced aloneness and exile, and the rage at having to live with such a choice. But as Mason (1983, p. 143) reminds us, omnipotence has its own burdens. Its "crushing and suffocating quality," he notes, "also produces panic and explosion, in a desperate attempt to escape, even at the cost of disintegration. The internal effect of the omniscient suffocating super-ego could be likened to an attack of acute claustrophobia of the mind." This pain, suffocation, and claustrophobia were projected into Ms. A's own body, and manifested themselves explicitly in the fears of suffocation that brought her repeatedly to the emergency room and eventually to analysis.

The parable of the cave challenges us on many levels. One, the best known, is the question "What is real and what is illusion?" But another more fundamental question underlies that one, and Plato, at least, does not shrink from it: Can we afford to tell the difference? What does it cost us to face reality, and what does it cost us to hide from it? As analysts we must not shrink from those questions either. Our job is to free our patients from their entrapment in intrapsychic caves. In doing so, we confront them with confusing, dazzling, and sometimes terrifying realities—internal and external—that they have never experienced before, or have rejected and "unexperienced." They may, and often do, react with anger and disbelief as Plato's escapee does. One of the premises of psychoanalysis is that the freedom of reality is worth the anxiety it costs. The price we pay for relief

492

is a heavy one—our original vision, which we must give up in our search for better relationships, greater self-knowledge, and the ability to tolerate ambivalence, intimacy, and loss. If we refuse to pay it, we invoke a feeling of aloneness, of helplessness, isolation and fear, and we go on paying that price forever.

References

Bick, E. (1968). "The experience of the skin in early object-relations," *Int. J. Psycho-Anal.*, 49:484–486.

Bion, W.R. (1957). "Differentiation of the psychotic from the non-psychotic personalities." In *Second Thoughts: Selected Papers in Psycho-Analysis*. London: Heinemann, 1967 (pp. 43–64). (Reprinted London: Karnac, 1984).

Bion, W.R. (1959). "Attacks on linking." In Second Thoughts: Selected Papers on Psycho-Analysis. London: Heinemann, 1967 (pp. 93–109). (Reprinted London: Karnac, 1984.)

Bion, W.R. (1962a) *Learning from Experience. London*: Heinemann. (Reprinted London: Karnac Fifth Printing, 2003).

Bion, W.R. (1962b). "A theory of thinking." In *Second Thoughts: Selected Papers on Psycho-Analysis*. London: Heinemann, 1967 (pp. 110–119). (Reprinted London: Karnac, 1984).

Freud, S. (1917e) [1915]). Mourning and melancholia. In: J. Strachey (ed.), *S.E.*, 14. London: Hogarth Press (pp. 237–258).

Glasser, M. (1979). "From the analysis of a transvestite." *Int. R. Psycho-Anal.* 6:163–173.

Klein, M. (1940). Mourning and Its Relation to Manic-Depressive States, In: *The Writings of Melanie Klein, Volume 1, Love Guilt and Reparation and Other Works 1921-1945* (pp.344–369). The Free Press: 1984 MacMillan, New York, The Melanie Klein Trust (1975).

Klein, M. (1946). Notes on Some Schizoid Mechanisms, In: *The Writings of Melanie Klein, Volume III, Envy and Gratitude and Other Works 1946-1963 Vol. III* (pp. 1–24). The Free Press: 1984 MacMillan, New York, The Melanie Klein Trust (1975).

Mason, A. (1983). "Suffocating superego." In: *Do I Dare Disturb the Universe? A Memorial to Wilfred Bion*, ed J. S. Grotstein. London: Karnac, pp.139–166.

Meltzer, D. (1966). "The relation of anal masturbation to projective identification." *Int. J. Psycho-Anal.* 47:335–342.

Money-Kyrle, R.E. 1968. "Cognitive development." *Int. J. Psycho-Anal.* 49:691–698.

Pick, I.B. (1985). "Working through in the countertransference." *Int. J. Psycho-Anal.* 66:157–166.

Rey, H. 1994. "Femininity, sexuality and inner space." In: *Universals of Psychoanalysis in the Treatment of Psychotic and Borderline States*, ed. J. Magagna. London: Free Association Books. 1994, pp. 263–277.

Rey, H. 1994. "The schizoid mode of being and the space-time continuum (before metaphor)." In *Universals of Psychoanalysis in the Treatment of Psychotic and Borderline States*, ed. J. Magagna. London: Free Association Books, pp. 8–31.

Rey, H. 1994. "Reparation," in *Universals of Psychoanalysis in the Treatment of Psychotic and Borderline States*, ed. J. Magagna. London: Free Association Books, 1994, pp. 207–228.

Sloate. P.L. (2010). "Superego and sexuality: An analysis of a psychosomatic solution." *Psychoanalytic Inquiry* 30(5): 457–473.

Sloate, P.L. (2015) "Transforming The Sadistic Superego In Psychosomatic Illness" Ed. Phyllis L. Sloate, PhD, FIPA CIPS Book Series: *The Boundaries of Psychoanalysis*, Karnac, forthcoming 2015.

Steiner, J. (1995). "A Tribute to Henri Rey." *Psychoanalytic Psychotherapy* 9:145–148.

Winnicott, D.W. (1951) "Transitional Objects and Transitional Phenomena: A Study Of The First Not-Me Possession." *Int. J. Psycho-Anal.* 34: 89–97.

On Divergence and Diversity: Regarding Gay Men and the Male-Gendered Pre-Oedipal Good Object

by Raymond Hoffman

In his discussions of the libidinal drive and its object, Freud (1905) explicitly delineated an expansive array of combinations, including among them active libidinal aims toward a female object, active libidinal aims toward a male object, passive libidinal aims toward a female object, and passive libidinal aims toward a male object. Yet throughout the history of psychoanalytic literature, this comprehensiveness, which I appreciate and admire, has been generally displaced in favor of narrow focus on a single expected mode of attachment in early life. Even where it is explicitly acknowledged that primary attachment may be a product of interaction with a variety of others and therefore a composite of numerous influences, primary attachment is described almost universally as attachment to the mother. Bollas (1987), for example, states that his focus in The Shadow of the Object is "the human subject's recording of the early experiences of the object" (p. 3), and includes in this "the voice of the mother, or the mood of the father" (p. 1), yet he immediately assures us that "the infant's experience of his first object ... is, of course, the mother" although she in known "less as a discrete object with particular qualities than as a process linked to the infant's being and the alteration of his being" (p. 4). By definition, the default psychoanalytic view of primary attachment is attachment to a female object, which encourages the related assumption that later revisions to the object of primary attachment in fantasy should result universally in a "mother," in relation to whom all subsequent object relations are referenced and interpreted. This view constricts our thinking and diminishes our awareness of the widely varying environmental and psychological realities in which people grow up. Furthermore, I believe, it both underlies and reinforces a pathologizing narrative in which homosexuality in men is seen as indicative of perversion, narcissism, part-object-relatedness, or genital anxieties that defensively distort and disguise heterosexual object ties. Too frequently, this is the narrative that continues to guide the way analysts listen to and theorize about their gay male patients. Even when analysts attempt not to automatically pathologize, this assumption remains, and exerts its many influences.

My own personal analysis and my treatment of male homosexual patients have led me to see things differently. In this paper I will propose an alternative view of the primary preoedipal object and explore some of its implications for later development, especially in the area of sexual orientation and choices. Specifically, I will posit that a child may make his or her primary preoedipal attachment to either a female- or male-gendered object, and that the latter alternative (and later identifications that arise from it) should not be seen as pathological. I will call this fork in the developmental road a preoedipal divergence.

A few caveats as I begin. First, I am not suggesting that a history of primary attachment to a male object is the root of all male homosexuality. Such an assertion would be immediately disproven by a single case of a male homosexual who clearly had been pre-oedipally attached primarily to his mother, and I could easily produce such cases myself, from among my patients and from among my personal acquaintances. As has been explicated by earlier observers (Phillips, 2003), it is as misguided to search for a unitary phenomenology of male homosexual object choice and sexuality as it is to generalize about adults in heterosexual relationships; to do so is to ignore the dramatic differences that exist among individuals, who may have little in common beyond the gender of their partners. And while it is true that generalizations about the psychopathological significance of male homosexual object choice and sexuality ignore the relational and intrapsychic strengths of healthy homosexuals, that doesn't mean that we should replace one set of generalizations with another. When an acquaintance once enthused to me about how she loved and admired gay men, I responded, not facetiously, "I wouldn't rush to generalize. Some of us are narcissists and perverts." (As are, obviously, some heterosexuals.) Yet, as many previous observers have noted, selection bias has been a major source of distortion in the analytic discourse on male homosexuality. Psychoanalytic experience with homosexuals generally comes from patients who come to treatment to address their distress and dissatisfaction; there is little clinical exposure to the lives and relationships of contented homosexual individuals who do not feel the need for psychotherapy. I have wisecracked that no one should generalize about male homosexuals who hasn't dated a few dozen of them, but there is more than a bit of seriousness in this advice. A visit to a Pride Day celebration or a gay men's chorus concert reveals more of the rich heterogeneity of gay men than perhaps years in an analyst's consulting room.

Another confound in our discourse has been the tendency toward over- or under-identification with the patient. That is, all psychoanalytic theorists, heterosexual or not, must guard against assumptions that their patients are, or are not, like them. No analyst should ever think that "out of my knowledge of how I am organized and what the choice of a male-gendered oedipal-stage object would mean to me, I can assert a universal organization and meaning, or expect such an organization and meaning in my patient." As I try to make sense for myself of the gap between the writings of heterosexuals about male homosexuality and my own experience as a male homosexual and as an analyst of gay male patients, I have come to recognize the importance of Erik Erikson's observation (1959) that identity formation, ours and our patients', requires not only embrace of the "like me," but also fervent repudiation of the "not me." Clear-eyed analysis, therefore, demands that we recognize both the affirmations and the repudiations, including those involved in the establishment of an internalized primary attachment object. It also suggests that as psychoanalysts we will do better to use an observed point of developmental divergence not to assert or define pathology, but rather to teach us something: about how early experiences of affirmation and repudiation inform later processes of identity consolidation, and how they affect our visceral assumptions about what is normative. This outlook is appropriate to the analytic study not only of the gender of the objects of oedipal-stage strivings, but also of earlier gender identifications and object choices.

That observation brings me back to my primary point. I believe that the stage of primary attachment is a developmental point at which both "me" and "not-me" identifications exist, and that the idea of a preoedipal divergence recognizes and reflect the ways these identifications aggregate differently in different individuals. Analytic theorizing will improve when we expand our default assumptions about the gender of the object in the preoedipal stages of development. To conceive of libidinal vicissitudes exclusively as functions of a primary attachment to a female-gendered object is meaningless (and distorting) in the context of a person whose primary attachment is to a male-gendered object, and psychoanalysis has not established any reason to reject altogether the possibility of primary attachment to a male-gendered object. Isay (1989) has described the frequent presentation with gay men in therapy or analysis of evidence of homoerotic fantasies from at least four or five years of age, and Lewes (1998) has described the finding in some gay men that "no amount of probing, no phase in the vicissitudes of the transference, is ever able to uncover a significant phallic libidinal tie to the mother" (p. 345–6). Lewes was puzzled because he thought "it must be true that the initial libidinal object must have been the mother, at least in the oral stage" (p. 346). The work of Isay and Lewes leaves us to contemplate the question: When did the object in the orientation become one gendered as male?

Again, it is not my intention to replace one inaccurate and overly general view of primary attachment (and its sexual implications) with an equally inaccurate and overly general converse, and I am not asserting that the origin of male homosexuality always lies in primary attachment to the father or another male figure in early development. There is still much to be understood about primary attachment and its relationship to eventual sexual object choice. I am only seeking to dislodge the conventional assumption that is so widespread as to be nearly universal—that primary attachment is always to an object of female gender. There have been glimmers of contemplation in our literature that a primary attachment might be formed to a non-maternal object (Agger, 1988), but little more than that.

Drive theory has long been criticized for neglecting the realities of the child's environment. Fortunately we no longer have to rely on drive theory alone to account for the way an individual's libidinal aims develop, and a psychoanalytic theory that fully incorporates the insights of self-psychology, object relations, ego psychology, and attachment and drive theories should not maintain a one-dimensional view of how an adaptive individual genders the pre-oedipal good object over the course of development. Although our field is increasingly synthesizing the perspectives offered by multiple psychologies and by genetics, we have not yet fully thought through their implications with regard to object choice and gender, especially preoedipally. It is time to explore the possibility of a male-gendered primary object in a wider theoretical and experiential context.

Consider what the normative bias I am describing with regard to gender in the preoedipal attachment must feel like to an individual whose experience of primary attachment is to an object that is not the mother or even a mother, but a male. It's not hard to imagine how this could happen. There might be an absence of female caretakers, or a differential of availability or suitability between male and female caretakers. The child might construct a composite object of attachment out of different aspects of the caretaking environment and gender it internally as a male object. We may discover that genetic or other biological endowments predispose an individual to gender their attachment objects as male rather than female, just as a child born into an environment in which all primary caretakers are male might make a composite object of attachment that is nevertheless represented as female-gendered. As the primary caretaking gay male parent of a son who has less often had a biologically female caretaker than a male one, neither of these possibilities seems far-fetched to me. Nor do I suggest that this list of potential reasons is exhaustive.

In any case, the assumption that a child's primary attachment must be to "the mother" throughout pre-oedipal development simply does not correspond with the realities of, or the abundance of possibilities offered by, a world rich in fathers, grandparents, siblings, aunts, uncles, and nannies. One male patient of mine came to treatment in a suicidal crisis of guilt because the man who married his grandmother in late mid-life, taking her away from the patient's childhood home, had finally died, at an advanced age, of natural causes. Happily for this man, he was able in analysis to recognize his deep possessiveness towards his grandmother, who had been to him, up until her remarriage, a more satisfying object than his mother. I doubt that I am the only analyst who has had a male patient present in a crisis precipitated by oedipal conflict centered on a non-maternal object of primary attachment.

It also seems a workaday observation in my life as a gay male analyst seeing gay male patients that early preference for a male object can arise in a variety of parenting scenarios, including those with seemingly ordinary good-enough mothers who are simply not preferred to fathers or other male figures, as well as those with absent or withdrawn (for instance, schizophrenic or severely depressed) mothers, those with what Fonagy would call "non-mentalising" borderline mothers, or those with narcissistically self-preoccupied mothers. Sometimes a male object is the best available, or for some reason the one preferred by the individual. In the absence of a good-enough object of either gender, or among good-enough objects of both genders, a child may establish a composite object, and gender it according to his or her experience and endowment. A woman patient of mine, who had what she herself characterized as profound difficulties in attachment to her severely "not-good-enough" mother, described frequently how hard it was for her to approach the moment of getting to sleep—a psychological transition, as I will discuss in a moment, in which the felt presence of a good object is very important. The one comfort she could find was in isolated memories of approaching her parents' bed in the night and being allowed to crawl in and stay next to her mother while the mother slept. Only when her mother was asleep could my patient experience her as not engaged in an active process of shutting out her very being. My patient would say that she could recall being fed in early life, but never being seen.

This woman had not found in her mother, or in anyone else, a good-enough object to accompany her in the transition to sleep. Nor did she seem to have found or constructed a specific or composite alternative to the absent maternal good object. I could imagine this failure, but it was hard for me to relate to it. As we analyzed her sleep problem for its roots (in experience, in fantasy, and in internal conflict), I became ever more aware that my own sense of preoedipal attachment to a male good object is a composite representation, drawn from relational aspects of different individuals. It includes the male object who most consistently "saw" me reciprocally and as a differentiated other, the people who fed me—in actuality a series of females and males holding baby bottles—and the person with whom I slept at night—my brother. These streams of experience seem to have ultimately gendered as male my primary object of attachment, a reliable and good object whose experienced presence spared me my patient's experience of insomnia, as well as her profound sense of isolation, pessimism, and aggrievedness. It also may be, given that I have two heterosexual brothers who were reared in a similar (but not identical) environment that my genes may have predisposed me to this particular gendering of my primary attachment object. The future will undoubtedly tell us more about such possibilities. In any case, theoretical exploration of the connection between sleep and early attachment has shed some light on the way this kind of attachment and gendering can take place, and in turn on another important aspect of heteronormative bias.

ii

Isakower (1938) and Lewis (1946), in their discussions of what have become familiar to us as the Isakower phenomenon and the dream screen, respectively, both described an adult fantasy of oral satiation experienced by adults in the initiation of sleep. Isakower and Lewin both posited that in falling asleep, the would-be sleeper unites with a wishful hallucination of the breast at the end of suckling. The hopeful sleeper, Isakower (1938) tells us, falls asleep by "reveling in the hallucinatory possession of an object that has been lost.... The hallucinatory revival of these long-abandoned or lost objects is conditioned by a complete regression of the ego.... It cannot be denied that phantasies of a later date concerning the situation in the uterus, at birth and at the mother's breast are also involved in this regressive movement..." (p. 344–345).

Spitz (1955) took issue with Isakower and Lewin. He was convinced that the Isakower phenomenon and the dream screen do not represent the breast, but rather the visually-perceived human face, and that the regressive image of breasts and nipples is actually a condensation of breast and nipples with the human face and its two eyes. Spitz based this belief on his observation that a nursing baby looks not at the nipple and breast (or bottle), but at the face of the person feeding him. Furthermore, he pointed out, the earliest perceptions of contented nursing are undoubtedly not so unilaterally visual as a breast hallucination would imply, but likely include the multiple sensitivities of the oral cavity to touch, taste, smell, and the sensations of swallowing.

In this context it is reasonable to challenge too Melanie Klein's conception of the breast as the exemplar of early primary object relatedness, which I see as a related example of the way a female-gender-specific view of primary attachment can lead analysts to an unnecessarily narrow hearing of our patients. Certainly "the breast" (either as a real object or as a metaphor for the nurturing other in its totality) is a confusing construct when the object of primary preoedipal attachment has been experienced as male-gendered. And, as Winnicott (1953) has pointed out:

When it is said that the first object is the breast, the word 'breast' is used, I believe, to stand for the technique of mothering as well as for the actual flesh. It is not impossible for a mother to be a good enough mother (in my way of putting it) with a bottle for the actual feeding (p. 95).

The more encompassing view suggested by Spitz and Winnicott includes the significance of the caretaker's gaze in attachment to and internalization of the first object, and opens the door to a sense of how a male-gendered early attachment might develop. This view is ultimately not only less anatomically specific, but also less inherently gendered, as seen in the work of Winnicott (1971), and Beebe and Lachman (1988), among others.

Their differences notwithstanding, Lewin, Isakower, and Spitz are united in the belief that it is the fantasy and memory of the preoedipal good object that enable us to regress into blissful sleep, and into fantasied and remembered union. They share an interest, too, in the ongoing revisions of the preoedipal good object as development proceeds. Reading them, it seems to me that for an individual whose primary attachment is to a male-gendered object, the fantasy that enables sleep might well be one of oral satisfaction at a male source of satiation, later organized as a fantasy of satiated sucking on the penis. Superficially this sucking might resemble, or be described as, fellatio, but it should be more accurately understood as a preoedipal and pregenital source of male-gendered oral gratification—that is, a male nipple or breast, condensed, as Spitz would have it, with the visual gaze of the father or other caretaker. In other words, it would be a wishful fantasy of the penis that is regressively oral rather than libidinally genital. A regressive fantasy like this offers the same union with a lost primary object of attachment that Isakower, Lewin, and Spitz propose, except that—perhaps early on, perhaps as a "phantasy of later date" (Isakower, p. 345)—it has become predominantly male- rather than female-gendered.

Like Isakower, I am using two meanings of "regressive" here. The movement away from the cathexis of external stimuli (characteristic of the waking state) and toward the cathexis of internal mental representations (characteristic of sleep) is one type of psychic regression to which he refers. But in addition, Isakower points out, "infantile [genital] masturbation, practiced while the child is going to sleep, is accompanied by incestuous phantasies which the superego repudiates" (p. 344). He notes that structural conflict between superego and id leads to a substitution being made "for the disturbing genital instinctual wish directed toward the incestuous object" (p. 344). In this assertion he introduces a second type of regression—from the libidinally genital to the libidinally oral.

Isakower's comment here lends itself to the speculation—as many drive theorists have made—that such oedipal conflict is prompting an additional defensive disguise, a switch in object from the mother to the father to hide the true forbidden incestuous wish. But to assert this in a general way is to privilege our theories about conflict over our theories about attachment and object-relatedness in a way that is not necessarily supported by the data of analysis. This is one example of the vestigial authority drive theory retains as we work to absorb alternative models into our theorizing. I suppose one must acknowledge that any gendered object in the mind of the individual has imbedded in its creation defensive disguises and does not in fact lead us to the primary object in the world, but we have not generally defined anyone's primary preoedipal object as the object in the world instead of the object in the mind of the individual.

It is perhaps worth mentioning that the use of the good object of Isakower, Lewin and Spitz in the initiation of sleep, whether we symbolize it as breast, nipple, face, or penis, is not the same as the part-object "sleeping pill" that Joyce McDougall (1989) describes in her investigations of sexual addiction and the mode of primitive defense she describes as disaffectation. I make this point explicitly because of the tendency of psychoanalytic discussions to veer off, whenever given the chance, into the pathologizing of homosexual phenomena, and into the generalizing of a pathology present in some homosexuals to all homosexuals.

The healthy male homosexual's love for his same-sex object is characterized by pleasure in all the sensations of the other's body, as a healthy heterosexual lover's would be. The smell, the taste, the male hair patterns of the partner, along with the touch of his skin and the feel of his musculature, are all perceived and enjoyed as intimate aspects of an entire beloved person. This observation too, I think, supports the possibility that some individuals have an internal representation of a male source of oral-stage gratification. As per Spitz above, pleasures like these—the pleasures of the oral cavity and the visual, tactile, and olfactory perceptions that follow it—are precisely the traces one would expect of the earliest primal experiences of pleasure with a male object. In less well-integrated male homosexuals, on the other hand, the sexual act is isolated from attachment to a whole object and from earliest ties to oral gratification. (I have gay friends who referred to one section of a local country-western dance bar as "the no-kissing corner." It was populated by the men who thought it "queer" to kiss during sex and who would never want to cuddle or spend the night after a sexual encounter, so therefore my friends avoided it. I think it is clear that the integration of oedipal and preoedipal, genital and oral, trends—as in wanting to lie down to sleep with the same person with whom you share the discharge of orgasm—is adaptive to any individual seeking relational happiness. No matter how handsome the inhabitants of the no-kissing corner appeared, to engage with them was to court disappointment. This pair of observations corroborates my supposition that homosexual object choice may arise out of preoedipal attachment to an object that is male-gendered, and that such a primary attachment often supports healthy object relationships. Some homosexuals, like some heterosexuals, may avoid relational intimacy, but this avoidance is not implicit in the choice of a same-sex object.

Isakower, Lewin, and Spitz, through their insights into the fantasy of regressively reclaiming and possessing a gratifying early attachment object, open a window onto a broader understanding of the more-or-less contented homosexuality of the gay men who occupy the seats next to us in lecture halls and on buses, and into the presentation, in so many gay male patients seeking treatment, of typical oedipal-level neuroses, as Isay (1989), Goldsmith (2001), and Phillips, (2003), have previously observed.

It is a truism through much of the psychoanalytic developmental literature that to reach a heterosexual object choice, a female child must switch her primary object interest from a female to a male, and that a male child does not have to make this switch. But if a child's primary object of preoedipal attachment is experienced as male, it stands to reason that the "switching" requirements involved for heterosexual object choice would be reversed. A significant number of the male homosexual patients that I have seen in analysis or long-term therapy have presented, from start to finish, with neuroses typical of oedipal-level conflict; that is, an erotic attachment to one parent and an ambivalent rivalry towards the other. When the erotic attachment is toward a male object, however, such constellations have historically, and infelicitously, been characterized by analysts as a "negative" oedipal configuration. Phillips (2003) has addressed previously the bias inherent in the label and the concept of the "negative" oedipal, without positing exactly the possibility of the early divergence I am discussing. I am in agreement with him that the assumption that a male's choice of a male sexual object demonstrates an intermediary stage, a regression, or an extra level of defensive distortion is neither necessary nor clinically useful, and stigmatizes homosexuality as essentially different from heterosexuality. Our theoreticians have been reluctant to postulate that attachment to a male object may be based less in defense than in gratification, and that such an attachment would likely engage a reversal of the expected triangular configuration. That is, maternal identification may serve the same purpose for homosexual boys as paternal identification does for heterosexual boys—defending against the dangers of oedipal rivalry with, and aggressive impulses toward, the triangulated parent. It is not necessarily best seen as the stunted seed of what should have been a primary object orientation toward a female object.

Here, too, Klein's descriptions of infantile ambivalence toward and envy of the breast, and her assertions about maternal breasts and paternal penises and the early oedipal implications of the child's relationship to them, are difficult to accord with my own experience and with the experiences described by certain of my homosexual male patients. One gay male in analysis, who was generally positively attached to his father of infancy and to a current male partner, described the persecutory object of his childhood in a dream of a Cyclops monster that chased him through a haystack after he attacked it with a hatchet. Whereas Klein, I believe, would view this dream as characteristic of an early paranoid relation to the maternal breast, in this patient's context it did not suggest interpretation of a triangulated positive oedipal conflict or the "negative" oedipal conflict often observed in gay oedipal constellations. This patient came to understand his dream as involving a paranoid relation to a paternal penis pursing him in a "haystack" of pubic hair, and understood it most fruitfully as a projection of his aggression onto a source of deprivation, frustration, and humiliation.

iii

The traditional analytic view of gender in primary object attachment is still shaping not only how we hear our patients, but also how we view artistic and cultural productions. In a recent review of the movie Brokeback Mountain, Shill (2007) asserts that Jack Twist and Ennis Del Mar, the star-crossed lovers at the center of the story, are hungry for a lost maternal object, and that they fantasize finding it in a male object for reasons that Shill explores only to the extent that they coincide with his assumption of primary maternal attachment. He posits that Jack and Ennis adopt

510

an oedipal attachment to a male figure in an attempt to recover a lost maternal object through identification. While I agree that identification can serve to defend against the acknowledgement or experience of loss, I think that there are more compelling ways to view the movie, if one admits the possibility of non-maternal objects of preoedipal attachment, and that Shill's theory that the characters in the movie are compensating for maternal absence is simply not supported by evidence in the movie.

Brokeback Mountain deals with two men, both unmarried, who initiate a sexual relationship. Although each goes on to marry a woman, their own sexual relationship continues over many years. I think there is ample evidence that the interplay among the movie's characters actually revolves not around the loss of a female object, but around Ennis's inhibitions about laying claim to a valued male object of attachment.

Jack is able to act upon his love for a man; he can even imagine setting up a little ranching operation near his parents' spread where he and Ennis could live out their days together despite the opprobrium of society and his father, and the scorn of his rejected wife. Although Shill asserts—in support of his theory of mourned maternal absence—that nothing is known of Jack's mother, she actually does appear in the movie, and one can speculate that she has been, while not Jack's primary oedipal goal, at least as good in her role as his oedipal rival as one could expect a parent to be, especially within the cultural context of the time. (She is not portrayed as conveying to Jack that he is prohibited from possession not only of his father, but also of any other man.) No evidence of her absence either as primary object or as object of oedipal identification is easily gleaned from the movie.

Both of Ennis's parents are dead, having been killed in a car accident. Which of them might have been his primary object of attachment and which his oedipal rival is not stated or demonstrated. What is demonstrated is that Ennis remembers having been taken by his father

511

to see the decomposing body of a gay rancher who had been dragged to death by a rope around his genitals for the transgression of living with his male lover. Thus, the movie makes clear, it was seared irrevocably into Ennis's mind that a man who lays claim to a male object will be catastrophically punished. In this respect, it seems that Ennis's oedipal complex may take the "plicate" form described by Lewes, in which "a single figure, the father, plays two diametrically opposed and simultaneous roles—the exciter and the prohibitor of erotic arousal" (1998, p. 347). At the end of their first summer together as hired hands herding sheep on Brokeback Mountain, Ennis pretends to be indifferent to his impending separation from Jack. But as soon as Jack has driven out of his sight, he turns into an alley between two buildings, vomits, and crumples over in grief. When Jack is killed in an accident with an exploding tire, the film reveals Ennis's fantasy that Jack was actually beaten to death by a group of homophobic men in punishment for his sexual transgressions. At the end of the movie, presented with his daughter's decision to marry the man with whom she's in love, Ennis decides, after initial hesitation, that he will attend the wedding. The last words of the movie, as Ennis looks at his and Jack's shirts in his closet, intertwined as he had found them and retrieved them from Jack's childhood bedroom closet, are "Jack, I swear...." The viewer is left to fill in the end of that sentence, which, in my understanding, would go something like this: "I swear to stop doing what I have always done—walking away from the people I love, out of fear." Out of his love for his daughter, he fights his initial impulse, which is to go on the spring roundup and thereby deny his love, rather than go to her wedding.

In Shill's view, the early scenes of the movie depict a barren and objectless world, reflective of the lost attachment to the mother. As a gay man and analyst, I bring to the film a different attitude about male homosexuality (not to mention, as a farm-reared Midwesterner, a different attitude toward rural places). For me, those scenes depict a present attachment—of both men to the mountain, to the landscape, to ranching, and, in a conflicted but nevertheless exciting sexual bond, to each other. It seems to me relevant that the original story was written by Annie Proulx. Perhaps excitement about genital relations with a male object of attachment, and the specter of oedipal conflict producing prohibitions on possession of the oedipal father, are filtered out less by barriers set up during identity formation for this heterosexual woman author and for this gay male viewer than they would be for a heterosexual male viewer.

iv

Finally, I want to consider how some common colloquial uses of language relate to the repudiation of the "not-me" in identity consolidation, especially as it pertains to the normative bias I am exploring here. These expressions shed some light on why individuals preoedipally attached to females might find such attachment to a male difficult to think about.

For instance, we can understand "You suck!" as a general term of disparagement implying a regression to orality from a later stage. Sometimes the insult of "sucking" is reinforced by alliance with the taboos on anal pleasure that are instituted in the progression from oral and anal stages to the phallic stage. (I am thinking of such disdainful comments as "those Orioles really suck ass.") Repudiation of these regressive trends is part and parcel of the insult intended in the phrases uttered. There is a different kind of insult intended, however, in the epithet "Cocksucker!" Certainly it implies a repudiation of oral sexual intercourse with a male-gendered object, but it seems to me that the force of the insult relates to an earlier divergence and repudiation—at the oral level, not the genital one, and at a level reaching back earlier than sexual identity per se. The level of profanity ascribed to this term distinguishes it from the more general deprecation of sucking or of activities below the waistline. Might you see a tabloid headline screaming: "Them Yankees Suck!"? Yes. But "Them Yankees are Cocksuckers!"? Not anytime soon. I think the additional increment of denunciation is incurred not just because cocksucking may be a genital activity or even because of the sexual object choice it implies (note that it is no less censorious when applied to heterosexuals), but precisely because it evokes the more fundamental level of primary oral-stage attachment or disavowal. The underlying thought would be, "Suckers are bad enough, but you cocksuckers are really beyond the pale." The insult is not just about orality, it's about the wrong kind of orality. I think this distinction lends some clarification to the difference in heterosexual male attitudes toward images of female versus male homosexual activity. Female homosexuality crosses a barrier of identification at the genital level but not at the oral developmental level—a woman sucking a woman's breast or licking her genitals is not taboo in the way a man sucking another man's penis is taboo, because in the mind of the heterosexual male it does not undo a repudiation that reaches all the way back to oral-stage identification. (Similarly, the obvious repudiation of anal pleasures in the reaction of heterosexual males to images or thoughts of male penile-anal intercourse adds something to our understanding of the consolidation of heterosexuality in males and the divergence between male heterosexuals and homosexuals, but it does not, I think, sufficiently capture what we might understand possibly to be the full preoedipal divergence between them.)

A thought experiment: equal teams of straight boys and gay boys engaged in playground taunts, with no watchful teacher or parent in sight. The response of the straight boys to the taunt of "cocksucker!" would be outrage, while the response of the gay boys would on some level be "Yeah? So what?" I venture that it is about this group that psychoanalytic theory has yet to say very much that rings true: those contented, orally and genitally male-seeking males who think of their loves not as a travesty of heterosexual love, but in fact as its equal.

Conclusion

Freud thought that we all begin with an early polymorphous potential that gradually narrows down over time as we make our choices of sexual object and mode of gratification. His view left open many possible ways to understand how male sexual object choice unfolds, and what it means. Yet our theory has ignored most of those ways, dismissing them repeatedly in favor of a restrictive vision of the pregenital attachments and relationships that underlie our genital ones. To close them off in this way is to limit—indeed, to undermine—psychoanalytic understanding.

We know that early and ongoing processes of both affirmation and repudiation shape both our identifications and our ultimate attitudes about what is "right" and "normal" and what is not as we navigate our preoedipal and oedipal object worlds. There is no benefit in glossing over or oversimplifying either the many uses or the many forms of self- and object-representation. I would not wish to make the error of postulating no effect where the "mother" of earliest infancy might be in the psyche of a person with a male-gendered pre-oedipal primary object, just as we should not postulate no effect where a primary male object might be. Bollas's writings about the "shadow of the object" can contribute usefully to the full analysis of an individual who had reasons to choose a primary male object over an available or absent female one. We must also be alert, as with the analysis of heterosexual female patients, to the benefit that will accrue in retrieving the mother from behind the projected hostility of the triangulated homosexual boy, or from behind his reaction formation to that hostility. But to eliminate the possibility that an individual might have a primary male-gendered preoedipal good object of attachment is to discount the resourcefulness of human beings, the widely varying environments in which they grow up, and the reality

516

of their great diversity. It also leads us, needlessly, to pathologize where pathology is not in evidence.

A transformative personal analysis depends on accurate diagnostic thinking and effective interpretation. This requires us as analysts to "get it right," and by "right" I mean not the understanding that our biases lead us to expect, but the one our patient recognizes as accurate. It also requires us to think comprehensively about what goes on in the patient's mind, without foreclosing on either the particulars or on the primary dynamic interplay among them. So far, underlying assumptions in the psychoanalytic literature make it perilously easy to vacate the place where a good paternal or otherwise male primary object of attachment may exist, leaving nothing there. To accept these assumptions unexamined can only handicap us in our analytic functioning, whether they embody simple heterosexist expectations, or developmental beliefs about the adaptive individual in his or her environment that are less nuanced than those to which theories other than drive theory might lead us. Still, our institutes continue to perpetuate exactly these assumptions as we train our candidates. It is time to reopen our awareness, and consider that there are many possible ways that a child can come into the world and find a mother, a father—or any other primary preoedipal good object of whatever gender. This finding is an active process, and too important to be artificially dismissed as automatic or foreordained. As Isakower, Lewin, and Spitz suggested, it is likely the achievement that allows us, daily, over the long haul of our adaptive, productive, and intimate lives, to lay ourselves down to restful and contented sleep. And that, with any luck, will take place cuddled next to someone who represents our own many and individual strivings.

References

Beebe, B., Lachmann, F.M. (1988). The Contribution of Mother-Infant Mutual Influence to the Origins of Self- and Object Representations. *Psychoanal. Psychol.*, 5:305–337.

Erikson, E.H. (1980). *Identity and the Life Cycle.* New York: Norton.

Freud, S. (1905). Three Essays on the Theory of Sexuality. S.E. 7.

Goldsmith, S. J. (2001). Oedipus or Orestes? Homosexual men, their mothers, and other women revisited. *J. Amer. Psychoanal. Assn.* 49:1269–87.

Isakower, O. (1938). A Contribution to the Patho-Psychology of Phenomena Associated with Falling Asleep. *Int. J. Psycho-Anal.*, 19: 331–345.

Isay, R. A. (1989). *Being homosexual. Gay men and their development.* New York: Farrar Strauss Giroux.

Klein, M. (1975). *The Collected Works of Melanie Klein.* London: Hogarth Press.

Lewes, K. (1998). A special oedipal mechanism in the development of male homosexuality. *Psychoanal. Psychol.* 15: 341–349.

Lewin, B.D. (1946). Sleep, the Mouth, and the Dream Screen. *Psychoanal. Q.*, 15:419–434.

McDougall, Joyce. (1989). Affects, Affect Dispersal, and Disaffectation. In *Theatres of the Body: A Psychoanalytic Approach to Psychosomatic Illness.* New York: Norton.

Phillips, S.H. (2003). Homosexuality: Coming out of the confusion. *International Journal of Psychoanalysis*, 84:1431–1450.

Shill, M. "Review of Brokeback Mountain." *International Psychoanalysis.* N.p., 23 April 2007. Web.

Spitz, R.A. (1955). The Primal Cavity—a Contribution to the Genesis of Perception and its Role for Psychoanalytic Theory. *Psychoanal. St. Child*, 10:215–240.

Winnicott, D.W. (1953). Transitional Objects and Transitional Phenomena. *Int. J. Psychoanal.* 34:89–97.

Winnicott, D.W. (1971). The Mirror Role of the Mother and Family in Child Development. *Playing and Reality*. London: Tavistock Publications.

www.ingramcontent.com/pod-product-compliance
Lightning Source LLC
Chambersburg PA
CBHW051707020426
42333CB00014B/879